GLOSSARY-INDEX
for
A COURSE IN MIRACLES

(Keyed to First Edition of *A Course in Miracles*)

GLOSSARY-INDEX
for
A COURSE IN MIRACLES

Fourth Edition, Revised and Enlarged

(Keyed to First Edition of *A Course in Miracles*)

KENNETH WAPNICK, Ph.D.

Foundation for "A Course in Miracles"

Foundation for "A Course in Miracles"
1275 Tennanah Lake Road
Roscoe, NY 12776-5905

Printed in the United States of America

Library of Congress Cataloging-in-Publication Data

Wapnick, Kenneth
Glossary-index for a Course in miracles / Kenneth Wapnick. -- 4th ed. rev. and enl.
p. cm.
ISBN 0-933291-03-5 (hard)
1. Course in miracles--Indexes. 2. Spiritual life--Indexes.
I. Title.
BP605.C68W3563 1993
299'.93--dc20 93-5296

Contents

Preface vii

Introduction 1

Part I: Theory 7

Part II: Glossary-Index 21

Part III: Scriptural Index

Abbreviations 221

A Course in Miracles

text 225

workbook for students 252

manual for teachers 264

"Psychotherapy: Purpose, Process and Practice" 267

"The Song of Prayer" 268

Bible

Old Testament 271

New Testament 296

Preface

This fourth edition has been newly typeset and includes the following changes:

1) Each reference in the Glossary-Index and the Scriptural Index has been carefully checked and re-checked, and errors corrected that had been present since the first printing of the first edition. In addition, new references have been added to many existing terms, and some have been deleted.

2) References have been expanded to include the two scribed pamphlets, "Psychotherapy: Purpose, Process and Practice" and "The Song of Prayer." The pagination from the first edition of the pamphlets has been used.

3) Each definition has been reviewed, and modifications and additions have been made where appropriate. Also, some changes and additions have been made to the Theory section.

4) Eight new terms have been added to the Glossary-Index: **anti-Christ, child, joining, looking at the ego, oneness, process, sleep, split**.

5) Included now in the Scriptural Index are portions of biblical passage(s) or, in the case of lengthy passages, the main theme corresponding to the Course reference. This will facilitate identification of these passages.

I should like to thank our very fine Foundation staff for their help in preparing this fourth edition, especially Elizabeth Schmit and Jeffrey Seibert for their painstaking check of Course references, Jeffrey also for examining the cross-referencing system in the Scriptural Index and making the necessary corrections and revisions, Linda McGuffie (not on our staff) for her careful checking of all scriptural references, Loral Reeves who skillfully designed and formatted the book on the computer, and Rosemarie LoSasso, who checked over and reviewed every aspect of the book, and with her usual conscientiousness and dedication supervised the entire publication of this new edition from beginning to end.

Finally, I am grateful to the many unnamed people who over the years have contributed suggestions and corrections to this *Glossary-Index*.

Preface to Third Edition

This third edition has been entirely re-typeset, with the following minor changes:

1) Two lines have been added near the end of the original Preface, one line to explain the abbreviations used in the Glossary and one line to explain the use of letters in citing verses from the Bible.*

2) Two terms (denial, holy instant) have been added to the chart in the section on Theory.

3) Typographical errors have been corrected and minor stylistic changes made.

4) Three page references have been added in the Glossary.

5) Twelve scriptural references have been added and inserted in their appropriate places in both sections of the Scriptural Index.

I am grateful to Rosemarie LoSasso for her careful and conscientious supervision of the publication of this third edition.

*** Changed in the Fourth Edition.**

Preface to Second Edition

This second edition has been revised and enlarged in the following ways:

1) The Preface has been slightly changed to improve readability.

2) In the section on Theory, a paragraph has been added to the text.

3) Six terms have been added to the Glossary-Index. These include: awakening, joy (happiness, gladness), laughter, light, not to make error real, and peace.

The definitions of thirteen of the existing terms have been expanded, and page references have been added throughout.

4) Sixty-five scriptural references in the Course have been added, forty-four of which are to Mt 7:7b,8b (Seek and you shall find). These have been inserted in their appropriate places in both sections of the Scriptural Index. In addition, the Index has been redesigned to ease the identification of the references.

I am grateful to the many people who contributed their suggestions and corrections to the first edition, which stimulated this revised and enlarged edition.

First Edition - Acknowledgments

I would like to express my gratitude and appreciation to Sister Joan Metzner, Joan Pantesco, Sharon Reis, my wife Gloria, and countless others who have helped in the preparation of the manuscript; and to the Foundation for Inner Peace, publishers of *A Course in Miracles*, for permission to publish this *Glossary-Index*.

INTRODUCTION

Unlike most thought systems, *A Course in Miracles* does not proceed in a truly linear fashion with its theoretical structure built upon increasingly complex ideas. Rather, the Course's development is more circular with its themes treated symphonically: introduced, set aside, reintroduced, and developed. This results in an interlocking matrix in which every part is integral and essential to the whole, while implicitly containing that whole within itself.

This structure establishes a process of learning instead of merely setting forth a theoretical system. The process resembles the ascent up a spiral staircase. The reader is led in a circular pattern, each revolution leading higher until the top of the spiral is reached, which opens unto God. Thus, the same material consistently recurs, both within the Course as a thought system as well as in learning opportunities in our personal lives. Each revolution, as it were, leads us closer to our spiritual goal. The last two paragraphs of the first chapter in the text particularly emphasize this cumulative impact of the Course's learning process.

Through careful study of the text, along with the daily practice that the workbook provides, the student is gradually prepared for the deeper experiences of God towards which *A Course in Miracles* points. Intellectual mastery of its thought system will not suffice to bring about the perceptual and experiential transformation that is the aim of the Course.

This *Glossary-Index* was prepared as a guide for students of *A Course in Miracles*. It is not a substitute for working through the material itself. Rather, it is intended as an aid in studying and understanding the Course's thought system. This book is divided into three sections. The first, Theory, briefly summarizes the Course's theoretical system, presenting the interrelationships among the more important terms to be defined. These words are in bold type. Following this summary is an alphabetical listing of these and additional terms, in five divisions: One-mindedness, wrong-mindedness, right-mindedness, related terms, and symbols. Some terms, incidentally, appear in more than one listing.

The second section, the Glossary-Index, presents all the terms in alphabetical order. Each is defined as it is used in the Course. Several words, especially those pertaining to One-mindedness, have no precise meaning in this world and their definitions can only be approximated here. As *A Course in Miracles* says: "words are but symbols of symbols. They are thus twice removed from reality" (manual, p. 51). It should be noted that many of the terms have different meanings or connotations outside the Course, and these should not be confused with the Course's usage. Moreover, some words have differing uses in *A Course in Miracles* itself, reflecting knowledge or perception (e.g., extension), right- or wrong-mindedness (e.g., denial).

Following the definition is a selected and subheaded index of the principal pages in the text, workbook, manual, and the two pamphlets "Psychotherapy: Purpose, Process and Practice" and "The Song of Prayer" where the terms are most meaningfully discussed. The most important of these references are in bold type. Unlike a concordance, not every reference for a term is noted. In general, there is only a single subheading for each passage indexed; however, multiple subheadings have been included when they are particularly important in that passage. Occasionally a term is referenced when it is described, though the term itself is not mentioned; e.g., the reference for projection in the manual, p. 43, is subheaded under guilt. The capitalization used in the Course is followed in this book. Thus, the Persons of the Trinity—God, Christ (Son of God), Holy Spirit—are always capitalized, as are all pronouns referring to Them. Pronouns referring to the Son of God in his separated state are in lower case. Words that directly relate to the Trinity, such as Love, Will, Heaven, etc., are capitalized, though their pronouns are not.

The final section, the Scriptural Index, lists all scriptural references in *A Course in Miracles*, taken from the King James Version, the version used in the Course. The first part lists these references sequentially as they are found in the three books and two pamphlets. The second lists them as they are found sequentially in the Bible. Many of the references are found in more than one book of the Bible, but only the more important or widely known of these have been cross-referenced.

Abbreviations used are as follows:

T: text
W: workbook
M: manual for teachers

P: "Psychotherapy: Purpose, Process and Practice"
S: "The Song of Prayer"

w-m: wrong-mindedness
r-m: right-mindedness

When a new section is begun in the middle of a page, the listings are separated; e.g., the subheading *Holy Spirit* under *justice*: T: 497-501, 501-502.

Scriptural abbreviations are found on page 221. The letter a, b, or c after the verse number refers to the first, second, or third part respectively of that verse.

Part I

THEORY

THEORY

A Course in Miracles distinguishes two worlds: God and the ego, **knowledge** and **perception, truth** and **illusion**. Strictly speaking, every aspect of the post-separation world of perception reflects the **ego**. However, the Course further subdivides the world of perception into wrong- and right-mindedness. Within this framework the Course almost always uses the word "ego" to denote wrong-mindedness, while right-mindedness is the domain of the Holy Spirit, Who teaches forgiveness as the correction for the ego. Thus, we can speak of three thought systems: **One-mindedness**, which belongs to knowledge, and **wrong-** and **right-mindedness** which reflect the world of perception. Our discussion will follow this tripartite view of **mind**.

The accompanying chart summarizes the Course's description of the mind. It should be examined in conjunction with the following references from the Course which deal with the relationship of spirit to mind, spirit to ego, and the three levels of mind:

text:	p. 10, ¶4
	p. 37, ¶3 through p. 39, top ¶
	p. 48, ¶1,2
	p. 122, ¶2,3 through p. 123, ¶2
workbook:	p. 167, ¶3-5
manual:	pp. 75-76

A Course in Miracles, therefore, is written on two levels, reflecting two basic divisions. The first level presents the difference between the One Mind and the separated mind, while the second contrasts wrong- and right-mindedness within the separated mind. On this first level, for example, the world and body are illusions made by the ego, and thus symbolize the separation. The second level relates to this world where we believe we are. Here, the world and the body are neutral and can serve one of two purposes. To the wrong-minded ego they are instruments to reinforce separation; to the right mind they are the Holy Spirit's teaching devices through which we learn His lessons of forgiveness. On this level, illusions refer to the misperceptions of the ego; e.g., seeing attack instead of a call for love, sin instead of error.

Thus, the Course focuses on our thoughts, not their external manifestations which are really projections of these thoughts. As it says: "This is a course in cause and not effect" (text, p. 432). We are urged *not* to

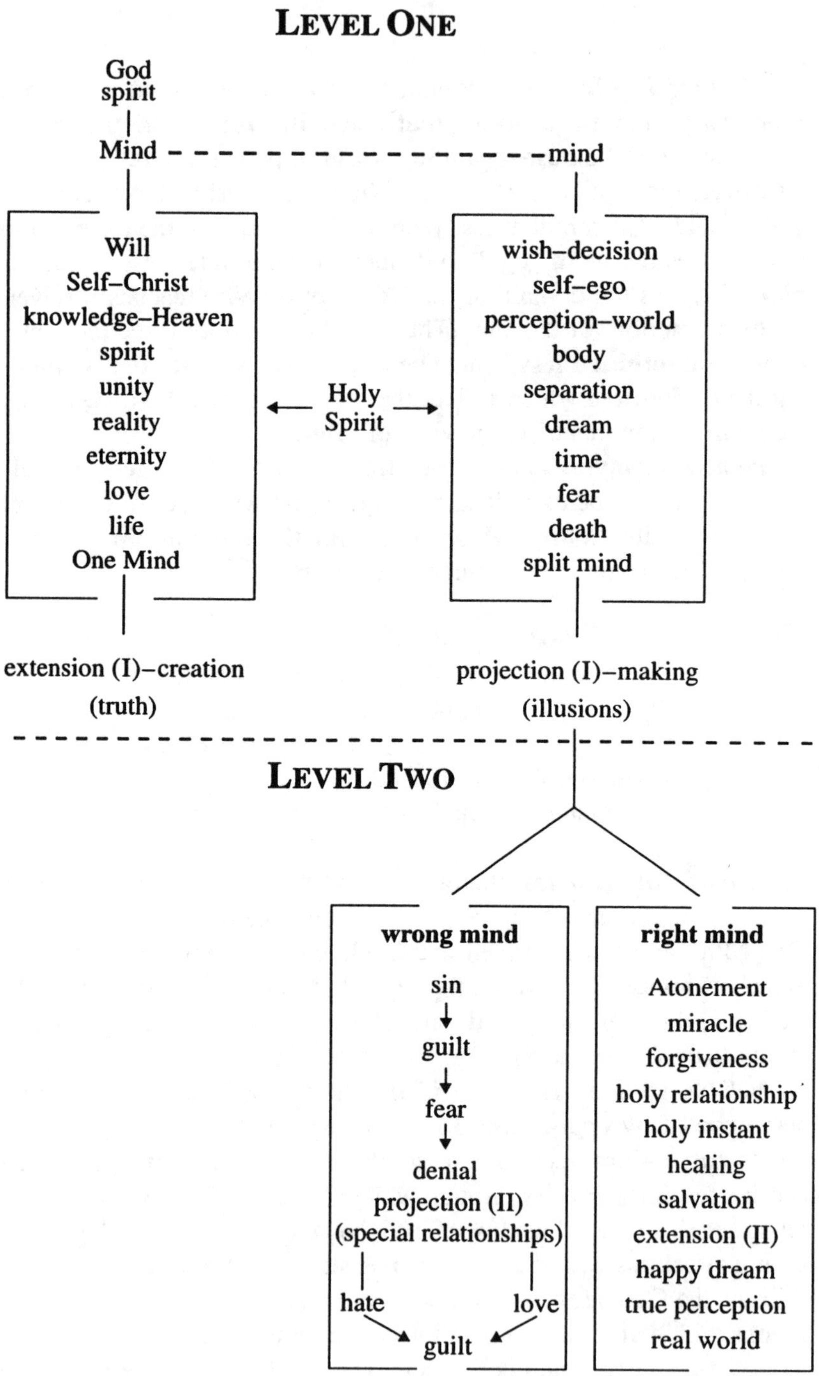
LEVEL ONE
God
spirit
Mind
mind
Will
Self–Christ
knowledge–Heaven
spirit
unity
reality
eternity
love
life
One Mind
Holy
Spirit
wish–decision
self–ego
perception–world
body
separation
dream
time
fear
death
split mind
extension (I)–creation
(truth)
projection (I)–making
(illusions)
LEVEL TWO
wrong mind
sin
guilt
fear
denial
projection (II)
(special relationships)
hate
love
guilt
right mind
Atonement
miracle
forgiveness
holy relationship
holy instant
healing
salvation
extension (II)
happy dream
true perception
real world

seek to change the world (**effect**), but to change our mind (**cause**) about the world (text, p. 415). When lesson 193 states: "I will forgive, and this will disappear" (workbook, p. 359), what is meant is that our perception of the problem and any pain that comes to us from this perception disappear, not necessarily the physical expression of the problem. For example, if rain threatens proposed plans and brings upset or disappointment, we should not pray for sunshine, but rather for help in looking at the inclement weather as an opportunity we have chosen to learn a lesson in forgiveness the Holy Spirit can teach us. This is not to deny that the ego can make or affect a physical world. However, as this physical world is inherently illusory, a result of our thoughts, the Course's emphasis is on correcting these mistaken or miscreative thoughts, which are always the true source of any problem. This correction then allows the Holy Spirit's Love to direct our behavior in the world.

One-mindedness

The One-mindedness of Christ is the world of **Heaven** or knowledge: the pre-separation world of **spirit**, **love**, truth, eternity, infinity, and reality, where the **oneness** of God's **creation**—the sum of all His **Thoughts**—is unbroken. It is the natural state of direct **communication** with God and His creation that existed before the mind of God's Son thought of separation. In this state the perfect unity of the **Trinity** is maintained.

The Trinity consists of: 1) **God**, the Father; 2) His **Son**, **Christ**, our true **Self**; and 3) the **Holy Spirit**, the **Voice for God**. Included in the Second Person of the Trinity are our **creations**, the extensions of our Self or spirit. The Second Person of the Trinity is not exclusively identified with **Jesus**, who is part of Christ, as we all are.

Wrong-mindedness

The ego consists of three fundamental concepts: **sin**: the belief that we have separated ourselves from God; **guilt**: the experience of having sinned, of having done something wrong which emanates from our belief that we have attacked God by usurping His role as First Cause, making ourselves our own first cause; and **fear**: the emotion that inevitably follows guilt, coming from our belief in sin and based on our thought that we deserve to be punished by the ego's made-up god of vengeance.

To ensure its survival, the ego continually attracts guilt to itself, since guilt proves sin's reality and it is sin that gave the ego birth. Once it has established guilt as real the ego teaches us never to approach or even look at it, for it says we would either be destroyed by an angry, vengeful god—a god that the ego made, in fact, to suit its purpose—intent on punishing us for our sin against him, or else annihilated in the oblivion of our own nothingness. This fear keeps the guilt and sin intact, for without seeing them as decisions of our minds we can never change our belief in them.

Left with the anxiety and terror brought on by the fear of God, our only recourse is to turn to the ego for help, since God has become our enemy. The ego's plan of salvation from guilt has two parts: the first is **denial**, wherein we push our guilt out of awareness, hoping that by not seeing the problem it will not be there. Second, after the guilt is denied, we project it out from us onto another, **magically** hoping to be free from the guilt by unconsciously placing it outside ourselves.

Projection has two principal forms: **special hate** and **special love relationships**. In special hate relationships our self-hatred or guilt is transferred onto others, making them responsible for the misery we feel. Our **anger** or **attack** attempts to justify the projection, reinforcing others' guilt for the sins we projected from ourselves. Special love relationships have the same goal of projecting guilt, though the form differs greatly. Our guilt teaches we are empty, unfulfilled, incomplete, and needful, all aspects of the **scarcity principle**. Believing this lack can never be corrected, we seek outside ourselves for those people who can complete us. Special love, thus, takes this form: I have certain special needs that God cannot meet, but you, a special person with special attributes, can meet them for me. When you do, I shall love you. If you do not, my love will turn to hate.

The ego's world becomes divided into enemies (special hate) or savior-**idols** (special love), and the true Identity of Christ in others is obscured. **Judgment**, always based on the past rather than acceptance in the present, is the ego's guiding principle. Through special relationships the ego sustains its existence by maintaining guilt, since using others to meet our needs constitutes an attack, and attack in any form reinforces guilt. This sets into motion the guilt-attack cycle, wherein the greater our guilt, the greater the need to project it by attacking others through special relationships, which merely adds to the guilt, increasing the need to project it.

The ego's wrong-mindedness is a **dream** of **separation**, most clearly expressed in the physical **world** which was made as "an attack on God" (workbook, p. 403). The **body's** existence is one of **sickness, suffering**, and **death**, which witness to the seeming reality of the body as opposed to spirit, which can never suffer pain, or die. **Crucifixion** is the Course's symbol of the ego, representing the belief in attack and **sacrifice**, where one's gain depends on another's loss. All aspects of the separated world are illusions, since what is of God can never be separate from Him, and therefore what seems separate from God cannot be real. This is expressed by the Course principle **"ideas leave not their source"**: we are an Idea (or Thought) in the **Mind of God** that has never left its Source.

Right-mindedness

God's **Answer** to the separation is the Holy Spirit, and His plan to undo the ego is called the **Atonement**. *A Course in Miracles* employs many terms that reflect the Holy Spirit's plan, and each is a virtual synonym for the other. They include: **miracle, forgiveness, salvation, healing, real world, true perception, vision, face of Christ, reason, justice, holy instant, holy relationship, function, happy dream, Second Coming, Word of God, Last (Final) Judgment, resurrection,** redemption, correction, **awakening**, and undoing.

These terms, belonging to the separated world of perception, refer to the **process** (the miracle) that corrects our misperceptions, shifting from hearing the ego's voice of sin, guilt, and fear, to the Holy Spirit's Voice of forgiveness. In this way, special or unholy relationships become holy. Without these relationships we would have no way of being freed from the guilt the ego has taught us to bury through denial, and retain through projection. The Holy Spirit turns the tables on the ego by changing its purpose for projection into an opportunity to see this denied guilt in another, thereby bringing it back within which allows us finally to change our minds about it.

While the practice of forgiveness, or undoing guilt, is usually experienced as complex and long term, it can be understood essentially as a three-step process (see, e.g., text, p. 83; workbook, pp. 34,118,365). The first step reverses the projection as we realize that the guilt is not in another but in ourselves. Second, now that the guilt has been brought to our attention and we recognize that its source is in us, we undo this **decision** by choosing to see ourselves as guiltless Sons of God, rather than guilty sons of the ego. These two steps are our responsibility; the final one is the Holy Spirit's, Who is able to take the guilt from us now that we have released it to Him, **looking** at it with His Love beside us, and thus without judgment and guilt. This looking without judgment, in gentle **laughter**, is the meaning of forgiveness. Using the workbook as our guide, we become trained over time to hear the Holy Spirit's Voice, learning that all things are opportunities to learn forgiveness (workbook, p. 357-59).

Illustrative of this process-aspect of forgiveness are the references under **periods of unsettling** and **bringing darkness (illusions) to the light (truth)**, as well as workbook lesson 284. These reflect the almost inevitable difficulty that results when one begins to take the Holy Spirit's lessons seriously, and allows the deeply denied guilt to begin to surface in one's consciousness.

When our guilt is finally undone, right-mindedness having corrected wrong-mindedness, the **bridge** to the real world is complete. The **memory of God** dawns within our minds, as all interferences to it have been removed and we see the face of Christ in all people. This world of illusion and separation ends as God takes the **last step**, reaching down and lifting us unto Himself. Restored to the One-mindedness of Christ, "we are home, where... [God] would have us be" (text, p. 622).

One-mindedness

abundance
Christ
communication
communion
creation
creations
extension
function
gift
God
gratitude
Great Rays
Heaven (Kingdom of God, Heaven)
Holy Spirit (Answer, Voice for God)
"ideas leave not their source"
innocence
invulnerability
judgment
knowledge
Last (Final) Judgment
laws of God
light
love
mind
Mind of God
Name of God
One-mindedness
oneness
Self
Son of God
spirit
Thoughts of God
Trinity
Will of God

Wrong-mindedness

- anti-Christ
- attack (anger)
- body
- crucifixion
- death
- defenses
- denial
- devil
- dissociation
- dream
- ego
- fear
- gap
- gift
- giving–receiving
- guilt
- hell
- "ideas leave not their source"
- idol
- illusion
- innocence
- judgment
- magic
- means–end
- perception
- projection
- sacrifice
- scarcity principle
- separation
- sickness
- sin
- sleep
- Son of God
- special relationship
- split
- suffering (pain)
- temptation
- time
- world
- wrong-mindedness

Right-mindedness

accepting the Atonement
a little willingness
Atonement
awakening
body
communication
death
defenses
denial
extension
face of Christ
forgiveness
free will (1)
free will (2)
function
gift
giving–receiving
grace
Great Rays
gratitude
happy dream
healing
holy instant
holy relationship
"I am as God created me"
"ideas leave not their source"
innocence
invulnerability
joining
joy (happiness, gladness)
judgment
justice
Last (Final) Judgment
last step
laughter
laws of God
light
looking at the ego
love
means–end
memory of God
miracle
no order of difficulty in miracles
not to make error real
oneness
peace
perception
prayer
process
projection
real world
reason
resurrection

Right-mindedness (continued)

- revelation
- right-mindedness
- salvation
- Second Coming
- Son of God
- teacher of God
- Thoughts of God
- time
- true perception
- vision
- Word of God
- world

Related Terms

A Course in Miracles

bringing darkness (illusions) to the light (truth)

cause–effect

Christmas

decision

Easter

faith

form–content

having–being

humility–arrogance

Jesus

make–create

periods of unsettling

questions

senseless musings

teaching–learning

truth–illusion

wish–will

Symbols

altar

angels

bridge

child

lilies

song of Heaven

star

thorns

toys

war

Part II

GLOSSARY-INDEX

abundance

Heaven's principle that contrasts with the ego's belief in scarcity; God's Son can never lack anything or be in need, since God's gifts, given eternally in creation, are always with him.

(Note—since abundance and scarcity are usually discussed together, *scarcity* and related ego concepts are not cross-referenced below.)

---

charity
T: 52

Christ
T: 10

creation
T: 9,517

extension
T: 119,**120**

God
T: **56**,64,**120**,555

grandeur
T: 166

innocence
T: 33

real world
W: 88,408

Sonship
T: 9,10,206
W: 307

truth
T: **9**

accepting the Atonement

accepting the unreality of the separation, sin and guilt, sickness and death, by following the specific curriculum of forgiving our special relationships—taught by the Holy Spirit—that corrects our mistakes; this is our one responsibility, our function in the Atonement.

---

ego
T: 132

fear
T: 15

forgiveness
T: 251,**393-94**
M: 46

guilt
T: 222,246,251

healing
T: 373
M: 19,53,55

holy relationship
T: 448
P: 6,18

identity
W: 260-62

invulnerability
T: **356-57**

miracle worker
T: **22**,79
M: 21,46

resurrection
M: 65

salvation
W: 437,449

separation
T: 122,220,**555**

sin
T: 362
W: 179,461
M: 35

time
T: 18

the Course frequently refers to itself; its goal is not love or God, but the undoing, through forgiveness, of the interferences of guilt and fear that prevent our acceptance of Him; its primary focus, therefore, is on the ego and its undoing, rather than on Christ or spirit.

---

cause–effect
T: 432

consistency
T: 409
W: 287

decision
T: 320,509,609

doubt
W: 307

ego
T: 122,440,442,456
M: **73**

forgiveness
T: **619**
M: 15,**50**

free will
T: intro.
M: 4

giving–receiving
W: 185,222
M: 13

goal
T: 509
W: 65-66,226,315,329,388
M: 26,65

holy instant
M: 58

holy relationship
T: 363

Holy Spirit
T: 161,205
M: 67-68

identity
T: 149,275,312
W: 225,321-22

Jesus
M: 56,84

knowledge
T: 128,369
W: 257

learning
T: 288,416,464,480,609,619
M: 1

love
T: intro.,228
W: 225

mind-training
T: 13
W: 1-2

peace
T: 128,224,464
W: 328

philosophy/theology
M: 73

practicality
T: 147,196
M: 38,68

process
W: 477

reincarnation
M: 57

resistance
T: 192,196,224,228,460-61,466, 494

simplicity
T: 195,289,440,508
W: 60
M: 73

world
W: 236-37,239

a little willingness

this, joined with the Holy Spirit, is all the Atonement requires; our ego seems to make the undoing of guilt impossible, and on our own it would be, but the willingness to forgive allows the Holy Spirit to undo it for us; looking with the Holy Spirit at our guilt without judgment.

A Course in Miracles
T: 417,464

decision
T: 25

forgiveness
T: 516,572,616-17

God
P: 11

holy instant
T: 288,335,**354-56**

Holy Spirit
T: 26,145,183,196,268,291,316,
328,**357-58,497**

miracle
T: 158,557

real world
T: 195,237,323

salvation
T: 516
W: 364

Second Coming
W: 439

vision
T: 299-300,441

altar

the part of the mind that chooses God or the ego; not an external structure, but an attitude or devotion.

w-m: used rarely as symbol of the ego's presence: drips with blood.

r-m: symbol of God's Presence in us; the meeting place of God and His Son: strewn with the lilies of forgiveness.

Atonement
T: 18-19,34,**207**,244

belief
T: 102

Christ
T: 187,213
M: 83

church
T: 86

defilement
T: 18,22-23

ego
T: 238,296,419
W: 457

forgiveness
T: 488,**510**
W: 346,397,460

gifts
T: 270
W: 183

God
T: 173,246,288,454,575
W: 72,275,346,463
M: 82
S: 2

grace
T: 374
W: 315

holiness
T: 287-88,579

holy relationship
T: 264,373-74
W: 334

Holy Spirit
T: 70,114,269,283-84

knowledge
T: 36

lilies–thorns
T: **397-99**,412

mind/spirit
T: 2,108

prayer
S: 2

Self
T: 186
W: 444

Son of God
T: **36**,193,269,579
W: 447
M: 82

special relationships
T: 319

true perception
T: 36,**213**
M: **82**

angels

extensions of God's Thought; symbol of the light and protection of God that always surround us, since we in truth have never left Him; not to be confused with the popular idea of celestial beings, which are inherently illusory.

Christ
W: 441
S: 14

gifts
W: 448

God
W: 478

holy relationship
T: 390
W: 298

light
T: 522
W: 235

Name of God
W: 334

anger

(see: *attack*)

Answer

(see: *Holy Spirit*)

anti-Christ

symbol for the ego and the belief that there is a power that can oppose the omnipotence of God and deny the reality of Christ.

(Note—not to be confused with the Christian term denoting the real presence of evil [or the devil] in the world.)

---

ego
T: 575-76,584
W:254

idol
T: 575-76

Atonement

the Holy Spirit's plan of correction to undo the ego and heal the belief in separation; came into being after the separation, and will be completed when every separated Son has fulfilled his part in the Atonement by total forgiveness; its principle is that the separation never occurred.

---

correction
T: 29
M: 46

defense
T: 16-17,17-18

face of Christ
W: 421

fear
T: 2-3,7,74

forgiveness
T: 7,**156-57**,260
M: 73

God
T: 300,325

guilt
T: 356
W: 263

guiltlessness
T: 259,261

healing
W: 263
M: **53-54**

holy relationship
P: 23

Holy Spirit
T: **68**,243-44,357
M: 67,85

illusions
M: **4**

Jesus
T: **6-7**,62,76
M: 85

last step
T: 300

miracles
T: 2-4,8,9,20-21

psychotherapy
P: 7

real world
T: 329

resurrection
T: 32

sacrifice
T: 32-34

separation
T: 69,**90**,331

sharing
T: 75,157

Atonement (continued)

sin
T: 362-63

special relationships
T: 324,333

teaching
T: 262-64
M: 6

time
T: 16-17,283
M: 4,58

attack

the attempt to justify the projection of guilt onto others, demonstrating their sinfulness and guilt so that we may feel free of it; because attack is always a projection of responsibility for the separation, it is never justified; also used to denote the thought of separation from God, for which we believe God will attack and punish us in return.

(Note—"attack" and "anger" are used as virtual synonyms.)

---

love
T: 202
W: 114,349
M: 21

magic
M: **42-44**,45

mind
T: 206-207,472
W: **297-98**

miracle
T: 462-63
W: 137-38

peace
M: 49

projection
T: **84,85-88**,89,119
W: 33,**364-65**

sacrifice
T: 296,302-303,504

separation
S: 6

sickness
T: 525-26,528,560

sin
T: 374-75,455,490-91,**606**
W: 329-30

special relationships
T: **295-97**,313-16,464-66

world
T: 400
W: 277,403

awakening

the Course speaks of the separation as being a dream from which we need to awaken; salvation therefore consists of hearing the Holy Spirit—the Call to awaken—in ourselves and in our brothers: thus accepting the oneness with each other that undoes the separation which gave rise to the dream in the beginning.

---

death–resurrection
T: 86-87,541
W: 300
M: 65-66

dream
T: **169**,203-204,229,250,327, **350-52**,**541-43**,577
W: 243,279,435,447

God
T: 105,139,171,403
W: 313,445,462

guilt
T: 187,243,262

Holy Spirit
T: 71,94,96,131,146-47,162, **212-13**,240,402,521
W: 315
M: 61

Jesus
T: **194**,204,287

light
T: 15,254,568
W: 263

love
T: 111,236,260

mind
W: **312**

miracle
T: 2,123,**551-52**,569

peace
T: 238,570
W: 458

real world/forgiveness
W: 354,369,433

special relationships
T: 469-70,471

spiritual vision
T: 18,22

body

level I: the embodiment of the ego; the thought of separation projected by the mind and becoming form; the witness to the seeming reality of the separation by being a limitation on love, excluding it from our awareness; includes both our physical bodies as well as our personalities.

level II: inherently neutral, neither "good" nor "evil"; its purpose is given it by the mind.

w-m: the symbol of guilt and attack

r-m: the means of teaching and learning forgiveness, whereby the ego's guilt is undone; the instrument of salvation through which the Holy Spirit speaks.

---

appetites
T: 52-53

Christ
T: 482,482-83

death
M: 63-64
S: **15**,16

dream
T: **543-44**
W: 415

ego
T: 59-60,93,300,364-65,409
W: 122-23,372

fear
T: 422
W: 297-98

forgiveness
T: **526-28**
W: 355
M: 81

guilt
T: **359-60**,368,384,386-87

healing
T: 111,146,371-72,561-62
W: 246,252-53,415
S: 18

holy instant
T: 300-301

Holy Spirit
T: 140-43,301,407-408
W: 155,372-73

instrument of salvation
T: 145-46,473-75
W: **282,322**,401,436,436,439, 469,**471**
M: 30-31,69,86
P: 11,17
S: 14

magic
S: 17

body (continued)

mind
T: 20,22,359-62,423,558-59, **559-60**
W: **245-46**,372
M: **23-24**
P: **12-13**

neutrality
T: 389,472,538,564,606
W: **435**

perception
T: 38

projection
T: 552
W: 298

sacrifice
T: 305,422-23,504-505

separation
T: 371-72,560,563-64

sickness
T: 144-46,566-67
W: 251-53
M: 16-17
P: 13

sin
T: 363,606-607
W: 409

Son of God
W: **415**

special relationships
T: 321,331,407-409,472,479-80

suffering
T: 386-87,537
W: 132

temptation
T: 619
W: 105

world
T: 367-68,614-15
M: 81

bridge

symbol for the transition from perception to knowledge, and thus is equated variously with the Holy Spirit, the real world, and God's last step; used also to denote the shift from false to true perception and the real world.

---

creations
T: 313,315

forgiveness
W: 243
M: 79

God
T: **314-17**,320,550,554

Holy Spirit
T: 72-73,90,316
W: 168,272,427

Jesus
T: 5,62-63

peace
W: 375

real world
T: **321-23,328-29**

time–eternity
T: 17,316-17,328-29

truth–illusions
W: 370

vision
W: 293

bringing darkness (illusions) to the light (truth)

the process of undoing denial and dissociation, expressing the decision to bring our guilt to the light of the Holy Spirit to be looked at and forgiven, rather than fearfully keeping it in the darkness of our unconscious minds where it could never be seen and undone; living in illusions brings sickness and pain, bringing them to truth is healing and salvation.

Atonement
T: **270-71**

Christ
T: 620
W: 421

Christ's vision
W: 440,442

conflict
T: 454
W: 459

death
T: 336
M: 64

dissociation
T: **266-68**

error
T: 16,455,490
W: 189

fear
T: 45-46,**264-66**
W: 182

forgiveness
T: 449
W: 174-75,242-43,420,457
M: 65,82

guilt
T: 225,295

healing
T: 159
W: 250,252,264
M: 19

Heaven–hell
W: 258

holy instant
T: 418,**533-35**
W: 395

holy relationship
T: 354

Holy Spirit
T: 227,253-54,269,276-77,**328**, 367,524,545-46
W: 427

bringing darkness (illusions) to the light (truth) (continued)

problem–answer
W: 141

sin
T: 375-76,411

special relationships
T: 314

teachers of God
M: 18

cause and effect are mutually dependent, since the existence of one determines the existence of the other; moreover, if something is not a cause it cannot exist, since all being has effects.

knowledge: God is the only *Cause*, and His Son is His *Effect*.

perception: the thought of separation—sin—is the *cause* of the dream of suffering and death, which is sin's *effect*; forgiveness undoes sin by demonstrating that sin has no effect; i.e., the peace of God and our loving relationship with Him is totally unaffected by what others have done to us; therefore, not having effects, sin cannot be a cause and thus cannot exist.

---

attack
T: 209-10,523

dream
T: 473,**539-42**,**551-53**,**553-55**,
555-57

ego
T: 312

fear
T: 188,258,519-20
W: 231
M: 44
P: 1

forgiveness
T: 157-58,435,**528-29**
S: 15

God
T: 28,151,256,550,**550**

guilt
T: **256**,547
W: 287

healing
T: 565

magic
M: 40
S: 6-7,16

miracle
T: 24,517,538,549,552-53,598

nothingness
T: 532

sickness
T: 514-15,551,560
W: 250-51

sin
T: 258,**527**
W: 179

Son of God
T: 420,550
W: 454

thoughts
T: 27,415
W: 26,28,30

time
T: 520-21,548-49

world
T: 539-42,**544-46**
W: 34-35,49,351-52,445
P: 2

metaphor to describe the "little wisdom" of the separated Sons, who are like little children who do not understand the world, and therefore need to be taught by their elder brother Jesus to distinguish what is true from what is false, the world of reality from the world of fantasy; if we were spiritually advanced adults we would not need the help that *A Course in Miracles* provides.

Christ

the Second Person of the Trinity; the one Son of God or totality of the Sonship; the Self That God created by extension of His spirit; though Christ creates as does His Father, He is not the Father since God created Christ, but Christ did not create God.

(Note—not to be equated exclusively with Jesus.)

see: *creations, vision*

---

risen Christ
T: 192,396-97,522

Second Coming
T: 58
W: 439

Self
T: 292
W: **421**

Son of God
T: 187,**197**

strength
T: 620
W: 103

time of Christ
T: 302,304,306

touch
T: 235
W: 309-10

Christmas

the holiday commemorating the traditional birth of Jesus; used as a symbol for the rebirth of Christ in ourselves: the "time of Christ."

Bethlehem
T: 390

Jesus
T: 286,**301-302**,305-306

manger
T: 287

Prince of Peace
T: 286-87,305

time of Christ
T: 301-302,**304-306**

communication

knowledge: synonymous with creation, an expression of our unified relationship to God which can be likened to a flow of spirit and love; only spirit can communicate, unlike the ego, which is separate by nature.

true perception: we experience communication in our right minds through the Holy Spirit, allowing His Love to be shared through us.

Atonement
T: 263

body
T: **140-43**,300-301,360
W: 122
M: 65

creation
T: **63-64**,150

forgiveness
T: **297-98**

God–Son
T: 259,269
W: 78,229,335

holy instant
T: 289,294

Holy Spirit
T: 4,70,**97**,250,261-62,265-66, 274

mind
T: **111**,289,305-306,405

miracle
T: 20-21

psychic powers
M: 59-60

revelation
T: 4,4,64

separation
T: 70,95,265

spirit
T: 48,63

symbols
T: 597
W: 337

communion

the joining of Father, Son, and Holy Spirit, Whose union seemed broken by the separation; awareness of this union of spirit is restored to us through the holy relationship; not to be confused with the traditional Catholic understanding of the term, which emphasizes the sharing of the *body* (not the mind) of Jesus in the liturgy of the Eucharist at Mass, through the transubstantiation of bread and wine into his body and blood.

---

body
T: 140,**384**

communication
T: 97

fear
T: 8

holy relationship/Jesus
T: 383,**385-86**
P: 6

Holy Spirit
T: 74,114,384

miracle
T: 9,41

creation

the extension of God's being or spirit, the Cause, that resulted in His Son, the Effect; described as the First Coming of Christ; it is the Son's function in Heaven to create, as it was God's in creating Him.

(Note—exists only at the level of knowledge, and is not equivalent to creation or creativity as the terms are used in the world of perception.)

see: *creations*

---

creations

the extensions of our spirit; the effects of our creating, analogous to the creation when God created His Son by extending Himself; as extensions of Christ, our creations are part of the Second Person of the Trinity; creation is ongoing in Heaven, beyond time and space, and independent of the Son's lack of awareness of it in this world.

see: *creation*

Atonement
T: 77

creation
T: 30,168-69,270,272,315,
478,**550**
W:237-38,451

dissociation
T: 63,162

extension
T: **14,104-105**,180-81,286

forgiveness
T: 510,572-73

God
T: 124,127,162-63,178,242,298,
420,468
W:454

Holy Spirit
T: 68,123,131,300,**312**

joy
T: 113,117,489

spirit
T: 54,**122-23**

Trinity
T: **138**,139

crucifixion

a symbol of the ego's attack on God and therefore on His Son, witnessing to the "reality" of suffering, sacrifice, victimization, and death which the world seems to manifest; also refers to the killing of Jesus, an extreme example that taught that our true Identity of love can never be destroyed, for death has no power over life.

(Note—since crucifixion and resurrection are usually discussed together, "resurrection" is not cross-referenced below.)

---

decision
T: **192-94**,255

ego
T: 224,225,264

faithlessness
T: 345

forgiveness
T: **396**,397-99,518

Jesus
T: 32-33,**84-88**,193-94,396
W:322

message
T: 47,87

projection
T: 85-87
W:364

sacrifice
T: **32-34,525-27**

suffering
T: 395
W:457

world
T: 220

death

w-m: the final witness to the seeming reality of the body and the separation from our Creator, Who is life; if the body dies then it must have lived, which means its maker—the ego—must be real and alive as well; also seen by the ego as the ultimate punishment for our sin of separation from God.

r-m: the quiet laying down of the body after it has fulfilled its purpose as a teaching device.

---

attack
T: 228
W: 298

attraction
T: **388-91**,392

body
T: 96-97,389-90,574
W: 435
S: 15

decision
T: 46,388
W: 274
M: 16,31

dream
T: 571
M: 77

ego
T: 216-17,**280-81**,387-88

forgiveness-to-destroy
S: 13

God
T: 572-73
W: 122,**302-303**
M: 49-50,**63-64**,84

healing
S: **16-17**

Holy Spirit
T: 538-39
M: 31

Jesus
T: 97,193,217
M: 55

life
T: 46,228-29,541
W: 258,**311-12**
M: 49-50,63

resurrection
M: 65

separation
M: 47

sin
T: 383,494,498,607
W: 179

special relationships
T: 335-36,474

decision

the last remaining freedom as prisoners of this world is our power to decide; while unknown in Heaven, decision is necessary here as it was our decision to be separate from our Source that must be corrected; this is accomplished by choosing the Holy Spirit instead of the ego, right-mindedness instead of wrong-mindedness.

see: *free will*

---

body
T: 476-77,614

Christ
T: 619-20

death
T: 388
W: 274

dissociation
T: 169-70

dreams–awakening
T: 541-42,568-69

forgiveness
W: 460
S: 11

healing
T: 182-83

Heaven–hell
W: **257-59**,352
M: 51

holiness
T: 413,415

Holy Spirit
T: 69-71,**83**,101,**255-59**,**260**, 285-86

imprisonment–freedom
T: 215,303-304,430

Jesus
T: 39,71,134-35,287

joy
T: 82-83,489
W: 351-52

littleness–magnitude
T: 285-86

mind
T: 53,114,134

miracle
T: 256,598-99
W: 137-38

pain
W: 429

projection/extension
T: **215-16**

real world–world
T: 509
W: 229-30,231-32

right- and wrong-mindedness
M: 75

rules
T: 581-84

self-concept
T: 612-13

separation
T: 79

sickness
W: **250-51**
M: **16-18**,53

sin/error
T: 489
W: 470
P: 8

Son of God
T: **418**,440

time
T: intro.,178
M: 4

truth–illusions
T: 332,603
W: **239-41**,**274-76**,284-85,339-40

vision
T: 405
W: 31,42,43,319

world
T: 607-609

defenses

w-m: the dynamics we use to "protect" ourselves from our guilt, fear, and seeming attack of others, the most important of which are denial and projection; by their very nature "defenses do what they would defend," as they reinforce the belief in our own vulnerability which merely increases our fear and belief that we need defense.

r-m: reinterpreted as the means to free us from fear; e.g., denial denies "the denial of truth," and projecting our guilt enables us to be aware of what we have denied, so that we may truly forgive it.

Atonement
T: 16-17,17-18

attack
T: 93,461
W: **245-46**,277,318
M: 49

crucifixion
T: 32

defenselessness
W: 243,**277-80**,332-33
M: **12-13**

denial
T: 16,118

fear
T: 202

holy instant
T: 335

Holy Spirit
T: **268**

illusion
T: **445-47**
W: 278

invulnerability
T: 267-68
M: 39

magic
P: **9**

planning
W: **246-49**

sickness
W: **250-53**

sin
T: 399,446

special relationships
T: 334-35

theology
M: 73

time
W: 252,329

denial

w-m: avoiding guilt by pushing the decision that made it out of awareness, rendering it inaccessible to correction or Atonement; roughly equivalent to repression; protects the ego's belief that *it* is our source and not God.

r-m: used to deny error and affirm truth: to deny "the denial of truth."

---

body
T: 20,372,387

defenses
W: **250-51**

ego
T: **59-60**,115,191

fear
T: **202**,224,436-37

God
T: **175-78**,181,186

guilt
P: 13

Holy Spirit
T: **118**

illusions
T: 172

mind
T: 118

projection
T: 16,89,121,206,224,387, **539-42**
M: 43

right mind/miracle worker
T: 16,**203-205**

separation
T: 28
W: 139,219
M: 43

truth
T: 151,183,432-33
P: 10

vision
T: 232
W: 154

devil

a projection of the ego, which attempts to deny responsibility for our sin and guilt by projecting them onto an external agent, which therefore seems to affect us by its "evil."

---

ego
M: 60

God
T: **44-45**

separation
T: 45

sin
W: 179

dissociation

an ego defense that separates the ego from the Holy Spirit—the wrong mind from the right mind—splitting off what seems fearful, which merely reinforces the fear that is the ego's goal; the ego's attempt to separate two conflicting thought systems and keep them both in our minds, so that *its* thought system of darkness is safe from undoing by the light.

see: *split*

---

creations
T: 63

ego/fear
T: **280-81**

ego–spirit
T: **61-62**

Holy Spirit
T: 72

knowledge
T: **169-70**,427

mind
W: 167

projection
T: 88-89,215

separation
T: 88,**267**

truth
T: 136

dream

the post-separation state in which the Son of God dreams a world of sin, guilt, and fear, believing this to be reality and Heaven the dream; the Son, being the dreamer, is the *cause* of the world which is the *effect*, although this relationship between cause and effect appears reversed in this world, where we seem to be the effect or victim of the world; occasionally used to denote sleeping dreams, although there is no real difference between them and waking ones, for both belong to the illusory world of perception.

see: *happy dream*, *sleep*

---

attack
T: 431,539-42

body
T: 543-45
W: 415

cause–effect
T: **539-43**,**543-45**,**551-53**,553-56

crucifixion
T: 194

darkness
T: 232,352-54

death
T: 571
M: 63-64

ego
T: 48,94
M: 77

fear
T: 558,569
W: 458
P: 19

forgiveness
W: 427

form–content
T: 351,568-69
W: 339
S: 14

God
T: 94
W: 426

idol
T: 574,577-79

judgment
T: 577-80

separation
T: 14-15,552
S: 17

sickness
T: 551-53,553-55,555-57
W: 263

sin
M: 83

sleeping dreams
T: 15,169,**350-52**

special relationships
T: 471

teacher of God
M: 31

time
W: 312

Easter

the holiday commemorating the resurrection of Jesus; since the resurrection symbolizes ego transcendence in its overcoming of death, Easter is used as a symbol for the Son of God's offering and acceptance of redemption (or ego transcendence) through forgiveness.

---

forgiveness
T: 396,398-99
W: 273

Jesus
T: **396-97**

resurrection
T: **394-95**

salvation
T: 397
W: 249

ego

the belief in the reality of the separated or false self, made as substitute for the Self Which God created; the thought of separation that gives rise to sin, guilt, fear, and a thought system based on specialness to protect itself; the part of the mind that believes it is separate from the Mind of Christ; this split mind has two parts: wrong- and right-mindedness; almost always used to denote "wrong-mindedness," but can include the part of the split mind that can learn to choose right-mindedness.

(Note—not to be equated with the "ego" of psychoanalysis, but can be roughly equated with the entire psyche, of which the psychoanalytic "ego" is a part.)

---

separation
T: 37,55,189-91
W: **457**

sickness
T: 144-45,171-72
P: 9

sin
T: **375-76**,423-24

special relationships
T: **295-97**,307,337-38

spirit
T: 47,48-51,54-55

time
T: 72-73,229-30,280-81

wish–will
T: 124-25
W: 125-26

world
T: 74,400

wrong-mindedness
T: 56
M: 75

extension

knowledge: the ongoing process of creation, wherein spirit extends itself: God creating Christ; since Heaven is beyond time and space, "extension" cannot be understood as a temporal or spatial process.

true perception: extending the Holy Spirit or Christ's vision in the form of forgiveness or peace; the Holy Spirit's use of the law of mind, contrasted with the ego's projection; since ideas leave not their source, what is extended remains in the mind, where it is reflected in the world of illusion.

---

creating
T: **14-15**,**105**,117,138-39, 180-81,286
W:451

creation
T: 90,462

forgiveness
T: 449,568

giving
W:345-46

holy relationship
T: 435-36

Holy Spirit
T: 91,120,**153**

law of mind
T: **106-107**,**120**,215

mind
T: 90-91,142

miracle
T: 309,**535**,549

peace
T: 379,386
W:51

projection
T: 14-15,106,179

spirit
T: **122-23**

vision
W:45,**47**,55,293

Will of God
T: 131-32
W:133,456,456

face of Christ

symbol of forgiveness; the face of true innocence seen in another when we look through Christ's vision, free from our projections of guilt; thus it is the extension to others of the guiltlessness we see in ourselves, independent of what our physical eyes may see.

(Note—not to be confused with the face of Jesus, nor with anything external.)

---

fear
T: 391

forgiveness
T: 403-404
W: **213**,370,**421**
M: 15,65,**79-80**
P: 11

healing
M: 54

holy instant
T: 405-406,536
W: 316

Holy Spirit
W: 272
M: 85

idol
T: 576

memory of God
T: 592
W: 213
M: 83

sin
T: **444**,510,521
S: 8

vision/true perception
T: 405,476,**617-19**
W: 272-73,420
M: 66,81-82
S: 10

faith

the expression of where we choose to place our trust; we are free to have faith in the ego or the Holy Spirit, in the illusion of sin in others, or in the truth of their holiness as Sons of God.

---

belief
T: 243,421-23,427

body
T: 386,422-23
W: 154-55

experience
W: 455

faithlessness
T: 343-44,**371-74**,562

healing
T: 373-74

holy instant
T: 345

holy relationship
T: 338,**343-44**,373-74,393

Holy Spirit
T: 342,357,373-74,419
W: 197,412

justice
T: 497

love–illusion
W: 79

miracle
T: 175
W: 463

problem solving
T: 342-43

sin
T: 419,421-23

sinlessness
W: **329-30**

teacher of God
M: 14

truth–illusion
T: 344,372

vision
T: **421-23**

fear

the emotion of the ego, contrasted with love, the emotion given us by God; originates in the expected punishment for our sins, which our guilt demands; the resulting terror over what we believe we deserve leads us—through the dynamics of denial and projection—to defend ourselves by attacking others, which merely reinforces our sense of vulnerability and fear, establishing a vicious circle of fear and defense.

---

punishment
T: 77,376,460

sin
T: 376,520
W: 414

sinlessness
T: **423-25**

special relationships
T: 315,466

thoughts
T: 27-28
W: 461

world
T: 367-68
W: 21,231,402

forgiveness

looking at our specialness with the Holy Spirit or Jesus, without guilt or judgment; our special function that shifts perception of another as "enemy" (special hate) or "savior-idol" (special love) to brother or friend, removing all projections of guilt from him; the expression of the miracle or vision of Christ, that sees all people united in the Sonship of God, looking beyond the seeming differences that reflect separation: thus, perceiving sin as real makes true forgiveness impossible; the recognition that what we thought was done to us we did to ourselves, since we are responsible for our scripts, and therefore only we can deprive ourselves of the peace of God: thus, we forgive others for what they have *not* done to us, not for what they have done.

see: *looking at the ego*

Atonement
T: 156-57

attack
W: 137-38,369-71

death
T: 529
S: 16

ego
T: 157

face of Christ
W: 213
M: 15,**79-80**
S: 12-13

forgiveness-to-destroy
T: 24,528-29,**593-94**
W: **222-23,242**
S: 2,**9-10**,11,**11-13**

function
T: 260,**492-94**
W: 103,344,355-56,374

God
T: 326,470-71,585-86
W: 73,99
P: **5**

guilt
M: 81-82

happy dream
T: 542-43,579-80,590
W: 263,294,369,412

healing
T: 528-31
W: 254-56
M: 53-54
P: **12**
S: 15,15,20

holy relationship
T: 393-95,448-50,491-92

Holy Spirit
T: **157-58**,488
W: 391

illusions
T: 325-26,568
W: 369-70
M: 79

invulnerability
T: **256**
W: 456

love
W: 344
S: 19

miracles
W: 137-38,463

perception
T: 41
W: 460,460

prayer
T: 40
S: **3-4**,9,19

psychotherapy
P: 1,**13**,14,19

real world
T: **328-30**,**368-70**,452,509-11,
590-92,593-94
W: 130-31,408,420,420,433

salvation
W: 174-76,213-15
S: **13-14**

sin
T: 593-95
W: 210-12,242-44,**391**
S: **9-11**

special relationships
T: 330-33,**470-71**
P: 21

suffering
W: **357-59**

teacher of God
P: 5

time
T:572

world
W: 105,403
M: 35-36

form–content

the world's multitude of forms conceals the simplicity of their content: truth or illusion, love or fear; the ego attempts to convince us our problems are on the level of form, so that their underlying content—fear—escapes notice and correction; the Holy Spirit corrects all our seeming problems at their source—the mind—healing the ego's content of fear with His Love and demonstrating that there is no order of difficulty in miracles or problem solving.

A Course in Miracles
M: 3

attack
T: 458-60,460,461
M: 21

death
W: 311

dream
T: 351
W: 339-40

ego
T: 274
M: 77

fear
T: 230,302,347,569
W: 402

forgiveness
W: 243,344,**357-59**

forgiveness-to-destroy
S: 11

God
M: 79
S: 2,3

healing
P: 6

Holy Spirit
T: 73-74,**106-107**,483-84,487, **506-507**
W: 105

idol
T: 577,586-87

illusions
T: 348,453-54,609
M: 64

miracle
T: 20
W: 466

problems
W: 139,141

psychotherapy
P: 17

reason
T: **442-43**

religion
P: 5

sickness
W: 263-64
M: 18
P: 9

special function
T: 495

special relationships
T: 319-20,335-36

suffering
T: 545

existent only in the illusory world of perception, where it appears that the Son of God has the power to separate himself from God; since on the perceptual level we chose to be separate, we can also choose to change our minds; this freedom of choice—between wrong- and right-mindedness—is the only one possible in this world; in the non-dualistic state of Heaven's perfect oneness, choosing cannot exist, and therefore free will as it is usually understood is meaningless in reality.

(Note—not to be confused with "freedom of will," which reflects that the Will of God can *not* be imprisoned by the ego, and therefore must always remain free.)

see: *free will (2)*

---

free will (2)

an aspect of our free will within the illusion: we are free to believe what reality is, but since reality was created by God we are not free to change it in any way; our thoughts do not affect reality, but do affect what we believe and experience to be reality.

see: *free will (1)*

---

creating
T: 123,162

ego
T: 116-17

God
T: 18,70,151,168,174,175,352
W: 395

knowledge
T: 68,244

life–death
T: 182,505,576

mind
T: 64,69,359,472,**572**

reality
T: 13,129,217-18,327,425,512

self-creating
T: **43-44,45**

sin
T: 489

soul
T: 212

truth
T: **74**,124,**515-16**,615

Will of God
T: 82,**125**,138,249,359

function

knowledge: creation, the extension of God's Love or spirit; God creates His Son, Christ, Who in turn creates as does His Father; our function of creating, ongoing throughout eternity, is restored to our awareness when the Atonement is completed.

perception: forgiveness, healing, salvation, the acceptance of the Atonement for ourselves; our "special function" is to forgive our special relationships; the function of the Holy Spirit is to carry out the plan of the Atonement, reminding each Son of God of his special function.

Atonement
M: 53

Christ
S: 14

creating
T: 117,123,**138-39**,156,214,228, 572-73

forgiveness
T: **260**
W: 103,104,105-106,**355-56**,456

healing
T: 156,214,228
W: 255-56
M: 54

holy relationship
T: 350,448-49

Holy Spirit
T: 216,449
W: 109-10,281,391
M: 67

psychotherapy
P: 15,17

salvation
W: 107,**174-76**,177-78,**342-44**, 449

sin
T: 527

special function
T: 262,**403-404**,**493-94**,495-97, 500,505-506,507-508,509
W: 172-73

teacher of God
W: 278
M: 11,15,**18**,35-36,37,40

vision
W: 56

gap

the illusory space between ourselves and God, and ourselves and others, brought about by the belief in separation; in this space arise the dreams of sickness and hate, since projection onto bodies must always follow the mind's belief in separation.

---

body
T: 559-60,**563-64**,568

bridge
T: 313

dream
T: 556-57,590

idol
T: 575-76,587

sickness
T: **554-55**,557-58,561-62

world
T: 558-59

gift

knowledge: the gifts of God are love, eternal life, and freedom, which can never be withdrawn, though they can be denied in the dreaming of the world.

perception: w-m: the ego's gifts are fear, suffering, and death, though they often are not seen for what they are; the ego's gifts are "bought" through sacrifice.

r-m: God's gifts are translated by the Holy Spirit into forgiveness and joy, which are given us as we give them to others.

see: *giving–receiving*

---

altar
T: 270
W: 183

brother
T: 177,543,571
W: 448,448

Christ
W: 442

ego–God
T: 55,120
W: 110

forgiveness
T: 406,449
W: **214-15**,**367-68**,437,459

freedom
T: 135
W: 369

God
T: 104,116,181
W: **185-86**,223,**308-10**,429,437, 437
S: 11

grace
W: 316

gratitude
W: 216-17,367-68

healing
M: 19,21-22

Holy Spirit
T: 257,271,406,449
W: 427

Jesus
T: 135,397-98
M: 55

lilies–thorns
T: **397-99**

limitless
T: 518
M: 68

miracles
W: 466

real world
T: 621

special relationships
T: 472

teacher of God
M: 12,21

world
W: 185,277

giving–receiving

w-m: if one gives he has less, reinforcing the ego's belief in scarcity and sacrifice, and exemplifying its principle of "giving to get," wherein it gives away so that it can get more of something else in return; believing it can give its actual gifts of guilt and fear away, the ego's version of giving is really projection.

r-m: giving and receiving are identical, reflecting Heaven's principle of abundance and the law of extension: spirit can never lose, since when one gives love one receives it; the Holy Spirit's gifts are qualitative, not quantitative, and thus are increased as they are shared; the same principle works on the ego level, for as one gives guilt away (projection) one receives it.

see: *gift*

---

abundance
T: 52,118-19
P: 22

bargain
T: 104,154

creation
W: **185**

extension–projection
T: 120-21

forgiveness
T: **394-95**
W: 211,213,**222-24**,369,465

God
T: 181

healing
T: 256
W: 256
M: 19,54

holy relationship
T: 403,430,445,448,567
M: 5

Holy Spirit
T: 72,97-98,162,402
W: 436,473

idea
T: 67,72
W: **345-46**

law of love
W: 394,465,466,468

miracle
T: 1-2,163,503
W: 293-94,466

sacrifice
T: 52
W: 345-46

teacher of God
W: **281-83**
M: 13,**19-20**,21,42

vision
T: 621
W: **191-92**,292

Word of God
W: 188

world
W: 185

God

the First Person in the Trinity; the Creator, the Source of all being or life; the Father, Whose Fatherhood is established by the existence of His Son, Christ; the First Cause, Whose Son is His Effect; God's essence is spirit, which is shared with all creation, whose unity is the state of Heaven.

---

body
T: 97,364,462

Cause–Effect
T: 28,256,**259**,550,**550**
W: **454**

Christ
T: 152,**187**,213,292
W: 421

creation
T: 14,63-64,**104-105**
W: 414,**451**

crucifixion
T: 32-33

death
T: 217,389
M: 63-64

dependency
T: 190

ego
T: 77-78,179
W: 122-23

Father
T: 178
W: 393
S: **19-20**

fear
T: 149,303,**391-93**,558,563-65, 602
S: 19

forgiveness
T: 326,471
W: **73**,412

healing
T: 105,109-11
S: 18,19

holy instant
T: 294

Holy Spirit
T: 68,**69-71**,78,241,274,299
W: 427
M: 85-86
P: 17

Jesus
T: 5,39,621-22
M: 55-56

judgment–justice
T: 29-30,**498-99**
W: **445**
M: 37,47-48
S: 14

last step
T: 105,199,241,532,591
M: 65,75

laws
T: 95,174,293
W: 132-33

laws of chaos
T: 174,455-58

loneliness
T: 19,64,298,514

love
T: 151,217-19,226-27,294-95, 391-92
W: 73,313-14,349-50

miracles
T: 1-4

perception–knowledge
W: 67
P: 5

prodigal son
T: 138

relationship
T: 299,333
P: 1,5-6,**11-12**

sacrifice
T: 33,303

salvation
W: 120-21

sickness
T: **171**,558

special relationships
T: 10,317-18,466,470-71

Thought
T: 78,333,587-88,609
W: 306-307

Will
T: 133,**180-82**
W: 128,179-80,308-309
S: 13

world
T: 28-29,138,194,476
W: 308,403
M: 81

grace

our natural state as spirit, awareness of which returns to us when we complete our lessons of forgiveness; an aspect of God's Love in this world; past learning for it cannot be taught, but the goal of learning, for all lessons point to its love.

Atonement
T: 33

forgiveness
T: 492

healing
T: 374
W: 255

holy instant
W: **316-17**

holy relationship
T: **373-74**,383,445

Holy Spirit
W: 317,427

Jesus
T: 383

Love
W: **313-14**,**315**,467

miracle
T: 8,520
W: 334,463,468

salvation
W: 316,437

Son of God
T: **126**,193

spirit
T: 7

teacher of God
M: 69

vision
T: 492
W: 313

gratitude

knowledge: God is grateful to His creation for completing Him, and along with the Holy Spirit and Jesus, He is grateful for our efforts to return to Him; should be understood as a metaphor for God's Love, since in reality He has no separated consciousness which can feel gratitude for another.

true perception: the expression of thanks to our Creator for our existence, and to all "living things" that offer the opportunity for remembering Him; our gratitude to each other reflects our recognition that salvation comes through forgiveness, and thus becomes the way to remember God.

see: *song of Heaven*

---

brother (Son of God)
T: **62-63**,66,114,201,235-36,315, **339-40**,430,486
W: 196,362-63,**367-68**

Christ (from)
T: 592
W: 368
M: 12

God (from)
T: 177,306,**486**,522,537
W: 216-17,232,368
S: 20

God (to)
T: 88,235
W: 216-17,**362-63**
M: **55**,88
S: 3

Holy Spirit (from)
T: 339,352
M: 86

Holy Spirit (to)
T: 379
W: 352,369
M: 68

Jesus
T: 88,135,621-22
M: 55

Jesus (from)
T: 352
M: 68-69

miracle
T: 3

psychotherapy
P: 21

song
T: 622
W: 216,435,444
M: 12
S: 1,4

Great Rays

knowledge: the extension of the light of God, our true reality as Christ; the Great Rays are of the spirit, having nothing to do with the body at all.

true perception: the presence of the light of Christ in the separated mind; seemingly split off from the Great Rays of God which are unseen, this light is manifest as a spark in each Son, made visible through forgiveness of our special relationships.

---

body
T: 299-300,**321-22**

dream
T: 567-68

ego
T: 179

face of Christ
T: 391

Heaven
T: 354
M: 87

holy instant
T: **299-300**

Son of God
T: 185
W: 474

spark
T: **175**,176,**183-84**,322,354

special relationships
T: 321

guilt

the feeling experienced in relation to sin; its reflection from our minds is seen in all the negative feelings and beliefs we have about ourselves, mostly unconscious; rests on a sense of inherent unworthiness, seemingly beyond even the forgiving power of God, Who we erroneously believe demands punishment for our seeming sin of separation against Him; following the ego's counsel that to look on guilt would destroy us, we deny its presence in our minds, and then project it outward in the form of attack, either onto others as anger or onto our own bodies as sickness.

see: *scarcity principle*

---

attack
T: 223,**242-44**,460,606
S: **5-6**

attraction
T: 295-97,382,387

body
T: 359-60,368,384,387

death
T: 216-17

decision
T: 82-83,255-58

denial
T: 224-25

ego
T: **77-79**,223-25,229,244
W: 240
P: 1-2

fear
T: **382-83**,387,437,594,602
M: 67

forgiveness
T: 260,368-69,594-95
W: **242-44**
M: 81-82
P: 12

forgiveness-to-destroy
S: **12**

healing
P: 10

hell
T: 280-81
W: 60

projection
T: **223-24**,244-45,359,544-55
S: 5

psychotherapy
P: **14-15**

sacrifice
T: 304-305

separation
T: 79,220,290
M: **43**

sickness
T: **525-27**,553
W: 263
M: 17
P: **8**,13

sin
T: 375-76,376-77
M: 81

special relationships
T: **245-47**,290-91,292,**295-97**, 314,**317-19**

time
T: 79,**221-22**

world
T: 220,244,**367-68**,526,544-45, 590-91,601

happy dream

the Holy Spirit's correction for the ego's dream of pain and suffering; though still illusory, the happy dream leads beyond all other illusions to the truth; it is the dream of forgiveness in which the real world is ultimately seen and salvation attained.

Christ
W: 294

forgiveness
T: 568,571-72
W: **369**,412

healing
T: 555
W: 254

Holy Spirit
T: 147,414,**542-43**,569-70
W: 263,290,355,427

miracle
T: 552-53,598
M: 78

real world
T: **579**

resurrection
M: 65

salvation
T: 590
W: 397

special–holy relationships
T: **351-52**,357-58

having–being

the state of the Kingdom, where there is no distinction between what we have and what we are; an expression of the principle of abundance: all that we have comes from God and can never be lost or lacking, including our Identity as His Son; an integral part of the three "Lessons of the Holy Spirit."

---

ego–Holy Spirit
T: **56**

God
T: 110,133,516

Holy Spirit
T: **99-100**,102-103

Kingdom
T: 56,64,108

life
T: 118

mind–spirit
T: 67

Son of God
T: **182**,275

healing

the correction in the mind of the belief in sickness that makes the separation and the body seem real; the effect of joining with another in forgiveness, shifting perception from separate bodies—the source of all sickness—to our shared purpose of healing in this world; since healing is based on the belief that our true Identity is spirit, not the body, sickness of any kind must be illusory, as only a body or ego can suffer; healing thus reflects the principle that there is no order of difficulty in miracles.

Atonement
T: 19
W: 263
M: 53-54

faith
T: 371-73

fear
T: 19-20,112,152,528,530,535

forgiveness
T: **528-31**
M: **53-54**
P: 12
S: **15**

God
T: 105-106,109-10

happy dream
T: 554-55
W: 254

holy instant
T: 536

Holy Spirit
T: 72,109-11,111-13,**536-37**
W: 264

Jesus
T: 134
M: 55

joining–separation
T: 110,134,171-73,**182-83**,
555-57,560
P: 6
S: **18**

mind–body
T: 111-14,371-72,550-51,**553**,
561-62
W: 246-47,252-53,**263-65**
M: 16-17
P: 4

miracle
T: 19,529,535,553

psychotherapy
P: 8,**11-12**,**13-14**,18-20

sickness
W: **254-56**
M: 16-17

teacher of God
M: 18,19-20,21-22
S: 18-19

Teacher of teachers
P: **7**

time
T: 23

unhealed healer
T: 159-61
P: **14**,15,21

world
S: 16

Heaven

the non-dualistic world of knowledge, wherein dwell God and His creation in the perfect unity of His Will and spirit; though exclusive of the world of perception, Heaven can be reflected here in the holy relationship and the real world.

see: *knowledge*

Atonement
T: 74,77,448

body
T: 97,364,366,505

changelessness
T: 249,262,282,570

communication
T: 107

creations/extension
T: 101,**104-105**,106-107,117, 120,123,242,313,315,489

decision
T: 511
W: 232,233-34,**257-59**

ego
T: 56,**74-75**,280-81

forgiveness
T: 509-11,516,**591**
W: 243,359,374,464

grace
W: 316

gratitude
T: 395,522

guilt
T: 77,248,261,263

having–being
T: 56,94,108

healing
T: 105-106,272

hell
T: 228,280-83,305,318,440, 459-60,491-92,496
W: 248

holy instant
T: 282-83,335

holy relationship
T: **349**,357,378,380-81,399,402, 425,448,**521-22**

Holy Spirit
T: 69,91,100,107,131,281-82, 367,429
W: 290

illusions
T: 172,440,459

inheritance
T: 44,209,262-63

Jesus
T: 104-105,247-48,349

joy
T: 65,113,126,323

justice
T: 501,509
M: 47-48

light
T: 91,452,488,521-22,585
W: 177,408,418,429

love
T: 93,317
W: 344,359,430

miracle
T: 241-42

peace
T: 128,249-50,272,385,573

real world
T: 196,271,452,508-509,621
W: 125,293,408,442

sin
T: 378,403,441,498,510-11

Son of God (Self)
T: 79,127,178,313,358-59,490
W: 469
S: 17

special relationships
T: 291,317-18

teacher of God
T: 127
M: 36

Thoughts of God
T: 75,587

truth
T: 103,107,110,250

unity
T: 54,270,**359**,518

vision
T: 378,413,421

will–Will
T: 124,130,270,352,585
W: 342

within
T: **54**,197,304
W: 135

world
T: 137-38,248-49,317

hell

the ego's illusory picture of a world beyond death which would punish us for our sins; hell thus becomes the guilt of the past projected onto the future, bypassing the present; also used to denote the ego thought system.

---

body
W: 415

decision
T: 509,619
W: 232,257-58
M: 12,51,78

dream
W: 339
M: 66

ego
T: **280-81**
W: 69

fear
T: **617**
W: 364

forgiveness
T: 471
W: 374,**464**

guilt
T: 281
W: **60**
M: 14-15

Heaven
T: 228,496,523
W: 233-34

Holy Spirit
T: **281**
W: 477
M: 67

Jesus
M: 83

projection
S: 5

sacrifice
W: 248

sin
T: 498,515
M: 2

special relationships
T: 318,469,471

suffering
M: 65

teacher of God
M: 36

unreality
T: 228,281
W: 339,464

holy instant

the instant outside time in which we choose forgiveness instead of guilt, the miracle instead of a grievance, the Holy Spirit instead of the ego; the expression of our little willingness to live in the present, which opens into eternity, rather than holding on to the past and fearing the future, which keeps us in hell; also used to denote the ultimate holy instant, the real world, the culmination of all the holy instants we have chosen along the way.

---

body
T: **299-301**,361-62,362

Christ
T: 302
W: 331-33,443

communication
T: 289,294,297-98

faith
T: **293-94**,345,373-74

forgiveness
T: 326

grace
W: 316-17

Great Rays
T: 299-300

guilt
T: 297-98,302,321

healing
T: 429,535-36

Heaven
T: 335-37

holy relationship
T: 337,339-40,363,369,**405-406**, 434

Holy Spirit
T: **281-83**,283-84,298,323, **324-26**,356,358
W: 476
S: 20

Jesus
T: 289,294

judgment
T: 290,419

miracle
T: 282-83,535
W: 316

practice
T: 282,284-85,**288-90**

problem solving
T: **533-35**

salvation
W: 404

special relationships
T: **290-92**

suffering
W: 360

willingness
T: 289,291,323,**354-56**,358

world
W: 337

holy relationship

the Holy Spirit's means to undo the unholy or special relationship by shifting the goal of guilt to the goal of forgiveness or truth; the process of forgiveness by which one who had perceived another as separate joins with him in his mind through Christ's vision.

---

body
T: 405
W: 415

Christ
T: 437-38,441,604-605

faith
T: 338-39,343-44

forgiveness
T: 393-95,435,448-50,491-92
S: 14

holy instant
T: 337,340

Holy Spirit
T: **337-40**,407-408,447-48
M: 5
P: 5

Jesus
T: 132,353-54,383,385-86

joining
T: **404-405**,435-36
W: **339-40**
M: **5-7**
P: 6
S: 6

light
T: 353-54,441,448

prayer
S: 7,8

psychotherapy
P: 1,3,**4**,5-6,**6**,7,**10-12**,13,**13-16**, 17-18,**18-20**,21,**22-23**

real world
T: 337

sin
T: 443-44,**444-45**

special function
T: 350,**403-404**,493-94,507

special relationships
T: **406-409**,435

vision
T: 405-406,441

Holy Spirit

the Third Person of the Trinity Who is metaphorically described in the Course as God's Answer to the separation; the Communication Link between God and His separated Sons, bridging the gap between the Mind of Christ and our split mind; the memory of God and His Son we took with us into our dream; the One Who sees our illusions (perception), leading us through them to the truth (knowledge); the Voice for God Who speaks for Him and for our real Self, reminding us of the Identity we forgot; also referred to as Bridge, Comforter, Guide, Mediator, Teacher, and Translator.

Answer
T: 69,167

Atonement
T: 68,69,244
M: 85

body
T: 97
S: 15

Bridge
T: 72,90,316
W: 168

Christ
T: 233
W: 421

Comforter
T: 184-85

Communication Link
T: 70,88,140,171,250
M: 85

forgiveness
T: 155-56,**157-58**,298,**487-88**, **530-31**

gratitude
T: 339,352,379
W: 352,369

Great Rays
T: 299

Guide
T: 70,124-25,**257-59**
W: 285-86,385,477-78
M: 39,46,67,85

happy dreams
T: 238-40,357-58,414

healing
T: 69,72
M: 19
S: 18

hearing
T: 153-54,172-73,183

hell
T: 281

holy instant
T: 323
W: 476

holy relationship
T: 379,**407-408**
M: 5
P: 1,22

Interpreter
T: 80-81,196,200-202,229-30,
266,291,308,597
M: 47,65

Jesus
T: 67,71,215
M: 85-86

judgment
T: 101,200-202,273-75
W: 271-73

justice
T: 498-502,506-507

Lessons
T: 95-103

Mediator
T: 6,**68**,**72-74**,122,238,261-62,
299
W: 67,**427**
M: 85

memory
T: 547-48

miracle
T: 97,214,538-39

right-mindedness
T: 70
W: 78
M: 75

psychotherapy
P: 4,7,17,18-19

salvation
T: 258,330,411
W: 168,316,369

sin
T: 377,402-403

special function
T: 403-404,**493**,500,506
W: 173

special relationships
T: 291-92,334,467

suffering
T: 545-46

Teacher
T: 210-11,283-84,311,483-84
W: 165
M: 67-68

teacher of God
W: 220-21,**281-82**,436
M: 25,36,69,86
P: 2

time
T: 281-83,511
W: 170

Translator
T: 97,106-107,110,157,268,
274-75,283-84,310
W: 290,355

Trinity
T: 67,72,483

Voice for God
T: **70**
W: 78,187,271-73,**342-44**
M: **85-86**

world
T: 329,487-88
W: 105

humility–arrogance

humility is of the right mind, which recognizes its dependence on God, while arrogance is of the wrong mind, which feels it is in competition with Him; spirit rests in the grandeur of God, from Whom it derives its power, while the ego's grandiosity comes from believing that *it* is God, with the power to determine our function in God's plan; in this way the ego confuses humility with arrogance, telling us we are unworthy to be God's instruments of salvation.

---

ego
T: 50,156

forgiveness-to-destroy
S: **11-12**

function
W: 101,281,**342-44**

grandeur–grandiosity
T: **165-67**

healing
S: 18

holy instant
T: 355

Holy Spirit
T: 308

Jesus
T: 286-87

littleness–magnitude
T: **285-88**,288

love
T: 178

prayer
S: 7-8

sin
T: 375,378,389,501

teacher of God
M: 36

truth
W: 450

wish–will
T: 449,518

world
W: 236-37,**274-75**

"I am as God created me"

an expression of the principle of the Atonement; the statement that acknowledges that the separation from God never truly occurred; denial of this principle reinforces belief in our separated ego self and body; accepting it heals the separation, restoring to awareness our true Identity as God's Son, our Self.

---

arrogance
T: 518

Atonement
W: 261-62
M: 55

body
W: 376

Cause–Effect
W: 454

changelessness
T: 587
W: 274,396,425

Christ
T: 233-34
W: 421,441,471
M: 85
S: 14

decision
W: 260

ego
M: 77

forgiveness
W: 356,408,441,468

freedom
T: 513
W: 93

Great Rays
W: 474

guiltlessness
T: 222,234

holiness
W: 430,438
M: 66

Holy Spirit
M: 67-68

illusions
T: 469-70
W: 422

judgment
W: 405,419
M: 54

justice
T: 507

light
W: 101,401

love
W: 402,423,428

mind
T: 102

resurrection
T: 193

sacrifice
W: 452,465

salvation
W: 160,**162-63**,**195-96**,**300-301**

Self
W: 368,416,431

sin
T: 375

suffering
T: 177,**620-21**
W: 407,428
M: 18

truth
T: 453
W: 252,353

unity
W: 164,341,443,451
M: 30

will
W: 444

world
T: 476
W: 237-38

the expression of the law of cause and effect, for cause and effect cannot be separate: an idea cannot leave the mind that thought it.

knowledge: the extension of God's Thought, His Son, has never left its Source, for what is of God can never be separate from Him.

perception: the world of separation has never left its source in the separated mind, though it appears to be external to it; thus, there is no material world, only a projected illusion of one.

- w-m: projecting guilt from our minds by attack reinforces its presence in the mind that thought it.
- r-m: extending the Love of the Holy Spirit through forgiveness—seeing Him in others—increases the awareness of His loving Presence in ourselves.

---

attack
T: 472
W: 40,318

body
T: 443
W: 122,395
S: 15

Christ
W: 294,421

creation
T: 90,517
W: 291

creations
T: 312

extension
T: 91

giving
T: 67
W: 345

Holy Spirit
T: 389

idol
T: 575-76

life–death
T: 388
W: **311-12**

love–fear
T: 114

mind
T: 374,433
W: 71

"ideas leave not their source" (continued)

projection
T: **515,517**

salvation
W: 148,168

separation
T: **372**,440-41

sharing
T: 75,92

sin
W: 287

Thought of God
T: 587,**609**
W: 306,414,426,454

world
W: 231,236-37,403

idol

symbol of the substitution of the ego for our true Self or God; a false belief that there can be something other than, or more than God, and thus separate from Him, a belief which is then projected onto the special relationship: people, things, or ideas; the anti-Christ.

---

anti-Christ
T: **575-77**

body
T: 407-409
W: 425

death
T: **573-75**
W: 302

decision
T: 584,**586-88**

dream
T: 577-78

fear
T: 113,579
W: **318-20**

holy relationship
T: 592-93

illusions
T: 588-90
W: 119

Jesus
M: 84

real world
T: 590-92

self-concept
T: 610
W: 101,147

sickness
T: **171-73**,594-95

special relationships
T: 586

illusion

something that is believed to be real but is not; the ultimate illusion is the separation from God, upon which rest all the manifestations of the separated world which may be understood as distortions in perception; i.e., seeing attack instead of a call for love, sin instead of error; the illusions of the world reinforce the belief that the body has a value in and of itself, a source of either pleasure or pain; forgiveness is the final illusion as it forgives what never was, and leads beyond all illusion to the truth of God.

---

attack
T: 143,226,**588-90**

death
M: 63-64

decision
T: **509**,609

defense
T: 445-47
W: **245-46**,266,278
M: 39

ego
W: 21
M: 77-78

fear
T: **188**,318-19

forgiveness
T: **325-26**,470-71,568
W: 73,243,369-70

form–content
T: 63,230

holy instant
T: 325-26

Holy Spirit
T: 115,137

mind
T: 115,118,556
W: 71-72,110
M: 75

miracle
W: 152

resurrection
M: 65-66

sacrifice
W: 452

sin
T: 327,515,541

special relationships
T: **314-16**,**318-20**,344

truth
T: 103,327-28,438-39,**453-54**, 558
W: **189-90**,284-85

innocence

knowledge: used rarely to denote God or His attributes.

perception: w-m: the face of innocence the ego employs to conceal its true intent of attack, making others guilty for seemingly having inflicted suffering upon an innocent victim.

r-m: the Holy Spirit's correction for our belief in sinfulness; awareness of our innocence and purity as God's Son is restored to us through the forgiveness of our guilt and attainment of true perception.

Atonement
T: **33,262-64**

attack
T: 489,491,525

child
W: 331

dream
T: 542

face of Christ
W: 370

face of innocence
T: 517,523,552,**610-11**

forgiveness
T: **525-26**
W: 99

God
T: 34,262,304,549
W: 346,372,444

guilt–guiltlessness
T: 244,259,451,523,**546**,602

healing
T: 529-30

holy relationship
T: 399,507,543

Holy Spirit
T: **290**,393,499-500

invulnerability
T: 33,390,402,451-52

Jesus
T: 33

justice
T: 502

mind
T: 550-51

real world
T: 401,422-23,601
W: 349-50

salvation
M: 3

Self
T: 500
W: 346

sin
T: 425,505,559

true perception
T: 34-35

truth
W: 243

vision
T: 618
W: 417

invulnerability

our natural state as a Son of God; our true nature being spirit and not the body, nothing of the ego's world can harm us; recognizing our invulnerability becomes the basis for our defenselessness, the condition for forgiveness.

Atonement
T: 256-57

attack
T: 84-85,92,**209-10**,461,489
W: **40**,115,150

defenselessness
W: **277-78**
M: 13

forgiveness
W: **103**,210,213

gentleness
M: 11-12

God
T: 175,217,461,479
W: **75-76**,79,150,361,405,416, 456

guiltlessness
T: 222-23,**256**
W: 172

holy instant
T: 604-605

Holy Spirit
T: 88,92
W: 424
M: 39

innocence
T: 390,451

Jesus
T: 84-87,137

love
T: 171
W: 415

real world
W: 433

sickness
T: 144

sinlessness
W: **461**,464

spirit
T: 9,51,615

unity/wholeness
T: 54,75
W: 451

Jesus

the source of the Course, its first person or "I"; the one who first completed his part in the Atonement, enabling him to be in charge of the whole plan; transcending his ego, Jesus has become identified with Christ and can now serve as our model for learning and an ever-present help when we call upon him in our desire to forgive.

(Note—not to be exclusively identified with Christ, the Second Person of the Trinity.)

Jesus (continued)

holy relationship
T: 153-54,333,353-54,385-86, 394-95,402

Holy Spirit
T: 71,75,215,240,395
M: 85-86

illusions
W: 119

light
T: 113-14,133-34

miracle
T: 6-8,15-16,23

model
T: 39,71,84,84-88
M: 55-56,83-84

resurrection
T: 39,47,193,204,217,264
W: **322**
M: 83-84

sacrifice
T: 302,305-306

Second Coming
T: 58

sickness
T: 147,172

teacher
T: 49,75-76,264,287
W: 322

time
T: 24,29

world
T: 134

despite the dream of separation, the Sons of God remain joined with each other as Christ, and joined with God in perfect oneness; however, since we share the illusion of being separate, we must first share the illusion of joining with each other, which reflects the process of forgiveness occurring in our minds; only then can we awaken and remember that we are already joined; joining with Jesus or the Holy Spirit is the prerequisite for joining with our brothers.

(Note—not to be confused with external joining)

---

miracle
T: 404-405,553-55

prayer
P: 14
S: 6-7,7-8

psychotherapy
P: 7,13,14

real world
T: 352,592-93

Sonship
T: 234-36,242

teacher of God
M: 12,30,38,61

world
T: 540

joy (happiness, gladness)

joy is one of the characteristics of a teacher of God, shared with all of Heaven; happiness is God's Will for us, attained through fulfilling our function of forgiveness and awakening from the dream of death.

---

decision
T: **82-83**,170,417,**433**,**433-34**

depression/misery
T: 57,141-43,439-41

extension
T: 74,105,113,117,123,450

forgiveness/function
T: 333
W: 105,**109-10**,146,212

God/Heaven
T: 64-65,95-96,126,**138-39**,225, 486,510-11
W: 63,183-84,**185-86**,352,472

guilt
T: 79,244

healing
T: **66**,66-67,112,565-66

holy relationship
T: 339-40,399,401,405,**412**,444

Holy Spirit
T: 68,69,71,93,124-26,131, **161-62**,237,252-54,256
W: 187

love
T: 311
W: 182

real world
T: 238,323,328,573,591-92
W: 440
M: 36

resurrection/Easter
T: 193,396-97

spirit
T: 50,62

teacher of God
T: 263-64
M: 1-2,**12-13**

vision
T: 473-74,489

Will of God
T: 12,130,131,133,136,163, 184-85
W: **177-78**,179-80,181,357,382, 400

world
T: 89,416,573
W: 248,278-79

judgment

knowledge: strictly speaking God does not judge, since what He creates is perfect and at one with Him; the Course's references to God's Judgment reflect His recognition of His Son *as* His Son, forever loved and one with Him.

perception: w-m: condemnation, whereby people are separated into those to be hated and those to be "loved," a judgment always based upon the past.

r-m: vision, whereby people are seen either as expressing love or calling for it, a judgment inspired by the Holy Spirit and always based upon the present.

see: *Last (Final) Judgment*

---

attack
T: 220,581-82
W: 467

body
T: 410-11
W: **271-72**

dream
T: 577-80

ego
T: 58,80,144-45,273-74

fear
T: 596

forgiveness
W: **369-71**,391,470

God
T: 29-30
W: **445**
M: 28,**37**,47-48

Holy Spirit
T: 101,155-56,200-202,**273-75**
W: 220,272-73,**446**,467
M: 25,66

love
T: 499-500
W: 225

past
T: 290

perception
T: **41-44**,216
W: 81,446
M: 23

psychotherapy
P: 14-15,18,**19**

sickness
P: 7-8

special relationships
T: 466

justice

the Holy Spirit's correction for the world's injustice; the belief that God's Sons are equally loved and equally holy, undoing the judgments based on separation; the end of sacrifice and the belief that one's gain is another's loss; called "the rock on which salvation rests."

---

attack
T: **522-24**

forgiveness
T: 509

God
T: 505,507,512
M: 47-48

Holy Spirit
T: **497-501,501-502**

judgment
T: 578

mercy
T: 43

miracle
T: 502-503,506-507

sin
T: 497-501

Kingdom of God, Heaven

(see: *Heaven*)

knowledge

Heaven, or the pre-separation world of God and His unified creation in which there are no differences or forms, and thus it is exclusive of the world of perception; not to be confused with the common use of "knowledge," which implies the dualism of a subject who *knows* and an object which is *known*; in the Course it reflects the pure experience of non-duality, with no subject-object dichotomy.

(Note—since perception and knowledge are usually discussed together, *perception* is not cross-referenced below.)

see: *Heaven*

---

revelation
T: 36

spirit
T: 38-39,47,48

true perception
T: **35-37**,54,61,68,219,240-42
W: 25
M: **81-82**

truth
T: 515
W: 409

wholeness
T: 41,144,240

world
W: 403

Last (Final) Judgment

knowledge: contrasted with the traditional Christian view of judgment and punishment to reflect God's loving relationship with *all* His Sons: His Final Judgment.

true perception: contrasted with the traditional Christian view of judgment and punishment and equated with the end of the Atonement when, following the Second Coming, the final distinction is made between truth and illusion, all guilt is undone, and awareness is restored to us as Christ—the Son of the living God.

---

fear
T: **29-30**,158

God
W:**445**
M:37

Holy Spirit
T: 249
M:66

miracle
T: 30

perception–knowledge
T: 41
W:**445**

Second Coming
W:439

truth–illusion
T: 508-509

last step

this step, belonging to God, occurs when the Atonement is complete and all ego interferences have been removed; when nothing remains to separate us from God, He takes the last step, raising us unto Himself; strictly speaking God does not take steps, and the term actually refers to *our* experience of returning to our Source Which we never truly left.

Atonement
T: 300

face of Christ
M: 79

forgiveness
T: 260,532,**591**
W: 99,**359**

grace
W: 313,315

Holy Spirit
T: 68,102,**105**,379
W: 388

Jesus
T: 62

memory of God
T: 550

miracle
T: 242,554

real world
T: **199**
W: 229,432-33
M: 75
S: 8

resurrection
M: 65

true perception
T: 241
M: 82

laughter

the Course asks us not to take the ego and its world seriously, for this makes them real in our minds; rather, we are urged to laugh gently at the ego thought system and all its seeming consequences, remembering at last to laugh at the "tiny, mad idea."

---

cause–effect
T: **545**

fear
T: 198
W: 64

forgiveness
T: 394
W: 242

guilt/sin
T: 542
W: 272,279,287

judgment
T: 42

sacrifice
W: **345-46**

self
W: 309

suffering
T: 530
W: 362

teacher of God
W: **177**,284

tears
T: 526
W: 88,334,358
M: 27,36

time
T: **544**,549

laws of God

the principles that express God's existence and the extension of His Kingdom.

knowledge: include creation, love, truth, and eternal life.

true perception: reflected in this world as forgiveness, the miracle, healing, and freedom, in contrast with the ego's laws of projection, specialness, suffering, and death—the laws of chaos.

---

body
W: 292,425,425

Christ
W: 471

creation
T: 114,169,489

death
T: 476
W: 255

decision
W: 239-40

ego
T: 78,243

extension–projection
T: **106-107,120-21**

forgiveness
T: 493
W: 369

freedom
T: **174**
W: 93-94,151

giving
T: 118
W: 293,463,468
P: **22**

healing
T: 109-10,476,529,537

holy instant
T: 293

holy relationship
T: **403-404**,406,477

Holy Spirit
T: 106-107,120
W: 281

inviolate
T: 133,151,168,181,537

laws of chaos
T: 174,458

love
T: 236,487
W: 225-26,**465**

miracle
T: 539
W: 135,**466**

perception
T: 487,489

protection
T: 168,186,589

truth
T: 515

world
T: 126
W: **132-33**
M: 8,45

light

knowledge: metaphor to describe the essence of spirit—God and Christ.

true perception: metaphor to describe the vision of Christ, or forgiveness, which joins us in holy relationships and removes the darkened veils of guilt that keep us rooted in the ego's dream.

see: *bringing darkness (illusions) to the light (truth)*
Great Rays

Atonement
T: 17,33

body
T: 479-80,483,485-87,488

darkness
T: 9,55,233-36,273,304,489-90, 492-93
W: 151,170-71
M: 3

dream
T: 15,578

enlightenment
T: 47,113,131,203,213
W: 347

forgiveness
T: 452,510,567-68
W: 94,103,104,144,145,211,458

God/Heaven
T: 45-46,58,142,185-86,186, 521-22,585,587-88,622
W: 69-70,97,162,394,402,408, 429

guilt
T: 244,246-48,263,368

healing
T: 66,203,256
W: 191

holy instant
T: 405,513

holy relationship
T: 350,**352-54**,399,401-402,441, 444,**448-50**,462-63,605
W: 278

Holy Spirit
T: 69,73,100,239,253-54
M: 85

Jesus
T: **133-34**,385-86

mind
T: 108-109,127,153,160-61

miracle
T: 3,41,242
W: 137-38,154-56,157-58,466
M: 77

real world
T: **235-36**,368-69
W: 125,130-31,235,248-49,331, 349

veil/cloud
T: 294,391,576,617-19
W: 63,91,**116-17**,119,166

vision
T: **232-33**,241,412,**417**
W: 25,292,418

world
T: 71,91
W: 101-102,144,177,218-19, **287-88**,289-90,**347-48**

lilies

the Course's symbol of forgiveness and the innocence of God's Son; the gift of forgiveness that we offer each other, contrasted with the ego's gift of thorns (attack, crucifixion).

---

altar
T: 412
W: 346

face of Christ
T: **396**

innocence
T: 399

Jesus
T: **397-98**

light
W: 457

miracle
W: 463

truth
W: 460

vision
W: 294

looking at the ego

the essence of forgiveness: looking with the Holy Spirit's or Jesus' non-judgmental gentleness and patience at our ego thought system; since it is guilt that prevents us from looking at our specialness, thus sustaining the ego and keeping its true nature hidden, it is looking without judgment at our attack thoughts that undoes the ego: thus, looking at the ego without guilt and fear is the essence of the Atonement.

see: *bringing darkness (illusions) to the light (truth)*

---

looking at the ego (continued)

love

knowledge: the essence of God's being and relationship to His creation, which is unchanging and eternal; beyond definition and teaching, and can only be experienced or known once the barriers of guilt have been removed through forgiveness.

true perception: impossible in the illusory world of perception, yet expressed here through forgiveness; the emotion given by God, in contrast to the ego's emotion of fear, and reflected in any expression of true joining with another.

A Course in Miracles
T: intro.,228

Atonement
T: 16,26,325

attack
T: 114,209-11,458-59,461-63, 522
W: **114-15**
M: **21**

body
T: 12,**359**,**364-66**,**406-409**, 564-65

charity
T: 23

Christ
T: 187,203-204,**213**,592

creating
T: 104-105,113-14,138,169
S: 1

death
T: 389-90
M: 63-64

ego
T: 115,207-208,290

extension
T: 104,120,181,222,292,464,550

faith
T: 373,421

fear
T: 12,66,190,**202**,**225-27**,**230-33**, 302-303,347,382-83,391-92, **563-64**
W: 182,318-19
P: 9

forgiveness
T: 369,492,568
W: **73**,344,358-59

God
T: 119,151,176-77,**217-19**,
226-27,261,294-95,321
W: 174-76,**225-26**

grace
W: 313-14,315

gratitude
T: 201
W: 362-63,437

guilt
T: 220-21,221,**246-47**,297,382

happy dream
T: 238,570

healing
T: 147,537

holy instant
T: **290-92**,293-94,305,366

Holy Spirit
T: 163-64,258,264,273-75,300
W: 427,436

identity
T: 87,92,111,115
W: 112-13,321,396,428,469

invulnerability
T: 171,217
W: **79**,415,417,467

Jesus
T: 104-105,247-48,305-306
M: 55

judgment
T: 411
W: 470

justice
T: 499-501,507-508

law
T: 236
W: 466,468

messengers
T: 215,**382-83**

miracle
T: 1,3,539
W: 472

prayer
S: 2

real world
T: 195,207,237
W: **349-50**

sacrifice
T: 302-303,304-306,507

sharing
T: 75,178,217

sickness
T: 203

sin
T: 9,82,377,494-95

sinlessness
T: 451
W: 100,400

special relationships
T: **313-17**,**317-20**,464-66,466-69

magic

the attempt to solve a problem where it is not, i.e., trying to solve a problem in the mind through physical or "mindless" measures: the ego's strategy to keep the real problem—the belief in separation—from God's Answer; guilt is projected outside our minds onto others (attack) or our bodies (sickness) and sought to be corrected there, rather than being undone in our minds by bringing it to the Holy Spirit; referred to as "false healing" in "The Song of Prayer."

---

attack
M: **42-44**,45

body
W: 157

defenses
W: 172,250,258

ego
T: 29,53

guilt
M: 43-44

healing
T: 111-12,160
S: 16,**16**,17,**17-18**

Holy Spirit
T: 96
M: 59-60

mindlessness
T: 2,21
M: 64

psychotherapy
P: **3**

sickness
T: **19-20**,21,78,173
W: 263-64
P: **8-9**

special relationships
T: 457

temptation
M: 39-41

time
W: 291

world
T: 494
W: 79,132-33

spirit creates, while the ego makes.

knowledge: creation occurs only within the world of knowledge, creating truth.

perception: making, also referred to as miscreating, leads only to illusions; used rarely for the Holy Spirit, Who is described as the Maker of the real world.

see: *creation*

---

ego–Holy Spirit
T: **78**

ego–spirit
T: **49-50**

fear–love
T: 28,114

forgiveness
T: 369

healing
T: 23-24

Holy Spirit
T: 487-89

mind
T: **29,38**,77

projection–extension
T: 179

Self
W: 160

separation
T: 37,**39-40**

teacher of God
M: 12,18

thought
T: 1,44
W: 26

wish–will
W: 125

world
T: 195

despite the multitude of means in the world, there remain but two ends or goals: truth or illusion; the body can serve either end, as the mind elects.

w-m: the body is used as a means to bring about the goal of sin and guilt, reinforcing illusion through the special relationship.

r-m: the body is used as a means to achieve the goal of forgiveness, leading us to truth through the holy relationship.

---

body
T: **143-46**,362,386,405
W: 409,**415**,435

forgiveness
W: 145,**412**

God
T: 479-80
W: 413,413

grace
W: 313

holy relationship
T: 340,357

Holy Spirit
T: **409-11,422**
W: 427,440

perception
T: **479-81**,483

reason
T: 429,440

salvation
W: 449

truth
T: **340-42**,346

vision
W: 420

world
T: 608
W: 38

memory of God

the Atonement's final stage, which follows seeing the face of Christ in all our brothers and precedes the last step, taken by God Himself; we remember God through forgiveness, undoing all beliefs in separation that obscured His Presence to us.

---

body
T: 453

Christ's vision
W: 422

decision
T: 218
W: 339

face of Christ
T: **510**,521,592
W: 213
M: **79**

fear
T: 225,391,549-50
W: 77

forgiveness
T: 369-70
W: 99,397,427,460,468
P: **5**

function
W: 451,475

grace
W: 313

gratitude
W: 448

guilt
T: 223,225,246

healing
T: **203**

holy instant
T: 294,549

holy relationship
P: 5-6

innocence
T: 602

Jesus
T: 135
M: 83

last step
T: 550
W: **433**

psychotherapy
P: 16

resurrection
M: 65

sacrifice
T: 504-505,507

memory of God (continued)

special function
T: 508

true perception
M: 82

mind

knowledge: the activating agent of spirit, to which it is roughly equivalent, supplying its creative energy.

perception: the agent of choice; we are free to believe that our minds can be separated or split off from the Mind of God (wrong-mindedness), or that they can be returned to it (right-mindedness); thus, the split mind can be understood as having three parts: the wrong mind, the right mind, and the part of the mind (decision maker) that chooses between them; not to be confused with the brain, which is a physical organ and thus an aspect of our bodily self.

see: *Mind of God, split*

---

abstraction
T: 63
W: 297

attack
T: 114,359-60

body
T: **19-20**,21-22,**359-60**,371,386
W: 167,**245-47**,355
M: **23-24**
P: **12-13**

creation
T: 20,21,27

death
W: 311-12

decision
T: 114,**134-35**,168,207
M: **16-17**

denial
T: 118

ego
T: 60,**115-16**,208

extension
T: 91-92,117,142-43

guilt
T: 77-78
W: 118

healing
T: 160,553
P: 1

Holy Spirit
W: 372

Jesus
T: 39,134-35

joining
T: 186,**359-60**,553-54
W: 29

law of mind
T: 90-91,106,215

make–create
T: 38,44-45

mind training
T: 13
W: 1,164-65

miracle
T: 549,553

sickness
T: 142
W: 247
M: 16-17
P: 8

sin
T: 423,**606-607**

spirit
T: 10,38
W: **167**,170,456
M: **75**

world
T: 206-207
W: **236-38**,351-52

Mind of God

equated with the creative function of God which represents the activating agent of spirit, supplying its creative energy; as an extension of God, the Mind of Christ—God's Thought—shares in the attributes of the Mind of God—One-mindedness; after the separation, the Mind of Christ *appeared* to be split in two: Mind and mind.

---

changelessness
T: 168,201,320,357

Christ
T: 68
M: 75

creation
T: 58,120,**180-81**,495

guiltlessness
T: 222

healing
T: 371

Holy Spirit
T: **68**,72,91,241,262
W: 174,316

identity
T: 163,166-67,240
W: 261

innocence
T: 262

Jesus
T: **71**,75-76,113

light
T: 354,485-86
W: 418

love
T: 177
W: 217

miracle
T: 549

sinlessness
W: 55

thoughts
W: 67,**71-72**,98,168,266-67

Thoughts
T: 90,185,476
W: 92,426,454

Trinity
T: 35

unity
T: 113,136,175,587-88
W: 58

will
T: 69,471

miracle

the change of mind that shifts our perception from the ego's world of sin, guilt, and fear, to the Holy Spirit's world of forgiveness; reverses projection by restoring to the mind its causative function, allowing us to choose again; transcends the laws of this world to reflect the laws of God; accomplished by our joining with the Holy Spirit or Jesus, being the means of healing our own and others' minds.

(Note—not to be confused with the traditional understanding of miracles as changes in external phenomena.)

---

mind
T: 426

principles
T: **1-4,23-24**

revelation
T: 4-5

salvation
W: 153

sin
T: **538-39**

time
T: 6,10,30,162-63,547
W: 170

vision
T: 36
W: 154-56,**293-94**

Name of God

used as a symbol for the Identity of God, Which Self we share as His Son; the symbol of God's holiness, which is our own as well.

Christ
T: 201,286
M: 54

creations
T: 178,184-85

forgiveness
W: 402

Holy Spirit
T: 81,212,295,379
W: 138,316

illusions
T: 316

Jesus
T: 147,333
M: **55**

love
W: 428

psychotherapy
P: 17

salvation
W: 187,397

Son of God
T: 147
W: **334-35**,379,393,393,416,431, 472
M: 18,87

Teacher of teachers
M: 61

unity
T: 518
W: 261,**337-38**

no order of difficulty in miracles

the first principle of miracles; something is either true or false, with no real levels existing within each category; there is no order of difficulty in correcting illusions as they are all equally unreal, requiring only the miracle's shift from illusion to truth; similarly, there is no order of difficulty in healing as any form of sickness (illusion), even unto death, is undone in the mind—where it truly is—when brought to the truth there; the correction for the ego's first law of chaos: there is a hierarchy of illusions.

---

not to make error real

one of the key elements in the Holy Spirit's plan of forgiveness, correcting the ego's plan to make sin real which inevitably leads us either to erect defenses against it out of fear, or to forgive it falsely; true forgiveness, on the other hand, recognizes the error as a call for love and correction; making the error real, as when we falsely empathize with another, or magically hope to solve an external problem, roots us still further in the ego's thought system, while seeing all problems or forms of suffering as external reflections of internal guilt allows the true healing of the mind to occur.

---

attack
T: 156

cause–effect
T: 550-53
W: 63

ego
T: **155-57,191**

forgiveness
T: 156,**156-58**

Holy Spirit
T: **246**

Holy Spirit's judgment
T: **200-202**,203-205

illusions
T: 328,597-99

investment
T: 205-206

magic
M: 40,42-44

miracle
T: 552-53,**597-99**

sickness–healing
T: 173-75,550-51
W: 250-51
P: **9**

sin
T: 258,419
W: 179-80,287
S: **9-10**

unhealed healer
T: 159-61

One-mindedness

the Mind of God or Christ; the extension of God which is the unified Mind of the Sonship; transcending both right- and wrong-mindedness, it exists only at the level of knowledge and Heaven.

Christ
T: 37-38
M: **75**

Holy Spirit
T: 53,68

oneness

knowledge: the reality of God and Christ, Whose perfect unity constitutes Heaven.

perception: reflected in the world through forgiveness, the undoing of our belief in separate interests; our joining together with others, through the undoing of our thoughts of specialness, is simply the acceptance of our inherent oneness as God's Son; sharing this purpose of forgiveness is our one and only function, reflecting our function of creating in Heaven.

see: *One-mindedness*

Father-Son
T: 8,35,116,131-32,**139**,181-82, 182,246,248,385,**406**,**420**, 449-50,467,475-76,561
W: **218-19**,**237-38**,338,341,378, 402,421,454,456
M: 80
S: 1,14

forgiveness
T: 222
M: 79,81

God
T: 88,180,259,304,306,508, 516,563
W: 91-92,146,315
P: 14

holy instant
T: 289,292,293

holy relationship
T: 198,405,486-87

Holy Spirit
T: 269-70,278,312,531,556-57
M: 85

Jesus
T: 39,134,**136-37**
W: 394

Kingdom
T: 41,46,54,91,105,107,122, **122-23**,**358-59**,402,517-18
W: 346

love
T: 66,219,317-19,382,430
W: 225

mind
T: 82,256-57

miracle
T: 69

Self
T: 365
W: 160,**164-66**,167-69,170,254, 321,411

Sonship
T: **29**,**74-76**,102,147-48,162, 174,185-86,235,**315-17**,**332**, **347**,**349-50**,475
W: 94,261-62,296,362-63,416, **451**,469,471
M: 30
S: 4,18

Thoughts
T: 90,**586-88**,609-10

Trinity
T: 35,37,**135-36**,241,**483-84**

truth
T: 266

pain

(see: *suffering*)

peace

the goal of the Course; the condition for attaining knowledge and returning home; obscured by four obstacles—our attraction to attack (guilt), pain, death, and the fear of God—which are overcome by teaching and learning forgiveness.

A Course in Miracles
T: 128,464

Atonement
T: 83,163,244,257,404

attack
T: 193,380-82,502
W: 416

body
T: 12,15,384-85

Christ
T: 213,478
W: 332-33,442

death
T: 388,541

Easter
T: 396

eternity
T: 73-74,79,105

extension
T: 117,123,207,216,379,490
W: 51,**406**,474

forgiveness
T: 11,473,572
W: 104,114,210,**213-14**,470,474
M: 49,79

God/Heaven
T: 119,133,173,174-75,184, 185-86,186-87,235,**248-50**, 288,391-92
W: 79,183-84,185-86,193-94, 319-20,392,412

holy instant
T: 361-62

holy relationship
T: 350,395,448-49,475,477,518, 570-72

idols
T: 573-74,576

Jesus
T: 137,172,204,294,305-306,621
W: 394
M: 84

judgment
T: 42,434

obstacles
T: **379-95**
W: 319,358-59,363,365

peace of God
T: intro.,16,120,238-40
W: **339-41,347-48**,374-75,380, 387,396,419,423,466
M: **49-50**

salvation
T: 206,412
W: 118

special relationships
T: 227-28,245-47,315,467,473,
473

teaching
T: 92,98-100,102,**263-64**
M: 10-11

truth
T: **276-79**,341-42,345-46,371

war
T: 70,108,128,**452-55**,461,
464-65,488,535,565
W: 397
M: **28-29**,36,49

perception

level I: the post-separation, dualistic world of form and differences, mutually exclusive of the non-dualistic world of knowledge; this world arises from our belief in separation and has no reality outside of this thought.

level II: comes from projection: what we see inwardly determines what we see outside ourselves; crucial to perception, therefore, is our *interpretation* of "reality," rather than what seems to be objectively real.

w-m: perception of sin and guilt reinforces the belief in the reality of the separation.

r-m: perception of opportunities to forgive serves to undo the belief in the reality of the separation.

(Note—since perception and knowledge are often discussed together, "knowledge" is not cross-referenced below.)

see: *true perception*

---

learning
M: 8

mind
T: 38,425,427

miracle
T: 35-36
W: 463,466

part–whole
T: 144,240-41

prayer
T: 41

projection
T: 206-207,231,**415**,480
W: 81,441

real world
T: 194-95,219,368-70
W: **433**

specific
T: 51

thoughts
W: 25,28

world
T: 251
W: 336,403
M: 81

our guilt and fear cannot be undone without dealing with them through the opportunities for forgiveness used by the Holy Spirit; this honest looking within our minds with the Holy Spirit or Jesus—a process the ego counsels *against*—is what leads to the periods of discomfort and anxiety we almost inevitably feel in the process of shifting from wrong- to right-mindedness.

---

darkness–light
T: 179,186-87,353,401-402

development of trust
M: **8-10**

ego
T: 48,52,**164**,165-66

fear/terror
T: 28,225-26,367,392,408
W: 365
S: **5**

Holy Spirit
T: 98,345,611-12

illusions
T: 10-11
M: 87

learning
W: 23,80

perception–vision
T: 18,22-23,98
W: 15

special relationships
T: **322,337-38**,409,409-10,421, 444,**469-70**,613

prayer

belongs to the world of perception, as popularly understood, for it asks God for something we believe we need; our only real prayer, on the other hand, is for forgiveness, as this restores to our awareness that we already have what we need; as used in the Course itself, does not include the experiences of communion with God that come during periods of quietness or meditation; compared to a ladder in "The Song of Prayer," emphasizing both the process of forgiveness as well as the communion between God and Christ, the Song that is the very end of the ladder.

Bible
T: 152

forgiveness
T: **40**
S: **5-6**,**6-7**,9,14,19

Holy Spirit
T: **152-55**
M: 67-68

humility
S: 7-8

joining
W: 417
P: 14

justice
M: 48

love
S: 1

miracle
T: **1**,40

Name of God
W: 335,389

perception
T: 41

process
S: **1-3**,**3-4**

song
S: 1,11

words
M: **51-52**

process

A Course in Miracles emphasizes that within the dream of separation forgiveness occurs over time, and is therefore a process of growth; our fear of God's Love is so great that we cling to our specialness as protection, and thus we must learn gently and patiently that the ego's guilt and attack reinforce pain, while the Holy Spirit's forgiveness leads to joy.

(Note—since the workbook as a whole is concerned with the *process* of learning the Course's curriculum, only the more important references have been included below.)

see: *periods of unsettling*

---

miracle
T: 6
W: 170

prayer
S: 1,3,**4**,8,15

psychotherapy
P: 20

reawakening
T: 67,186-87

teacher of God
M: 1-2,8-15,**25**,43-44,57-58

teaching/learning
T: 47-48,52,61-62,196,**600-601**, 606
W: 43,289,300,328
M: 6-7,38

time/holy instant
T: 28-29,282-83,284,288, 324-25,354-55,404,404-406, 513,519-21,535-36
W: 291
M: 3

truth
T: 316,374,613-14
W: 284-86,**429**

undoing
T: 83,**97-98**,**98-100**,**100-103**

vision
W: 219

world
W: 236-37

projection

the fundamental law of mind: projection makes perception—what we see inwardly determines what we see outside our minds.

w-m: reinforces guilt by displacing it onto someone else, attacking it there and denying its presence in ourselves; an attempt to shift responsibility for separation from ourselves to others.

r-m: the principle of extension, undoing guilt by allowing the forgiveness of the Holy Spirit to be extended (projected) through us.

---

attack
T: **84**,85,89,231
W:33,40,**318-19**,364-65

authority problem
T: 43

body
T: 359-60,387

cause–effect
T: 552
W:28,49

crucifixion
T: 87-88

dream
T: **539-43,543-46**

ego
T: 89,91,119,120-21
W: **120**

extension/law of mind
T: 14,90,106,120,179,215

fear
T: 77,351
W:21,231,298
P: 15

forgiveness
T: 491-92
W:391
P: 13
S: **10**

God
W:114,122-23

guilt
T: 220,**223-24**,244,**244-45**
W:118
M:43
S: **5-6**

perception
T: 231,**415**
W:4,13,231,**454**

sacrifice
T: 32-33,498,523

separation
T: **88-89**

sin
T: 606,610-11

special relationships
T: 314-15,317-20,330-31,443-44

world
T: **206-207**,243,**347-48**,413-14, 415,540,**544-45**
W: 18,19,53,236-37
P: 2

questions

the Course presents our basic decision to choose between God and the ego in the form of different questions.

---

communication
T: 289

dream
W: 340

forgiveness
T: **411**,488,572
W: **243-44**
S: 14

God–ego
T: 78,179,**184**,286
W: 288,296

Holy Spirit
M: 78

identity
W: 260

problem–answer
T: **196**

purpose
T: 61,**341**,413,479

real world
T: 431-32

sin–truth
T: 432-33

Will of God
T: 139

world
T: 400

real world

the state of mind in which, through total forgiveness, the world of perception is released from the projections of guilt we had placed upon it: thus, it is the mind that has changed, not the world, and we see through the vision of Christ which blesses rather than condemns; the Holy Spirit's happy dream; the end of the Atonement, undoing our thoughts of separation and allowing God to take the last step.

---

reason

right-mindedness; thinking in accordance with the Holy Spirit, choosing to follow His guidance and learn His lessons of forgiveness, seeing sinlessness rather than sin, and choosing vision instead of judgment.

(Note—not to be confused with rationalism.)

---

resurrection

the awakening from the dream of death; the total change in mind that transcends the ego and its perceptions of the world, the body, and death, allowing us to identify completely with our true Self; also refers to the resurrection of Jesus.

(Note—since crucifixion and resurrection are often discussed together, "crucifixion" is not cross-referenced below.)

---

revelation

the direct communication from God to His Son which reflects the original form of communication present in our creation; it proceeds from God to His Son, but is not reciprocal; brief return to this state is possible in this world.

---

communication
T: 4,**64-65**

ego
T: 55

fear
T: 3,4,13

grace
W: 317

healing
T: 66-67

Jesus/Holy Spirit
T: 5-6

knowledge
T: 36

miracle
T: **3**,4,**4-5**

time
T: 4,23
W: 291-92,315

unity
W: 291,**315-16**

right-mindedness

the part of our separated minds that contains the Holy Spirit—the Voice of forgiveness and reason; we are repeatedly asked to choose it instead of wrong-mindedness, to follow the Holy Spirit's guidance rather than the ego's, and thus return to the One-mindedness of Christ.

---

sacrifice

a central belief in the ego's thought system: someone must lose if another is to gain; the principle of giving up in order to receive (giving to get); e.g., in order to receive God's Love we must pay a price, usually in the form of suffering to expiate our guilt (sin); in order to receive another's love, we must pay for it through the special love bargain; the reversal of the principle of salvation or justice: no one loses and everyone gains.

---

salvation
T: 460,**496-97**,517

special relationships
T: 296-97,**318-19**

suffering
T: 525
W: 179,346

teacher of God
T: 416
W: **284-85**
M: 8-10,**32-34**

truth
W: 157

vision
W: 42,56,355-56

salvation

the Atonement, or undoing of the separation; we are "saved" from our *belief* in the reality of sin and guilt through the change of mind that forgiveness and the miracle bring about.

---

cause–effect
T: **545-46**,552

compromise
T: 460-61

face of Christ
M: 79

forgiveness
T: 590
W: 73,103,**174-76**,213-14,344, 437
M: 35

function
W: 174-76,177-78,316,342-44, 449

God
T: 220,288
W: 120-21

guilt
T: 257-58
W: **118-19**

happy dream
T: 329-30,590
W: **397**

healing
W: 254
P: 10

holiness
T: 443
W: 56,60

holy relationship
T: 63,132,385
P: 22

Holy Spirit
T: 258
W: 168,316,369

illusions
T: 320
W: 119

justice
T: 503
M: 47-48

mind
T: 206-207
W: **236-37**,274

miracle
T: 598
W: 170

perception
T: 509
W: 67

real world
T: 195,330,508-509

reason
T: 442

right-mindedness
T: 53

rock of salvation
T: **496-97**

sacrifice
T: 519
W: 465

simplicity
T: 304,600
W: 135,153

sin
W: 179

teacher of God
M: 3,6

thoughts
W: 23,26,34

vision
T: 411,614

world
T: 493,586,614

scarcity principle

an aspect of guilt; the belief that we are empty and incomplete, lacking what we need; this leads to our seeking idols or special relationships to fill the scarcity we experience within ourselves; inevitably projected into feelings of deprivation, wherein we believe others are depriving us of the peace which in reality *we* have taken from ourselves; in contrast to God's principle of abundance.

---

attack
T: 119

body
T: **305,573-74**

decision
T: 57

ego
T: **52**,206

God
T: 561
W: 307

Holy Spirit
T: 76

love
T: 293

miracle
T: 3

need
M: 35

perception
T: 4,40-41

prayer
S: **3**

projection
T: 14,24

psychotherapy
P: 19

separation
T: **11**,39

sin
T: 78

special relationships/idols
T: 319,435,574-75,586
P: 22

truth–error
T: 9

Second Coming

the healing of the mind of the Sonship; the collective return to awareness of our reality as the one Son of God, which we had at our creation, the First Coming; precedes the Last Judgment, after which this world of illusion ends.

---

awareness of reality
T: 158-59

ego
T: 58

forgiveness
W: **439**

Jesus
T: **58**

Last Judgment
T: 158
W: 439,445

Self

our true Identity as Son of God; synonymous with Christ, the Second Person of the Trinity, and contrasted with the ego self we made as a substitute for God's creation; used rarely to refer to the Self of God.

---

attack
T: 465
W: 114,329

body
W: 415

Christ/Son
T: 73,**292**,620
W: 158,162,166,170,196,410, 411,**421**,441

ego/self
T: 52,365-66,613
W: 160,**167-68**

fear
W: 295-96

forgiveness
T: 474-75

God
T: 292
W: 334,**411**

healing
W: 254-56

Holy Spirit
W: 168,210,477

humility
S: 7

illusions
T: 12,558

Jesus
W: 322

love
W: 112-13,321,410,415

salvation
T: 186
W: 135,236-37

sinlessness
W: 330

unity
W: **164-66**,346

world
W: 225,227,410,411

senseless musings

most often used to denote attempts by the ego to understand ideas from the world of knowledge that are beyond our comprehension; occasionally used for attempts to understand the ego thought system.

---

ego
T: 51,117
W: 81
M: **73**

forgiveness
S: 13

God/Heaven
T: 185,261,480,591
M: 56
S: 4

identity
W: **261**,469

knowledge
T: **369**

oneness
T: 508
W: **316**

salvation
T: 590,614-15
M: 35,61-62

Teacher of teachers
M: 61

separation

the belief in sin that affirms an identity separate from our Creator; seemed to happen once, and the thought system which arose from that idea is represented by the ego; results in a world of perception and form, of pain, suffering, and death, real in time, but unknown in eternity.

Atonement
T: 16,18,90,331

attack
T: 226,449-50

body
T: 359,**371-72**,561,563-64,614

decision
T: 320

dissociation
T: 88

ego
T: 55,77,190-91
W: 457

fear
T: 50
W: 231

guilt
T: **220,290**

Holy Spirit
T: 68,331-32,334

magic
M: 43
S: **17-18**

mind/thought
T: 45,241,440
W: 87

origin
T: **14-15**,45,552

perception
T: 37-38,41
W: 336

projection
T: **88-89**,552

salvation
W: 177,397

sickness
T: 514,**553-54**
W: 254
M: 54

sin
T: 428-29

world
T: 207
W: 237-38

sickness

a conflict in the mind (guilt) displaced onto the body; the ego's attempt to defend itself against truth (spirit) by focusing attention on the body; a sick body is the *effect* of the sick or split mind that is its *cause*, representing the ego's desire to make others guilty by sacrificing oneself, projecting responsibility for the attack onto them.

see: *suffering*

Atonement
W: 263
M: 53-54

attack
T: 144-45,560

body
T: **144-46**,566-67
W: 251-53

cause–effect
T: 551,553,553-55
S: **15-16**

decision
W: **250-53**
M: 16-18,53

God
T: **171-73**,173-75,182,558

guilt
T: **525-27**
W: 263
M: 17
P: 13

healing
T: 372,557
W: 118,254-56,263-64

love
T: 203

magic
T: 20,78

mind
T: 19-20,**146-48**,553,553
M: **16-18**
P: **7-10**

miracle
T: 2,552-53,594-95

separation
T: 142,182,**553-54**,555-57, 557-58
W: **254**
M: 54
S: 18

sin
T: 514-15
W: 472

sin

the belief in the reality of our separation from God, seen by the ego as an act incapable of correction because it represents our attack on our Creator, Who would therefore never forgive us; leads to guilt, which demands punishment; equivalent to separation, and the central concept in the ego's thought system, from which all others logically follow; to the Holy Spirit, an error in our thinking to be corrected and therefore forgiven and healed.

Atonement
T: 362-63

attack
T: 490-91

body
T: 409,410-11,538-39,**606-607**

death
T: 375,383,388-89,494,498
W: 179

defenses
T: 82,399,446

error
T: **374-76,376-78**,428-29,
442-43,501
M: 45

fear
T: 15,**423-24**,451,520
W: 414

forgiveness
T: 488-89
W: 210,**242-44**,391
M: 83

forgiveness-to-destroy
S: 9,**11-12**

guilt
T: 78,376-77
M: 43,81

illusion
T: 327,515
W: **179-80**,242,**409**
M: 81

projection
T: 517,606,610-11

punishment
T: 374-77,455-56

sacrifice
T: 422-23,497-98,500

separation
T: 428-29,586

sickness
T: 514-15,525-27
W: 472

special relationships
T: 421-22,435,443-44,**467**,470, 472-73,474

suffering
T: 539

world
T: 413-14,494-96
W: 330
M: 35

sleep

usually denotes the state of separation from God, in Whom we are awake as Christ; our experiences within the ego thought system constitute our dreams of specialness, in which we believe we have accomplished the impossible of separating from our Creator; less frequently used in the popular sense of physical sleep, where it is emphasized that there is no difference between our sleeping dreams at night and our "waking" ones during the day.

see: *dreams*

Adam
T: 15

death
T: 182,541
W: 354,428

dreams
T: **169**,574

ego
T: 248
W: 114

forgiveness
W: 412

God
T: 326
W: 313

guilt
T: 261

happy dreams
T: 542-43
W: 263

Holy Spirit
T: 71,212-13,250

mind
T: 27
W: **311-12**

miracle
T: 551,568-69

nightmares
T: 94,194,236

physical
T: **146-47**,169,304

real world
W: 433

sickness
T: **146**

sleeping dreams
T: 232,350-52

special relationships
T: 351-52,471

teacher of God
M: 61,66

will
T: 69

Son of God

knowledge: the Second Person of the Trinity; the Christ Who is our true Self.

perception: our identity as separated Sons, or the Son of God as ego with a wrong and right mind; the biblical phrase "son of man" is used rarely to denote the Son as separated.

Cause–Effect
T: 420,550

Christ/Self
T: **187**,**620**
W: 160,162,195-96,**421**,471
M: 30,75

creation
T: 14,88,560
W: 266,**451**

crucifixion
T: 193-94

forgiveness
T: 595
W: 138

God
T: 10,182,269,298-99,406,406
W: **445**
S: 19-20

grace
T: 126

guiltlessness
T: 221-23,225,261,601-602
M: 3

Heaven
T: 505

holy relationship
T: 349,404,408

Identity
W: **353-54**,410,**469**
S: 3

immortality
T: 182,572

Jesus
T: 5,76

light
W: 101

Name
T: 147
W: 138,316

son of man
T: 87,225,481,482
M: 30

Sonship
T: 29,180,186

Trinity
T: 35

unity
T: 75,136,198
W: 164,261

song of Heaven

symbol of the love and gratitude that unites God and His Sons, who once believed they were separate from their Creator; in "The Song of Prayer," used as a symbol of the soundless communion between God and Christ.

---

ancient
T: **416-17**
W:298

Christ
T: 475
W:304

Easter
T: 398

form–content
S: **2**

freedom
T: 248,339,425,505

gratitude
T: 235,**510**,622
M:12

healing
S: 18

holy relationship
T: 337,511

Holy Spirit
W:369-70

love
T: 467,505,511,602
S: 20

praise
T: 248,446

prayer
S: 1,11

resurrection
M:66

salvation
T: 621

special relationships
T: 467

time
T: 512,579
M:87

special relationships

relationships onto which we project guilt, substituting them for love and our true relationship with God; the defenses that reinforce belief in the scarcity principle while appearing to be undoing it—doing what they would defend against—for special relationships attempt to fill up the perceived lack in ourselves by taking from others who are inevitably seen as separate, thereby reinforcing a guilt that ultimately comes from our believed separation from God: the thought of attack that is the original source of our sense of lack; all relationships in this world begin as special since they begin with the perception of separation and differences, which must then be corrected by the Holy Spirit through forgiveness, making the relationship holy; specialness has two forms: special hate justifies the projection of guilt by attack; special love conceals the attack within the illusion of love, where we believe our special needs are met by special people with special attributes, for which we love them: in this sense, special love is roughly equivalent to dependency, which breeds contempt or hatred.

---

attack
T: **294-97**,**313-16**,472-73,473-75

body
T: 321,330-31,406-409,472,
476-78

death
T: 335-36,474

dreams
T: 351

ego
T: 307,**333-36**,400

fear
T: 315,466

forgiveness
T: 468,**470-71**,488,492-94

forgiveness-to-destroy
S: **12**

God
T: 10,294,**317-20**,471
S: 6

guilt
T: 245,247,290-91,292,295-97,
314,317-19,321-23

healing
T: 529
S: 18

holy instant
T: **290-92**

holy relationship
T: **337-40**

special relationships (continued)

Holy Spirit
T: 291-92,298,323,334,483,493

past
T: 323-24,**330-33**
S: 7

psychotherapy
P: 20

sacrifice
T: 296,318-19

scarcity
T: 435,573-75,**586**
P: 22

separation
T: 290,563-64

sin
T: 435,443-44,**466-70**,472-73

substitution
T: 291,347-48,**464-66**

spirit

the nature of our true reality which, being of God, is changeless and eternal; contrasted with the body, the embodiment of the ego, which changes and dies; the Thought in God's Mind which is the unified Christ.

---

body
T: 22,392,**614-15**
W: 167

communication
T: 9,63

creating
T: 10,38,54,67,**122-23**

ego
T: 47,**48-51**,53,62

God
T: 41
M: 75

grace
T: 7

Holy Spirit
T: 73,122

immortality
T: 54

mind
T: 9-10,**38**
W: **167-68**,439,456
M: **75**

miracle
T: 1-3

Self
W: 167-68,**170-71**

soul
M: 75

without enumerating them as such, the Course describes four levels of splits, which are mirrored in the world by our special relationships: 1) the original thought of separation when we believed we had *split* ourselves off from God, leading to the belief in two minds: the Mind of Christ and the split mind; 2) the further *split* of the split mind into the wrong and right minds: the homes of the ego and the Holy Spirit; 3) the *splitting* off of the wrong from the right mind through the belief in the ego's thought system of sin, guilt, and fear; the Holy Spirit's Love now being buried beneath the ego's specialness, with God feared rather than accepted; 4) the final ontological *split* wherein the guilt in our minds is denied and projected out, making a separated world of attack and death, a world which appears to be split off from the mind that thought it.

see: *dissociation*

---

abstract–concrete
T: 63
W: 297

attack–guilt
T: 121,**220**,**223-24**
W: 318,**364-65**
M: 33

behavior
T: 25-26,200

body
T: 142,146,359,**364-65**,372,
573-74

creations
T: 168-69

ego
T: 77

ego–Holy Spirit
T: 43,**69-70**,110,116,**129**
W: 110,120

fear
T: 25-26,149

God/Heaven
T: 96,117,149-50,217,367,
454-55
W: 114,195,234

Holy Spirit
T: 45,201
W: **397**

love
T: 207-208,**209-10**,211,499

oneness/wholeness
T: 57,134,174,269,309,342,484
W: 164,362-63
M: 47

perception
T: 37-38,90,190-91,**231-32**,
442-43

projection
T: **88-90,206-207**,215

Self
T: 123,365
W: **167**,170,260

separation
T: 11,73,88
M: 75

sickness
T: 148,171,557-58
W: 118,**250-51**,254

sin
T: **377-78**,515-16

special–holy relationships
T: 197-98,291,313-14,331,347,
349-50,470,486-87,**530-31**

world
T: 206-207,**347-48**
W: **336**

star

symbol of Christ, of the light and Presence of God that always shines in us, and which forgiveness reveals.

Christmas
T: **304**

grace
W: 334

psychotherapy
P: 15

real world
M: 87-88

teacher of God
W: 243

Thought of God
T: **587-88**

truth
T: 615

suffering

one of the basic ego witnesses to the reality of the body and the non-existence of spirit, since the body appears to experience suffering or pain; to be in pain, therefore, is to deny God, while being aware of our true invulnerability as God's Son is to deny the reality of pain.

(Note—suffering and pain are used as virtual synonyms.)

see: *sickness*

---

teacher of God

at the instant we decide to join with another, a decision to join the Atonement, we become teachers of God; teaching the Holy Spirit's lesson of forgiveness, we learn it for ourselves, recognizing that our Teacher is the Holy Spirit Who teaches through us by our example of forgiveness and peace; also referred to as "miracle worker," "messenger," and "minister of God"; used as a synonym for students of *A Course in Miracles*.

A Course in Miracles
M: 38-39,67

Atonement
T: 22
M: **53-54**

body
W: 289-90,373
M: **30-31**

characteristics
M: **8-15**

Christ
W: 309-10,471

death
W: 303
M: 63-64

defenselessness
W: **278-80**
P: **9-10**

forgiveness
P: 5
S: 9

giving
W: **281-83**
M: 21

God
S: **20**

gratitude
W: 216-17,363

healing
W: 255-56
M: 18,19-20,21-22,53-54
S: **18-19**

Holy Spirit
W: 419,**436**
M: 38-39,51-52,67-69
P: 2,7

Jesus
T: 62,65
W: 322
M: 84,86

judgment
M: 25-27,37

light
T: 354
W: 104,144,218,347-48,406
M: 3

magic
M: 39-41,**42-44**

miracle
T: 21-24
W: 468

psychotherapy
P: 4,**6**,10,15,17-18,18-20

pupils
M: 4-5,6-7

reincarnation
M: 57-58

salvation
W: 172-73,177-78,345,**469**

Teacher of teachers
M: 61,84
P: **7**,10-11,20

Word of God
W: 220,424

world
W: 284-86
M: 1-2,35-36,61

teaching–learning

what we believe we are is what we always teach, and what we teach reinforces our belief; thus teaching and learning occur all the time, are really identical, and therefore cannot be separated from each other; our choice of what we teach and learn comes from our identity as spirit or ego.

Atonement
T: **262-64**,275
M: 6

attack
T: 92
M: 42

body
T: 145-46,566-67,606-607

change/contrast
T: 249,252-53,335-36,613-16

decision
W: 257

ego
T: 48-49,91-92,108,311-12

equality
T: 47,69,86,98,162
W: 436
M: **1-2**

forgiveness
W: **210-11**,357-59
M: 15

God
T: 95,259,**275-79**
W: 357-59

grace
W: 315

guilt–guiltlessness
T: 255-59,262-64,601
M: 3

happy learner
T: 252-54,262

holy relationship
M: 4-5

Holy Spirit
T: 95-103,107,109-10,129-30, 141,155-56,**210**,211,221, 278-79,280,311,536-37, 611-12
W: 210-11

Jesus
T: 48-51,75-76,**84-88**,264
W: 322

learning handicaps
T: 210

levels
M: **6-7**

love
T: intro.,87,92

mind
T: 48,98-99,111

peace
T: 100,263-64,276-79

projection
T: 106

psychotherapy
P: 4,17-18

Self
T: 312-13

transfer
T: 210,536-37
W: 1-2

truth
T: 251,251-52,252-54,275-76

vision–knowledge
W: 289-90,291-92

world
T: **600-603**
W: 336-37

temptation

seeing ourselves and others as egos or bodies, denying our true Identity as Christ by wishing to make illusions real.

---

attack
T: 87,462,488,606
W: 121,160,299,361
M: 21

body
T: 619
W: 105

decision
T: 602,**619-21**

ego
T: 337-38

God
T: 326,497
W: 389

guilt
T: 523,599

illusions
T: **598-99**
W: 101,105,422

Jesus
T: 87,622

littleness–glory
T: 451-52

psychic powers
M: 59-60

salvation
W: 118

self
T: **618-19**
W: 171

teacher of God
M: **39-40**,55

world
T: 476
W: 133,139,227-28

thorns

the Course's symbol of crucifixion, the sin and guilt of God's Son; the gift of the ego which projects guilt onto others and attacks them for it; contrasted with lilies, the gift of forgiveness.

---

body
T: **397-99**
W:298

crucifixion
T: 396,525

Holy Spirit
T: 506-507

Thoughts of God

knowledge: the non-spatial extension of God's Mind or spirit; includes all of creation, our true Self as well as our own creations; being part of God, His Thoughts share in His attributes: unified, eternal, formless, creative, and changeless.

true perception: used infrequently to refer to thoughts of the real world; e.g., peace, salvation, healing, and the miracle.

---

time

level I: an integral part of the ego's illusory world of separation, in contrast to eternity, which exists only in Heaven; while time appears to be linear, it is all contained in a tiny instant which has already been corrected and undone by the Holy Spirit, and in truth never happened at all.

level II: w-m: the means of maintaining the ego by preserving the sins of the past through guilt, projected by fear of punishment into the future, and overlooking the present which is the closest approximation to eternity.

r-m: the means of undoing the ego by forgiving the past through the holy instant, the medium of miracles; when forgiveness is complete, the world of time has fulfilled the Holy Spirit's purpose and will simply disappear.

Atonement/plan
T: 17,283
W: 174,248,**291**,316

carpet
T: **221**

cause–effect
T: **548-50**

decision
T: intro.,440,488
W: 258

ego
T: 72-73,**229-30**,280-81

eternity
T: 79,168,178,186
W: 399

forgiveness
T: 330-32,493,572

God
T: 180
M: 4,68

guilt
T: 79,221-22

holy instant
T: 234-35,281-83,325,340,362, 405-406
W: 360,443

holy relationship
T: 363

Holy Spirit
T: 229-30,**280-83**,511-13
W: 433

illusions
T: 222
W: 233-34,252,312
M: 4
P: 20

miracle
T: 1-2,4,**6**,10,30
W: 170

past
T: 233-34,240,270,330-32
W: 11

perception
T: 35-36

revelation
T: 4
W: 291-92,**315-16**

Second Coming
W: 439

separation
T: 45,**511-13**,519
M: **4**

teacher of God
M: 3,6,35,38

symbol of the world of sin, reflecting its inherent meaninglessness and harmlessness, despite its seeming solidity and strength.

---

dream
T: 578-79

fear
T: 564,590
W: **278-79**

gap
T: 564

guilt
W: 279

idols
T: 578,**589-90**

sin
W: 272,409

time
W: 466

war
W: 333

world
T: 368
W: 413
M: 32

Trinity

the unity of Its Levels is not understandable in this world; consists of 1) God, the Father and Creator, 2) His Son, Christ, our true Self, Which includes our creations, and 3) the Holy Spirit, the Voice for God.

---

creations
T: 138-39

God
T: 105,259

Holy Spirit
T: 67,72

Son of God
T: 35

unity
T: 35,37,135-36,**483**

true perception

seeing through the eyes of Christ, the vision of forgiveness which corrects the ego's misperceptions of separation by reflecting the true unity of the Son of God; not to be equated with physical sight, it is the attitude that undoes the projections of guilt, allowing us to look upon the real world in place of the world of sin, fear, suffering, and death.

see: *perception*

---

forgiveness
T: 329
W: 447
M: 81-82

gratitude
W: 232

holy relationship
T: 385-86,438

Holy Spirit
T: 110,249,495
W: **67**,357,420
M: 85

innocence
T: 34

knowledge
T: **35-37**,54,68,213,240-41
M: **81-82**

light
W: 25

miracle
T: 241

real world
T: 219
W: 330

right-mindedness
T: 53

world
W: 345

truth–illusion

something is either true or false, reality or illusion; there can be no compromise: we are either created by God or made by the ego; this principle explains why there is no order of difficulty in miracles, since all that is needed for healing or the miracle to occur is to shift from the illusions of the ego to the truth of the Holy Spirit.

A Course in Miracles
T: 34,320,440

Atonement
T: 243,325
M: 53

attack
T: 523
M: 42-43

body
T: 538

decision
T: **255**,332-33
W: 151,**239-40**,257,274-76,352

dream
T: 352,568-69

ego
T: 116
P: 4

fear
T: 190
W: 295

forgiveness
W: 243

form–content
T: 391,453-55,455,459
M: 22

God
T: 494
W: 351
M: 79
P: 2

healing
T: **372**
W: 254,**263-65**
M: 19,**23-24**
S: 17

Holy Spirit
T: 3,74,**99-100**,100,147,217-18, 253-54,341
W: 110,445

Jesus
T: 55
M: 83

Last Judgment
T: 30-31,**508-509**

life–death
T: 46
W: 302-303,311
M: **63-64**

perception
T: 195,515
W: 43

reason
T: 439-40

sacrifice
M: 33

salvation
T: 320,516,600
W: 174,274

sin–sinlessness
W: 55

special relationships
T: 314-15

spirit–ego, body
T: **48**,63,614
W: 167

thoughts
W: 26

world
W: 231-32,237

vision

the perception of Christ or the Holy Spirit that sees beyond the body to the spirit that is our true Identity; the vision of forgiveness and sinlessness through which is seen the real world; purely internal, reflecting a decision to accept reality rather than judge it; a shift in attitude from the ego's purpose for the body (specialness) to the Holy Spirit's (forgiveness), and thus is not to be equated with physical sight.

Atonement
T: 18

body
T: 476
W: 292

Christ
T: 212-13,232-33,241
W: 291-92,442

decision
T: 614
W: 31,42-43,422

extension
W: **45**,**47**,55

faith
T: 421-23

forgiveness
W: 131,137-38,292,294,355-56, 420
P: 14

God
W: 65
S: 10

holy relationship
P: 5-6

Holy Spirit
T: 212-13,398,412-14
W: 272,403
M: 85

innocence
T: **618-19**
W: 346,417

Jesus
M: 56,83

judgment
T: 405,419
W: 81

justice
M: 48

light
T: **232-33**,241,**417**
W: 25,191,313

miracle
T: 36
W: 154-56,**293-94**

projection
W: 13,16

real world
T: 212-13,218-19,621
M: 75

reason
T: 442

sinlessness
T: **410-11**,**411-14**,441,467-68
W: 447

Voice for God

(see: *Holy Spirit*)

symbol of the ego's belief in conflict between itself and its image of a vengeful God Who seeks to destroy it; this conflict is projected onto the experience of ourselves at war with the world and with everyone in it.

---

death
M: 63

ego
T: 108,128,**430-31**

God
T: **452-55**,461

illusions
T: **248**,453-55

miracle
T: **462-63,535**

peace
T: 70,488,565
M: 49

Self
T: 542,558

sin
T: 451

special relationships
T: 464-66,487

Thought of God
T: 588

truth
T: 603
W: 252

Will of God

the expression of God's being, which can only create; though seeming to be split by the separation and the ego's wishes, its wholeness and unity with the will of the Sonship remain unchanged and unbroken.

---

changelessness
T: 133,494
M: 3

Christ
T: 237,246
W: 291,368
M: 75

creation
T: 63-64,150,174
W: 389,451
M: 75

ego/self
T: 110,355,419,452
W: 159,457

extension/creations
T: 123,**131-32**,138-39,181-82
W: 133,357,450,**456**

fear
T: **149-50**,182

forgiveness
T: 516
W: 357,391,458
M: 79

happiness/joy
T: 12,131,182
W: 177-78,179-80,181,400

holy relationship
T: 438,593

Holy Spirit
T: 70-71,130,149-50,353, 483-84,601

Identity
T: 119,125,**130-31**,136

immortality
T: 182,194,209
W: 302-303

Jesus
T: **134-35**,**136-37**,139,287,621

magic
W: 132
M: 40,43

miracle
T: 125,136

peace
T: 133,174,250,464
M: 50

real world
T: 352
W: 88,125

resurrection
T: 193

salvation
T: 138,163

sickness/suffering
T: 173-74,176,184-85,237-38, 497
W:174-75,455

sin
T: 378,389,512-13,**515-16**, 594-95
W:409

sinlessness
W:330,459

special relationships
T: 466,467,470-71,477

unity
T: 34-35,136,148,150-51,182, 182,270,380,426-27,**486-87**
W: **128-29**,221,342,406,444,454
M: 18

vision
W: 65,97,131

wish–will
T: 124-25,189,590
W: 91-92,443
M: 79
S: 7

world
W: 308

wish–will

the ego wishes, spirit wills.

knowledge: willing expresses creation, which is truth.

perception: wishing can reflect wrong- or right-mindedness, both inherently illusory, since wishing implies that there exists a reality other than the unity of Heaven.

---

death–life
T: 518

decision
T: **124-25**

dream
T: 590

forgiveness
M: 79

free will
T: 44,134-35

learning
T: 601

make–create
T: 473

mind
T: 38,**517**

spirit
T: 122-23

truth
T: 515
W: 91-92

world
T: 207
W: **125-26**

Word of God

God's "answer" to the separation; used variously for different aspects of this answer: e.g., forgiveness, peace, Atonement, and the Holy Spirit.

(Note—does not refer to Jesus or Christ, as it does in the Bible.)

---

world

level I: the *effect* of the ego's belief in separation, which is its *cause*; the thought of separation and attack on God given form; being the expression of the belief in time and space, it was not created by God, Who transcends time and space entirely; unless specifically referring to the world of knowledge, refers only to perception, the post-separation domain of the ego.

level II: w-m: a prison of separation which reinforces the ego's belief in sin and guilt, perpetuating the seeming existence of this world.

r-m: a classroom wherein we learn our lessons of forgiveness, the Holy Spirit's teaching device to help us transcend the world; thus the purpose of the world is to teach us that there is no world.

see: *real world*

---

attack
W: **34-35**,125,277,403

body
T: 543-44,614-15
W: 123
M: 16-17,81

death
T: 220,572-73
M: 63-64

dream
T: 350-52,**539-43**,551-53

fear
T: 592
W: 21,231-32,245,403

forgiveness
T: 487-88,510,585-86
W: 105

forgiveness (cont.)
M: 35-36
P: 5
S: 11

God
T: 137-38,194,609
W: 23-24,274-75,308
M: 28,81

guilt
T: **220**,367-68,526,601

healing
T: 19,476
W: 237

Holy Spirit
T: 74,495-96
W: 403
M: 59

idea
T: 67

illusion
T: 367-68
W: 85,284,308,336-37,402,**403**

insanity
T: 251

judgment
T: 400-401
M: 25,26

love
T: 226
W: 225-26

mind
W: **236-38**

projection
T: 206-207,243-44,**347-48**,
413-14,415,539-42,544-46
W: 18,21

sacrifice
T: 504-506
M: 32-33

self-concept
T: 610-14

separation
T: 48,207,554-55,562
W: 336-37

sin
T: 494-96,517
W: 330

suffering
T: 539-40
W: 351-52

valueless
W: 227-28,239-41,394
P: 22

wrong-mindedness

the part of our separated and split minds that contains the ego—the voice of sin, guilt, fear, and attack; we are repeatedly asked to choose right-mindedness instead of wrong-mindedness, which imprisons us still further in the world of separation.

---

ego
T: **37-38**,56,59
W: 110
M: **75**

fear
T: 22

right-mindedness
T: 22,38,53

sickness
T: 19

Part III

SCRIPTURAL INDEX

(King James Version)

ABBREVIATIONS FOR SCRIPTURAL REFERENCES

Old Testament

Gn	Genesis
Ex	Exodus
Lv	Leviticus
Nb	Numbers
Dt	Deuteronomy
Jos	Joshua
Jg	Judges
1 K	1 Kings
Jb	Job
Ps	Psalms
Pr	Proverbs
Qo	Ecclesiastes
Is	Isaiah
Jr	Jeremiah
Ezk	Ezekiel
Dn	Daniel
Ho	Hosea
Jl	Joel

New Testament

Mt	Matthew
Mk	Mark
Lk	Luke
Jn	John
Ac	Acts
Rm	Romans
1 Co	1 Corinthians
2 Co	2 Corinthians
Ga	Galatians
Ep	Ephesians
Ph	Philippians
Col	Colossians
1 Th	1 Thessalonians
1 Tm	1 Timothy
2 Tm	2 Timothy
Heb	Hebrews
1 P	1 Peter
1 Jn	1 John
Rv	Revelation

A Course in Miracles

text
workbook for students
manual for teachers

"Psychotherapy: Purpose, Process and Practice"

"The Song of Prayer"

Page	*Quote*	*Bible Reference*
2	Miracles bear witness to truth	Jn 1:7-8; 18:37c
2	as blessed to give as to receive	Ac 20:35
2	loving your neighbor as yourself	Lv 19:18; Mt 22:39
2	heal the sick and raise the dead	Is 26:19; 35:5-6; Mt 10:1,8a; 11:5
2	likeness of your Creator	Gn 1:26-27
5	elder brother [Jesus]	Rm 8:29
5	"No man cometh...but by me"	Jn 14:6b
5	elder brother [Jesus]	Rm 8:29
5	"I and my Father are one"	Jn 10:30; 14:20
5	the Father is greater	Jn 14:28c
6	you do it to *yourself* and me	Mt 25:40
6	"Heaven and earth...pass away"	Mt 24:35
6-7	the resurrection and the life	Jn 11:25a
7	This is how a man must think	Pr 23:7
7	"Lead us not into temptation"	Mt 6:13a
7	The Golden Rule	Mt 7:12
8	bring in the stranger	Mt25:35; Heb13:2
9	"There is no death"	Rv 21:4b; 2 Tm 1:10
9	I came to fulfill the law	Mt 5:17
9	Those who witness for me	Ac 1:8; Is 43:10,12
10	"Except ye...little children"	Mt 18:3
10	"God is not mocked"	Jb 13:9; Ga 6:7b
10	cannot serve two masters	Mt 6:24
10	choosing to follow Him [Christ]	Mt 4:19
10	All shallow roots	Lk 8:13
11	the Golden Rule	Mt 7:12
11	"separation"..."fall"	Gn 3:1-7

Page	Quote	Bible Reference
12	*Perfect love casts out fear*	1 Jn 4:18b
12	this faith *is* His gift	Ep 2:8
12	All real pleasure...God's Will	Ps 40:8
12	who know not what they do	Lk 23:34
14	likeness to your Creator	Gn 1:26-27
14	the twinkling of an eye	1 Co 15:52a
14-15	The Garden of Eden	Gn: Chaps. 2-3
15	a deep sleep fell upon Adam	Gn 2:21
15	the deep sleep fell upon Adam	Gn 2:21
15	you *are* free	Jn 8:32
15	find it...searching	Mt 7:7b,8b; Dt 4:29
15	I have asked...perform miracles	Mt 10:1,8a; 11:5
15	cannot be performed in...fear	Mt 17:19-20
16	your heart...your treasure	Mt 6:21
16	"peace of God...understanding"	Ph 4:7
16	a two-edged sword	Ps 149:6; Rv 1:16
17	"The meek shall inherit the earth"	Mt 5:5; Ps 37:11
18	body as a temple	1 Co 6:19; 3:16
19	daily bread	Mt 6:11
24	"Father forgive them..."	Lk 23:34
24	"Be of one mind"	2 Co 13:11
24	"Do this in remembrance of me"	Lk 22:19; 1 Co 11:24-25
24	*I do not have to worry*	Mt 10:19
27	belief...move mountains	Mt 17:20a,b; 1 Co 13:2
28	the darkness is abolished	1 Jn 1:5; 2:8

Page	Quote	Bible Reference
28-29	"For God so loved the world..."	Jn 3:16
29-31	Last Judgment	Mt 11:22
30	God Himself...it was good	Gn 1:31
32	"Vengeance is Mine..."	Dt 32:35; Rm 12:19
33	Adam...Garden of Eden	Gn 3:23-24
33	be merciful even as your Father	Lk 6:36
33	"lamb of God...sins of the world"	Jn 1:29
33	The lion and the lamb	Is 11:6; 65:25
33	"Blessed are the pure..."	Mt 5:8; Ps 24:4
33	lamb "taketh away...world"	Jn 1:29
33	light abolishes forms of darkness	1 Jn 1:5; 2:8
34	Atonement, not sacrifice	Ho 6:6; Mt 9:13
34	likeness of His Own	Gn 1:26-27
35	commends his spirit	Lk 23:46; Ps 31:5
35	their hearts are pure	Mt 5:8; Ps 24:4
35	"When He shall...as He is"	1 Jn 3:2
36	Bible tells you to know yourself	Mt 7:3-5; 23:25-26
37	"Alpha and Omega..."	Rv 21:6; 22:13
37	"Before Abraham was I am"	Jn 8:58
37	"Fear God...commandments"	Qo 12:13; Dt 5:29
39	"Many are called...are chosen"	Mt 20:16b; 22:14
39	find rest unto their souls	Mt 11:29b; Jr 6:16
40	truth that shall set you free	Jn 8:32
40	"God created man...likeness"	Gn 1:26-27
41	Last Judgment	Mt 11:22

Page	*Quote*	*Bible Reference*
41	Last Judgment	Mt 11:22
41	"Judge not that ye be not judged"	Mt 7:1
43	"root of all evil"	1 Tm 6:10
44	"Seek ye first..."	Mt 6:33
44-45	"devil"...opposition to God	Mt 4:1-11; Rv 12:7-10
45	"sell" him their souls	Mt 16:26
45	The fruit...garden	Gn 2:16-17
46	There is no death	Rv 21:4b; 2 Tm 1:10
46	The branch that bears no fruit	Jn 15:2
46	Your kingdom is not of this world	Jn 18:36
47	twice as far as he asks	Mt 5:41
47	"Be still and know that I am God"	Ps 46:10
49	be still and know that God is real	Ps 46:10
49	you are His beloved Son	Mt 3:17; 17:5
49	God is not the author of fear	1 Co 14:33
50	Do not try to make...house stand	Mt 7:24-27
50	Its weakness is your strength	2Co 12:9b; Ph 4:13
50	Of your ego you can do nothing	Jn 5:19,30
50	The meek shall inherit the earth	Mt 5:5; Ps 37:11
51	if I had not once been tempted	Mt 4:1-11; Heb 2:18
51	*I have overcome the world*	Jn 16:33
52	Be patient a while	Ps 46:10
54	"Kingdom...is within you"	Lk 17:21
54	*the ego will not prevail against it*	Mt 16:18b

Page	*Quote*	*Bible Reference*
55	The Bible gives...you must ask	Mt 7:7a,8a; 21:22
55-56	no other gods before Him	Ex 20:3
56	Holy One	Ps 16:10; Mk 1:24
56	Holy One	Ps 16:10; Mk 1:24
57	The glass...is dark indeed	1 Co 13:12
57	darkened glass	1 Co 13:12
58	To the ego's dark glass	1 Co 13:12
58	the Holy One shine...in peace	Ps 16:10; Mk 1:24; Nb 6:25-26
58	Second Coming	Mt 16:27; 25:31
58	second [Coming]	Mt 16:27; 25:31
58	Second Coming	Mt 16:27; 25:31
59	your brother...in my name	Mt 18:20
59	I raised the dead	Jn 11:43-44; Mt 9:24-25
59	All things work together for good	Rm 8:28
60	"Seek and ye shall find"	Mt 7:7b,8b; Dt 4:29
62	Holy One	Ps 16:10; Mk 1:24
64	The Bible...should praise God	Ps 150:1-6; Rm 15:11
66	love his neighbor	Lv 19:18; Mt 22:39
67	"May the mind...in Christ Jesus"	Ph 2:5
67	the Comforter	Jn 14:16a
67	"If I go...He will abide with you"	Jn 14:16b; 15:4,10; 16:7
70	God did not leave...comfortless	Jn 14:18
70	What profiteth...soul	Mt 16:26
70	God's Will...earth...Heaven	Mt 6:10b,c

Page	*Quote*	*Bible Reference*
71	all power in Heaven and earth	Mt 28:18
71	the light of the world with me	Mt 5:14; Jn 8:12
71	"My yoke is easy..."	Mt 11:30
74	truth...set you free	Jn 8:32
74	in remembrance of me	Lk 22:19; 1 Co 11:24-25
74	The ego cannot prevail	Mt 16:18b
75	thoughts can make you...free	Jn 8:32
75	the Kingdom of Heaven	Mt 19:14
75	The Mind that was in me	Ph 2:5
75	"turning the other cheek"	Mt 5:39
76	I will never leave you	Heb 13:5
76	rendering unto God	Mt 22:21
76	depart in peace	Lk 2:29
76	I have loved you as I loved myself	Lv 19:18; Mt 22:39
76	have our being	Ac 17:28
80	The Mind that was in me	Ph 2:5
80	"As ye sow, so shall ye reap"	Ga 6:7c; 2 Co 9:6
80	"Vengeance...sayeth the Lord"	Dt 32:35; Rm 12:19
80	"I will visit the sins..."	Ex 34:7
80	"The wicked shall perish"	Ps 37:20
81	bearing false witness	Ex 20:16; Mt 19:18
81	"thine is the Kingdom"	Mt 6:13b
81	"I am come as a light..."	Jn 12:46
82	cast your cares upon Him	1 P 5:7
82	moved mountains...faith	Mt 17:20a,b; 1 Co 13:2
82	healed the sick...the dead	Is 26:19; 35:5-6; Mt 10:1,8a; 11:5

Page	*Quote*	*Bible Reference*
82	God commended His Spirit	Lk 23:46; Ps 31:5
84-88	Crucifixion [of Jesus]	Mt 27:26-50
86	"agony in the garden"	Lk 22:39-46
86	build my church	Mt 16:18a
86	the way, the truth and the life	Jn 14:6a
87	"wrath of God"	Ezk 7:19; Jn 3:36
87	"...peace...sword"	Mt 10:34
87	"Betrayest...with a kiss?"	Lk 22:48
87	The "punishment"...upon Judas	Mt 26:24
87-88	the Apostles...understand later	Jn 16:12
88	learned of me	Mt 11:29a
90	everything was created by Him	Jn 1:3
90	He uses everything for good	Rm 8:28
90	The ego cannot prevail	Mt 16:18b
91	The ego is legion	Mk 5:9
91	light of the world	Mt 5:14; Jn 8:12
91	light of the world	Mt 5:14; Jn 8:12
92	the truth that will set you free	Jn 8:32
97	To be of one mind	1 P 3:8; Rm 12:16
105	your joy may be complete	Jn 15:11; 16:24
105	true...forever	Heb 13:8
107	"I am with you always"	Mt 28:20
108	the way, the truth and the life	Jn 14:6a
110	Seek ye first	Mt 6:33
110	God is All in all	1 Co 15:28; Ep 1:23

Page	*Quote*	*Bible Reference*
110	All being is in Him	Ac 17:28
113	remembrance of me	Lk 22:19; 1 Co 11:24-25
113	Blessed are you	Mt 5:3-11
113	Come therefore unto me	Mt 11:28a
119	Sons of the living God	Jn 6:69
119	His beloved Sons	Mt 3:17; 17:5
120	All power and glory are yours	Mt 6:13b
122	spirit's own fullness	Ep 3:19
122	The ego cannot prevail	Mt 16:18b
125	not left you comfortless	Jn 14:18
126	Following Him	Mt 4:19
127	"What is truth?"	Jn 18:38
130-31	power and glory	Mt 6:13b
131	Glory to God in the highest	Lk 2:14
131	Ask and it shall be given you	Mt 7:7a,8a; 21:22
131-33	power and glory	Mt 6:13b
132	For I am…with you	Mt 28:20
132	in remembrance of *you*	Lk 22:19; 1 Co 11:24-25
132	imprisoned or released	Mt 16:19b; Jn 20:23
133	Yet He is All in all	1 Co 15:28; Ep 1:23
133	I am come as a light	Jn 12:46
133	I am with you always	Mt 28:20
133	I am the light of the world	Mt 5:14; Jn 8:12

Page	*Quote*	*Bible Reference*
133	to overcome the world	Jn 16:33
134	The remembrance of me	Lk 22:19; 1 Co 11:24-25
134	of Him Who sent me	Jn 8:16; 20:21b
134	The world…reject me	Jn 15:18
135	Of yourself you can do nothing	Jn 5:19,30
135	I will always remember you	Lk 22:19; 1 Co 11:24-25
136	likeness of God	Gn 1:26-27
138	over His Kingdom…no power	Jn 18:36
138	the prodigal son	Lk 15:11-32
139	Whom God has joined	Mt 19:6
140	Your heart…your treasure	Mt 6:21
141	power and glory	Mt 6:13b
141	Rejoice…you can do nothing	Jn 5:19,30
141	power and glory	Mt 6:13b
141	"The Word…made flesh"	Jn 1:14
142	temple of the Holy Spirit	1 Co 6:19; 3:16
142	through the body, but not *in* it	Jn 15:19; 17:14,16,18
143	thought cannot be made flesh	Jn 1:14
146	sickness…unto death	Jn 11:4
147	be perfect	Mt 5:48
147	to heal all errors	Is 26:19; 35:5-6; Mt 10:1,8a; 11:5
147	take no thought of the body	1 Co 6:15-20
147	accomplish all…in my name	Jn 14:13-14; 16:23

Page	*Quote*	*Bible Reference*
150	alien tongues	Gn 11:1-9; 1 Co 12:10,28
151	God is Love	1 Jn 4:8,16
152	all prayer is answered	Mt 7:7a,8a; 21:22
153	This light can shine into yours	Mt 5:16
154	What you give...exact measure	Mt 7:2
157	is not *of* you but *for* you	Jn 15:19;17:14,16,18
158	Last Judgment	Mt 11:22
158-59	Second Coming	Mt 16:27; 25:31
160	"Let there be light"	Gn 1:3
161	*By their fruits...know them*	Mt 7:16
162	What you offer...to Him	Mt 25:40
162	what you do to my brother	Mt 25:40
169	love your creations as yourself	Lv 19:18; Mt 22:39
169	your banishment is not of God	Gn 3:23-24
171	What Comforter can there be	Jn 14:16a
172	"My peace I give unto you"	Jn 14:27a
172	faith...make you whole	Mt 9:22
172	God is not jealous	Ex 20:5; 34:14
172-73	no other gods before Him	Ex 20:3
173-74	other gods before Him	Ex 20:3
174	no other laws beside His	Ex 20:3
175	the wages of sin *is* death	Rm 6:23

Page	*Quote*	*Bible Reference*
176	Who alone is his Help	Ps 115:9; 121:2
176	of yourself you can do nothing	Jn 5:19,30
176	be troubled over nothing	Jn 14:1
180	no beginnings...in God	Heb 7:3
180	I and my Father...one with you	Jn 10:30; 14:20
182	Blessed are you	Mt 5:3-11
183	know not what you do	Lk 23:34
183	your guest will abide with you	Jn 14:16b; 15:4,10
184	the Comforter of God	Jn 14:16a
184	Your Comforter will rest you	Mt 11:28b,29b
184	root of all evil	1 Tm 6:10
184	he knows not what he does	Lk 23:34
184	your joy would be complete	Jn 15:11; 16:24
185	The children of light	Lk 16:8; 1 Th 5:5
185	no other gods	Ex 20:3
185	God's Comforter can comfort	Jn 14:16a
187	But love yourself	Jn 13:34
187	Come unto me	Mt 11:28a
187	Blessed is the Son of God	Ps 118:26; Mt 21:9
187	Peace be unto you	Jn 20:19,21a,26
188	Be not afraid	Jn 6:20
192	false witness	Ex 20:16; Mt 19:18
192	"Blessed are ye...still believe"	Jn 20:29
192	ascends to the Father	Jn 20:17
193	I am *your* resurrection...*your* life	Jn 11:25a
193	ascend unto the Father together	Jn 20:17
193	as it was...ever shall be	Heb 13:8

Page	*Quote*	*Bible Reference*
193	Father has given you all	Lk 15:31
193	nails…thorn	Mt 27:29,35
194	nailed…crown of thorns	Mt 27:29,35
194	your redeemer liveth	Jb 19:25
194	To God all things are possible	Mt 19:26
194	a new Heaven and a new earth	Is 65:17; Rv 21:1
196	become as little children	Mt 18:3
196	you will see it as it is	1 Jn 3:2
196	if you ask you will receive	Mt 7:7a,8a; 21:22
197	Blessed are you	Mt 5:3-11
197	Kingdom…*is* within you	Lk 17:21
198	If you perceive offense	Mt 5:29
203	know your brother as yourself	Lv 19:18; Mt 22:39
204	A little while…will see me	Jn 16:16
204	There is no fear in perfect love	1 Jn 4:18a,b
204	The Lord is with you	Lk 1:28; Jg 6:12
204	Yet your Redeemer liveth	Jb 19:25
204	abideth in you	Jn 14:16b; 15:4,10
205	sell all you have…follow me	Mt 19:21
207-208	seek…find	Mt 7:7b,8b; Dt 4:29
209	death is your treasure…purchase	Mt 13:44-46
209	Your inheritance…nor sold	Gn 25:31-33
210	of yourself you cannot learn	Jn 5:19,30
210	"Seek and do not find"	Mt 7:7b,8b; Dt 4:29
211-12	lose your own soul	Mk 8:36

Page	*Quote*	*Bible Reference*
212	world...profits nothing	Pr 10:2; Jn 6:63
215	seek...find	Mt 7:7b,8b; Dt 4:29
220	Adam's "sin"	Gn 3:23-24
221-22	seeking...finds	Mt 7:7b,8b; Dt 4:29
222	Goodness and mercy	Ps 23:6
225	joy in Heaven...homecoming	Lk 15:7
225	son of man	Ezk 2:1; Mt 8:20
227	departing in peace	Lk 2:29
227	returning to the Father	Jn 14:12,28b
228	dust...you were made	Gn 2:7; 3:19
232	You who know not what you do	Lk 23:34
232	And He...return unto the Father	Jn 14:12,28b
233	risen in Him to the Father	Col 2:12; 3:1
234	born again	Jn 3:3,7
234	born again	Jn 3:3,7
234	born again	Jn 3:3,7
234	find it if you seek it	Mt 7:7b,8b; Dt 4:29
235	Now is the time of salvation	2 Co 6:2
235	only light...no darkness	1 Jn 1:5; 2:8
235	the light is in you	Mt 5:14; Jn 8:12
237	to return to dust	Gn 2:7; 3:19
238	peace of God...understanding	Ph 4:7
238	you have need of nothing	Mt 6:8,32

Page	*Quote*	*Bible Reference*
240	My peace I give you	Jn 14:27a
242	seeking…find	Mt 7:7b,8b; Dt 4:29
242	the gates of Heaven	Gn 28:17
243	For faith is…treasured	Mt 6:21
244	great is the joy in Heaven	Lk 15:7
245	born again	Jn 3:3,7
247	There is no fear in love	1 Jn 4:18a
247	No one who condemns a brother	1 Jn 2:9; 4:20
247	*be still*	Ps 46:10
247	I thank You, Father	Mt 11:25; Jn 11:41
247	my faith…on what I treasure	Mt 6:21
248	the gates of Heaven	Gn 28:17
249	They will not prevail against	Mt 16:18b
249-50	If that suffices Him…for you	2 Co 12:9a
250	His certainty suffices	2 Co 12:9a
251	Yes, you are blessed indeed	Mt 5:3-11
253	the "treasure" that you seek	Mt 6:21
253	the light…into the darkness	Jn 1:5; Lk 1:79
253	lets it shine on you	Nb 6:25
254	and built on truth	Mt 7:24-27
254	you will not look back	Gn 19:26; Lk 9:62
256	replace darkness…and fear	1 Jn 1:5; 2:8; 4:18a,b
256	If he…binds himself	Mt 16:19b; Jn 20:23
258	the innocence that sets you free	Jn 8:32

Page	*Quote*	*Bible Reference*
259	*He leadeth me and knows the way*	Ps 23:2-3
262	You know not what you do	Lk 23:34
263	Peace, then, be unto everyone	Jn 20:19,21a,26
264	Abide with me	Jn 14:16b; 15:4,10
264	Blessed are you	Mt 5:3-11
264	holy ground	Ex 3:5
264	Judge not	Mt 7:1
266	You know not what you say	Lk 23:34
268	All honor to you through Him	Rv 5:12,13; 1Tm 6:16
274	two or more join together	Mt 18:20
274	seeks…find	Mt 7:7b,8b; Dt 4:29
275	His Son, given all power by Him	Mt 28:18
277	no needs his Father will not meet	Mt 6:8,32
283	ascend unto your Father	Jn 20:17
283	Blessed is God's Teacher	Mt 5:3-11
284	For you are…and will forever be	Heb 13:8
284	weakness…strength	2 Co 12:9b; Ph 4:13
284	strength…weakness	2 Co 12:9b; Ph 4:13
286	The power and the glory	Mt 6:13b
286	All honor…of God	Rv 5:12,13; 1 Tm 6:16
287	the Prince of Peace	Is 9:6
287	Welcome me not into a manger	Lk 2:7
287	My Kingdom is not of this world	Jn 18:36

Page	*Quote*	*Bible Reference*
287	My Kingdom...is in you	Lk 17:21
287	abide with you	Jn 14:16b; 15:4,10
287	needs not seek to find	Mt 7:7b,8b; Dt 4:29
287	release...be bound	Mt 16:19b; Jn 20:23
291	love, where fear...is not perfect	1 Jn 4:18a,b
293	perfect love is in you	Lk 17:21; 1 Jn 4:18b
293	seek...cannot find	Mt 7:7b,8b; Dt 4:29
293	For the instant...he is not bound	Mt 16:19b; Jn 20:23
299	everyone seek, and find	Mt 7:7b,8b; Dt 4:29
305	seeking...you find not love	Mt 7:7b,8b; Dt 4:29
305	The Prince of Peace	Is 9:6
310	glad tidings	Lk 1:19; 8:1
311	joyful tidings	Lk 1:19; 8:1
311	"By their fruits..."	Mt 7:16
313	His Kingdom has no limits	Dn 7:27
313	Your bridge is builded stronger	Mt 7:24-27
315	seek and find	Mt 7:7b,8b; Dt 4:29
318	"Seek but do not find"	Mt 7:7b,8b; Dt 4:29
318	seeks...finds	Mt 7:7b,8b; Dt 4:29
320	raise other gods before Him	Ex 20:3
322	it will abide with you	Jn 14:16b; 15:4,10
325	Release your brothers	Mt 16:19b; Jn 20:23
325	His help suffices	2 Co 12:9a
326	Seek and *find* His message	Mt 7:7b,8b; Dt 4:29

Page	*Quote*	*Bible Reference*
326	*Forgive us…Amen.*	Mt 6:9-13
327	The betrayal of the Son of God	Lk 22:48
327	cannot be faithful to two masters	Mt 6:24
332	seeks and finds	Mt 7:7b,8b; Dt 4:29
332	Whom God has joined	Mt 19:6
336	Let us ascend…to the Father	Jn 20:17
336-37	the power and the glory	Mt 6:13b
339	justification for your faith	Rm 3:28; 5:1
339	will leave you comfortless	Jn 14:18
341	deception cannot prevail	Mt 16:18b
348	"God is not fear, but Love"	1 Jn 4:8,16,18a
348	the living God	Jn 6:69
349	holy ground	Ex 3:5
352	The light…cannot put it out	Jn 1:5; Lk 1:79
353	Who walks beside you	Lk 24:13-16
357	"Thy Will be done"	Mt 6:10b; 26:39,42
357	love your brother as yourself	Lv 19:18; Mt 22:39
365-66	The desert becomes a garden	Is 51:3
366	living water	Jn 4:10; 7:38
367	bear witness	Jn 1:7-8; 18:37c
373	faith is always justified	Rm 3:28; 5:1
373	Faith is the gift of God	Ep 2:8
374	glad tidings	Lk 1:19; 8:1

Page	*Quote*	*Bible Reference*
375	For the wages of sin *is* death	Rm 6:23
378	your brother as yourself	Lv 19:18; Mt 22:39
378	weary ones can come and rest	Mt 11:28b,29b
382	Perception...two masters	Mt 6:24
383	communion....I will join you there	Mt 26:29; Lk 22:30
385	I...overcame the world	Jn 16:33
386	seek...and not find	Mt 7:7b,8b; Dt 4:29
388	seeking...find	Mt 7:7b,8b; Dt 4:29
390	babe of Bethlehem	Lk 2:12
390	the resurrection and the life	Jn 11:25a
394	the power to forgive your sin	Mt 16:19b; Jn 20:23
394	faith and hope and mercy	1 Co 13:13
395	He leadeth you and me	Ps 23:2-3
395	garden of...agony and death	Lk 22:39-46
395	rise again	Mt 20:19
395	not to be lost but found	Lk 15:24,32
396	wander into the temptation	Mt 6:13a
396	I was a stranger...took me in	Mt 25:35; Heb 13:2
397	is against me still	Mt 12:30; Lk 9:50
398	There *is* no fear in love	1 Jn 4:18a
398	Let us lift up our eyes	Ps 121:1
402	enter with him to Paradise	Lk 23:43
402	faith...is justified	Rm 3:28; 5:1
402	no fear in perfect love	1 Jn 4:18a,b

Page	*Quote*	*Bible Reference*
402	the pure in heart see God	Mt 5:8; Ps 24:4
402	Son to lead them to the Father	Jn 14:6b
404	The ark of peace	Gn 7:9
404	making straight your path	Is 40:3; Jn 1:23
406	What is he	Ps 8:4; Heb 2:6
406-409	The Temple of the Holy Spirit	1 Co 6:19; 3:16
407	Love...known...misunderstood	1 Co 13:4-7
408	You are an idolater no longer	Ep 2:19
408	look you not back	Gn 19:26; Lk 9:62
408	Everlasting Arms	Dt 33:27
415	As a man thinketh	Pr 23:7
421	faith can move mountains	Mt 17:20a,b; 1 Co 13:2
422	sought to find it	Mt 7:7b,8b; Dt 4:29
422	its recognition is at hand	Mt 3:2; 4:17
425	The still, small Voice	1 K 19:12
427	the great deceiver's needs	Rv 12:9; 20:7-10
429	condemn the Son of God	Mt 16:19b; Jn 20:23
430	To give is...to receive	Ac 20:35
430	God is not mocked	Jb 13:9; Ga 6:7b
430	you are for him or against him	Mt 12:30; Lk 9:50
431	do not know...whom they hate	Lk 23:34
431	*seek*...find	Mt 7:7b,8b; Dt 4:29
431	seek...find	Mt 7:7b,8b; Dt 4:29

Page	*Quote*	*Bible Reference*
435	whom God hath joined	Mt 19:6
437	For no two brothers can unite	Mt 18:20
442	rock on which its church is built	Mt 16:18a
446	separate whom He has joined	Mt 19:6
447	seek…found	Mt 7:7b,8b; Dt 4:29
451	fear no evil	Ps 23:4
451	lead God's Son into temptation	Mt 6:13a
454	house of God…itself divided	Mt 12:25
454	Holy One	Ps 16:10; Mk 1:24
454	temple…becomes a house of sin	Jr 7:11; Mt 21:13
456	Sin cannot be remitted	Mt 26:28; Ac 2:38
457	this priceless pearl	Mt 13:46
463	have a mind as one	Ph 2:2
464	He will not fail	Dt 31:6,8
468	the power to forgive	Mt 9:6
468	the key to Heaven	Mt 16:19a
469	You *are* your brother's	Gn 4:9
469	the gates of hell	Mt 16:18b
469	The key you threw away	Mt 16:19a
470	given your brother's birthright	Gn 25:31-33
470	What rests on nothing	Mt 7:24-27
471	a flaming sword	Gn 3:24
471	"Thy will be done"	Mt 6:10b; 26:39,42

Page	Quote	Bible Reference
471	Holy One	Ps 16:10; Mk 1:24
471	come forth…dream of death	Jn 11:11,43
471	Curse God and die	Jb 2:9
471	the print of nails	Jn 20:25
471	The print of nails	Jn 20:25
472	Of itself…can do nothing	Jn 5:19,30
472	treasure house barren and empty	Mt 6:19
473	So are you bound	Mt 16:19b; Jn 20:23
474	hated him before it hated you	Jn 15:18
476	your brother…release you both	Mt 16:19b; Jn 20:23
476	lives and shares His Being	Ac 17:28
478	This is your son, beloved of you	Mt 3:17; 17:5
480	"…my own beloved son…"	Mt 3:17; 17:5
481	The son of man	Ezk 2:1; Mt 8:20
482	The son of man	Ezk 2:1; Mt 8:20
482	everlasting Love	Jr 31:3
483	see your brother as yourself	Lv 19:18; Mt 22:39
484	seek…found	Mt 7:7b,8b; Dt 4:29
489	that his joy might be increased	Jn 15:11; 16:24
490	In you is all of Heaven	Lk 17:21
491	returning unto God…His Own	Mt 22:21
494	the cost of sin is death	Rm 6:23
495	For God and His beloved Son	Mt 3:17; 17:5

Page	*Quote*	*Bible Reference*
497	the rock on which salvation rests	Mt 16:18a
497	one divided still against himself	Mt 12:25
497	only little faith is asked of you	Mt 17:20a
498	Vengeance is alien to God's Mind	Dt 32:35; Rm 12:19
498	lightning bolts...angry Hand	Ps 144:6-7; 18:13-14
499	Heaven's gate	Gn 28:17
499	stand at God's right Hand	Ps 110:1; Mk 16:19
499	power to forgive...sin	Mt 9:6
500	Judge not	Mt 7:1
501	you know not what it is	Lk 23:34
501	Heaven...treasures	Mt 6:20
504	see him as you see yourself	Lv 19:18; Mt 22:39
505	He is the same forever	Heb 13:8
505	Born again	Jn 3:3,7
508	the gate of Heaven	Gn 28:17
508	gate where Oneness is	Gn 28:17
508-509	final judgment	Mt 11:22
509	gate...Heaven	Gn 28:17
510	holy place on which you stand	Ex 3:5
510	gate of Heaven	Gn 28:17
510	Heaven's gate	Gn 28:17
511	how great...the joy in Heaven	Lk 15:7
511	gate of Heaven	Gn 28:17
511	Heaven's gate	Gn 28:17
512	the dead...be peacefully forgotten	Mt 8:22

Page	*Quote*	*Bible Reference*
513	Heaven's gate	Gn 28:17
514	in Whom all power...rests	Mt 28:18
514	gifts that are not of this world	Jn 14:27b; 18:36
515	in this world, but not a part of it	Jn 15:19; 17:14,16,18
517-18	What God calls...forever one	Mt 19:6
520	everything brings good	Rm 8:28
520	What profits freedom	Mt 16:26
521	holy ground	Ex 3:5
521	ground so holy	Ex 3:5
522	temple of the living God	1 Co 6:19; 3:16
523	you do not know him *as* yourself	Lv 19:18; Mt 22:39
525	fear no evil	Ps 23:4
525	a crown of thorns	Mt 27:29
525	His beloved Son	Mt 3:17; 17:5
526	every tear is wiped away	Is 25:8; Rv 7:17; 21:4a
528	forgive him his transgressions	Mt 6:12,14
528	Good cannot *be* returned for evil	Mt 5:44
528	removed it from his own [eyes]	Mt 7:3-5
529	the last trumpet	1 Co 15:52b; Jl 2:1
529	there is no death	Rv 21:4b; 2 Tm 1:10
532	eyes...seen or ears have heard	Is 64:4; 1 Co 2:9
535	Be not afraid	Jn 6:20

Page	*Quote*	*Bible Reference*
537	Peace be to you	Jn 20:19,21a,26
538	Sin's witnesses...call of death	Rm 6:23
538	truth he represents	Jn 1:7-8; 18:37c
539	The dying live, the dead arise	Is 26:19; 35:5-6; Mt 10:1,8a; 11:5
539	he knows not what he does	Lk 23:34
540-41	Seek not...to *find*	Mt 7:7b,8b; Dt 4:29
542	there is no death	Rv 21:4b; 2 Tm 1:10
545	others do...you did to them	Mt 7:12
554	treasures...thieves	Mt 6:19
555	Be not afraid	Jn 6:20
555	door is open...the feast of plenty	Lk 14:16-23
555	lean years	Gn 41:27
556-57	what is joined in Him is...one	Mt 19:6
557	I thank You, Father	Mt 11:25; Jn 11:41
558	fear...love	1 Jn 4:18a
560	"You are beloved of Me..."	Mt 3:17; 17:5
560	"...Be you perfect as Myself..."	Mt 5:48
561	what is joined cannot be separate	Mt 19:6
561	who can build his home	Mt 7:24-27
562	It is like the house...itself alone	Mt 7:24-27
562	ark of safety	Gn 7:9
564	"God is Love"	1 Jn 4:8,16

Page	*Quote*	*Bible Reference*
565	self be lost by being found	Lk 15:24,32
566	the holy ground	Ex 3:5
567	from sickness and from death	Jn 11:4
568	Whom you forgive	Mt 16:19b; Jn 20:23
570-71	Be...still and hear God's Voice	Ps 46:10
571	Behold His Son	Jn 19:5
571	his Father's house	Jn 14:2
571	how blessed are you	Mt 5:3-11
572	He will be as he was and as he is	Heb 13:8
572	Heaven would not pass away	Mt 24:35
573	There is no death	Rv 21:4b; 2 Tm 1:10
573	world will bind your feet...hands	Jn 11:44
573-75	Seek Not Outside Yourself	Mt 7:7b,8b; Dt 4:29
575	there is no death	Rv 21:4b; 2 Tm 1:10
575-76	anti-Christ	1 Jn 2:18,22
577	If Heaven is within	Lk 17:21
577	bow down in worship...no life	Ex 32:1-8
577-78	Judge not	Mt 7:1
578-79	toys...put away	1 Co 13:11
584	anti-Christ	1 Jn 2:18,22
584	Whose kingdom is the world	Mt 6:24
584	as you have received...you give	Mt 10:8b
585	whom God so loves	Jn 3:16
592	they still look back	Gn 19:26; Lk 9:62

Page	*Quote*	*Bible Reference*
592	the gate of Heaven	Gn 28:17
592	His Father's house	Jn 14:2
592	Look back no longer	Gn 19:26; Lk 9:62
592	coins of suffering	Mt 26:15
592	Do not look back	Gn 19:26; Lk 9:62
593	Be merciful	Lk 6:36
594	God is just	Is 45:21
595	*I thank You, Father*	Mt 11:25; Jn 11:41
595	graven image	Ex 20:4
597	Interpreter...common language	Gn 11:1-9; 1 Co 12:10,28
598	What you ask *is* given you	Mt 7:7a,8a; 21:22
599	And when He has appeared	1 Jn 3:2
600-601	Voice...small and still	1 K 19:12
601	Voice, so small and still	1 K 19:12
602	God is Love	1 Jn 4:8,16
602	be still	Ps 46:10
603	born again	Jn 3:3,7
604	be still	Ps 46:10
604	Be still and listen	Ps 46:10
604	Be very still an instant	Ps 46:10
605	He asks and you receive	Mt 7:7a,8a; 21:22
607	God has said...no sacrifice	Ho 6:6; Mt 9:13
611	seek...find	Mt 7:7b,8b; Dt 4:29

Page	*Quote*	*Bible Reference*
614	flesh...spirit	Jn 3:6
615	Your will be done	Mt 6:10b,c
615	"Your will be done"	Mt 6:10b; 26:39,42
615	forgiven it its trespasses	Mt 6:12,14
615	Your will be done	Mt 6:10b,c
615	Your will be done	Mt 6:10b; 26:39,42
617	you see...nothing with clarity	1 Co 13:12
618	likeness...whose image	Gn 1:26-27
620	your weakness...Christ in you	2Co 12:9b; Ph4:13
620	He...not leave you comfortless	Jn 14:18
620	cannot prevail against	Mt 16:18b
621	I thank You, Father	Mt 11:25; Jn 11:41
622	in Your likeness	Gn 1:26-27
622	lives and moves in You	Ac 17:28

Page	Quote	Bible Reference
26	own likeness	Gn 1:26-27
31	great indeed...your reward	Mt 5:12
31	the resurrection and the life	Jn 11:25a
31	all power is given	Mt 28:18
59	dominion over all	Gn 1:28
73	forgive...binding themselves	Mt 16:19b; Jn 20:23
75	Of yourself...these things	Jn 5:19,30
77	His strength...your weakness	2 Co 12:9b; Ph 4:13
78	Be very still	Ps 46:10
79	Such is the Kingdom	Mt 19:14
86	cannot prevail	Mt 16:18b
86	no other gods	Ex 20:3
101	depart in peace	Lk 2:29
101-102	the light of the world	Mt 5:14; Jn 8:12
102	to build a firm foundation	Lk 6:48
103	the light of the world	Mt 5:14; Jn 8:12
103	the light of the world	Mt 5:14; Jn 8:12
103	strength of Christ in you	2 Co 12:9b; Ph 4:13
103	*the light of the world*	Mt 5:14; Jn 8:12
104	The light of the world	Mt 5:14; Jn 8:12
104	How blessed are you	Mt 5:3-11
104	the light of the world	Mt 5:14; Jn 8:12
104	*the light of the world*	Mt 5:14; Jn 8:12
105	"...wander into temptation"	Mt 6:13a

Page	*Quote*	*Bible Reference*
105	the light of the world	Mt 5:14; Jn 8:12
112	you are the light of the world	Mt 5:14; Jn 8:12
114	God in their own image	Gn 1:26-27
116-17	the light of the world	Mt 5:14; Jn 8:12
117	the power of God	Mt 22:29
117	His Will and yours be done	Mt 6:10b; 26:39,42
120	"Seek but do not find"	Mt 7:7b,8b; Dt 4:29
121	All things are possible to God	Mt 19:26
124	Ask and you will be answered	Mt 7:7a,8a; 21:22
124	Seek and you will find	Mt 7:7b,8b; Dt 4:29
125-27	I will there be light	Gn 1:3
126	nothing can prevail against it	Mt 16:18b
130	glad tidings	Lk 1:19; 8:1
132	seek salvation...find it	Mt 7:7b,8b; Dt 4:29
133	truth that keeps us free	Jn 8:32
135	the Kingdom...is within you	Lk 17:21
135	the Will of God be done	Mt 6:10b; 26:39,42
143	the way, the truth and the life	Jn 14:6a
144	the light of the world	Mt 5:14; Jn 8:12
144	Let me be still	Ps 46:10
144	*the light of the world*	Mt 5:14; Jn 8:12
144	*the light of the world*	Mt 5:14; Jn 8:12
144	the light of the world	Mt 5:14; Jn 8:12

Page	*Quote*	*Bible Reference*
145	the light of the world	Mt 5:14; Jn 8:12
145	the light of the world	Mt 5:14; Jn 8:12
145	the light of the world	Mt 5:14; Jn 8:12
145	*the light of the world*	Mt 5:14; Jn 8:12
147	likeness of my Creator	Gn 1:26-27
147	likeness of my Creator	Gn 1:26-27
148	the light of the world	Mt 5:14; Jn 8:12
148	*The light of the world*	Mt 5:14; Jn 8:12
150	I will there be light	Gn 1:3
154	impossible...you are not alone	Mt 19:26
157	eyes that cannot see	Mk 8:18; Jr 5:21
157	God...should be light	Gn 1:3
157-58	strength...weakness	2 Co 12:9b; Ph4:13
162	God has...promised...ask	Mt 7:7a,8a; 21:22
170	He is with you always	Mt 28:20
173	on earth as...Heaven	Mt 6:10b,c
174-76	God...Love	1 Jn 4:8,16
177	Your joy must be complete	Jn 15:11; 16:24
181	seek this...find it	Mt 7:7b,8b; Dt 4:29
182	God, being Love	1 Jn 4:8,16
182	God...being Love	1 Jn 4:8,16
182	*God, being Love*	1 Jn 4:8,16
182	God, being Love	1 Jn 4:8,16
182	*God, being Love*	1 Jn 4:8,16

Page	*Quote*	*Bible Reference*
187-88	be still	Ps 46:10
189	From dust to dust	Gn 2:7; 3:19
193	Let it be still	Ps 46:10
193-94	born again	Jn 3:3,7
195	truth ... set you free	Jn 8:32
196	graven images ... worshipped	Ex 20:4
196	Seek Him ... find Him	Mt 7:7b,8b; Dt 4:29
196	Word of God ... sets you free	Jn 8:32
196	key ... gate of Heaven	Mt 16:19a
204	*My function here is to forgive*	Mt 16:19b; Jn 20:23
206	God, being Love	1 Jn 4:8,16
206	God, being Love	1 Jn 4:8,16
207	be still	Ps 46:10
207	*be still*	Ps 46:10
207	be still	Ps 46:10
210	bears witness	Jn 1:7-8; 18:37c
213	Seek ... You will not find	Mt 7:7b,8b; Dt 4:29
219	transfiguration	Mt 17:2
219	the glass	1 Co 13:12
220	the tidings of salvation	Lk 1:19; 8:1
221	be still	Ps 46:10
221	be still	Ps 46:10
225	Seek not ... to find your Self	Mt 7:7b,8b; Dt 4:29

Page	*Quote*	*Bible Reference*
226	He will abide with you	Jn 14:16b; 15:4,10
227-28	be still	Ps 46:10
231	be sought...not be found	Mt 7:7b,8b; Dt 4:29
231	seeking what can not be found	Mt 7:7b,8b; Dt 4:29
233-35	seek...find	Mt 7:7b,8b; Dt 4:29
236	seeking...want to find	Mt 7:7b,8b; Dt 4:29
237	sick are healed...dead arise	Is 26:19; 35:5-6; Mt 10:1,8a; 11:5
241	the gate of Heaven	Gn 28:17
242	as white as snow	Is 1:18
243	Heaven's gate	Gn 28:17
246	its [body] value...dust	Gn 2:6-7
252	truth...set us free	Jn 8:32
254	anti-Christ	1 Jn 2:18,22
261	he knows not what he is	Lk 23:34
263	Peace be to you	Jn 20:19,21a,26
264	but seek it...must be found	Mt 7:7b,8b; Dt 4:29
264	We will be still	Ps 46:10
267	the Lord of Hosts	Ps 46:7,11
272	bear false witness	Ex 20:16; Mt 19:18
272	within the Holy, holy as Itself	Ex 26:33
273	your transfiguration	Mt 17:2

Page	*Quote*	*Bible Reference*
277	You know not what you do	Lk 23:34
277-78	Christ's strength...weakness	2 Co 12:9b; Ph 4:13
278	Be still a moment	Ps 46:10
278	God has elected all, but few	Mt 20:16b; 22:14
280	We rise up strong in Christ	2 Co 12:9b; Ph 4:13
280	Be not afraid nor timid	Jn 6:20
284	living in the world...not here	Jn 15:19; 17:14,16,18
284	serve them...serve yourself	Lv 19:18; Mt 22:39
285	truth...lighting up the path	Is 42:16
285	ransom from illusion	Ps 49:7; Mt20:28
287	Where you are He is	Jn 14:3
287	apart from Him and live	Ac 17:28
287	unto Its likeness	Gn 1:26-27
290	Holy One	Ps 16:10; Mk 1:24
292	its image...its likeness	Gn 1:26-27
293	The darkened glass	1 Co 13:12
293	on earth, as...in Heaven	Mt 6:10b,c
293	and the blind can see	Is 26:19; 35:5-6; Mt 10:1,8a; 11:5
293	received but for the asking	Mt 7:7a,8a; 21:22
294	holy ground	Ex 3:5
295	fear...created in His likeness	Gn 1:26-27
295	search...find	Mt 7:7b,8b; Dt 4:29
296	Whom God has joined	Mt 19:6
296	denies...brother is denying Him	Mt 25:45
296	the gift of sight	Mk 10:51-52

Page	Quote	Bible Reference
298	nails which pierce	Jn 20:25
298	lift the crown of thorns	Mt 27:29
300	trumpet of awakening…its call	1 Co 15:52b; Jl 2:1
300	will never look on death	Jn 8:51; 11:25b,26
302-303	There is no death	Rv 21:4b; 2 Tm 1:10
303	*We live and move in You alone*	Ac 17:28
306	Ask…and it is given you	Mt 7:7a,8a; 21:22
311	There is no death	Rv 21:4b; 2 Tm 1:10
311	There is no death	Rv 21:4b; 2 Tm 1:10
311	There is no death	Rv 21:4b; 2 Tm 1:10
312	As we were…forever be	Heb 13:8
313	never-changing Love	Jr 31:3
315-16	bear witness	Jn 1:7-8; 18:37c
316	the time…is now at hand	Mt 3:2; 4:17
319	gods of vengeance	Dt 32:35; Rm 12:19
321	*be quiet and…be still*	Ps 46:10
321-22	*God is but Love*	1 Jn 4:8,16
322	Hallowed your name	Mt 6:9
324-27	God is but Love	1 Jn 4:8,16
331	seeking…find	Mt 7:7b,8b; Dt 4:29
331	His Father's house	Jn 14:2
331	holy ground	Ex 3:5
331-33	be still an instant	Ps 46:10

Page	*Quote*	*Bible Reference*
332	profits nothing	Pr 10:2; Jn 6:63
334	The sick...blind...deaf	Is 26:19; 35:5-6; Mt 10:1,8a; 11:5
334	tears of pain are dried	Is 25:8; Rv7:17;21:4a
335	Let all thoughts be still	Ps 46:10
339	Many...few	Mt 20:16b; 22:14
339	should any two agree	Mt 18:19
340	seeks...find	Mt 7:7b,8b; Dt 4:29
342	the Will of God is done	Mt 6:10b,c
350	Be still	Ps 46:10
350	Is it not He...the way to Him	Jn 14:5
350	Ask and receive	Mt 7:7a,8a; 21:22
350	*Your Will...be done in us*	Mt 6:10b,c
354	Son of God has come in glory	Mt 16:27; 25:31
354	redeem the lost...the helpless	Mt 18:11
354	All power is given unto you	Mt 28:18
354	nothing that you cannot do	Mt 17:20c
354	They must await...you are free	Mt 16:19b; Jn 20:23
356	born again in Christ	Jn 3:3,7
356	Release instead of bind	Mt 16:19b; Jn 20:23
358	all tears be wiped away	Is 25:8; Rv 7:17; 21:4a
358	Give...and give a little more	Mt 19:21
358	arise...our Father's house	Lk 15:18
358	our Father's house	Jn 14:2
359	Heaven's gate	Gn 28:17

Page	*Quote*	*Bible Reference*
360	Heaven's gate	Gn 28:17
362	It will never be...bound	Mt 16:19b; Jn 20:23
367	know not what...do	Lk 23:34
367	The world...offer it release	Mt 16:19b; Jn 20:23
368	live and move in Him	Ac 17:28
370	on earth and...holy home	Mt 6:10b,c
370	as you forgive the trespasses	Mt 6:12,14
374	You will be bound...as he is	Mt 16:19b; Jn 20:23
374-75	Seek...find	Mt 7:7b,8b; Dt 4:29
375	gate of Heaven	Gn 28:17
375	the path is straight	Is 40:3; Jn 1:23
378	I will be still an instant	Ps 46:10
381	*I will be still*	Ps 46:10
387	*Be still, my mind*	Ps 46:10
389	search for truth...found	Mt 7:7b,8b; Dt 4:29
389	we need but be still	Ps 46:10
392	Let all my thoughts be still	Ps 46:10
392	let our thoughts be still	Ps 46:10
392	I live and move in Him	Ac 17:28
396	I seek...and find It	Mt 7:7b,8b; Dt 4:29
396	seek and find	Mt 7:7b,8b; Dt 4:29
396	*seek...find*	Mt 7:7b,8b; Dt 4:29
398	*seek...to find*	Mt 7:7b,8b; Dt 4:29
398	seek...to find	Mt 7:7b,8b; Dt 4:29

Page	*Quote*	*Bible Reference*
401	arise in glory…shine	Is 60:1
403	find…seek	Mt 7:7b,8b; Dt 4:29
406	if I have hatred in my heart	1 Jn 2:9; 4:20
409	loves him…everlasting Love	Jr 31:3
409	How long, O holy Son of God	Ps 89:46; 13:1
410	I sought…I find myself	Mt 7:7b,8b; Dt 4:29
411	every voice but God's be still	Ps 46:10
412	bear witness to the truth	Jn 1:7-8; 18:37c
416	my refuge and my strength	Ps 46:1
416	*Let me not seek…and find*	Mt 7:7b,8b; Dt 4:29
416	be sought and found	Mt 7:7b,8b; Dt 4:29
417	our Father's house	Jn 14:2
417	*before me and…beside me*	Ps 139:5
418	This day we enter into paradise	Lk 23:43
421	let us seek to find	Mt 7:7b,8b; Dt 4:29
425	Let me not bind Your Son	Mt 16:19b; Jn 20:23
431	seek and find	Mt 7:7b,8b; Dt 4:29
434	God's Will is done	Mt 6:10b,c
434	We will seek…find	Mt 7:7b,8b; Dt 4:29
436	seek and find	Mt 7:7b,8b; Dt 4:29
439	Second Coming	Mt 16:27; 25:31
439	Second Coming	Mt 16:27; 25:31
439	Second Coming	Mt 16:27; 25:31

Page	*Quote*	*Bible Reference*
439	Second Coming	Mt 16:27; 25:31
439	Second Coming's way	Mt 16:27; 25:31
439	Last Judgment	Mt 11:22
439	Second Coming	Mt 16:27; 25:31
439	Second Coming	Mt 16:27; 25:31
439	Second Coming	Mt 16:27; 25:31
440	God...wipe away all tears	Is 25:8; Rv 7:17; 21:4a
441	The holy Christ is born in me	Jn 3:3,7
441	He is born again in me	Jn 3:3,7
445	Last Judgment	Mt 11:22
445	Second Coming	Mt 16:27; 25:31
445	Final Judgment	Mt 11:22
445	Last Judgment	Mt 11:22
445	Final Judgment	Mt 11:22
445	Be not afraid of love	Jn 6:20
445	wipe away all tears	Is 25:8; Rv 7:17; 21:4a
445	Final Judgment	Mt 11:22
450	I came...salvation...world	Jn 18:37b
450	My Father...power unto me	Mt 28:18
450	in earth and Heaven	Mt 28:18
451	let God's Will...on earth	Mt 6:10b,c
452	the likeness of Himself	Gn 1:26-27
452	Holy One	Ps 16:10; Mk 1:24
453	*Your beloved Son*	Mt 3:17; 17:5
454	therefore seeks to find	Mt 7:7b,8b; Dt 4:29
454	*as it is in Heaven, so on earth*	Mt 6:10b,c

Page	*Quote*	*Bible Reference*
455	second place to gain the first	Mt 19:30; 20:16a
458	Fear binds....sets it free	Mt 16:19b; Jn 20:23
458	*bind...release*	Mt 16:19b; Jn 20:23
459	I go to find	Mt 7:7b,8b; Dt 4:29
459	*I seek*	Mt 7:7b,8b; Dt 4:29
461	His beloved Son	Mt 3:17; 17:5
464	*gate of Heaven*	Gn 28:17
466	*I do not seek...would find*	Mt 7:7b,8b; Dt 4:29
466	*I would abide in You*	Jn 14:16b; 15:4,10
467	Be very still	Ps 46:10
467	Your grace suffices me	2 Co 12:9a
468	Our Father knows our needs	Mt 6:8,32
469	the gate of Heaven	Gn 28:17
469	it is written on our hearts	Rm 2:15
469	glad tidings	Lk 1:19; 8:1
469	the gate of Heaven	Gn 28:17
470	*not left me comfortless*	Jn 14:18
473	*be still, remembering*	Ps 46:10
475	the way, the truth and life	Jn 14:6a
476	"...all I have is his"	Lk 15:31
477-78	For we go homeward	Lk 15:20
478	never leave you comfortless	Jn 14:18

Page	*Quote*	*Bible Reference*
3	light has entered the darkness	Jn 1:5; Lk 1:79
3	bringer of salvation	Lk 1:77
3	Many hear...few will answer	Mt 20:16b; 22:14
5	any two who join together	Mt 18:20
8	*in* them but not *of* them	Jn 15:19; 17:14,16,18
14	seeking...it finds	Mt 7:7b,8b; Dt 4:29
15	glad tidings	Lk 1:19; 8:1
15	Blessed indeed are they	Mt 5:3-11
15	bringers of salvation	Lk 1:77
26	judge anything rightly	Jn 7:24
30	son of man	Ezk 2:1; Mt 8:20
32	to seek without finding	Mt 7:7b,8b; Dt 4:29
33	"Seek but do not find"	Mt 7:7b,8b; Dt 4:29
36	His Will be done	Mt 6:10b; 26:39,42
37	Final Judgment	Mt 11:22
37	Final Judgment	Mt 11:22
37	Final Judgment	Mt 11:22
37	Judge not	Mt 7:1
37	Final Judgment	Mt 11:22
37	Learn to be quiet...stillness	Ps 46:10
37	There is no deceit in God	Is 37:10; Jr 20:7
37	His promises are sure	Lk 24:49; Ps 105:42
41	the gate of Heaven	Gn 28:17
44	There is no death	Rv 21:4b; 2Tm 1:10

Page	*Quote*	*Bible Reference*
48	What had been lost…found	Lk 15:24,32
49	peace…not of this world	Jn 14:27a,b; 18:36
49	fail to find…but seeks	Mt 7:7b,8b; Dt 4:29
51	What you ask for you receive	Mt 7:7a,8a; 21:22
54	"This is my beloved Son"	Mt 3:17; 17:5
55	"Ask…Jesus Christ"	Jn 14:13-14; 16:23
55	Remember his promises	Jn 14:13-14; 16:23
56	he is with you…always here	Mt 28:20
59	the walls…fall	Jos 6:20
60	withheld from love…fear	1 Jn 4:18a
61	His Word…everyone's heart	Rm 2:15
64	"…overcome…death"	1 Co 15:26
66	Final Judgment	Mt 11:22
67	"Of myself I can do nothing"	Jn 5:19,30
68	translate…into His language	Rm 8:26
68	A loving father…His Son	Mt 7:9-11
68	your weakness is His strength	2 Co 12:9b; Ph 4:13
69	of all things visible	Col 1:16
79	God knows what His Son needs	Mt 6:8,32
79	Heaven…outside the gate	Gn 28:17
82	Hallowed your name and His	Mt 6:9
83	Their names are legion	Mk 5:9

Page	*Quote*	*Bible Reference*
84	*There is no death*	Rv 21:4b; 2Tm 1:10
85	Jesus...ascended into Heaven	Ac 1:8-9; 2:1-4
85	in His likeness or spirit	Gn 1:26-27
85	All power in Heaven and earth	Mt 28:18
85	a far country	Lk 15:13
87	the Holy of the Holies	Ex 26:33
87	loves you as He loves Himself	Lv 19:18; Mt 22:39
87	Ask...help to roll the stone away	Mt28:2;Jn11:38-39
87	Be not afraid	Jn 6:20
87	morning star	Rv 2:28; 22:16

"Psychotherapy: Purpose, Process and Practice"

Page	*Quote*	*Bible Reference*
1	the Way, the Truth and the Life	Jn 14:6a
5	the temple of the Holy Spirit	1 Co 6:19; 3:16
6	If any two are joined	Mt 18:20
6	Let him be still	Ps 46:10
8	asked for and…received	Mt 7:7a,8a; 21:22
11	helpless of ourselves	Jn 5:19,30
11	forgive…trespasses	Mt 6:12,14
14	Physician, heal thyself	Lk 4:23
15	all power in earth and Heaven	Mt 28:18
19	God is said to have looked	Gn 1:31
22	to him who hath…given	Mt 13:12
22	Relationships…temple	1 Co 6:19; 3:16
22	Physician…heal thyself	Lk 4:23
23	glad tidings of salvation	Lk 1:19; 8:1
23	God sent His Son	Rm 8:3

"The Song of Prayer"

Page	*Quote*	*Bible Reference*
1	Ask...to receive	Mt 7:7a,8a; 21:22
2	sought first the Kingdom	Mt 6:33
2	have no gods before Him	Ex 20:3
3	prays without ceasing	Th 5:17
3	Ask and you have received	Mt 7:7a,8a; 21:22
9	seek and find	Mt 7:7b,8b; Dt 4:29
9	Forgiveness-to-destroy *is* death	Rm 6:23
10	as you see the Son	Mt 25:40
13	Christ is for all...in all	1 Co 15:28; Ep 1:23
13	arise...your Father's house	Lk 15:18
13	your Father's house	Jn 14:2
14	He will not leave you comfortless	Jn 14:18
15	back to dust...will return	Gn 2:7; 3:19
16	depart in peace	Lk 2:29
18	no fear...for love has entered	1 Jn 4:18a
19	His likeness	Gn 1:26,27
19	as you choose...and God to you	Mt 25:40
19	Vengeance is His	Dt 32:35; Rm 12:19
20	Be still an instant	Ps 46:10
20	the thorns fall...bleeding brow	Mt 27:29

Bible

Old Testament

New Testament

OLD TESTAMENT

Genesis

Chapter and Verse	*Quote*	*Course Reference*
1:3	Let there be light	T: 160
		W: 125-27
		W: 150
		W: 157
1:26-27	make man in our image	T: 2
		T: 14
		T: 34
		T: 40
		T: 136
		T: 618
		T: 622
		W: 26
		W: 114
		W: 147
		W: 147
		W: 287
		W: 292
		W: 295
		W: 452
		M: 85
		S: 19
1:28	dominion over [all]	W: 59
1:31	God…good	T: 30
		P: 19
Chapters 2-3	garden of Eden	T: 14-15
2:6-7	God formed man…dust	W: 246

Chapter and Verse	*Quote*	*Course Reference*
2:7 (3:19)	God formed man...dust	T: 228
		T: 237
		W: 189
		S: 15
2:16-17	tree...good and evil	T: 45
2:21	deep sleep...Adam	T: 15
		T: 15
3:1-7	the fall	T: 11
3:19 (see Gn 2:7)	dust thou art	
3:23-24	God...garden of Eden	T: 33
		T: 169
		T: 220
3:24	flaming sword	T: 471
4:9	Am I my brother's keeper?	T: 469
7:9	Noah's ark	T: 404
		T: 562
11:1-9 (1 Co 12:10,28)	tower of Babel	T: 150
		T: 597
19:26 (Lk 9:62)	his wife looked back	T: 254
		T: 408
		T: 592
		T: 592
		T: 592

Chapter and Verse	*Quote*	*Course Reference*
25:31-33	Jacob–birthright	T: 209
		T: 470
28:17	the gate of heaven	T: 242
		T: 248
		T: 499
		T: 508
		T: 508
		T: 509-10
		T: 511
		T: 511
		T: 513
		T: 592
		W: 241
		W: 243
		W: 359
		W: 360
		W: 375
		W: 464
		W: 469
		W: 469
		M: 41
		M: 79
41:27	years of famine	T: 555

Exodus

Chapter and Verse	*Quote*	*Course Reference*
3:5	holy ground	T: 264
		T: 349
		T: 510
		T: 521
		T: 521
		T: 566
		W: 294
		W: 331
20:3	no other gods	T: 55-56
		T: 172-73
		T: 173-74
		T: 185
		T: 320
		W: 86
		S: 2
20:4	Thou shalt…graven image	T: 595
		W: 196
20:5 (34:14)	I…am a jealous God	T: 172
20:16 (Mt 19:18)	false witness	T: 81
		T: 192
		W: 272
26:33	the holy place	W: 272
		M: 87
32:1-8	molten calf…worshipped	T: 577
34:7	iniquity of the fathers	T: 80

Chapter and Verse	*Quote*	*Course Reference*
34:14 (see 20:5)	the Lord…jealous God	

Chapter and Verse	*Quote*	*Course Reference*
19:18 (Mt 22:39)	thy neighbour as thyself.................	T: 2
	....	T: 66
	....	T: 76
	....	T: 169
	....	T: 203
	....	T: 357
	....	T: 378
	....	T: 483
	....	T: 504
	....	T: 523
	....	W: 284
	....	M: 87

Numbers

Chapter and Verse	*Quote*	*Course Reference*
6:25	Lord...face shine upon thee	T: 253
6:25-26	shine upon thee...peace.................	T: 58

Deuteronomy

Chapter and Verse	*Quote*	*Course Reference*
4:29 (see Mt 7:7b,8b)	seek the Lord...find him	
5:29 (see Qo 12:13)	fear me...commandments	
31:6,8	he will not fail thee	T: 464
32:35 (Rm 12:19)	To me belongeth vengeance	T: 32
	....	T: 80
	....	T: 498
	....	W: 319
	....	S: 19
33:27	everlasting arms	T: 408

Joshua

Chapter and Verse	*Quote*	*Course Reference*
6:20	sound of the trumpet...wall...........	M: 59

Chapter and Verse	*Quote*	*Course Reference*
6:12 (see Lk 1:28)	The Lord is with thee	

1 Kings

Chapter and Verse	*Quote*	*Course Reference*
19:12	a still small voice	T: 425
	....	T: 600-601
	....	T: 601

Job

Chapter and Verse	*Quote*	*Course Reference*
2:9	curse God, and die	T: 471
13:9 (Ga 6:7b)	as one man mocketh another	T: 10
	....	T: 430
19:25	my redeemer liveth	T: 194
	....	T: 204

Chapter and Verse	*Quote*	*Course Reference*
8:4 (Heb 2:6)	What is man	T: 406
13:1 (see 89:46)	how long…hide thy face	
16:10 (Mk 1:24)	Holy One	T: 56
	....	T: 56
	....	T: 58
	....	T: 62
	....	T: 454
	....	T: 471
	....	W: 290
	....	W: 452
18:13-14 (see 144:6-7)	Lord…lightnings	
23:2-3	he leadeth me	T: 259
	....	T: 395
23:4	I will fear no evil	T: 451
	....	T: 525
23:6	goodness and mercy…follow	T: 222
24:4 (see Mt 5:8)	a pure heart	
31:5 (see Lk 23:46)	I commit my spirit	
37:11 (see Mt 5:5)	meek shall inherit the earth	
37:20	the wicked shall perish	T: 80

Chapter and Verse	*Quote*	*Course Reference*
40:8	I delight to do thy will	T: 12
46:1	God...refuge and strength	W: 416
46:7,11	The Lord of hosts..........................	W: 267
46:10	Be still...I am God	T: 47
	....	T: 49
	....	T: 52
	....	T: 247
	....	T: 570-71
	....	T: 602
	....	T: 604
	....	T: 604
	....	T: 604
	....	W: 78
	....	W: 144
	....	W: 187-88
	....	W: 193
	....	W: 207
	....	W: 207
	....	W: 207
	....	W: 221
	....	W: 221
	....	W: 227-28
	....	W: 264
	....	W: 278
	....	W: 321
	....	W: 331-33
	....	W: 335

Chapter and Verse	*Quote*	*Course Reference*
46:10 (cont.)	Be still...I am God	W: 350
		W: 378
		W: 381
		W: 387
		W: 389
		W: 392
		W: 392
		W: 411
		W: 467
		W: 473
		M: 37
		P: 6
		S: 20
49:7 (Mt 20:28)	ransom for him	W: 285
89:46 (13:1)	How long, Lord?	W: 409
105:42 (see Lk 24:49)	remembered his...promise	
110:1 (Mk 16:19)	Sit thou at my right hand	T: 499
115:9 (121:2)	trust thou in the Lord	T: 176
118:26 (Mt 21:9)	Blessed...name of the Lord	T: 187
121:1	I will lift up mine eyes	T: 398
121:2 (see 115:9)	My help...from the Lord	

Chapter and Verse	*Quote*	*Course Reference*
139:5	Thou...behind and before	W:417
144:6-7 (18:13-14)	Cast forth lightning.........................	T: 498
149:6 (Rv 1:16)	a two-edged sword..........................	T: 16
150:1-6 (Rm 15:11)	Praise ye the Lord...........................	T: 64

Proverbs

Chapter and Verse	*Quote*	*Course Reference*
10:2 (Jn 6:63)	Treasures...profit nothing	T: 212
	....	W: 332
23:7	as he thinketh in his heart	T: 7
	....	T: 415

Chapter and Verse	*Quote*	*Course Reference*
12:13 (Dt 5:29)	Fear God…commandments	T: 37

Chapter and Verse	*Quote*	*Course Reference*
1:18	white as snow	W: 242
9:6	The Prince of Peace	T: 287
	....	T: 305
11:6 (65:25)	wolf…dwell with the lamb............	T: 33
25:8 (Rv 7:17; 21:4a)	God will wipe away tears	T: 526
	....	W: 334
	....	W: 358
	....	W: 440
	....	W: 445
26:19; 35:5-6 (Mt 10:1,8a; 11:5)	dead…live…eyes…opened..........	T: 2
	....	T: 82
	....	T: 147
	....	T: 539
	....	W: 237
	....	W: 293
	....	W: 334
37:10 (Jr 20:7)	Let not thy God…deceive	M: 37
40:3 (Jn 1:23)	make straight…highway	T: 404
	....	W: 375
42:16	I will lead them in paths	W: 285
43:10,12 (see Ac 1:8)	Ye are my witnesses	

Isaiah (continued)

Chapter and Verse	*Quote*	*Course Reference*
45:21	a just God..	T: 594
51:3	desert...garden of the Lord	T: 365-66
60:1	Arise...thy light is come	W: 401
64:4 (1 Co 2:9)	not heard...neither...seen	T: 532
65:17 (Rv 21:1)	new heavens...new earth...............	T: 194
65:25 (see 11:6)	wolf...lamb...feed together	

Jeremiah

Chapter and Verse	*Quote*	*Course Reference*
5:21 (see Mk 8:18)	have eyes, and see not	
6:16 (see Mt 11:29b)	find rest for your souls	
7:11 (Mt 21:13)	house...den of robbers	T: 454
20:7 (see Is 37:10)	Lord, thou hast deceived me	
31:3	loved...everlasting love	T: 482
	....	W: 313
	....	W: 409

Chapter and Verse	*Quote*	*Course Reference*
2:1 (Mt 8:20)	Son of man....................................	T: 225
	....	T: 481
	....	T: 482
	....	M: 30
7:19 (Jn 3:36)	wrath of the Lord..........................	T: 87

Daniel

Chapter and Verse	*Quote*	*Course Reference*
7:27	kingdom…everlasting	T: 313

Hosea

Chapter and Verse	*Quote*	*Course Reference*
6:6 (Mt 9:13)	mercy…not sacrifice	T: 34
	....	T: 607

Joel

Chapter and Verse	*Quote*	*Course Reference*
2:1 (see 1 Co 15:52b)	Blow ye the trumpet in Zion	

NEW TESTAMENT

Matthew

Chapter and Verse	*Quote*	*Course Reference*
3:2 (4:17)	kingdom...is at hand	T: 422
	....	W: 316
3:17 (17:5)	This is my beloved Son	T: 49
	....	T: 119
	....	T: 478
	....	T: 480
	....	T: 495
	....	T: 525
	....	T: 560
	....	W: 453
	....	W: 461
	....	M: 54
4:1-11 (Rv 12:7-10)	the devil	T: 44-45
4:1-11 (Heb 2:18)	tempted of the devil	T: 51
4:17 (see 3:2)	kingdom...is at hand	
4:19	Follow me	T: 10
	....	T: 126
5:3-11	Blessed are	T: 113
	....	T: 182
	....	T: 197
	....	T: 251
	....	T: 264
	....	T: 283
	....	T: 571

Chapter and Verse	*Quote*	*Course Reference*
5:3-11 (cont.)	Blessed are..................................	W: 104
	....	M: 15
5:5 (Ps 37:11)	Blessed are the meek	T: 17
	....	T: 50
5:8 (Ps 24:4)	Blessed are the pure in heart..........	T: 33
	....	T: 35
	....	T: 402
5:12	great is your reward.......................	W: 31
5:14 (Jn 8:12)	the light of the world	T: 71
	....	T: 91
	....	T: 91
	....	T: 133
	....	T: 235
	....	W: 101-102
	....	W: 103
	....	W: 103
	....	W: 103
	....	W: 104
	....	W: 104
	....	W: 104
	....	W: 105
	....	W: 112
	....	W: 116-17
	....	W: 144
	....	W: 144
	....	W: 144
	....	W: 144

Chapter and Verse	*Quote*	*Course Reference*
5:14 (Jn 8:12) (cont.)	the light of the world	W: 145
	....	W: 145
	....	W: 145
	....	W: 145
	....	W: 148
	....	W: 148
5:16	Let your light so shine	T: 153
5:17	the law...fulfil	T: 9
5:29	if thy right eye offend thee	T: 198
5:39	thy right cheek...the other............	T: 75
5:41	go a mile...twain	T: 47
5:44	do good...that hate you	T: 528
5:48	Be ye therefore perfect	T: 147
	....	T: 560
6:8,32	Father knoweth...need	T: 238
	....	T: 277
	....	W: 468
	....	M: 79
6:9	Hallowed be thy name	W: 322
	....	M: 82
6:9-13	Our Father...Amen.	T: 326
6:10b (26:39,42)	Thy will be done	T: 357
	....	T: 471
	....	T: 615
	....	T: 615
	....	W: 117

Chapter and Verse	*Quote*	*Course Reference*
6:10b (26:39,42) (cont.)	Thy will be done...........................	W: 135
	....	M: 36
6:10b,c	Thy will...earth...heaven	T: 70
	....	T: 615
	....	T: 615
	....	W: 173
	....	W: 293
	....	W: 342
	....	W: 350
	....	W: 370
	....	W: 434
	....	W: 451
	....	W: 454
6:11	our daily bread............................	T: 19
6:12,14	forgive...trespasses	T: 528
	....	T: 615
	....	W: 370
	....	P: 11
6:13a	lead us not into temptation	T: 7
	....	T: 396
	....	T: 451
	....	W: 105
6:13b	thine is the kingdom	T: 81
	....	T: 120
	....	T: 130-31
	....	T: 131-33

Chapter and Verse	*Quote*	*Course Reference*
6:13b (cont.)	thine is the kingdom	T: 141
	....	T: 141
	....	T: 286
	....	T: 336-37
6:19	treasures...thieves	T: 472
	....	T: 554
6:20	treasures in heaven...thieves.........	T: 501
6:21	your treasure...your heart	T: 16
	....	T: 140
	....	T: 243
	....	T: 247
	....	T: 253
6:24	serve two masters	T: 10
	....	T: 327
	....	T: 382
	....	T: 584
6:33	seek ye first the kingdom..............	T: 44
	....	T: 110
	....	S: 2
7:1	Judge not...be not judged.............	T: 41
	....	T: 264
	....	T: 500
	....	T: 577-78
	....	M: 37
7:2	with what measure ye mete	T: 154
7:3-5	mote...brother's eye.....................	T: 528
7:3-5 (23:25-26)	mote...cup....................................	T: 36

Chapter and Verse	*Quote*	*Course Reference*
7:7a,8a (21:22)	Ask...be given you........................	T: 55
	....	T: 131
	....	T: 152
	....	T: 196
	....	T: 598
	....	T: 605
	....	W: 124
	....	W: 162
	....	W: 293
	....	W: 306
	....	W: 350
	....	M: 51
	....	P: 8
	....	S: 1
	....	S: 3
7:7b,8b (Dt 4:29)	seek, and ye shall find	T: 15
	....	T: 60
	....	T: 207-208
	....	T: 210
	....	T: 215
	....	T: 221-22
	....	T: 234
	....	T: 242
	....	T: 274
	....	T: 287
	....	T: 293
	....	T: 299

Chapter and Verse	*Quote*	*Course Reference*
7:7b,8b (Dt 4:29) (cont.)	seek, and ye shall find	T: 305
	....	T: 315
	....	T: 318
	....	T: 318
	....	T: 326
	....	T: 332
	....	T: 386
	....	T: 388
	....	T: 422
	....	T: 431
	....	T: 431
	....	T: 447
	....	T: 484
	....	T: 540-41
	....	T: 573-75
	....	T: 611
	....	W: 120
	....	W: 124
	....	W: 132
	....	W: 181
	....	W: 196
	....	W: 213
	....	W: 225
	....	W: 231
	....	W: 231
	....	W: 233-35

Chapter and Verse	*Quote*	*Course Reference*
7:7b,8b (Dt 4:29) (cont.)	seek, and ye shall find	W: 236
	....	W: 264
	....	W: 295
	....	W: 331
	....	W: 340
	....	W: 374-75
	....	W: 389
	....	W: 396
	....	W: 396
	....	W: 396
	....	W: 398
	....	W: 398
	....	W: 403
	....	W: 410
	....	W: 416
	....	W: 416
	....	W: 421
	....	W: 431
	....	W: 434
	....	W: 436
	....	W: 454
	....	W: 459
	....	W: 459
	....	W: 466
	....	M: 14
	....	M: 32

Chapter and Verse	*Quote*	*Course Reference*
7:7b,8b (Dt 4:29) (cont.)	seek, and ye shall find	M: 33
	....	M: 49
	....	S: 9
7:9-11	how much...your Father	M: 68
7:12	do ye even so to them	T: 7
	....	T: 11
	....	T: 545
7:16	know them by their fruits	T: 161
	....	T: 311
7:24-27	built his house upon a rock...........	T: 50
	....	T: 254
	....	T: 313
	....	T: 470
	....	T: 561-62
8:20 (see Ezk 2:1)	the Son of man	
8:22	let the dead bury their dead	T: 512
9:6	power...forgive sins	T: 468
	....	T: 499
9:13 (see Ho 6:6)	mercy, and not sacrifice	
9:22	faith hath made thee whole............	T: 172
9:24-25 (see Jn 11:43-44)	not dead, but sleepeth...arose	
10:1,8a; 11:5	he gave...power...to heal.............	T: 15
10:1,8a; 11:5 (see Is 26:19; 35:5-6)	Heal the sick...raise the dead	

Chapter and Verse	*Quote*	*Course Reference*
10:8b	freely…received, freely give	T: 584
10:19	take no thought how or what	T: 24
10:34	I came not to send peace…	T: 87
11:22	the day of judgment	T: 29-31
	....	T: 41
	....	T: 41
	....	T: 158
	....	T: 508-509
	....	W: 439
	....	W: 445
	....	W: 445
	....	W: 445
	....	W: 445
	....	W: 445
	....	M: 37
	....	M: 66
11:25 (Jn 11:41)	I thank thee, O Father	T: 247
	....	T: 557
	....	T: 595
	....	T: 621
11:28a	Come unto me.............................	T: 113
	....	T: 187
11:28b,29b	ye that labour…find rest..............	T: 184
	....	T: 378
11:29a	learn of me..................................	T: 88
11:29b (Jr 6:16)	find rest unto your souls	T: 39
11:30	my yoke is easy	T: 71

Chapter and Verse	*Quote*	*Course Reference*
12:25	house divided against itself	T: 454
	....	T: 497
12:30 (Lk 9:50)	He that is not with me..................	T: 397
	....	T: 430
13:12	whosoever hath...given................	P: 22
13:44-46	treasure...bought........................	T: 209
13:46	pearl of great price.......................	T: 457
16:18a	upon this rock...church................	T: 86
	....	T: 442
	....	T: 497
16:18b	gates of hell shall not prevail.........	T: 54
	....	T: 74
	....	T: 90
	....	T: 122
	....	T: 249
	....	T: 341
	....	T: 469
	....	T: 620
	....	W: 86
	....	W: 126
16:19a	keys of the kingdom	T: 468-69
	....	W: 196
16:19b (Jn 20:23)	bind...loose	T: 132
	....	T: 256
	....	T: 287
	....	T: 293

Chapter and Verse	*Quote*	*Course Reference*
16:19b (Jn 20:23) (cont.)	bind…loose	T: 325
		T: 394
		T: 429
		T: 473
		T: 476
		T: 568
		W: 73
		W: 204
		W: 354
		W: 356
		W: 362
		W: 367
		W: 374
		W: 425
		W: 458
		W: 458
16:26	profited…lose his own soul?	T: 45
		T: 70
		T: 520
16:27 (25:31)	Son of man…glory	T: 58
		T: 58
		T: 58
		T: 158
		T: 159
		W: 354
		W: 439

Chapter and Verse	*Quote*	*Course Reference*
16:27 (25:31) (cont.)	Son of man...glory	W: 439
		W: 439
		W: 439
		W: 439
		W: 439
		W: 439
		W: 439
		W: 445
17:2	transfigured	W: 219
		W: 273
17:5 (see 3:17)	This is my beloved Son	
17:19-20	Because of your unbelief	T: 15
17:20a	faith...mustard seed	T: 497
17:20a,b (1 Co 13:2)	faith...mountain	T: 27
		T: 82
		T: 421
17:20c	nothing shall be impossible	W: 354
18:3	become as little children	T: 10
		T: 196
18:11	save that which was lost	W: 354
18:19	if two of you shall agree	W: 339
18:20	two or three are gathered	T: 59
		T: 274
		T: 437
		M: 5

Chapter and Verse	*Quote*	*Course Reference*
18:20 (cont.)	two or three are gathered	P: 6
19:6	What...God hath joined	T: 139
	....	T: 332
	....	T: 435
	....	T: 446
	....	T: 517-18
	....	T: 556-57
	....	T: 561
	....	W: 296
19:14	such is the kingdom	T: 75
	....	W: 79
19:18 (see Ex 20:16)	bear false witness	
19:21	sell...follow me	T: 205
	....	W: 358
19:26	with God...possible	T: 194
	....	W: 121
	....	W: 154
19:30 (20:16a)	the last shall be first	W: 455
20:16a (see 19:30)	the last shall be first	
20:16b (22:14)	called...few chosen	T: 39
	....	W: 278
	....	W: 339
	....	M: 3
20:19	he shall rise again	T: 395

Matthew (continued)

Chapter and Verse	*Quote*	*Course Reference*
20:28 (see Ps 49:7)	his life a ransom for many	
21:9 (see Ps 118:26)	Blessed is he that cometh	
21:13 (see Jr 7:11)	house of prayer...thieves	
21:22 (see 7:7a,8a)	ask...ye shall receive	
22:14 (see 20:16b)	called...few are chosen	
22:21	Render...unto God	T: 76
	....	T: 491
22:29	the power of God	W: 117
22:39 (see Lv 19:18)	love thy neighbour as thyself	
23:25-26 (see 7:3-5)	cleanse first...within	
24:35	Heaven...pass away	T: 6
	....	T: 572
25:31 (see 16:27)	Son of man...glory	
25:35 (Heb 13:2)	I was a stranger	T: 8
	....	T: 396
25:40	as ye have done it unto one............	T: 6
	....	T: 162
	....	T: 162
	....	S: 10
	....	S: 19
25:45	as ye did it not to one.....................	W: 296

Chapter and Verse	*Quote*	*Course Reference*
26:15	thirty pieces of silver	T: 592
26:24	woe unto...betrayed	T: 87
26:28 (Ac 2:38)	the remission of sins	T: 456
26:29 (Lk 22:30)	I drink it new with you	T: 383
26:39,42 (see 6:10b)	thy will be done	
27:26-50	crucifixion..................................	T: 84-88
27:29	crown of thorns...........................	T: 525
	....	W: 298
	....	S: 20
27:29,35	crown of thorns...crucified	T: 193-94
28:2 (Jn 11:38,39)	rolled back the stone	M: 87
28:18	All power is given unto me	T: 71
	....	T: 275
	....	T: 514
	....	W: 31
	....	W: 354
	....	W: 450
	....	W: 450
	....	M: 85
	....	P: 15
28:20	I am with you always....................	T: 107
	....	T: 132
	....	T: 133
	....	W: 170
	....	M: 56

Mark

Chapter and Verse	*Quote*	*Course Reference*
1:24 (see Ps 16:10)	the Holy One	
5:9	My name is Legion........................	T: 91
	....	M: 83
8:18 (Jr 5:21)	Having eyes, see ye not?	W: 157
8:36	gain…lose his own soul	T: 211-12
10:51-52	that I might receive my sight.........	W: 296
16:19 (see Ps 110:1)	sat on the right hand of God	

Luke

Chapter and Verse	*Quote*	*Course Reference*
1:19 (8:1)	glad tidings	T: 310-11
		T: 374
		W: 130
		W: 220
		W: 469
		M: 15
		P: 23
1:28 (Jg 6:12)	the Lord is with thee	T: 204
1:77	knowledge of salvation	M: 3
		M: 15
1:79 (see Jn 1:5)	light to them… in darkness	
2:7	laid him in a manger	T: 287
2:12	babe…swaddling clothes	T: 390
2:14	Glory to God in the highest	T: 131
2:29	depart in peace	T: 76
		T: 227
		W: 101
		S: 16
4:23	Physician, heal thyself	P: 14
		P: 22
6:36	Be ye therefore merciful	T: 33
		T: 593
6:48	laid the foundation on a rock	W: 102
8:1 (see 1:19)	glad tidings	
8:13	these have no root	T: 10

Chapter and Verse	*Quote*	*Course Reference*
9:50 (see Mt 12:30)	not against us is for us	
9:62 (see Gn 19:26)	No man...looking back	
14:16-23	supper...house may be filled.........	T: 555
15:7	joy...sinner that repenteth	T: 225
	....	T: 244
	....	T: 511
15:11-32	A certain man had two sons...........	T: 138
15:13	a far country....................................	M: 85
15:18	arise and go to my father	W: 358
	....	S: 13
15:20	he...came to his father	W: 477-78
15:24,32	he was lost, and is found................	T: 395
	....	T: 565
	....	M: 48
15:31	all that I have is thine.....................	T: 193
	....	W: 476
16:8 (1 Th 5:5)	children of light	T: 185
17:21	kingdom of God is within..............	T: 54
	....	T: 197
	....	T: 287
	....	T: 293
	....	T: 490
	....	T: 577
	....	W: 135

Chapter and Verse	*Quote*	*Course Reference*
22:19 (1 Co 11:24-25)	in remembrance of me	T: 24
	....	T: 74
	....	T: 113
	....	T: 132
	....	T: 134-35
22:30 (see Mt 26:29)	eat and drink...table	
22:39-46	mount of Olives...agony	T: 86
	....	T: 395
22:48	Judas, betrayest thou...kiss	T: 87
	....	T: 327
23:34	Father, forgive them......................	T: 12
	....	T: 24
	....	T: 183
	....	T: 184
	....	T: 232
	....	T: 262
	....	T: 266
	....	T: 431
	....	T: 501
	....	T: 539
	....	W: 261
	....	W: 277
	....	W: 367
23:43	Today...with me in paradise..........	T: 402
	....	W: 418

Chapter and Verse	*Quote*	*Course Reference*
23:46 (Ps 31:5)	into thy hands…spirit....................	T: 35
	....	T: 82
24:13-16	Jesus…not know him....................	T: 353
24:49 (Ps 105:42)	promise of my Father.....................	M: 37

Chapter and Verse	*Quote*	*Course Reference*
1:3	All things were made by him.........	T: 90
1:5 (Lk 1:79)	light...darkness	T: 253
	....	T: 352
	....	M: 3
1:7-8 (18:37c)	bear witness...Light [truth]...........	T: 2
	....	T: 367
	....	T: 538
	....	W: 210
	....	W: 315-16
	....	W: 412
1:14	the Word was made flesh..............	T: 141
	....	T: 143
1:23 (see Is 40:3)	Make straight the way	
1:29	Lamb of God..................................	T: 33
	....	T: 33
3:3,7	born again......................................	T: 234
	....	T: 234
	....	T: 234
	....	T: 245
	....	T: 505
	....	T: 603
	....	W: 193-94
	....	W: 356
	....	W: 441
	....	W: 441
3:6	born of the flesh...Spirit...............	T: 614
3:16	For God so loved the world...........	T: 28-29

Chapter and Verse	*Quote*	*Course Reference*
3:16 (cont.)	For God so loved the world	T: 585
3:36 (see Ezk 7:19)	the wrath of God	
4:10 (7:38)	living water	T: 366
5:19,30	Son…nothing of himself	T: 50
	....	T: 135
	....	T: 141
	....	T: 176
	....	T: 210
	....	T: 472
	....	W: 75
	....	M: 67
	....	P: 11
6:20	be not afraid	T: 188
	....	T: 535
	....	T: 555
	....	W: 280
	....	W: 445
	....	M: 87
6:63 (see Pr 10:2)	the flesh profiteth nothing	
6:69	the Son of the living God..............	T: 119
	....	T: 348
7:24	Judge not…appearance	M: 26
7:38 (see 4:10)	living water	

Chapter and Verse	*Quote*	*Course Reference*
8:12 (see Mt 5:14)	the light of the world	
8:16 (20:21b)	the Father that sent me..................	T: 134
8:32	the truth shall make you free	T: 15
	....	T: 40
	....	T: 74
	....	T: 75
	....	T: 92
	....	T: 258
	....	W: 133
	....	W: 195
	....	W: 196
	....	W: 252
8:51 (11:25b,26)	he shall never see death	W: 300
8:58	Before Abraham was, I am...........	T: 37
10:30 (14:20)	I and my Father are one	T: 5
	....	T: 180
11:4	sickness is not unto death	T: 146
	....	T: 567
11:11 (11:43)	I go...awake him	T: 471
11:25a	I am the resurrection...life	T: 6-7
	....	T: 193
	....	T: 390
	....	W: 31
11:25b,26 (see 8:51)	shall never die	

Chapter and Verse	*Quote*	*Course Reference*
11:38,39 (see Mt 28:2)	Take ye away the stone	
11:41 (see Mt 11:25)	Father, I thank thee	
11:43 (see 11:11)	Lazarus, come forth	
11:43-44 (Mt 9:24-25)	he that was dead came forth	T: 59
11:44	bound hand and foot	T: 573
12:46	a light into the world......................	T: 81
	....	T: 133
13:34	love one another	T: 187
14:1	Let not your heart be troubled	T: 176
14:2	In my Father's house	T: 571
	....	T: 592
	....	W: 331
	....	W: 358
	....	W: 417
	....	S: 13
14:3	where I am...ye may be also.........	W: 287
14:5	how can we know the way............	W: 350
14:6a	way, the truth, and the life	T: 86
	....	T: 108
	....	W: 143
	....	W: 475
	....	P: 1
14:6b	no man cometh...but by me	T: 5

Chapter and Verse	*Quote*	*Course Reference*
14:6b (cont.)	no man cometh…but by me	T: 402
14:12,28b	I go unto my Father	T: 227
	....	T: 232
14:13-14 (16:23)	ask in my name	T: 147
	....	M: 55
	....	M: 55
14:16a	another Comforter	T: 67
	....	T: 171
	....	T: 184
	....	T: 185
14:16b (15:4,10)	abide with you for ever	T: 183
	....	T: 204
	....	T: 264
	....	T: 287
	....	T: 322
	....	W: 226
	....	W: 466
14:16b (15:4,10; 16:7)	abide with you…if I depart	T: 67
14:18	I will…comfortless	T: 70
	....	T: 125
	....	T: 339
	....	T: 620
	....	W: 470
	....	W: 478
	....	S: 14
14:20 (see 10:30)	I am in my Father…in you	

Chapter and Verse	*Quote*	*Course Reference*
14:27a	Peace I leave with you	T: 172
	....	T: 240
14:27a,b (18:36)	Peace...not as the world giveth.....	M: 49
14:27b	not as the world giveth	T: 514
14:28c	My Father is greater than I	T: 5
15:2	branch...beareth not fruit	T: 46
15:4,10 (see 14:16b)	Abide in me...my love	
15:11 (16:24)	that your joy might be full	T: 105
	....	T: 184
	....	T: 489
	....	W: 177
15:18	world...hated me	T: 134
	....	T: 474
15:19 (17:14,16,18)	ye are not of the world	T: 142
	....	T: 157
	....	T: 515
	....	W: 284
	....	M: 8
16:7 (see 14:16b)	if I depart, I will send him	
16:12	many things...cannot bear them....	T: 87-88
16:16	a little while...shall see me	T: 204
16:23 (see 14:13-14)	ask...in my name	
16:24 (see 15:11)	that your joy may be full	
16:33	I have overcome the world	T: 51

Chapter and Verse	*Quote*	*Course Reference*
16:33 (cont.)	I have overcome the world	T: 133
	....	T: 385
17:14,16,18 (see 15:19)	not of the world	
18:36	My kingdom...world.....................	T: 46
	....	T: 138
	....	T: 287
	....	T: 514
18:36 (14:27a,b)	not of this world...peace	M: 49
18:37b	came I into the world.....................	W: 450
18:37c (see 1:7-8)	bear witness unto the truth	
18:38	What is truth	T: 127
19:5	Behold the man...............................	T: 571
20:17	I ascend unto my Father	T: 192-93
	....	T: 283
	....	T: 336
20:19,21a,26	Peace be unto you..........................	T: 187
	....	T: 263
	....	T: 537
	....	W: 263
20:21b (see 8:16)	as my Father hath sent me	
20:23 (see Mt 16:19b)	sins ye remit...sins ye retain	
20:25	the print of the nails........................	T: 471
	....	T: 471

Chapter and Verse	*Quote*	*Course Reference*
20:25 (cont.)	the print of the nails........................	W: 298
20:29	Blessed...yet have believed	T: 192

Acts

Chapter and Verse	*Quote*	*Course Reference*
1:8 (Is 43:10,12)	be witnesses unto me	T: 9
1:8-9 (2:1-4)	Holy Ghost…taken up	M: 85
2:1-4 (see 1:8-9)	filled with the Holy Ghost	
2:38 (see Mt 26:28)	the remission of sins	
17:28	in him…have our being	T: 76
		T: 110
		T: 476
		T: 622
		W: 287
		W: 303
		W: 368
		W: 392
20:35	more blessed to give	T: 2
		T: 430

Chapter and Verse	*Quote*	*Course Reference*
2:15	written in their hearts	W: 469
		M: 61
3:28 (5:1)	justified by faith	T: 339
		T: 373
		T: 402
5:1 (see 3:28)	justified by faith	
6:23	the wages of sin is death	T: 175
		T: 375
		T: 494
		T: 538
		S: 9
8:3	Son...likeness of sinful flesh	P: 23
8:26	Spirit...groanings	M: 68
8:28	all things...for good	T: 59
		T: 90
		T: 520
8:29	firstborn...many brethren	T: 5
		T: 5
12:16 (see 1 P 3:8)	same mind...toward another	
12:19 (see Dt 32:35)	Vengeance is mine	
15:11 (see Ps 150:1-6)	Praise the Lord	

1 Corinthians

Chapter and Verse	*Quote*	*Course Reference*
2:9 (see Is 64:4)	Eye hath not seen...ear heard	
3:16 (see 6:19)	ye are the temple of God	
6:15-20	bodies...members of Christ...........	T: 147
6:19 (3:16)	temple of the Holy Ghost	T: 18
	....	T: 142
	....	T: 406-409
	....	T: 522
	....	P: 5
	....	P: 22
11:24-25 (see Lk 22:19)	in remembrance of me	
12:10,28 (see Gn 11:1-9)	diversities of tongues	
13:2 (see Mt 17:20a,b)	remove mountains	
13:4-7	Charity...truth	T: 407
13:11	I put away childish things..............	T: 578-79
13:12	see through a glass, darkly............	T: 57-58
	....	T: 617
	....	W: 219
	....	W: 293
13:13	faith, hope, charity.........................	T: 394
14:33	God is not the author	T: 49
15:26	last enemy...is death	M: 64

Chapter and Verse	*Quote*	*Course Reference*
15:28 (Ep 1:23)	God…all in all……	T: 110
	……	T: 133
	……	S: 13
15:52a	the twinkling of an eye……	T: 14
15:52b (Jl 2:1)	the trumpet shall sound……	T: 529
	……	W: 300

2 Corinthians

Chapter and Verse	*Quote*	*Course Reference*
6:2	now is the day of salvation	T: 235
9:6 (see Ga 6:7c)	soweth...reap	
12:9a	My grace is sufficient	T: 249-50
	....	T: 325
	....	W: 467
12:9b (Ph 4:13)	strength...weakness......................	T: 50
	....	T: 284
	....	T: 284
	....	T: 620
	....	W: 77
	....	W: 103
	....	W: 157-58
	....	W: 277-78
	....	W: 280
	....	M: 68
13:11	be of one mind	T: 24

Galatians

Chapter and Verse	*Quote*	*Course Reference*
6:7b (see Jb 13:9)	God is not mocked	
6:7c (2 Co 9:6)	soweth…reap..................................	T: 80

Ephesians

Chapter and Verse	*Quote*	*Course Reference*
1:23 (see 1 Co 15:28)	him that filleth all in all	
2:8	faith...gift of God..........................	T: 12
	....	T: 373
2:19	strangers and foreigners................	T: 408
3:19	the fulness of God..........................	T: 122

Philippians

Chapter and Verse	*Quote*	*Course Reference*
2:2	being...of one mind........................	T: 463
2:5	Let this mind...Christ Jesus	T: 67
	....	T: 75
	....	T: 80
4:7	peace...understanding	T: 16
	....	T: 238
4:13 (see 2 Co 12:9b)	I can do...through Christ	

Colossians

Chapter and Verse	*Quote*	*Course Reference*
1:16	visible and invisible........................	M: 69
2:12 (3:1)	ye are risen with him	T: 233
3:1 (see 2:12)	be risen with Christ	

1 Thessalonians

Chapter and Verse	*Quote*	*Course Reference*
5:5 (see Lk 16:8)	children of light	
5:17	Pray without ceasing......................	S: 3

Chapter and Verse	*Quote*	*Course Reference*
6:10	the root of all evil	T: 43
	....	T: 184
6:16 (see Rv 5:12-13)	honour and power everlasting	

2 Timothy

Chapter and Verse	*Quote*	*Course Reference*
1:10 (see Rv 21:4b)	Saviour...abolished death	

Hebrews

Chapter and Verse	*Quote*	*Course Reference*
2:6 (see Ps 8:4)	What is man...?	
2:18 (see Mt 4:1-11)	he...suffered being tempted	
7:3	neither beginning...nor end..........	T: 180
13:2 (see Mt 25:35)	entertain strangers	
13:5	I will never leave thee....................	T: 76
13:8	the same yesterday...forever.........	T: 105
	....	T: 193
	....	T: 284
	....	T: 505
	....	T: 572
	....	W: 312

1 Peter

Chapter and Verse	*Quote*	*Course Reference*
3:8 (Rm 12:16)	be ye all of one mind	T: 97
5:7	Casting...care upon him................	T: 82

Chapter and Verse	*Quote*	*Course Reference*
1:5 (2:8)	God is light...no darkness............	T: 28
	....	T: 33
	....	T: 235
	....	T: 256
2:8 (see 1:5)	darkness...light now shineth	
2:9 (4:20)	he that...hateth his brother...........	T: 247
	....	W: 406
2:18,22	antichrist....................................	T: 575-76
	....	T: 584
	....	W: 254
3:2	when he shall appear	T: 35
	....	T: 196
	....	T: 599
4:8,16	God is love..................................	T: 151
	....	T: 348
	....	T: 564
	....	T: 602
	....	W: 174-76
	....	W: 182
	....	W: 182
	....	W: 182
	....	W: 182
	....	W: 182
	....	W: 206
	....	W: 206

Chapter and Verse	*Quote*	*Course Reference*
4:8,16 (cont.)	God is love....................................	W: 321-22
	....	W: 324-27
4:18a	no fear in love................................	T: 247
	....	T: 348
	....	T: 398
	....	T: 558
	....	M: 60
	....	S: 18
4:18a,b	perfect love casteth out fear...........	T: 204
	....	T: 256
	....	T: 291
	....	T: 402
4:18b	perfect love casteth out fear...........	T: 12
	....	T: 293
4:20 (see 2:9)	hateth his brother	

Chapter and Verse	*Quote*	*Course Reference*
1:16 (see Ps 149:6)	a sharp two-edged sword	
2:28 (22:16)	the morning star	M: 87
5:12-13 (1 Tm 6:16)	honour...be unto him	T: 268
		T: 286
7:17 (see Is 25:8)	God shall wipe away all tears	
12:7-10 (see Mt 4:1-11)	the Devil...was cast out	
12:9 (20:7-10)	Satan...deceiveth	T: 427
20:7-10 (see 12:9)	Satan...deceive the nations	
21:1 (see Is 65:17)	new heaven...new earth	
21:4a (see Is 25:8)	God shall wipe away all tears	
21:4b (2 Tm 1:10)	there shall be no more death	T: 9
		T: 46
		T: 529
		T: 542
		T: 573
		T: 575
		W: 302-303
		W: 311
		W: 311

Chapter and Verse	*Quote*	*Course Reference*
21:4b (cont.) (2 Tm 1:10)	there shall be no more death..........	W: 311
	....	M: 44
	....	M: 84
21:6 (22:13)	Alpha and Omega..........................	T: 37
22:13 (see 21:6)	Alpha and Omega	
22:16 (see 2:28)	morning star	

GLOSSARY-INDEX
for
A COURSE IN MIRACLES

(Keyed to Second Edition of *A Course in Miracles*)

GLOSSARY-INDEX
for
A COURSE IN MIRACLES

Fourth Edition, Revised and Enlarged

(Keyed to Second Edition of *A Course in Miracles*)

KENNETH WAPNICK, Ph.D.

Foundation for "A Course in Miracles"

Foundation for "A Course in Miracles"
1275 Tennanah Lake Road
Roscoe, NY 12776-5905

Printed in the United States of America

Library of Congress Cataloging-in-Publication Data

Wapnick, Kenneth
Glossary-index for a Course in miracles / Kenneth Wapnick. -- 4th ed. rev. and enl.
p. cm.
ISBN 0-933291-03-5 (hard)
1. Course in miracles--Indexes. 2. Spiritual life--Indexes.
I. Title.
BP605.C68W3563 1993
299'.93--dc20 93-5296

Contents

Preface vii

Introduction 1

Part I: Theory 7

Part II: Glossary-Index 21

Part III: Scriptural Index

Abbreviations 231

A Course in Miracles

text 235

workbook for students 260

manual for teachers 272

clarification of terms 274

"Psychotherapy: Purpose, Process and Practice" 275

"The Song of Prayer" 276

Bible

Old Testament 279

New Testament 304

Preface

In many ways this fourth edition is a new book. Along with having been re-typeset, the book includes the following changes:

1) All the references have been changed to conform to the new numbering system of the second edition (third printing) of *A Course in Miracles*, which was published in 1992. All previous editions of the *Glossary-Index* were keyed to the first edition, and so references were provided only for the page numbers. This often made it difficult to locate the exact references. In the Glossary-Index section of this fourth edition, however, references are given for the specific paragraph(s) in the Course. In the Scriptural Index, references include sentence numbers as well. At the end of the Introduction there is a list of abbreviations and examples of the notations used.

2) References have also been expanded to include the two scribed pamphlets, "Psychotherapy: Purpose, Process and Practice" and "The Song of Prayer." These have also recently been published in second editions with the new numbering system.

3) Each reference in the Glossary-Index and the Scriptural Index has been carefully checked and re-checked, and errors corrected that had been present since the first printing of the first edition. In addition, new references have been added to many existing terms, and some have been deleted.

4) Each definition has been reviewed, and modifications and additions have been made where appropriate. Also, some changes and additions have been made to the Theory section.

5) Eight new terms have been added to the Glossary-Index: **anti-Christ, child, joining, looking at the ego, oneness, process, sleep, split**.

6) Included now in the Scriptural Index are portions of biblical passage(s) or, in the case of lengthy passages, the main theme corresponding to the Course reference. This will facilitate identification of these passages.

Such a vast undertaking as this fourth edition would never have been possible without the help of our very fine Foundation staff. I should like especially to thank Elizabeth Schmit and Jeffrey Seibert for their painstaking check of Course references, Jeffrey also for examining the

cross-referencing system in the Scriptural Index and making the necessary corrections and revisions, Linda McGuffie (not on our staff) for her careful checking of all scriptural references, Loral Reeves who skillfully designed and formatted the book on the computer, and Rosemarie LoSasso, who checked over and reviewed every aspect of the book, and with her usual conscientiousness and dedication supervised the entire publication of this new edition from beginning to end.

Finally, I am grateful to the many unnamed people who over the years have contributed suggestions and corrections to this *Glossary-Index*.

Preface to Third Edition

This third edition has been entirely re-typeset, with the following minor changes:

1) Two lines have been added near the end of the original Preface, one line to explain the abbreviations used in the Glossary and one line to explain the use of letters in citing verses from the Bible.*

2) Two terms (denial, holy instant) have been added to the chart in the section on Theory.

3) Typographical errors have been corrected and minor stylistic changes made.

4) Three page references have been added in the Glossary.

5) Twelve scriptural references have been added and inserted in their appropriate places in both sections of the Scriptural Index.

I am grateful to Rosemarie LoSasso for her careful and conscientious supervision of the publication of this third edition.

---

* Changed in the Fourth Edition.

Preface to Second Edition

This second edition has been revised and enlarged in the following ways:

1) The Preface has been slightly changed to improve readability.

2) In the section on Theory, a paragraph has been added to the text.

3) Six terms have been added to the Glossary-Index. These include: awakening, joy (happiness, gladness), laughter, light, not to make error real, and peace.

The definitions of thirteen of the existing terms have been expanded, and page references have been added throughout.

4) Sixty-five scriptural references in the Course have been added, forty-four of which are to Mt 7:7b,8b (Seek and you shall find). These have been inserted in their appropriate places in both sections of the Scriptural Index. In addition, the Index has been redesigned to ease the identification of the references.

I am grateful to the many people who contributed their suggestions and corrections to the first edition, which stimulated this revised and enlarged edition.

First Edition – Acknowledgments

I would like to express my gratitude and appreciation to Sister Joan Metzner, Joan Pantesco, Sharon Reis, my wife Gloria, and countless others who have helped in the preparation of the manuscript; and to the Foundation for Inner Peace, publishers of *A Course in Miracles*, for permission to publish this *Glossary-Index*.

INTRODUCTION

Unlike most thought systems, *A Course in Miracles* does not proceed in a truly linear fashion with its theoretical structure built upon increasingly complex ideas. Rather, the Course's development is more circular with its themes treated symphonically: introduced, set aside, reintroduced, and developed. This results in an interlocking matrix in which every part is integral and essential to the whole, while implicitly containing that whole within itself.

This structure establishes a process of learning instead of merely setting forth a theoretical system. The process resembles the ascent up a spiral staircase. The reader is led in a circular pattern, each revolution leading higher until the top of the spiral is reached, which opens unto God. Thus, the same material consistently recurs, both within the Course as a thought system as well as in learning opportunities in our personal lives. Each revolution, as it were, leads us closer to our spiritual goal. The last two paragraphs of the first chapter in the text particularly emphasize this cumulative impact of the Course's learning process.

Through careful study of the text, along with the daily practice that the workbook provides, the student is gradually prepared for the deeper experiences of God towards which *A Course in Miracles* points. Intellectual mastery of its thought system will not suffice to bring about the perceptual and experiential transformation that is the aim of the Course.

This *Glossary-Index* was prepared as a guide for students of *A Course in Miracles*. It is not a substitute for working through the material itself. Rather, it is intended as an aid in studying and understanding the Course's thought system. This book is divided into three sections. The first, Theory, briefly summarizes the Course's theoretical system, presenting the interrelationships among the more important terms to be defined. These words are in bold type. Following this summary is an alphabetical listing of these and additional terms, in five divisions: One-mindedness, wrong-mindedness, right-mindedness, related terms, and symbols. Some terms, incidentally, appear in more than one listing.

The second section, the Glossary-Index, presents all the terms in alphabetical order. Each is defined as it is used in the Course. Several words, especially those pertaining to One-mindedness, have no precise meaning in this world and their definitions can only be approximated here. As *A Course in Miracles* says: "words are but symbols of symbols. They are thus twice removed from reality" (M-21.1:9-10). It

should be noted that many of the terms have different meanings or connotations outside the Course, and these should not be confused with the Course's usage. Moreover, some words have differing uses in *A Course in Miracles* itself, reflecting knowledge or perception (e.g., extension), right- or wrong-mindedness (e.g., denial).

Following the definition is a selected and subheaded index of the principal passages in the text, workbook, manual, and the two pamphlets "Psychotherapy: Purpose, Process and Practice" and "The Song of Prayer" where the terms are most meaningfully discussed. The most important of these references are in bold type. Unlike a concordance, not every reference for a term is noted. In general, there is only a single subheading for each passage indexed; however, multiple subheadings have been included when they are particularly important in that passage. Occasionally a term is referenced when it is described, though the term itself is not mentioned; e.g., the reference for projection in the manual, M-17.5-7, is subheaded under guilt. The capitalization used in the Course is followed in this book. Thus, the Persons of the Trinity—God, Christ (Son of God), Holy Spirit—are always capitalized, as are all pronouns referring to Them. Pronouns referring to the Son of God in his separated state are in lower case. Words that directly relate to the Trinity, such as Love, Will, Heaven, etc., are capitalized, though their pronouns are not.

The final section, the Scriptural Index, lists all scriptural references in *A Course in Miracles*, taken from the King James Version, the version used in the Course. The first part lists these references sequentially as they are found in the three books and two pamphlets. The second lists them as they are found sequentially in the Bible. Many of the references are found in more than one book of the Bible, but only the more important or widely known of these have been cross-referenced.

Abbreviations used are as follows:

T:	text	In:	Introduction
W:	workbook	r:	Review (workbook)
M:	manual for teachers	FL:	Final lessons (workbook)
C:	clarification of terms	Ep:	Epilogue

P: "Psychotherapy: Purpose, Process and Practice"
S: "The Song of Prayer"

w-m: wrong-mindedness   r-m: right-mindedness

Examples of the notation used in references are as follows:

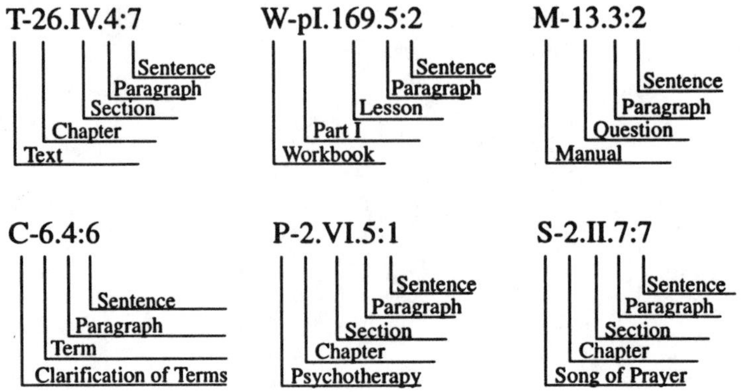

Scriptural abbreviations are found on page 231. The letter a, b, or c after the verse number refers to the first, second, or third part respectively of that verse.

Part I

THEORY

THEORY

A Course in Miracles distinguishes two worlds: God and the ego, **knowledge** and **perception**, **truth** and **illusion**. Strictly speaking, every aspect of the post-separation world of perception reflects the **ego**. However, the Course further subdivides the world of perception into wrong- and right-mindedness. Within this framework the Course almost always uses the word "ego" to denote wrong-mindedness, while right-mindedness is the domain of the Holy Spirit, Who teaches forgiveness as the correction for the ego. Thus, we can speak of three thought systems: **One-mindedness**, which belongs to knowledge, and **wrong-** and **right-mindedness** which reflect the world of perception. Our discussion will follow this tripartite view of **mind**.

The accompanying chart summarizes the Course's description of the mind. It should be examined in conjunction with the following references from the Course which deal with the relationship of spirit to mind, spirit to ego, and the three levels of mind:

T-1.V.5
T-3.IV.2-6
T-4.I.2-3
T-7.IX.1-4
W-pI.96.3-5
C-1

A Course in Miracles, therefore, is written on two levels, reflecting two basic divisions. The first level presents the difference between the One Mind and the separated mind, while the second contrasts wrong- and right-mindedness within the separated mind. On this first level, for example, the world and body are illusions made by the ego, and thus symbolize the separation. The second level relates to this world where we believe we are. Here, the world and the body are neutral and can serve one of two purposes. To the wrong-minded ego they are instruments to reinforce separation; to the right mind they are the Holy Spirit's teaching devices through which we learn His lessons of forgiveness. On this level, illusions refer to the misperceptions of the ego; e.g., seeing attack instead of a call for love, sin instead of error.

Thus, the Course focuses on our thoughts, not their external manifestations which are really projections of these thoughts. As it says: "This is a course in cause and not effect" (T-21.VII.7:8). We are urged *not* to

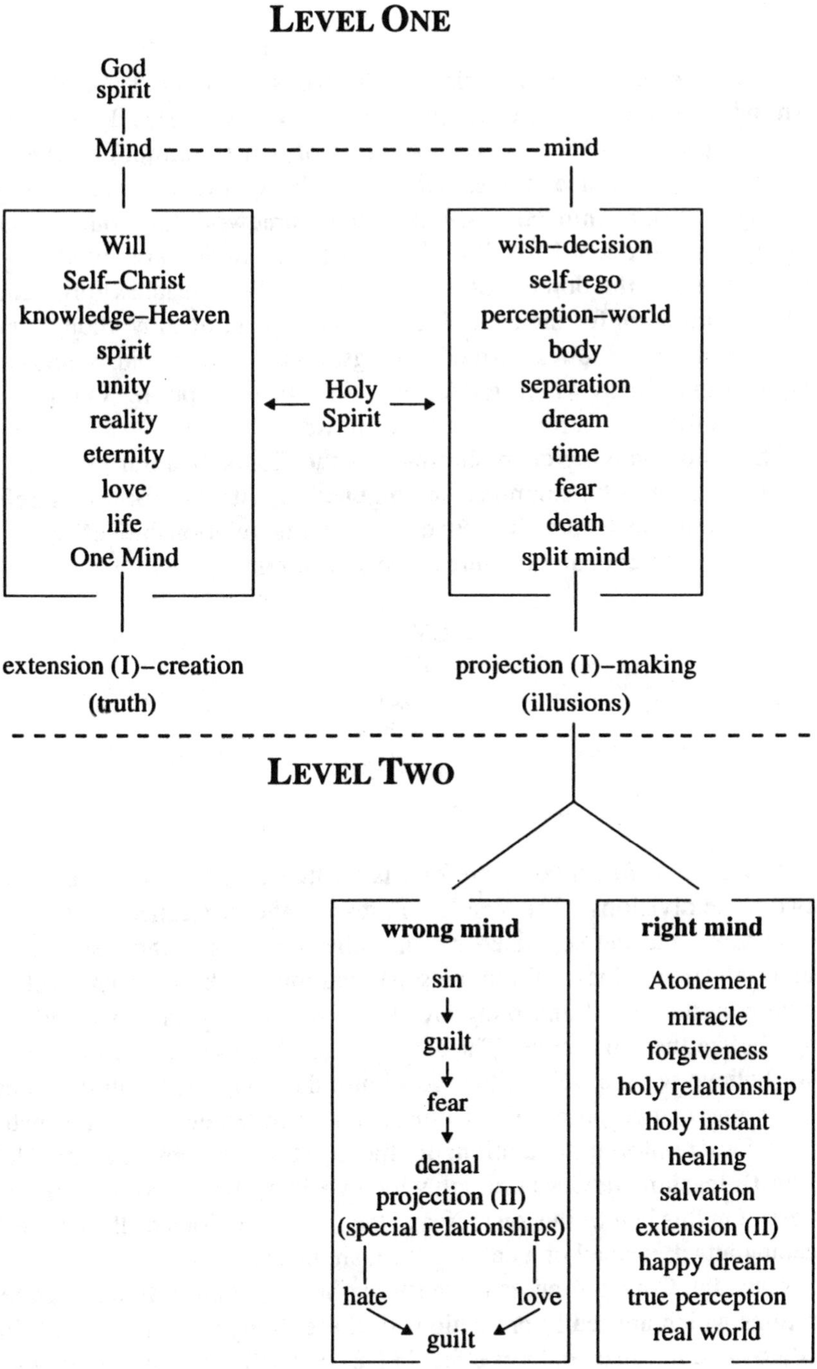
LEVEL ONE
God
spirit
Mind
mind
Will
Self–Christ
knowledge–Heaven
spirit
unity
reality
eternity
love
life
One Mind
Holy Spirit
wish–decision
self–ego
perception–world
body
separation
dream
time
fear
death
split mind
extension (I)–creation
(truth)
projection (I)–making
(illusions)
LEVEL TWO
wrong mind
sin
guilt
fear
denial
projection (II)
(special relationships)
hate
love
guilt
right mind
Atonement
miracle
forgiveness
holy relationship
holy instant
healing
salvation
extension (II)
happy dream
true perception
real world

seek to change the world (**effect**), but to change our mind (**cause**) about the world (T-21.In.1:7). When lesson 193 states: "I will forgive, and this will disappear" (W-pI.193.13:3), what is meant is that our perception of the problem and any pain that comes to us from this perception disappear, not necessarily the physical expression of the problem. For example, if rain threatens proposed plans and brings upset or disappointment, we should not pray for sunshine, but rather for help in looking at the inclement weather as an opportunity we have chosen to learn a lesson in forgiveness the Holy Spirit can teach us. This is not to deny that the ego can make or affect a physical world. However, as this physical world is inherently illusory, a result of our thoughts, the Course's emphasis is on correcting these mistaken or miscreative thoughts, which are always the true source of any problem. This correction then allows the Holy Spirit's Love to direct our behavior in the world.

One-mindedness

The One-mindedness of Christ is the world of **Heaven** or knowledge: the pre-separation world of **spirit**, **love**, truth, eternity, infinity, and reality, where the **oneness** of God's **creation**—the sum of all His **Thoughts**—is unbroken. It is the natural state of direct **communication** with God and His creation that existed before the mind of God's Son thought of separation. In this state the perfect unity of the **Trinity** is maintained.

The Trinity consists of: 1) **God**, the Father; 2) His **Son, Christ**, our true **Self**; and 3) the **Holy Spirit**, the **Voice for God**. Included in the Second Person of the Trinity are our **creations**, the extensions of our Self or spirit. The Second Person of the Trinity is not exclusively identified with **Jesus**, who is part of Christ, as we all are.

Wrong-mindedness

The ego consists of three fundamental concepts: **sin**: the belief that we have separated ourselves from God; **guilt**: the experience of having sinned, of having done something wrong which emanates from our belief that we have attacked God by usurping His role as First Cause, making ourselves our own first cause; and **fear**: the emotion that

inevitably follows guilt, coming from our belief in sin and based on our thought that we deserve to be punished by the ego's made-up god of vengeance.

To ensure its survival, the ego continually attracts guilt to itself, since guilt proves sin's reality and it is sin that gave the ego birth. Once it has established guilt as real the ego teaches us never to approach or even look at it, for it says we would either be destroyed by an angry, vengeful god—a god that the ego made, in fact, to suit its purpose—intent on punishing us for our sin against him, or else annihilated in the oblivion of our own nothingness. This fear keeps the guilt and sin intact, for without seeing them as decisions of our minds we can never change our belief in them.

Left with the anxiety and terror brought on by the fear of God, our only recourse is to turn to the ego for help, since God has become our enemy. The ego's plan of salvation from guilt has two parts: the first is **denial**, wherein we push our guilt out of awareness, hoping that by not seeing the problem it will not be there. Second, after the guilt is denied, we project it out from us onto another, **magically** hoping to be free from the guilt by unconsciously placing it outside ourselves.

Projection has two principal forms: **special hate** and **special love relationships**. In special hate relationships our self-hatred or guilt is transferred onto others, making them responsible for the misery we feel. Our **anger** or **attack** attempts to justify the projection, reinforcing others' guilt for the sins we projected from ourselves. Special love relationships have the same goal of projecting guilt, though the form differs greatly. Our guilt teaches we are empty, unfulfilled, incomplete, and needful, all aspects of the **scarcity principle**. Believing this lack can never be corrected, we seek outside ourselves for those people who can complete us. Special love, thus, takes this form: I have certain special needs that God cannot meet, but you, a special person with special attributes, can meet them for me. When you do, I shall love you. If you do not, my love will turn to hate.

The ego's world becomes divided into enemies (special hate) or savior-**idols** (special love), and the true Identity of Christ in others is obscured. **Judgment**, always based on the past rather than acceptance in the present, is the ego's guiding principle. Through special relationships the ego sustains its existence by maintaining guilt, since using others to meet our needs constitutes an attack, and attack in any form reinforces guilt. This sets into motion the guilt-attack cycle, wherein the greater our guilt, the greater the need to project it by attacking others

through special relationships, which merely adds to the guilt, increasing the need to project it.

The ego's wrong-mindedness is a **dream** of **separation,** most clearly expressed in the physical **world** which was made as "an attack on God" (W-pII.3.2:1). The **body's** existence is one of **sickness, suffering,** and **death,** which witness to the seeming reality of the body as opposed to spirit, which can never suffer pain, or die. **Crucifixion** is the Course's symbol of the ego, representing the belief in attack and **sacrifice,** where one's gain depends on another's loss. All aspects of the separated world are illusions, since what is of God can never be separate from Him, and therefore what seems separate from God cannot be real. This is expressed by the Course principle **"ideas leave not their source"**: we are an Idea (or Thought) in the **Mind of God** that has never left its Source.

Right-mindedness

God's **Answer** to the separation is the Holy Spirit, and His plan to undo the ego is called the **Atonement.** *A Course in Miracles* employs many terms that reflect the Holy Spirit's plan, and each is a virtual synonym for the other. They include: **miracle, forgiveness, salvation, healing, real world, true perception, vision, face of Christ, reason, justice, holy instant, holy relationship, function, happy dream, Second Coming, Word of God, Last (Final) Judgment, resurrection,** redemption, correction, **awakening,** and undoing.

These terms, belonging to the separated world of perception, refer to the **process** (the miracle) that corrects our misperceptions, shifting from hearing the ego's voice of sin, guilt, and fear, to the Holy Spirit's Voice of forgiveness. In this way, special or unholy relationships become holy. Without these relationships we would have no way of being freed from the guilt the ego has taught us to bury through denial, and retain through projection. The Holy Spirit turns the tables on the ego by changing its purpose for projection into an opportunity to see this denied guilt in another, thereby bringing it back within which allows us finally to change our minds about it.

While the practice of forgiveness, or undoing guilt, is usually experienced as complex and long term, it can be understood essentially as a three-step process (see, e.g., T-5.VII.6; W-pI.23.5; W-pI.70.1-4; W-pI.196.7-11). The first step reverses the projection as we realize that

the guilt is not in another but in ourselves. Second, now that the guilt has been brought to our attention and we recognize that its source is in us, we undo this **decision** by choosing to see ourselves as guiltless Sons of God, rather than guilty sons of the ego. These two steps are our responsibility; the final one is the Holy Spirit's, Who is able to take the guilt from us now that we have released it to Him, **looking** at it with His Love beside us, and thus without judgment and guilt. This looking without judgment, in gentle **laughter**, is the meaning of forgiveness. Using the workbook as our guide, we become trained over time to hear the Holy Spirit's Voice, learning that all things are opportunities to learn forgiveness (W-pI.193).

Illustrative of this process-aspect of forgiveness are the references under **periods of unsettling** and **bringing darkness (illusions) to the light (truth)**, as well as workbook lesson 284. These reflect the almost inevitable difficulty that results when one begins to take the Holy Spirit's lessons seriously, and allows the deeply denied guilt to begin to surface in one's consciousness.

When our guilt is finally undone, right-mindedness having corrected wrong-mindedness, the **bridge** to the real world is complete. The **memory of God** dawns within our minds, as all interferences to it have been removed and we see the face of Christ in all people. This world of illusion and separation ends as God takes the **last step**, reaching down and lifting us unto Himself. Restored to the One-mindedness of Christ, "we are home, where...[God] would have us be" (T-31.VIII.12:8).

One-mindedness

- abundance
- Christ
- communication
- communion
- creation
- creations
- extension
- function
- gift
- God
- gratitude
- Great Rays
- Heaven (Kingdom of God, Heaven)
- Holy Spirit (Answer, Voice for God)
- "ideas leave not their source"
- innocence
- invulnerability
- judgment
- knowledge
- Last (Final) Judgment
- laws of God
- light
- love
- mind
- Mind of God
- Name of God
- One-mindedness
- oneness
- Self
- Son of God
- spirit
- Thoughts of God
- Trinity
- Will of God

Wrong-mindedness

- anti-Christ
- attack (anger)
- body
- crucifixion
- death
- defenses
- denial
- devil
- dissociation
- dream
- ego
- fear
- gap
- gift
- giving–receiving
- guilt
- hell
- "ideas leave not their source"
- idol
- illusion
- innocence
- judgment
- magic
- means–end
- perception
- projection
- sacrifice
- scarcity principle
- separation
- sickness
- sin
- sleep
- Son of God
- special relationship
- split
- suffering (pain)
- temptation
- time
- world
- wrong-mindedness

Right-mindedness

accepting the Atonement
a little willingness
Atonement
awakening
body
communication
death
defenses
denial
extension
face of Christ
forgiveness
free will (1)
free will (2)
function
gift
giving–receiving
grace
Great Rays
gratitude
happy dream
healing
holy instant
holy relationship
"I am as God created me"
"ideas leave not their source"
innocence
invulnerability
joining
joy (happiness, gladness)
judgment
justice
Last (Final) Judgment
last step
laughter
laws of God
light
looking at the ego
love
means–end
memory of God
miracle
no order of difficulty in miracles
not to make error real
oneness
peace
perception
prayer
process
projection
real world
reason
resurrection

Right-mindedness (continued)

revelation	Thoughts of God
right-mindedness	time
salvation	true perception
Second Coming	vision
Son of God	Word of God
teacher of God	world

Related Terms

A Course in Miracles

bringing darkness (illusions) to the light (truth)

cause–effect

Christmas

decision

Easter

faith

form–content

having–being

humility–arrogance

Jesus

make–create

periods of unsettling

questions

senseless musings

teaching–learning

truth–illusion

wish–will

Symbols

altar

angels

bridge

child

lilies

song of Heaven

star

thorns

toys

war

Part II

GLOSSARY-INDEX

abundance

Heaven's principle that contrasts with the ego's belief in scarcity; God's Son can never lack anything or be in need, since God's gifts, given eternally in creation, are always with him.

(Note—since abundance and scarcity are usually discussed together, *scarcity* and related ego concepts are not cross-referenced below.)

---

charity
T-4.II.6-7

Christ
T-1.V.6

creation
T-1.IV.3; T-26.VII.13

extension
T-7.VII.7; **T-7.VIII.1**

God
T-4.III.9; T-4.VII.5; **T-7.VII.10**; T-28.III.9

grandeur
T-9.VIII.5

innocence
T-3.I.6

real world
W-pI.54.5; W-pII.249.1

Sonship
T-1.IV.4; T-1.V.4; T-12.III.5
W-pI.165.6

truth
T-1.IV.3

accepting the Atonement

accepting the unreality of the separation, sin and guilt, sickness and death, by following the specific curriculum of forgiving our special relationships—taught by the Holy Spirit—that corrects our mistakes; this is our one responsibility, our function in the Atonement.

---

ego
T-8.III.6

fear
T-2.I.4

forgiveness
T-14.I.1; **T-19.IV-D.9-12**
M-18.4

guilt
T-13.I.6; T-13.X.5-8; T-14.I.1

healing
T-19.I.9
M-6.1; M-22.1; M-23.2

holy relationship
T-22.VI.4-5
P-2.II.8; P-3.II.3

identity
W-pI.139

invulnerability
T-14.III.7-10

miracle worker
T-2.V.5; T-5.V.7
M-7.3; M-18.4

resurrection
M-28.1

salvation
W-pII.297.1; W-pII.318.2

separation
T-7.VIII.7; T-13.In.2; **T-28.IV.1**

sin
T-18.VII.1
W-pI.101.5; W-pII.337
M-14.3

time
T-2.III.3

the Course frequently refers to itself; its goal is not love or God, but the undoing, through forgiveness, of the interferences of guilt and fear that prevent our acceptance of Him; its primary focus, therefore, is on the ego and its undoing, rather than on Christ or spirit.

---

cause–effect
T-21.VII.7

consistency
T-20.VII.1
W-pI.156.2

decision
T-16.V.16; T-26.III.5: T-31.IV.8

doubt
W-pI.165.7

ego
T-7.VIII.7; T-22.II.6; T-22.III.2;
T-23.II.8
C-In.3-4

forgiveness
T-31.VII.15
M-4.X.2-3; **M-20.5**

free will
T-In.1
M-2.3

giving–receiving
W-pI.105.3; W-pI.126.1
M-4.VII.1

goal
T-26.III.5
W-pI.42; W-pI.127.6;

goal (continued)
W-pI.169.3; W-pI.181.4;
W-pII.In.1
M-10.3; M-28.3

holy instant
T-26.V.10
M-24.6

holy relationship
T-18.VII.6

Holy Spirit
T-9.V.9; T-12.II.10
M-29.2-4

identity
T-9.I.2; T-14.X.12; T-16.III.4
W-pI.127.4; W-pI.rV.In.5

Jesus
M-23.7
C-5.6

knowledge
T-8.I.1; T-18.IX.11
W-pI.138.5

learning
T-15.IV.1; T-21.I.3; T-24.In.2;
T-24.VII.8; T-31.IV.7;
T-31.VII.15
M-In.1-2

love
T-In.1; T-13.IV.1
W-pI.127.4

mind-training
T-1.VII.4
W-pI.In.

peace
T-8.I.1; T-13.II.7; T-24.In.1
W-pI.In(181-200).1

philosophy/theology
C-In.1-2

practicality
T-8.IX.8; T-11.VIII.5
M-16.4; M-29.5

process
W-Ep.1

reincarnation
M-24.3-4

resistance
T-11.VI.3; T-11.VIII.5;
T-13.II.6-7; T-13.IV.1: T-23.III.4;
T-24.I.8; T-25.VII.2

simplicity
T-11.VIII.1; T-15.IV.6; T-22.II.7;
T-26.III.1
W-pI.39.1-2
C-In.3

world
W-pI.132.5-8; W-pI.133.2

a little willingness

this, joined with the Holy Spirit, is all the Atonement requires; our ego seems to make the undoing of guilt impossible, and on our own it would be, but the willingness to forgive allows the Holy Spirit to undo it for us; looking with the Holy Spirit at our guilt without judgment.

A Course in Miracles
T-21.II.1; T-24.In.2

decision
T-2.VI.3

forgiveness
T-26.VII.10; T-29.VI.1; T-31.VII.5

God
P-2.V.6

holy instant
T-15.IV.2; T-17.IV.11: **T-18.IV**

Holy Spirit
T-2.VI.6; T-8.VIII.8; T-11.II.4-5; T-11.VIII.3; T-14.VII.5; T-15.V.5; T-16.IV.12; T-17.I.6; **T-18.V.2-6; T-25.VIII.1**

miracle
T-9.IV.6; T-28.IV.10

real world
T-11.VII.2; T-13.VII.4; T-16.VI.10

salvation
T-26.VII.10
W-pI.196.4

Second Coming
W-pII.9.1,5

vision
T-15.IX.1; T-22.II.13

altar

the part of the mind that chooses God or the ego; not an external structure, but an attitude or devotion.

w-m: used rarely as symbol of the ego's presence: drips with blood.

r-m: symbol of God's Presence in us; the meeting place of God and His Son: strewn with the lilies of forgiveness.

Atonement
T-2.III.1-2,4,5; T-3.I.8;
T-12.III.10; T-13.IX.7

belief
T-6.V-C.7

Christ
T-11.IV.6-7; T-12.VI.5-6
C-5.1

church
T-6.I.8

defilement
T-2.III.4; T-2.V.7-8

ego
T-13.VII.10; T-15.VII.9;
T-21.II.6-8
W-pII.12.4-5

forgiveness
T-25.III.6; **T-26.IV.3-5**
W-pI.187.9-11; W-pII.2.3;
W-pII.336.1

gifts
T-14.VIII.5
W-pI.104.1-2,4

God
T-10.III.11; T-13.X.9; T-15.IV.4;
T-23.I.11; T-29.VII.9; T-31.VIII.3
W-pI.45.8; W-pI.152.8;
W-pI.187.10; W-pII.13.3
C-4.8
S-1.I.5

grace
T-19.I.13
W-pI.169.1

holiness
T-15.III.9,12; T-29.IX.8

holy relationship
T-14.V.10; T-19.I.13-14
W-pI.183.5

Holy Spirit
T-5.II.8; T-7.V.11; T-14.VIII.2;
T-15.II.2

knowledge
T-3.III.5

lilies–thorns
T-20.II; T-20.VIII.4

mind/spirit
T-1.I.20; T-7.III.4

prayer
S-1.I.5

Self
T-11.IV.1,3
W-pII.309.2

Son of God
T-3.III.6; T-11.VI.5;
T-14.VIII.2; T-29.IX.8
W-pII.313.1
C-4.7

special relationships
T-16.V.11

true perception
T-3.III.6; **T-12.VI.7**
C-4.6

angels

extensions of God's Thought; symbol of the light and protection of God that always surround us, since we in truth have never left Him; not to be confused with the popular idea of celestial beings, which are inherently illusory.

Christ
W-pII.303.1
S-2.III.7

gifts
W-pII.316.1

God
W-Ep.6

holy relationship
T-19.IV-C.9
W-pI.161.9

light
T-26.IX.7
W-pI.131.13

Name of God
W-pI.183.2

anger

(see: *attack*)

Answer

(see: *Holy Spirit*)

anti-Christ

symbol for the ego and the belief that there is a power that can oppose the omnipotence of God and deny the reality of Christ.

(Note—not to be confused with the Christian term denoting the real presence of evil [or the devil] in the world.)

---

ego	*idol*
T-29.VIII.3,6; T-30.I.14 W-pI.137.6	T-29.VIII.3

Atonement

the Holy Spirit's plan of correction to undo the ego and heal the belief in separation; came into being after the separation, and will be completed when every separated Son has fulfilled his part in the Atonement by total forgiveness; its principle is that the separation never occurred.

---

correction
T-2.VII.6
M-18.4

defense
T-2.II.4,7; T-2.III.1-2

face of Christ
W-pII.6.4-5

fear
T-1.I.26; T-1.III.5; T-5.IV.1

forgiveness
T-1.III.3; **T-9.IV.1-2**; T-14.IV.3
C-In.1

God
T-15.IX.1; T-16.VII.10

guilt
T-18.IV.6
W-pI.140.4

guiltlessness
T-14.IV.1,9

healing
W-pI.140.4
M-22

holy relationship
P-3.III.8

Holy Spirit
T-5.I.5-6; T-13.IX.4-7;
T-18.V.1-2
M-29.3
C-6.2

illusions
M-2.2

Jesus
T-1.III.1-4; T-4.VI.6; T-5.IV.6
C-6.2

last step
T-15.IX.1

miracles
T-1.I.25,26,33,34,37,41,44;
T-1.III.7-9; T-1.IV.2; T-2.IV.5

psychotherapy
P-2.III.4

real world
T-17.II.3

resurrection
T-3.I.1

sacrifice
T-3.I.1-6,8

separation
T-5.II.2-3; **T-6.II.10**; T-17.III.5

sharing
T-5.IV.2; T-9.IV.3

sin
T-18.VII.1-5

special relationships
T-16.VII.5; T-17.III.10

teaching
T-14.V.2-11
M-3.3

time
T-2.II.4-6; T-15.II.1
M-2.2; M-24.6

attack

the attempt to justify the projection of guilt onto others, demonstrating their sinfulness and guilt so that we may feel free of it; because attack is always a projection of responsibility for the separation, it is never justified; also used to denote the thought of separation from God, for which we believe God will attack and punish us in return.

(Note—"attack" and "anger" are used as virtual synonyms.)

---

body
T-6.I.4; T-8.VII.1,3-5,11-16;
T-8.VIII.1-2,5; T-29.II.9
W-pI.72.1-7; W-pI.161.6-8

Christ
T-10.II.4-5; T-11.IV.5-6; T-25.V.2

defenses
W-pI.135.1; **W-pI.153.2-9**;
W-pI.170.1-5
P-2.In.1; **P-2.IV.9-10**

dream
T-18.II.1-4; T-29.IV.3-4

ego
T-7.VI.11; T-8.IX.6;
T-12.III.6,10; T-13.I.10-11;
T-19.IV-B.15
W-pI.71.2

fear
T-6.In.1; T-23.In.2
W-pI.170.1-10; W-pI.196.5-11
M-17

forgiveness
T-23.III.2-5; **T-30.VI.1-4**
W-pI.192.1-7

form
W-pI.21.2

God
T-11.IV.5; T-22.VI.11-12;
T-25.V.2-6
W-pI.72.1-10
S-1.III.2; S-2.I.3

guilt
T-15.VII.2-10; T-23.III
M-18.3

Holy Spirit
M-29.6

idol
T-30.IV.1

injustice
T-26.X; T-27.I.1-3

invulnerability
T-6.III.3; T-12.V.1-3; T-13.I.11
W-pI.26.1-4

Jesus
T-6.I.3-15

judgment
W-pII.347
M-4.IV.1

laws of chaos
T-23.II

love
T-12.I.8
W-pI.68.1-2; W-pI.189.3-4
M-7.4

magic
M-17; M-18.2

mind
T-12.III.7-10; T-24.IV.3
W-pI.161.1-9

miracle
T-23.IV.4-9
W-pI.78

peace
M-20.3-4

projection
T-6.In.1; **T-6.I.3,9,14,16**;
T-6.II.2-3; T-7.VII.8-9
W-pI.22.1; **W-pI.196.1-10**

sacrifice
T-15.VII.6-9; T-15.X.5-8;
T-26.I.1

separation
S-1.IV.1

sickness
T-27.I.3-4; T-27.II.1-3;
T-28.VI.4-5

sin
T-19.II.1-2; T-23.II.4; T-25.V.1;
T-31.III.1-2
W-pI.181.1-6

special relationships
T-15.VII.1-10; T-16.IV.1-11;
T-24.I

world
T-20.III.4-5
W-pI.153.1-4; W-pII.3.2

awakening

the Course speaks of the separation as being a dream from which we need to awaken; salvation therefore consists of hearing the Holy Spirit—the Call to awaken—in ourselves and in our brothers: thus accepting the oneness with each other that undoes the separation which gave rise to the dream in the beginning.

---

death–resurrection
T-6.I.7,12; T-27.VII.10
W-pI.162.2
M-28

dream
T-10.I.2; T-12.II.4-6; T-13.IV.6; T-13.XI.10; T-17.I.1; **T-18.II**; **T-27.VII.8-16**; T-29.IX.2
W-pI.134.11; W-pI.153.14; W-pII.294.2; W-pII.313.1

God
T-7.I.6; T-8.VI.9; T-10.III.2; T-20.IV.2
W-pI.168.1-3; W-pII.10.4-5; W-pII.340.2

guilt
T-11.IV.4; T-13.IX.1; T-14.V.2

Holy Spirit
T-5.II.10; T-6.IV.6; T-6.V.2; T-8.II.8; T-8.IX.3-4; T-9.VI.5; **T-12.VI.4-5**; T-13.VII.16; T-20.IV.1; T-26.IX.1
W-pI.169.3
M-26.3

Jesus
T-11.VI.9; T-12.II.7; T-15.III.9

light
T-2.I.4; T-14.II.8; T-29.III.5
W-pI.140.2

love
T-7.IV.7; T-13.VI.12-13; T-14.IV.5

mind
W-pI.167.8-12

miracle
T-1.I.20; T-7.IX.4; **T-28.II.4-9**; T-29.IV.2

peace
T-13.VII.9; T-29.V.3
W-pII.331.1

real world/forgiveness
W-pI.191.10; W-pI.198.3; W-pII.8.4

special relationships
T-24.II.14; T-24.III.7

spiritual vision
T.2.III.3; T-2.V.7

body

level I: the embodiment of the ego; the thought of separation projected by the mind and becoming form; the witness to the seeming reality of the separation by being a limitation on love, excluding it from our awareness; includes both our physical bodies as well as our personalities.

level II: inherently neutral, neither "good" nor "evil"; its purpose is given it by the mind.

w-m: the symbol of guilt and attack

r-m: the means of teaching and learning forgiveness, whereby the ego's guilt is undone; the instrument of salvation through which the Holy Spirit speaks.

---

appetites
T-4.II.7

Christ
T-25.In; T-25.I.1-4

death
M-27
S-3.I.1-3; S-3.II.1-3

dream
T-27.VIII.1-5
W-pII.5.3

ego
T-4.V.2-4; T-6.IV.4-5; T-15.IX.2;
T-18.VIII.3-7; T-20.VI.11
W-pI.72.2-8; W-pI.199.3-4

fear
T-21.III.7-8
W-pI.161.5-8

forgiveness
T-27.I.5-11
W-pI.192.4-5
C-4.5

guilt
T-18.VI.2-7; T-18.IX.5;
T-19.IV-B.1,12-13

healing
T-7.V.1; T-8.IX.1; T-19.I.3-6;
T-28.VII
W-pI.135.10; W-pI.136.16-18;
W-pII.5.4
S-3.III.6

holy instant
T-15.IX.3-7

Holy Spirit
T-8.VII.2-5,7-9,12-13;
T-15.IX.7; T-20.VI.5-7
W-pI.91.7; W-pI.199.6

instrument of salvation
T-8.VIII.9; T-24.V.3-9
W-pI.154.11; W-pI.rV.In.9;
W-pII.237.2; W-pII.295.1;
W-pII.296.1; W-pII.9.5;
W-pII.14.4; **W-pII.353**
M-12.3-5; M-29.8
C-6.5
P-2.V.5; P-3.I.2
S-2.III.5

magic
S-3.III.1-3

mind
T-2.IV.2-3; T-2.V.6;
T-18.VI.2-14; T-21.III.10;
T-28.V.4-5; **T-28.VI.1-5**
W-pI.135.4-9; W-pI.199.1
M-8.3-4,6
P-2.VI.2-4

neutrality
T-19.IV-C.5-6; T-24.IV.2;
T-27.VI.3; T-29.I.5; T-31.III.3-4;
W-pII.294

perception
T-3.IV.6

projection
T-28.II.8
W-pI.161.8

sacrifice
T-15.XI.5-7; T-21.III.9-12;
T-26.I.1-4

separation
T-19.I.3-7; T-28.VI.3; T-29.I.4-8

sickness
T-8.VIII.3-9; T-29.II.7-10
W-pI.136.8-20
M-5.I-II
P-2.VI.4

sin
T-18.VII.4; T-31.III.3-5
W-pII.4.1

Son of God
W-pII.5

special relationships
T-16.VI.4-5; T-17.III.2;
T-20.VI.4-12; T-24.IV.2;
T-24.VII.4,9-10

suffering
T-19.IV-B.9-16; T-27.VI.1
W-pI.76.5

temptation
T-31.VIII.1
W-pI.64.1-2

world
T-18.IX.3-7; T-31.VI.1-6
C-4.5

bridge

symbol for the transition from perception to knowledge, and thus is equated variously with the Holy Spirit, the real world, and God's last step; used also to denote the shift from false to true perception and the real world.

---

creations
T-16.III.8-9; T-16.IV.7-8

forgiveness
W-pI.134.10-11
C-3.2,5

God
T-16.IV.2,7-13; T-16.V.17;
T-28.I.15; T-28.III.3,6

Holy Spirit
T-5.III.1,7; T-6.II.7; T-16.IV.12
W-pI.96.8; W-pI.151.9; W-pII.7.1

Jesus
T-1.II.4; T-4.VI.7

peace
W-pI.200.8

real world
T-16.VI.5-12; **T-17.II.2**

time–eternity
T-2.II.6; T-16.IV.13; T-17.II.2

truth–illusions
W-pI.198.8

vision
W-pI.159.5

bringing darkness (illusions) to the light (truth)

the process of undoing denial and dissociation, expressing the decision to bring our guilt to the light of the Holy Spirit to be looked at and forgiven, rather than fearfully keeping it in the darkness of our unconscious minds where it could never be seen and undone; living in illusions brings sickness and pain, bringing them to truth is healing and salvation.

Atonement
T-14.IX.1-3

Christ
T-31.VIII.2
W-pII.6.4-5

Christ's vision
W-pII.302.1; W-pII.305.1

conflict
T-23.I.9
W-pII.333

death
T-17.IV.13-14
M-27.7

dissociation
T-14.VII

error
T-2.II.1; T-23.II.3; T-25.IV.5
W-pI.107.5

fear
T-3.VII.5; **T-14.VI**
W-pI.103.2

forgiveness
T-22.VI.9
W-pI.99.6-8; W-pI.134.6;
W-pII.270.1; W-pII.12.5
M-28.2
C-4.6

guilt
T-13.II.9; T-15.VII.3;

healing
T-9.V.3
W-pI.136.1,16; W-pI.140.7
M-6.1

Heaven–hell
W-pI.138.9-11

holy instant
T-21.II.4; **T-27.IV**
W-pII.227.1

holy relationship
T-18.III.6

Holy Spirit
T-13.III.7; T-14.II.4; T-14.VIII.1;
T-14.XI.4-9; **T-17.I.5-6**;
T-18.IX.1-2; T-26.X.6;
T-27.VIII.9-12
W-pII.7.1

problem–answer
W-pI.80.2-5

sin
T-19.II.6; T-20.VII.6

special relationships
T-16.IV.1

teachers of God
M-5.III.3

cause and effect are mutually dependent, since the existence of one determines the existence of the other; moreover, if something is not a cause it cannot exist, since all being has effects.

knowledge: God is the only *Cause*, and His Son is His *Effect*.

perception: the thought of separation—sin—is the *cause* of the dream of suffering and death, which is sin's *effect*; forgiveness undoes sin by demonstrating that sin has no effect; i.e., the peace of God and our loving relationship with Him is totally unaffected by what others have done to us; therefore, not having effects, sin cannot be a cause and thus cannot exist.

---

attack
T-12.V.1-3; T-26.X.2

dream
T-24.V.2; **T-27.VII.1-13**;
T-28.II.4-12; **T-28.III**; T-28.IV

ego
T-16.III.2

fear
T-11.V.2,4; T-14.III.15;
T-26.VIII.4-5
W-pI.130.4
M-17.9
P-1.1

forgiveness
T-9.IV.5; T-22.In.1; **T-27.II.1-6**
S-3.In

God
T-2.VII.3; T-9.I.9; T-14.III.8;
T-28.I.14; **T-28.II.1**

guilt
T-14.III.7-8; T-28.I.2
W-pI.156.1

healing
T-29.II.1-3

magic
M-16.9
S-1.IV.2; S-3.II.1

miracle
T-2.V.14; T-26.VII.14;
T-27.VI.5; T-28.I.9-10;
T-28.II.7-12; T-30.VIII.2

nothingness
T-27.III.3

sickness
T-26.VII.2-5; T-28.II.2-3;
T-28.VI.5
W-pI.136.1-6

sin
T-14.III.15; **T-27.I.9-10**
W-pI.101.5

Son of God
T-21.II.10-13; T-28.I.14
W-pII.326.I

thoughts
T-2.VII.1; T-21.In.1
W-pI.16.1-3; W-pI.17.1;
W-pI.19.1

time
T-26.VIII.6-9; T-28.I.5-9

world
T-27.VII.1-13; **T-27.VIII.5-13**
W-pI.23; W-pI.32.1-2;
W-pI.190.4-7; W-pII.10.2-3
P-1.4

metaphor to describe the "little wisdom" of the separated Sons, who are like little children who do not understand the world, and therefore need to be taught by their elder brother Jesus to distinguish what is true from what is false, the world of reality from the world of fantasy; if we were spiritually advanced adults we would not need the help that *A Course in Miracles* provides.

Christ
T-22.I.7-8
W-pI.182.4-12

ego
T-4.II.5; T-8.VIII.1; T-21.IV.8

fantasy–reality
T-6.V.4; **T-9.IV.10-12**;
T-11.VIII.13-14; T-13.V.7;
T-18.IX.7

holy relationship
T-19.IV-C.9-10; T-22.I.7-8

Holy Spirit
T-6.V.1-4; T-11.VIII.2-3,13-15

Jesus
T-4.I.13; T-8.V.4-5; T-13.II.8-9

lack of understanding
T-11.VIII.2-3,7-8; **T-22.I.6-8**

nightmares/dreams
T-6.V.1-2; **T-12.II.4-6**;
T-29.IX.4-10

parent-child
T-1.V.3; T-7.I.1; T-13.In.2-3
W-pI.rV.In.2-3
M-29.6
C-2.8

powerlessness
W-pI.rIV.In.4

projection
T-27.VIII.8

real world
W-pI.127.11

salvation
W-pI.153.12-13

toys/idols
T-29.IX.4-10; **T-30.IV.2-8**
W-pI.153.6-8; W-pII.4.4-5
M-13.4

Christ

the Second Person of the Trinity; the one Son of God or totality of the Sonship; the Self That God created by extension of His spirit; though Christ creates as does His Father, He is not the Father since God created Christ, but Christ did not create God.

(Note—not to be equated exclusively with Jesus.)

see: *creations, vision*

---

anti-Christ
T-29.VIII; T-30.I.14
W-pI.137.6

Atonement
T-12.III.10

attack
T-25.V.2

birth
W-pII.303.1; W-pII.308.1

body
T-24.VI.6-13; **T-25.In**; **T-25.I.1-4**
W-pI.161.12

completion
T-24.V

creation
T-4.IV.10

forgiveness
T-22.IV.3-4
W-pI.158.9; W-pI.159.8;
W-pI.192.8
S-2.III.2-3,5-6

Friend
T-19.IV-D.14; T-20.I.4

God
T-9.I.14; **T-11.IV.6-7**;
T-12.VI.6-7; T-31.VIII.12

guilt
T-13.I.1; T-13.VI.3

healing
T-11.VIII.9-12; T-12.II.3
S-3.IV.6-7

holy relationship
T-22.I.7-11; T-22.II.12-13;
T-31.II.6-9

Holy Spirit
T-13.V.11; T-25.I.5-6

Jesus
C-5.2-6; C-6.1

Mind
T-5.I.5; T-25.I.1
C-1.1,6

Presence
T-11.V.17; T-26.IX; T-26.X
W-pI.157.9

rebirth
T-22.II.12; T-31.II.9
W-pI.182; W-pI.192.8
C-Ep.5

risen Christ
T-11.VI.1; T-20.I; T-26.IX.8

Second Coming
T-4.IV.10
W-pII.9

Self
T-15.V.10
W-pII.6

Son of God
T-11.IV.7; **T-11.VIII.9**

strength
T-31.VIII.2-5
W-pI.62.3

time of Christ
T-15.X.2-4; T-15.XI.2,8

touch
T-13.VI.8
W-pI.166.12-15

Christmas

the holiday commemorating the traditional birth of Jesus; used as a symbol for the rebirth of Christ in ourselves: the "time of Christ."

Bethlehem
T-19.IV-C.10

Jesus
T-15.III.7; **T-15.X.1-4**;
T-15.XI.7-10

manger
T-15.III.9

Prince of Peace
T-15.III.8; T-15.XI.7

time of Christ
T-15.X.1-4; **T-15.XI**

communication

knowledge: synonymous with creation, an expression of our unified relationship to God which can be likened to a flow of spirit and love; only spirit can communicate, unlike the ego, which is separate by nature.

true perception: we experience communication in our right minds through the Holy Spirit, allowing His Love to be shared through us.

Atonement
T-14.V.5

body
T-8.VII; T-15.IX.2-7; T-18.VI.8
W-pI.72.2
M-28.1

creation
T-4.VII.3-6; T-9.I.6

forgiveness
T-15.VII.13-14

God–Son
T-14.III.18-19; T-14.VIII.2
W-pI.49.1; W-pI.129.4;
W-pI.183.11

holy instant
T-15.IV.6-8; T-15.VI.8

Holy Spirit
T-1.I.46; T-5.II.8; **T-6.V-A.5**;
T-13.XI.7-8; T-14.IV.10;
T-14.VI.5-8; T-14.X.11

mind
T-7.V.2-3; T-15.IV.6; T-15.XI.7;
T-20.V.5

miracle
T-2.IV.5

psychic powers
M-25.2,6

revelation
T-1.I.46; T-1.II.1; T-4.VII.7

separation
T-5.II.5; T-6.IV.12; T-14.VI.5

spirit
T-4.I.2; T-4.VII.3

symbols
T-30.VII.6-7
W-pI.184.9

communion

the joining of Father, Son, and Holy Spirit, Whose union seemed broken by the separation; awareness of this union of spirit is restored to us through the holy relationship; not to be confused with the traditional Catholic understanding of the term, which emphasizes the sharing of the *body* (not the mind) of Jesus in the liturgy of the Eucharist at Mass, through the transubstantiation of bread and wine into his body and blood.

---

body
T-7.V.10; T-8.VII.3;
T-19.IV-A.17

communication
T-6.V-A.5

fear
T-1.IV.1

holy relationship/Jesus
T-19.IV-A.16; **T-19.IV-B.4,7-8**
P-2.II.9

Holy Spirit
T-5.III.11; T-7.V.11; T-19.IV-B.3

miracle
T-1.IV.2; T-3.V.10

creation

the extension of God's being or spirit, the Cause, that resulted in His Son, the Effect; described as the First Coming of Christ; it is the Son's function in Heaven to create, as it was God's in creating Him.

(Note—exists only at the level of knowledge, and is not equivalent to creation or creativity as the terms are used in the world of perception.)

see: *creations*

---

communication
T-4.VII.3-6

eternal
P-3.II.4

extension
T-2.I.1-2; T-6.II.8; T-7.I.2-5; T-17.IV.1; T-19.III.6; T-23.IV.3
S-1.In.1

First Coming
T-4.IV.10; T-9.IV.9

forgiveness
W-pI.192.2-3

Holy Spirit
T-5.I.5; T-16.III.5; T-17.II.1

knowledge
T-14.VIII.4

laws of God
T-10.IV.5

Mind of God
T-4.VII.3; T-10.V.10; T-25.VII.4

oneness
T-8.III.3; T-24.VII.6

separation
T-13.VIII.3; T-28.V.6

sharing
T-4.VII.5; T-10.V.5

Son of God
T-5.IV.7; **T-28.II.1**
W-pII.11

understanding
T-14.IV.4

Will of God
T-8.II.6-7

Word of God
W-pII.276.1

creations

the extensions of our spirit; the effects of our creating, analogous to the creation when God created His Son by extending Himself; as extensions of Christ, our creations are part of the Second Person of the Trinity; creation is ongoing in Heaven, beyond time and space, and independent of the Son's lack of awareness of it in this world.

see: *creation*

Atonement
T-5.V.2

creation
T-2.VIII.3-4; T-10.I.1; T-14.VIII.4; T-14.X.1; T-16.IV.8; T-24.VII.1; **T-28.II.1**
W-pI.132.11-12; W-pII.11.2

dissociation
T-4.VI.7; T-9.VI.4

extension
T-2.I.1-2; **T-7.I.2-5**; T-11.I.3-7; T-15.III.7

forgiveness
T-26.IV.1; T-29.VI.4

God
T-7.X.1; T-7.XI.6-7; T-9.VI.4-7; T-10.V.13; T-13.VIII.9; T-15.VIII.2; T-21.II.12; T-24.II.6
W-pII.326.1

Holy Spirit
T-5.I.5; T-7.IX.5; T-8.II.8; T-15.IX.5; **T-16.III.5**

joy
T-7.V.9; T-7.VI.13; T-25.IV.2

spirit
T-4.III.1; **T-7.IX.2-3**

Trinity
T-8.VI.5-6,8

crucifixion

a symbol of the ego's attack on God and therefore on His Son, witnessing to the "reality" of suffering, sacrifice, victimization, and death which the world seems to manifest; also refers to the killing of Jesus, an extreme example that taught that our true Identity of love can never be destroyed, for death has no power over life.

(Note—since crucifixion and resurrection are usually discussed together, "resurrection" is not cross-referenced below.)

---

decision
T-11.VI.1-2,5-8; T-14.III.4

ego
T-13.II.6; T-13.III.1; T-14.V.10

faithlessness
T-17.VIII.4-5

forgiveness
T-20.I.1-3; T-20.II; T-26.VII.17

Jesus
T-3.I.1-5; **T-6.I**; T-11.VI.7-8;
T-20.I.2
W-pI.rV.In.6

message
T-4.In.3; T-6.I.13

projection
T-6.I.3,9,14-15
W-pI.196.1-5

sacrifice
T-3.I.1-8; **T-27.I.1-8**

suffering
T-19.IV-D.20
W-pII.12.4

world
T-13.In.4

death

w-m: the final witness to the seeming reality of the body and the separation from our Creator, Who is life; if the body dies then it must have lived, which means its maker—the ego—must be real and alive as well; also seen by the ego as the ultimate punishment for our sin of separation from God.

r-m: the quiet laying down of the body after it has fulfilled its purpose as a teaching device.

---

attack
T-13.IV.2
W-pI.161.7

attraction
T-19.IV-C; T-19.IV-D.4

body
T-6.V-A.1; T-19.IV-C.5-8;
T-29.VII.4
W-pII.294.1
S-3.I.1-2

decision
T-3.VII.6; T-19.IV-C.1
W-pI.152.1
M-5.I.2; M-12.5

dream
T-29.V.7
C-2.1

ego
T-12.VII.13-14; **T-15.I.3-4**;
T-19.IV-B.16-17

forgiveness-to-destroy
S-2.II.8

God
T-29.VI.2-4
W-pI.72.5; **W-pI.163**
M-20.5; **M-27**
C-5.6

healing
S-3.II.1-5

Holy Spirit
T-27.VI.4-6
M-12.5

Jesus
T-6.V-A.1; T-11.VI.7;
T-12.VII.15
M-23.2

life
T-3.VII.5-6; T-13.IV.3;
T-27.VII.9-10
W-pI.138.7; **W-pI.167.1-11**
M-20.4-5; M-27.4

resurrection
M-28.1-2

separation
M-19.4

sin
T-19.IV-A.17; T-25.VII.1-2;
T-25.VIII.3; T-31.III.5
W-pI.101.2-4

special relationships
T-17.IV.8-13; T-24.V.4

decision

the last remaining freedom as prisoners of this world is our power to decide; while unknown in Heaven, decision is necessary here as it was our decision to be separate from our Source that must be corrected; this is accomplished by choosing the Holy Spirit instead of the ego, right-mindedness instead of wrong-mindedness.

see: *free will*

---

body
T-24.VI.7; T-31.VI.1-3

Christ
T-31.VIII.1-5

death
T-19.IV-C.1
W-pI.152.1

dissociation
T-10.II.1-2

dreams–awakening
T-27.VII.8-11; T-29.IV.1

forgiveness
W-pII.335.1
S-2.I.8,10

healing
T-11.II.1-5

Heaven–hell
W-pI.138; W-pI.190.11
M-21.3

holiness
T-20.VIII.9; T-21.In.2

Holy Spirit
T-5.II.3,5-6,8-10; **T-5.VII.6**; T-6.V-C.4; **T-14.III.4-19**; **T-14.IV.5-6**; T-15.III.4-6

imprisonment–freedom
T-12.VII.9; T-15.X.9; T-21.VI.11

Jesus
T-3.IV.7; T-5.II.9-11; T-8.IV.5; T-15.III.10

joy
T-5.VII.5-6; T-25.IV.1
W-pI.190.6-11

littleness–magnitude
T-15.III.1-6

mind
T-4.II.7; T-7.VI.2; T-8.IV.5

miracle
T-14.III.5; T-30.VIII.4-6
W-pI.78

pain
W-pII.284.1

projection/extension
T-12.VII.7-12

real world–world
T-26.III.4
W-pI.129.6-9; W-pI.130.5-10

right- and wrong-mindedness
C-1.5-7

rules
T-30.I

self-concept
T-31.V.12-13

separation
T-5.V.8

sickness
W-pI.136.2-7
M-5; M-22.4

sin/error
T-25.III.9
W-pII.351
P-2.IV.1

Son of God
T-21.II.2-3; T-22.II.6

time
T-In.1; T.10.V.14
M-2.1-4

truth–illusions
T-17.III.9; T-31.II.2-3
W-pI.133.3-14; W-pI.152;
W-pI.155.3-12; W-pI.185.1-10

vision
T-20.V.4
W-pI.20.3; W-pI.27.1;
W-pI.28.1-5; W-pI.170.7-11

world
T-31.IV.1-8

defenses

w-m: the dynamics we use to "protect" ourselves from our guilt, fear, and seeming attack of others, the most important of which are denial and projection; by their very nature "defenses do what they would defend," as they reinforce the belief in our own vulnerability which merely increases our fear and belief that we need defense.

r-m: reinterpreted as the means to free us from fear; e.g., denial denies "the denial of truth," and projecting our guilt enables us to be aware of what we have denied, so that we may truly forgive it.

Atonement
T-2.II.4,7; T-2.III.1-2

attack
T-6.IV.4; T-23.III.5
W-pI.135.1-10; W-pI.153.1-5;
W-pI.170.1-5
M-20.4

crucifixion
T-3.I.2

defenselessness
W-pI.134.12; **W-pI.153**;
W-pI.182.7-12
M-4.VI
P-2.IV.9-10

denial
T-2.II.2; T-7.VII.1

fear
T-12.I.9

holy instant
T-17.IV.10-11

Holy Spirit
T-14.VII.5

illusion
T-22.V
W-pI.153.7

invulnerability
T-14.VII.5
M-16.6

magic
P-2.IV.6

planning
W-pI.135.11-26

sickness
W-pI.136

sin
T-20.III.1; T-22.V.2

special relationships
T-17.IV.5-8

theology
C-In.2

time
W-pI.136.13; W-pI.181.4-5

denial

w-m: avoiding guilt by pushing the decision that made it out of awareness, rendering it inaccessible to correction or Atonement; roughly equivalent to repression; protects the ego's belief that *it* is our source and not God.

r-m: used to deny error and affirm truth: to deny "the denial of truth."

---

body
T-2.IV.3; T-19.I.7; T-19.IV-B.14

defenses
W-pI.136.2-6

ego
T-4.V-2-4; T-7.VI.4; T-11.V.16

fear
T-12.I.8-10; T-13.II.4-5; T-22.I.4

God
T-10.V; T-11.I.8; T-11.IV.1-2

guilt
P-2.VI.4

Holy Spirit
T-7.VII.1

illusions
T-10.III.7

mind
T-7.VII.1

projection
T-2.II.2; T-6.II.2; T-7.VIII.3;
T-12.III.6; T-13.II.5;
T-19.IV-B.14; **T-27.VII.1-12**
M-17.6

right mind/miracle worker
T-2.II.2; **T-12.II**

separation
T-2.VII.5
W-pI.79.6; W-pI.124.7
M-17.5

truth
T-9.I.9,11-12; T-11.II.2-3;
T-21.VII.5,12
P-2.V.1

vision
T-13.V.8
W-pI.91.1-2

devil

a projection of the ego, which attempts to deny responsibility for our sin and guilt by projecting them onto an external agent, which therefore seems to affect us by its "evil."

---

ego
M-25.6

God
T-3.VII.2,5

separation
T-3.VII.5

sin
W-pI.101.5

dissociation

an ego defense that separates the ego from the Holy Spirit—the wrong mind from the right mind—splitting off what seems fearful, which merely reinforces the fear that is the ego's goal; the ego's attempt to separate two conflicting thought systems and keep them both in our minds, so that *its* thought system of darkness is safe from undoing by the light.

see: *split*

---

creations
T-4.VI.7

ego/fear
T-15.I.4

ego–spirit
T-4.VI.1,4

Holy Spirit
T-5.III.2

knowledge
T-10.II.1-2; T-21.V.7

mind
W-pI.96.4-5

projection
T-6.II.1-3; T-12.VII.7

separation
T-6.II.1; **T-14.VII.4**

truth
T-8.V.1

dream

the post-separation state in which the Son of God dreams a world of sin, guilt, and fear, believing this to be reality and Heaven the dream; the Son, being the dreamer, is the *cause* of the world which is the *effect,* although this relationship between cause and effect appears reversed in this world, where we seem to be the effect or victim of the world; occasionally used to denote sleeping dreams, although there is no real difference between them and waking ones, for both belong to the illusory world of perception.

see: *happy dream*, *sleep*

---

attack
T-21.VII.3-4; T-27.VII.1-13

body
T-27.VIII.1-10
W-pII.5.3

cause–effect
T-27.VII; **T-27.VIII.1-10**; **T-28.II.4-12**; T-28.III; T-28.IV.1-6

crucifixion
T-11.VI.8

darkness
T-13.V.8; T-18.III

death
T-29.V.7
M-27

ego
T-4.I.4, T-6.IV.6
C-2.1

fear
T-28.V.1-2; T-29.IV.2
W-pII.331.1
P-3.II.6

forgiveness
W-pII.7.4

form–content
T-18.II.5; T-29.IV.1-4
W-pI.185.4-5
S-2.III.4

God
T-6.IV.6
W-pII.279.1

idol
T-29.VII.6; T-29.IX.1-6

judgment
T-29.IX

separation
T-2.I.3-4: T-28.II.8-9
S-3.III.2

sickness
T-28.II.3-12; T-28.III; T-28.IV
W-pI.140.4

sin
C-5.4

sleeping dreams
T-2.I.4; T-10.I.2-3; **T-18.II**

special relationships
T-24.III.7

teacher of God
M-12.6

time
T-26.V.6
W-pI.167.9

Easter

the holiday commemorating the resurrection of Jesus; since the resurrection symbolizes ego transcendence in its overcoming of death, Easter is used as a symbol for the Son of God's offering and acceptance of redemption (or ego transcendence) through forgiveness.

---

forgiveness
T-20.I.1-2; T-20.II.6-10
W-p.I.151.16

Jesus
T-20.I.2-4

resurrection
T-19.IV-D.17-18

salvation
T-20.I.4
W-pI.135.25-26

sin
T-20.I.4

ego

the belief in the reality of the separated or false self, made as substitute for the Self Which God created; the thought of separation that gives rise to sin, guilt, fear, and a thought system based on specialness to protect itself; the part of the mind that believes it is separate from the Mind of Christ; this split mind has two parts: wrong- and right-mindedness; almost always used to denote "wrong-mindedness," but can include the part of the split mind that can learn to choose right-mindedness.

(Note—not to be equated with the "ego" of psychoanalysis, but can be roughly equated with the entire psyche, of which the psychoanalytic "ego" is a part.)

---

attack
T-7.VI.3,8,11; T-9.VII.4;
T-9.VIII.1-4; T-11.V.10,12-13,15

authority problem/autonomy
T-3.VI.7-8; **T-4.II.1-9**; T-11.In.2;
T-11.V.4-12; T-13.II.6;
T-15.VII.12
W-pI.72.2
S-3.IV.5

belief
T-4.II.4; T-4.VI.1; T-5.V.2-3;
T-7.VIII.4-7

body
T-4.II.7; **T-4.V.2-4**; T-6.IV.4-5
W-pI.199.3-4

death/hell
T-12.VII.13-14; **T-15.I.2-6**

fear
T-7.VI.4; T-11.V.1-4,8-12;
T-15.X.4

guilt
T-5.V.1-4; T-13.IX; T-15.VII.2-12
W-pI.133.11

Holy Spirit
T-5.III.5-11; T-6.IV.1,4; T-9.I.10
W-pI.66.2-9

illusions
T-23.I.3
W-pI.13.3
C-2.1-8
P-2.V.1

Jesus
T-4.I.3,13; T-4.III.2;
T-4.IV.8,10-11; T-4.VI.3

judgment
T-4.II.10; T-5.VI.4; T-14.X.7-9
W-pI.151.4

love
T-4.III.4; T-12.IV.1-3

plan of salvation
T-9.IV.4,8; T-9.V.1-7;
T-13.I.10-11
W-pI.71.1-6; W-pI.72.1-8

projection
T-6.II.2-4; T-7.VII.8-9;
T-7.VIII.1-5; T-8.VIII.1;
T-13.II.1-5

psychotherapy
P-2.In; **P-2.I.2-3**

separation
T-3.IV.2-3; T-4.III.3;
T-11.V.7,13-16
W-pII.12

sickness
T-8.VIII.3-7; T-10.III.4
P-2.IV.6

sin
T-19.II.4-8; T-21.IV.1-3

special relationships
T-15.VII.2-10; T-16.I.1-2;
T-17.V.4-7

spirit
T-4.In.1-2; T-4.I.2-3,6,7-13;
T-4.III.1,3

time
T-5.III.5-6; T-13.IV.4-8;
T-15.I.2-7

wish–will
T-7.X.4
W-pI.73.1-8

world
T-5.III.11; T-20.III.5

wrong-mindedness
T-4.III.10
C-1.6

extension

knowledge: the ongoing process of creation, wherein spirit extends itself: God creating Christ; since Heaven is beyond time and space, "extension" cannot be understood as a temporal or spatial process.

true perception: extending the Holy Spirit or Christ's vision in the form of forgiveness or peace; the Holy Spirit's use of the law of mind, contrasted with the ego's projection; since ideas leave not their source, what is extended remains in the mind, where it is reflected in the world of illusion.

---

creating
T-2.I.1-3; **T-7.I.5**; T-7.VI.12;
T-8.VI.6; T-11.I.3-7; T-15.III.7
W-pII.11.2

creation
T-6.II.8; T-23.IV.3

forgiveness
T-22.VI.8-9; T-29.III.4

giving
W-pI.187

holy relationship
T-22.In.3-4

Holy Spirit
T-6.II.11-12; T-7.VIII.1; **T-9.II.6**

law of mind
T-7.II.2-7; **T-7.VIII.1**; T-12.VII.7

mind
T-6.II.9-12; T-8.VII.10-12

miracle
T-16.II.1; **T-27.V.1**; T-28.I.11

peace
T-19.IV.1-3; T-19.IV-B.9
W-pI.34.1

projection
T-2.I.1-3; T-7.II.2-3; T-11.In.3

spirit
T-7.IX.1-4

vision
W-pI.29.1-3; **W-pI.30**;
W-pI.36.1; W-pI.159.4

Will of God
T-8.III.3
W-pI.76.11; W-pII.329.1;
W-pII.330.1

face of Christ

symbol of forgiveness; the face of true innocence seen in another when we look through Christ's vision, free from our projections of guilt; thus it is the extension to others of the guiltlessness we see in ourselves, independent of what our physical eyes may see.

(Note—not to be confused with the face of Jesus, nor with anything external.)

---

fear
T-19.IV-D.2

forgiveness
T-20.IV.5,7
W-pI.122.3; W-pI.198.10;
W-pII.6.4
M-4.X.2; M-28.2
C-3
P-2.V.7

healing
M-22.4

holy instant
T-20.V.6; T-27.V.6
W-pI.169.13

Holy Spirit
W-pI.151.8
C-6.3

idol
T-29.VIII.4

memory of God
T-30.V.7
W-pI.122.3
C-5.2

sin
T-22.IV.3; T-26.IV.3; T-26.IX.2
S-1.V.3

vision/true perception
T-20.V.4; T-24.VI.6;
T-31.VII.8-13
W-pI.151.8-12; W-pII.269
M-28.5-6
C-4.4-7
S-2.I.6

faith

the expression of where we choose to place our trust; we are free to have faith in the ego or the Holy Spirit, in the illusion of sin in others, or in the truth of their holiness as Sons of God.

---

belief
T-13.IX.2; T-21.III.3-12;
T-21.V.8-10

body
T-19.IV-B.11; T-21.III.7-12
W-pI.91.3-9

experience
W-pII.327

faithlessness
T-17.VII.3-10; **T-19.I.4-16**;
T-28.VII.5

healing
T-19.I.13

holy instant
T-17.VIII.1-3

holy relationship
T-17.V.6; **T-17.VII.4-10**;
T-19.I.12-15; T-19.IV-D.8-9

Holy Spirit
T-17.VI.6; T-18.V.2;
T-19.I.12-15; T-21.II.7
W-pI.rIII.In.6; W-pII.255.1

justice
T-25.VIII.2

love–illusion
W-pI.50.4

miracle
T-10.IV.7
W-pII.13.4

problem solving
T-17.VII.1-2

sin
T-21.II.9; T-21.III

sinlessness
W-pI.181.2-9

teacher of God
M-4.IX

truth–illusion
T-17.VII.9; T-19.I.5

vision
T-21.III.4-12

fear

the emotion of the ego, contrasted with love, the emotion given us by God; originates in the expected punishment for our sins, which our guilt demands; the resulting terror over what we believe we deserve leads us—through the dynamics of denial and projection—to defend ourselves by attacking others, which merely reinforces our sense of vulnerability and fear, establishing a vicious circle of fear and defense.

Atonement
T-5.IV.1

attack
T-6.In.1; T-6.I.3; **T-7.VII.8**
W-pI.68.2; W-pI.161.1,6-9
M-17.5-7

authority problem/ego autonomy
T-2.I.4; T-3.IV.3; T-3.VI.7-10;
T-3.VII.4; T-4.I.9

body
T-19.IV-B.13; T-21.III.7-8
W-pI.161.5-9

death
T-3.VII.5-6; T-15.I.4;
T-19.IV-C.3-11
M-27.2-6

defenses
W-pI.135.2-6; **W-pI.170.1-5**

dissociation
T-10.II.1-2

dreams
T-18.II.4

ego
T-4.I.10; T-5.III.4; T-5.V.1-3;
T-7.VI.4; **T-11.V.1-12**; T-15.I.4-7

forgiveness
T-9.IV.5; **T-19.IV-D.8-11**

God
T-13.III.2-10;
T-19.IV-D.1-4,9-12; T-22.VI.10;
T-23.II.5-7; T-23.IV.1
W-pI.103.2-3; W-pI.170.9-11;
W-pI.196.5-12
M-17.7

guilt
T-19.IV-A.10-15; T-22.I.4;
T-30.VI.4
M-29.3
S-1.III.4

healing
T-2.V.1-2,4,7-8; T-27.V.2

illusion
T-16.IV.6; T-16.V.8,14; T-23.II.20
P-2.IV.7

judgment
T-30.VII.3

love
T-1.VI.5; **T-12.I.8-10**;
T-12.II.8-9; T-13.V.1-5;
T-15.X.4-7; T-18.I.3
W-pI.160.1-4

mind
T-2.VI

punishment
T-5.V.3; T-19.III.2; T-23.III.1

sin
T-19.III.1-2; T-26.VIII.5
W-pII.259

sinlessness
T-21.IV

special relationships
T-16.IV.7; T-24.I.8

thoughts
T-2.VII.1-3
W-pII.338

world
T-18.IX.4
W-pI.13.1-4; W-pI.130.2-4;
W-pII.240

looking at our specialness with the Holy Spirit or Jesus, without guilt or judgment; our special function that shifts perception of another as "enemy" (special hate) or "savior-idol" (special love) to brother or friend, removing all projections of guilt from him; the expression of the miracle or vision of Christ, that sees all people united in the Sonship of God, looking beyond the seeming differences that reflect separation: thus, perceiving sin as real makes true forgiveness impossible; the recognition that what we thought was done to us we did to ourselves, since we are responsible for our scripts, and therefore only we can deprive ourselves of the peace of God: thus, we forgive others for what they have *not* done to us, not for what they have done.

see: *looking at the ego*

Atonement
T-9.IV.1-2

attack
W-pI.78; W-pI.198

death
T-27.II.6
S-3.II.4

ego
T-9.IV.4

face of Christ
W-pI.122.3
M-4.X.2
C-3
S-2.II.7

forgiveness-to-destroy
T-2.V.15; T-27.II.1-5;
T-30.VI.1-4
W-pI.126.1-7; **W-pI.134.1-5**
S-1.I.4; **S-2.I.1-2,7,9**; **S-2.II**

function
T-14.IV.3; **T-25.VI**
W-pI.62.1-5; W-pI.186.14;
W-pI.192; W-pI.200.6

God
T-16.VII.12; T-24.III.4-8;
T-30.II.4-5
W-pI.46.1-2; W-pI.60.1-2
P-2.II.2-4

guilt
C-4.5-6

happy dream
T-27.VII.14-16; T-29.IX.7-10;
T-30.IV.7-8
W-pI.140.3; W-pI.159.10;
W-pI.198.3; W-pII.256.1

healing
T-27.II
W-pI.137.5-15
M-22
P-2.VI.1
S-3.In; S-3.I.3; S-3.IV.9

holy relationship
T-19.IV-D.8-21; T-22.VI.7-15;
T-25.V.4-6

Holy Spirit
T-9.IV.2-6; T-25.III.5-8
W-pII.1.5

illusions
T-16.VII.9-12; T-29.III.3
W-pI.198.2-10
C-3.1-3

invulnerability
T-14.III.7
W-pII.330

love
W-pI.186.14
S-3.IV.2

miracles
W-pI.78; W-pII.13.1-3

perception
T-3.V.9
W-pII.335.1; W-pII.336.1

prayer
T-3.V.6
S-1.II.4-6,8; S-2.In; S-3.IV.4

psychotherapy
P-1.I.2; **P-2.VI.5-6**,7; P-2.VII.3;
P-3.II.4

real world
T-17.II; **T-18.IX.9-14**; T-23.In.6;
T-26.IV; T-30.V.1-7; T-30.VI.1-3
W-pI.75.3-11; W-pII.249.1;
W-pII.269.1; W-pII.270.1;
W-pII.8

salvation
W-pI.99; W-pI.122.5-14
S-2.III

sin
T-30.VI
W-pI.121.4-13; W-pI.134.1-16;
W-pII.1
S-2.I

special relationships
T-17.III; **T-24.III**
P-3.III.3

suffering
W-pI.193.4-13

teacher of God
P-2.II.1

time
T-26.V.6; T-29.VI.2-4

world
W-pI.64.1-3; W-pII.3
M-14

form–content

the world's multitude of forms conceals the simplicity of their content: truth or illusion, love or fear; the ego attempts to convince us our problems are on the level of form, so that their underlying content—fear—escapes notice and correction; the Holy Spirit corrects all our seeming problems at their source—the mind—healing the ego's content of fear with His Love and demonstrating that there is no order of difficulty in miracles or problem solving.

A Course in Miracles
M-1.3-4

attack
T-23.II.16-20; T-23.III.1-2;
T-23.IV.1
M-7.4

death
W-pI.167.2

dream
T-18.II.5
W-pI.185.3-9

ego
T-14.X.7-9
C-2.2-3

fear
T-13.V.1; T-15.X.4-5; T-18.I.3-4;
T-29.IV.2
W-pII.240.1

forgiveness
W-pI.134.7-9; W-pI.186.13-14;
W-pI.193.3-5,12-13

forgiveness-to-destroy
S-2.II.1

God
C-3.3
S-1.I.2-3; S-1.II.1

healing
P-2.II.6-7

Holy Spirit
T-5.III.10; **T-7.II.4-5**; T-25.I.5-7;
T-25.III.4; **T-26.II.1-7**
W-pI.64.2-5

idol
T-29.VIII.8; T-30.III.1-5

illusions
T-18.I.7; T-23.I.6-11; T-31.IV.8
M-27.7

miracle
T-2.IV.4
W-pII.345.1

problems
W-pI.79.2-6; W-pI.80.3

psychotherapy
P-3.I.3

reason
T-22.III.3-7

religion
P-2.II.2

sickness
W-pI.140.1-9
M-5.III.3
P-2.IV.7-8

special function
T-25.VII.7

special relationships
T-16.V.12; T-17.IV.8-15

suffering
T-27.VIII.10-11

existent only in the illusory world of perception, where it appears that the Son of God has the power to separate himself from God; since on the perceptual level we chose to be separate, we can also choose to change our minds; this freedom of choice—between wrong- and right-mindedness—is the only one possible in this world; in the non-dualistic state of Heaven's perfect oneness, choosing cannot exist, and therefore free will as it is usually understood is meaningless in reality.

(Note—not to be confused with "freedom of will," which reflects that the Will of God can *not* be imprisoned by the ego, and therefore must always remain free.)

see: *free will (2)*

---

free will (2)

an aspect of our free will within the illusion: we are free to believe what reality is, but since reality was created by God we are not free to change it in any way; our thoughts do not affect reality, but do affect what we believe and experience to be reality.

see: *free will (1)*

---

creating
T-7.IX.3; T-9.VI.4

ego
T-7.VI.9-11

God
T-2.III.3; T-5.II.5-6; T-9.I.11; T-10.In.1; T-10.IV.5; T-10.V.1; T-18.III.1
W-pII.227.1

knowledge
T-5.I.4; T-13.IX.8

life–death
T-11.I.9; T-26.I.7; T-29.VIII.4

mind
T-4.VII.3; T-5.II.1; T-18.VI.4; T-24.IV.2; **T-29.VI.3**

reality
T-1.VII.3; T-8.I.6; T-12.VIII.3; T-17.I.1; T-21.V.2; T-26.V.5

self-creating
T-3.VI.8-11; T-3.VII.4

sin
T-25.III.9

soul
T-12.VI.1

truth
T-5.IV.1; T-7.X.2; **T-26.VII.6**,9-10; T-31.VI.5

Will of God
T-5.VII.1; **T-7.X.4-7**; T-8.VI.2; T-13.XI.5; T-18.VI.5

function

knowledge: creation, the extension of God's Love or spirit; God creates His Son, Christ, Who in turn creates as does His Father; our function of creating, ongoing throughout eternity, is restored to our awareness when the Atonement is completed.

perception: forgiveness, healing, salvation, the acceptance of the Atonement for ourselves; our "special function" is to forgive our special relationships; the function of the Holy Spirit is to carry out the plan of the Atonement, reminding each Son of God of his special function.

Atonement
M-22.1-2

Christ
S-2.III.5-7

creating
T-7.VI.13; T-7.IX.3-4;
T-8.VI.6-8; T-9.III.8; T-12.VII.4;
T-13.IV.1; T-29.VI.4

forgiveness
T-14.IV.3-5
W-pI.62.1-5; W-pI.63;
W-pI.64.1-6; **W-pI.192**;
W-pII.330.1

healing
T-9.III.8; T-12.VII.4; T-13.IV.1
W-pI.137.13-15
M-22.6

holy relationship
T-18.I.13; T-22.VI.8

Holy Spirit
T-12.VII.12; T-22.VI.8-9
W-pI.66.2-10; W-pI.154.2-3;

Holy Spirit (continued)
W-pII.1.5
M-29.2-3

psychotherapy
P-2.VII.6; P-3.I.4

salvation
W-pI.65.1-2; **W-pI.99**; W-pI.100;
W-pI.186; W-pII.317

sin
T-27.I.9

special function
T-14.V.2; **T-20.IV.5-8**;
T-25.VI.3-7; T-25.VII.7-12;
T-25.VIII.11-14; T-26.I.5,8;
T-26.II.6-8; T-26.III.7
W-pI.98

teacher of God
W-pI.153.11
M-4.IV.1; M-4.X.3; **M-5.III**;
M-14.4-5; M-15; M-16.10-11

vision
W-pI.37.1

gap

the illusory space between ourselves and God, and ourselves and others, brought about by the belief in separation; in this space arise the dreams of sickness and hate, since projection onto bodies must always follow the mind's belief in separation.

---

body
T-28.VI.1-5; **T-29.I.4-9**;T-29.III.3

bridge
T-16.III.8-9

dream
T-28.IV.3-10; T-30.IV.8

idol
T-29.VIII.3-7; T-30.III.4

sickness
T-28.III.3-8; T-28.V.1-4; T-28.VII

world
T-28.V.4-7

knowledge: the gifts of God are love, eternal life, and freedom, which can never be withdrawn, though they can be denied in the dreaming of the world.

perception: w-m: the ego's gifts are fear, suffering, and death, though they often are not seen for what they are; the ego's gifts are "bought" through sacrifice.

r-m: God's gifts are translated by the Holy Spirit into forgiveness and joy, which are given us as we give them to others.

see: *giving–receiving*

---

altar
T-14.VIII.5
W-pI.104

brother
T-10.V.7; T-27.VII.15-16; T-29.V.5
W-pII.315; W-pII.316.1

Christ
W-pII.306

ego–God
T-4.III.3-5; T-7.VII.11
W-pI.66.8

forgiveness
T-20.V.6-7; T-22.VI.8-9
W-pI.122.7-14; **W-pI.197.1-6**; W-pII.297; W-pII.334

freedom
T-8.IV.7-8
W-pI.198.1

God
T-7.I.4; T-7.VI.10; T-11.I.7
W-pI.105; W-pI.126.7; **W-pI.166**; W-pII.284.2; W-pII.297.2; W-pII.298.2
S-2.I.8

grace
W-pI.169.12

gratitude
W-pI.123; W-pI.197

healing
M-6.2-4; M-7.1-4

Holy Spirit
T-14.III.11; T-14.IX.3; T-20.V.7; T-22.VI.8-9
W-pII.7

Jesus
T-8.IV.7; T-20.II.4-6
M-23.1-4

lilies–thorns
T-20.II

limitless
T-26.VII.18
M-29.5

miracles
W-pII.345.1

real world
T-31.VIII.8-10

special relationships
T-24.IV.3

teacher of God
M-4.V; M-7.1-4

world
W-pI.105.1-2; W-pI.153.1

giving–receiving

w-m: if one gives he has less, reinforcing the ego's belief in scarcity and sacrifice, and exemplifying its principle of "giving to get," wherein it gives away so that it can get more of something else in return; believing it can give its actual gifts of guilt and fear away, the ego's version of giving is really projection.

r-m: giving and receiving are identical, reflecting Heaven's principle of abundance and the law of extension: spirit can never lose, since when one gives love one receives it; the Holy Spirit's gifts are qualitative, not quantitative, and thus are increased as they are shared; the same principle works on the ego level, for as one gives guilt away (projection) one receives it.

see: *gift*

---

abundance
T-4.II.6-7; T-7.VII.5-7
P-3.III.5

bargain
T-7.I.4; T-9.II.11

creation
W-pI.105.4

extension–projection
T-7.VIII.1-3

forgiveness
T-19.IV-D.13-20
W-pI.121.9; W-pI.122.6;
W-pI.126; W-pI.198.1-2;
W-pII.344.1

God
T-11.I.6-7

healing
T-14.III.5
W-pI.137.15
M-6.2-4; M-22.6

holy relationship
T-20.IV.2-5; T-21.VI.9;
T-22.IV.5-7; T-22.VI.5-6;
T-29.III.1
M-2.5

Holy Spirit
T-5.III.2; T-6.V-A.5; T-9.VI.2;
T-20.IV.1
W-pII.295.2; W-pII.357

idea
T-5.I.1-2; T-5.III.2
W-pI.187

law of love
W-pII.225.1; W-pII.344.1;
W-pII.345.1; W-pII.349.1

miracle
T-1.I.9,11,16; T-9.VI.6;
T-25.IX.10
W-pI.159; W-pII.345.1

sacrifice
T-4.II.6
W-pI.187.6-8

teacher of God
W-pI.154.5-14
M-4.VII; **M-6.2-4**; M-7.1-3;
M-17.2

vision
T-31.VIII.8
W-pI.108.1-7; W-pI.158.10-11

Word of God
W-pI.106.10

world
W-pI.105.1-2

God

the First Person in the Trinity; the Creator, the Source of all being or life; the Father, Whose Fatherhood is established by the existence of His Son, Christ; the First Cause, Whose Son is His Effect; God's essence is spirit, which is shared with all creation, whose unity is the state of Heaven.

---

body
T-6.V-A.2; T-18.VIII.1-2;
T-23.IV.2-3

Cause–Effect
T-2.VII.3; T-14.III.8;
T-14.IV.1-2; T-28.I.14; **T-28.II.1**
W-pII.326.1

Christ
T-9.I.14; **T-11.IV.6-7**;
T-12.VI.5-6; T-15.V.10
W-pII.6

creation
T-2.I.1-2; T-4.VII.3-6; **T-7.I**
W-pII.260; **W-pII.11**

crucifixion
T-3.I.1-5

death
T-12.VII.14; T-19.IV-C.3-5
M-27

dependency
T-11.V.12

ego
T-5.V.2-6; T-11.In.1-2
W-pI.72.1-9

Father
T-10.V.12-13
W-pII.224
S-3.IV.6-10

fear
T-9.I.1-2; T-15.X.7-8;
T-19.IV-D.1-7,9-12; T-28.V.1;
T-29.I; T-31.I.10
S-3.IV.5

forgiveness
T-16.VII.11-12; T-24.III.5-8
W-pI.46.1-2; W-pII.256

healing
T-7.II.1; T-7.IV
S-3.III.5; S-3.IV.3

holy instant
T-15.VI.8

Holy Spirit
T-5.I.5-6; **T-5.II.1-12**; T-5.V.6;
T-13.VIII.4; T-14.X.10-11;
T-15.VIII.5-6
W-pII.7
C-6
P-3.I.2

Jesus
T-1.II.3-4; T-3.IV.7;
T-31.VIII.9-11
M-23

judgment–justice
T-2.VIII.2-3; **T-25.VIII.4-10**
W-pII.10.2-5
M-15; M-19.4-5
S-2.III.4

last step
T-7.I.6-7; T-11.VIII.15;
T-13.VIII.3; T-27.III.6;
T-30.V.3-4
M-28.1
C-1.5

laws
T-6.IV.11; T-10.IV.4-5; T-15.VI.5
W-pI.76.6-11

laws of chaos
T-10.IV.4-5; T-23.II.1-15

loneliness
T-2.III.5; T-4.VII.6; T-15.VIII.3;
T-26.VI.3

love
T-9.I.9,11; T-12.VIII.2-8;
T-13.III.2-8; T-15.VII.1;
T-19.IV-D.2-5
W-pI.46.2; W-pI.168; W-pI.189

miracles
T-1.I.2,4,11,19,21,24,27,29,31,
36,38,40,46

perception–knowledge
W-pI.43.1-3
P-2.II.4

prodigal son
T-8.VI.4

relationship
T-15.VIII.3-6; T-17.IV.1-2
P-1.1; P-2.II.5; **P-2.V.5-8**

sacrifice
T-3.I.4; T-15.X.7-8

salvation
W-pI.71

sickness
T-10.III.1-4; T-28.V.5

special relationships
T-1.V.3; T-16.V.4; T-24.I.7-9;
T-24.III.2-8

Thought
T-5.V.6; T-17.III.9; T-30.III.5-11;
T-31.IV.9-10
W-pI.165

Will
T-8.IV.1; **T-11.I.3-11**
W-pI.74.1-2; W-pI.101.6;
W-pI.166.1-2,10
S-2.III.1

world
T-2.VII.5; T-8.VI.2; T-11.VII.1;
T-24.VI.3
W-pI.166.2-3; W-pII.3.2
C-4.1-2

grace

our natural state as spirit, awareness of which returns to us when we complete our lessons of forgiveness; an aspect of God's Love in this world; past learning for it cannot be taught, but the goal of learning, for all lessons point to its love.

Atonement
T-3.I.6

forgiveness
T-25.VI.1

healing
T-19.I.13
W-pI.137.11

holy instant
W-pI.169.12-14

holy relationship
T-19.I.13; T-19.IV-A.16; T-22.IV.6

Holy Spirit
W-pI.169.15; W-pII.7.1

Jesus
T-19.IV-A.17

Love
W-pI.168; **W-pI.169.1-3**; W-pII.348

miracle
T-1.III.7-8; T-26.VIII.5
W-pI.183.3; W-pII.13.2; W-pII.349.2

salvation
W-pI.169.12; W-pII.297.2

Son of God
T-7.XI.1-2; T-11.VI.6

spirit
T-1.III.5

teacher of God
M-29.8

vision
T-25.VI.1-3
W-pI.168.4

gratitude

knowledge: God is grateful to His creation for completing Him, and along with the Holy Spirit and Jesus, He is grateful for our efforts to return to Him; should be understood as a metaphor for God's Love, since in reality He has no separated consciousness which can feel gratitude for another.

true perception: the expression of thanks to our Creator for our existence, and to all "living things" that offer the opportunity for remembering Him; our gratitude to each other reflects our recognition that salvation comes through forgiveness, and thus becomes the way to remember God.

see: *song of Heaven*

---

brother (Son of God)
T-4.VI.7; T-5.In.3; T-7.V.11; T-12.I.6; T-13.VI.10-11; T-16.IV.8; **T-17.V.11-15**; T-21.VI.10; T-25.II.9-10
W-pI.110.11; W-pI.195; **W-pI.197**

Christ (from)
T-30.V.8
W-pI.197.7
M-4.V

God (from)
T-10.V.7; T-15.XI.9; **T-25.II.9-10**; T-26.IX.7-8; T-27.V.11
W-pI.123.5-8; W-pI.130.9; W-pI.197.7-9
S-3.IV.9

God (to)
T-6.I.17; T-13.VI.8-9
W-pI.123; **W-pI.195**
M-23.4
C-Ep.5
S-1.I.7

Holy Spirit (from)
T-17.V.11; T-18.II.7
C-6.5

Holy Spirit (to)
T-19.IV.3
W-pI.190.11; W-pI.198.5
M-29.5

Jesus
T-6.I.17; T-8.IV.7; T-31.VIII.10-11
M-23.4-5

Jesus (from)
T-18.II.7
M-29.7-8

miracle
T-1.I.31

psychotherapy
P-3.III.4

song
T-31.VIII.11
W-pI.123.4; W-pII.293.2;
W-pII.310.2
M-4.V
S-1.In.1; S-1.II.7

Great Rays

knowledge: the extension of the light of God, our true reality as Christ; the Great Rays are of the spirit, having nothing to do with the body at all.

true perception: the presence of the light of Christ in the separated mind; seemingly split off from the Great Rays of God which are unseen, this light is manifest as a spark in each Son, made visible through forgiveness of our special relationships.

---

body
T-15.IX.1,3; **T-16.VI.4**,6

dream
T-29.III.3-5

ego
T-11.In.3

face of Christ
T-19.IV-D.2

Heaven
T-18.III.8
C-Ep.2

holy instant
T-15.IX.1,3

Son of God
T-11.III.4-5
W-pII.360

spark
T-10.IV.7-8; T-10.V.2;
T-11.II.5-6; T-16.VI.6; T-18.III.8

special relationships
T-16.VI.4

guilt

the feeling experienced in relation to sin; its reflection from our minds is seen in all the negative feelings and beliefs we have about ourselves, mostly unconscious; rests on a sense of inherent unworthiness, seemingly beyond even the forgiving power of God, Who we erroneously believe demands punishment for our seeming sin of separation against Him; following the ego's counsel that to look on guilt would destroy us, we deny its presence in our minds, and then project it outward in the form of attack, either onto others as anger or onto our own bodies as sickness.

see: *scarcity principle*

---

attack
T-13.I.10-11; **T-13.IX**;
T-23.III.1; T-31.III.2
S-1.III.3-4

attraction
T-15.VII.2-14; T-19.IV-A.10-11;
T-19.IV-B.12-13,16

body
T-18.VI.2-7; T-18.IX.5;
T-19.IV-B.1,13-16

death
T-12.VII.13-14

decision
T-5.VII.5-6; T-14.III.3-16

denial
T-13.II.4-8

ego
T-5.V; T-13.II; T-13.IV.4;
T-13.IX.8
W-pI.133.8-11
P-1.I.3

fear
T-19.IV-A.10-15;
T-19.IV-B.12-13; T-22.I.4;
T-30.VI.4; T-31.I.9-10
M-29.3

forgiveness
T-14.IV.3; T-18.IX.9-10,13;
T-30.VI.3-9
W-pI.134.5-17
C-4.5-6
P-2.VI.1

forgiveness-to-destroy
S-2.II.5

healing
P-2.IV.10-11

hell
T-15.I.4-7
W-pI.39.1-4

projection
T-13.II.1-5; T-13.X.1-3;
T-18.VI.2-4; T-27.VIII.7-8
S-1.III.1

psychotherapy
P-2.VII.4-5

sacrifice
T-15.XI.4

separation
T-5.V.8; T-13.In.1-2; T-15.V.2
M-17.5

sickness
T-27.I.4-8; T-28.II.11
W-pI.140.4
M-5.II.3-4
P-2.IV.1-3; P-2.VI.4-5

sin
T-19.II.2-6; T-19.III.1-3,7
C-4.5

special relationships
T-13.X.2-11; T-15.V.2-5;
T-15.VI.1; **T-15.VII.2-12**;
T-16.IV.3-4; **T-16.V.1-10**

time
T-5.VI.2; **T-13.I.3-9**

world
T-13.In.2-4; T-13.IX.7;
T-18.IX.4-9; T-27.I.6;
T-27.VIII.7-8; T-30.V.1-2;
T-31.I.4,7

happy dream

the Holy Spirit's correction for the ego's dream of pain and suffering; though still illusory, the happy dream leads beyond all other illusions to the truth; it is the dream of forgiveness in which the real world is ultimately seen and salvation attained.

Christ
W-pI.159.10

forgiveness
T-29.III.3-4; T-29.V.7-8
W-pI.198.3; W-pII.256.1

healing
T-28.III.8
W-pI.137.5

Holy Spirit
T-8.IX.3; T-20.VIII.10;
T-27.VII.13-14; T-29.IV.5-6
W-pI.140.3; W-pI.157.8;
W-pI.192.3; W-pII.7.4

miracle
T-28.II.10-12; T-30.VIII.2
C-2.7

real world
T-29.IX.7

resurrection
M-28.1

salvation
T-30.IV.7-8
W-pII.2.4-5

special–holy relationships
T-18.II.6-9; T-18.V.1-5

having–being

the state of the Kingdom, where there is no distinction between what we have and what we are; an expression of the principle of abundance: all that we have comes from God and can never be lost or lacking, including our Identity as His Son; an integral part of the three "Lessons of the Holy Spirit."

---

ego–Holy Spirit
T-4.III.9-10

God
T-7.IV.6; T-8.III.8; T-26.VII.11

Holy Spirit
T-6.V-B.3,7-8; T-6.V-C.5-10

Kingdom
T-4.III.9-10; T-4.VII.5; T-7.III.4

life
T-7.VII.5

mind–spirit
T-5.I.1

Son of God
T-11.II.1; T-14.XI.2

healing

the correction in the mind of the belief in sickness that makes the separation and the body seem real; the effect of joining with another in forgiveness, shifting perception from separate bodies—the source of all sickness—to our shared purpose of healing in this world; since healing is based on the belief that our true Identity is spirit, not the body, sickness of any kind must be illusory, as only a body or ego can suffer; healing thus reflects the principle that there is no order of difficulty in miracles.

Atonement
T-2.IV.1
W-pI.140.4
M-22

faith
T-19.I.2-10

fear
T-2.IV.1,4-5; T-7.V.5-6; T-9.II.2;
T-27.II.1,9; T-27.V.2

forgiveness
T-27.II
M-22
P-2.VI.1
S-3.In

God
T-7.II.1-2; T-7.IV.1-6

happy dream
T-28.III.7-9
W-pI.137.5

holy instant
T-27.V.5-6

Holy Spirit
T-5.III.1-2; T-7.IV; T-7.V.1-8;
T-27.V.8-10
W-pI.140.10

Jesus
T-8.IV.4-5
M-23.1-2

joining–separation
T-7.IV.5; T-8.IV.5; T-10.III.2-10;
T-11.II.1-4; T-28.IV; T-28.VI.5
P-2.II.6
S-3.III.4-6

mind–body
T-7.V; T-19.I.2-6; **T-28.II.2,11**;
T-28.VII.3-4
W-pI.135.9-12; W-pI.136.15-20;
W-pI.140
M-5.II
P-2.I.1

miracle
T-2.IV.1; T-27.II.5-7; T-27.V.1-4;
T-28.II.11

psychotherapy
P-2.IV.3-4; **P-2.V.4-8**;
P-2.VII.1-3; P-3.II

sickness
W-pI.137
M-5.II

teacher of God
M-5.III; M-6; M-7
S-3.IV.1-3

Teacher of teachers
P-2.III.3-4

time
T-2.V.9

unhealed healer
T-9.V
P-2.VII.4,7; P-3.III.1-3

world
S-3.I.5

Heaven

the non-dualistic world of knowledge, wherein dwell God and His creation in the perfect unity of His Will and spirit; though exclusive of the world of perception, Heaven can be reflected here in the holy relationship and the real world.

see: *knowledge*

Atonement
T-5.IV.1; T-5.V.2; T-22.VI.5

body
T-6.V-A.2; T-18.VIII.2,11;
T-26.I.7

changelessness
T-13.XI.6; T-14.V.1; T-15.I.10;
T-29.V.1-2

communication
T-7.II.7

creations/extension
T-6.V-C.4; **T-7.I.2-6**; T-7.II.2-7;
T-7.VI.12; T-7.VIII.1; T-7.IX.4;
T-13.VIII.9; T-16.III.6; T-16.IV.8;
T-25.IV.2

decision
T-26.V.1
W-pI.130.10-11; W-pI.131.3-10;
W-pI.138

ego
T-4.III.10; **T-5.IV.1-3**; T-15.I.3-7

forgiveness
T-26.IV; T-26.VII.9-10;
T-30.V.3-4
W-pI.134.10; W-pI.193.13;
W-pI.200.3-6; W-pII.342.1

grace
W-pI.169.12-13

gratitude
T-19.IV-D.19; T-26.IX.5-8

guilt
T-5.V.2; T-13.X.14; T-14.IV.9;
T-14.V.6

having–being
T-4.III.9; T-6.IV.7; T-7.III.4

healing
T-7.II.1-2; T-14.IX.8

hell
T-13.IV.2; T-15.I.3-14; T-15.XI.4;
T-16.V.4-8; T-22.II.7;
T-23.II.21-22; T-25.V.5-6;
T-25.VII.10
W-pI.135.24

holy instant
T-15.I.10-15; T-17.IV.11

holy relationship
T-18.I.11; T-18.V.3;
T-19.III.8-10; T-19.IV-A.3-6;
T-20.II.10-11; T-20.III.9-10;
T-21.IV.7; T-22.VI.5; **T-26.IX.1-6**

Holy Spirit
T-5.II.4; T-6.II.12-13; T-6.V-C.1; T-7.III.1; T-8.II.8; T-15.I.7-11; T-18.IX.1-2; T-21.VI.8
W-pI.157.8

illusions
T-10.III.7; T-22.II.8; T-23.II.19

inheritance
T-3.VI.11; T-12.IV.6-7; T-14.V.4

Jesus
T-7.I.5; T-13.X.13-14; T-18.I.12

joy
T-4.VII.8; T-7.V.9; T-7.XI.1; T-16.VI.11

justice
T-25.IX.1; T-26.IV.1
M-19.1,5

light
T-6.II.13; T-23.In.6; T-25.III.5-6; T-26.IX.4-6; T-30.II.3
W-pI.100.4; W-pII.249.1; W-pII.265.1; W-pII.283.1

love
T-6.IV.2; T-16.V.2-3
W-pI.186.14; W-pI.193.13; W-pII.286.1

miracle
T-13.VIII.3-10

peace
T-8.I.1,3; T-13.XI.7-8; T-14.X.1-2; T-19.IV-B.5; T-29.VII.1

real world
T-11.VIII.1; T-14.IX.5; T-23.In.6; T-26.III.2-5; T-31.VIII.8-9
W-pI.73.4; W-pI.159.3; W-pII.249.1; W-pII.306.1

sin
T-19.III.8-10; T-20.IV.2; T-22.II.13; T-25.VIII.6; T-26.IV.2-6

Son of God (Self)
T-5.VI.1; T-7.XI.4,7; T-10.V.11; T-16.III.7-9; T-18.VI.1; T-25.IV.5
W-pII.14.1
S-3.II.6

special relationships
T-15.V.7-8; T-16.V.2-8

teacher of God
T-7.XI.4
M-14.5

Thoughts of God
T-5.IV.3; T-30.III.8

truth
T-6.V-C.9; T-7.II.5; T-7.IV.7; T-13.XI.11

unity
T-4.III.1; T-14.VIII.5; **T-18.VI.1**; T-26.VII.15

vision
T-19.III.9-10; T-20.VIII.7; T-21.III.4

will–Will
T-7.X.2; T-8.II.6-7; T-14.VIII.5; T-18.II.9; T-30.II.1-3
W-pI.186.1

within
T-4.III.1; T-11.VIII.8; T-15.XI.2
W-pI.77.3

world
T-8.VI.1-3; T-13.XI.3-6; T-16.V.3

hell

the ego's illusory picture of a world beyond death which would punish us for our sins; hell thus becomes the guilt of the past projected onto the future, bypassing the present; also used to denote the ego thought system.

---

body
W-pII.5.4

decision
T-26.III.5; T-31.VII.14
W-pI.130.10-11;
W-pI.138.1-2,7-10
M-4.IV.2; M-21.3
C-2.10

dream
W-pI.185.2
M-28.6

ego
T-15.I.3-7
W-pI.44.5

fear
T-31.VII.7
W-pI.196.5

forgiveness
T-24.III.6-8
W-pI.200.3,6; **W-pII.342.1**

guilt
T-15.I.6
W-pI.39.1-4
M-4.X.1

Heaven
T-13.IV.1-2; T-25.VII.10;
T-26.X.2
W-pI.131.4-9

Holy Spirit
T-15.I.7
W-Ep.5
M-29.3

Jesus
C-5.5

projection
S-1.III.2

sacrifice
W-pI.135.24

sin
T-25.VIII.6; T-26.VII.7
M-In.5

special relationships
T-16.V.4-8; T-24.II.13;
T-24.III.6-8

suffering
M-28.2

teacher of God
M-14.5

unreality
T-13.IV.2; T-15.I.7
W-pI.185.2; W-pII.342.1

holy instant

the instant outside time in which we choose forgiveness instead of guilt, the miracle instead of a grievance, the Holy Spirit instead of the ego; the expression of our little willingness to live in the present, which opens into eternity, rather than holding on to the past and fearing the future, which keeps us in hell; also used to denote the ultimate holy instant, the real world, the culmination of all the holy instants we have chosen along the way.

---

body
T-15.IX; T-18.VI.13-14;
T-18.VII.2-3

Christ
T-15.X.2
W-pI.182.5-12; W-pII.308

communication
T-15.IV.6-8; T-15.VI.8;
T-15.VII.14

faith
T-15.VI.2-6; T-17.VIII.1-3;
T-19.I.10-14

forgiveness
T-16.VII.11

grace
W-pI.169.12-14

Great Rays
T-15.IX.1,3

guilt
T-15.VII.14; T-15.X.2; T-16.VI.3

healing
T-21.VI.7; T-27.V.1-6

Heaven
T-17.IV.11-16

holy relationship
T-17.V.1,10-15; T-18.VII.5;
T-18.IX.13; **T-20.V.5-6**;
T-21.VIII.5

Holy Spirit
T-15.I.8-15; T-15.II;
T-15.VIII.1-2; T-16.VI.12;
T-16.VII.6-11; T-18.IV.6-8;
T-18.V.6-7
W-pII.361-365
S-3.IV.7

Jesus
T-15.IV.5; T-15.VI.6

judgment
T-15.V.1; T-21.II.8

miracle
T-15.I.12-15; T-27.V.1-4
W-pI.169.12-13

practice
T-15.I.9-13; T-15.II.5-6; **T-15.IV**

problem solving
T-27.IV

salvation
W-pII.241.1

special relationships
T-15.V

suffering
W-pI.194.3-5

willingness
T-15.IV.5-8; T-15.V.5;
T-16.VI.12; **T-18.IV**; T-18.V.6

world
W-pI.184.10

holy relationship

the Holy Spirit's means to undo the unholy or special relationship by shifting the goal of guilt to the goal of forgiveness or truth; the process of forgiveness by which one who had perceived another as separate joins with him in his mind through Christ's vision.

---

body
T-20.V.5
W-pII.5.4

Christ
T-22.I.7-8,11; T-22.II.12-13;
T-31.II.7-9

faith
T-17.V.6-7; T-17.VII.4-10

forgiveness
T-19.IV-D.8-21; T-22.In.1;
T-22.VI.4-15; T-25.V.4-6
S-2.III.5

holy instant
T-17.V.1,12-15

Holy Spirit
T-17.V.2-15; T-20.VI.5-7,10;
T-22.VI.3-6
M-2.5
P-2.II.1

Jesus
T-8.III.4; T-18.III.4-7;
T-19.IV-A.16; T-19.IV-B.5-8

joining
T-20.V.1-2; T-22.In
W-pI.185.3-6
M-2.5; **M-3**

joining (continued)
P-2.II.6
S-1.III.5; S-1.IV.1

light
T-18.III.4-8; T-22.II.12;
T-22.VI.4-6

prayer
S-1.IV.3-4; S-1.V.3

psychotherapy
P-1.1-2; P-2.In.4; **P-2.I.**1,4;
P-2.II.5,**8-9**; P-2.III.2-3;
P-2.V.3-8; P-2.VI.7;
P-2.VII.1-3,7-9; P-3.I.4; **P-3.II**;
P-3.III.4,6-8

real world
T-17.V.2

sin
T-22.III.9; **T-22.IV.3-4**

special function
T-18.I.13; **T-20.IV.5-7**;
T-25.VI.4-7; T-26.II.6

special relationships
T-20.VI; T-22.In.2-3

vision
T-20.V.4-7; T-22.II.12-13

Holy Spirit

the Third Person of the Trinity Who is metaphorically described in the Course as God's Answer to the separation; the Communication Link between God and His separated Sons, bridging the gap between the Mind of Christ and our split mind; the memory of God and His Son we took with us into our dream; the One Who sees our illusions (perception), leading us through them to the truth (knowledge); the Voice for God Who speaks for Him and for our real Self, reminding us of the Identity we forgot; also referred to as Bridge, Comforter, Guide, Mediator, Teacher, and Translator.

Answer
T-5.II.2; T-9.VIII.11

Atonement
T-5.I.5-6; T-5.II.2; T-13.IX.6
C-6.2

body
T-6.V-A.2-5
S-3.I.4

Bridge
T-5.III.1; T-6.II.7; T-16.IV.12
W-pI.96.8

Christ
T-13.V.11
W-pII.6.3-4

Comforter
T-11.III.1-7

Communication Link
T-5.II.8; T-6.I.19; T-8.VII.2;
T-10.III.2; T-13.XI.8
C-6.3

forgiveness
T-9.III.3-8; **T-9.IV.5-6**;
T-15.VIII.1; **T-25.III.5-8**;
T-27.II.9-16

gratitude
T-17.V.11; T-18.II.7; T-19.IV.3
W-pI.190.11; W-pI.198.5

Great Rays
T-15.IX.1

Guide
T-5.II.8; T-7.X.3-7;
T-14.III.12-19
W-pI.155.10-14; W-pI.215.1;
W-Ep
M-16.7; M-18.4; M-29.2-3
C-6.4

happy dreams
T-13.VII.9-16; T-18.V.1-5;
T-20.VIII.10

healing
T-5.II.1-2; T-5.III.1-2
M-6.4
S-3.III.6

hearing
T-9.II.3-8; T-10.III.8-11;
T-11.II.5

hell
T-15.I.7

holy instant
T-16.VI.12
W-pII.361-365

holy relationship
T-19.IV.1; **T-20.VI.5-7,10**
M-2.5
P-1.1-2; P-3.III.8

Interpreter
T-5.VI.4-9; T-11.VIII.2;
T-12.I.3,5,8,10; T-13.IV.7-8;
T-14.VI.6-7; T-15.V.4; T-16.I.4;
T-30.VII.7
M-19.1-2; M-28.1

Jesus
T-5.I.3-4; T-5.II.10-12;
T-12.VII.6
C-6

judgment
T-6.V-C.2; T-12.I.3-10;
T-14.X.5-11
W-pI.151.3-13

justice
T-25.VIII.5-14; T-25.IX.3-7;
T-26.II.4-6

Lessons
T-6.V

Mediator
T-1.II.5; **T-5.I.5-7**; **T-5.III**;
T-7.IX.1; T-13.VII.10;
T-14.IV.9-10; T-15.VIII.5-6
W-pI.43.1; **W-pII.7**
C-6.3-4

memory
T-28.I.3-8

miracle
T-6.V-A.3-4; T-12.VII.1-4;
T-27.VI.4-6

right-mindedness
T-5.II.8
W-pI.49.1-2
C-1.5

psychotherapy
P-2.I.3; P-2.III.1; P-3.I.1-2;
P-3.II.3,5

salvation
T-14.III.13-14; T-17.II.8;
T-20.VII.9
W-pI.96.7-8; W-pI.169.9;
W-pI.198.5

sin
T-19.III.4-5; T-20.IV.1

special function
T-20.IV.6-8; **T-25.VI.4-7**;
T-25.VIII.11-14; T-26.I.8
W-pI.98.9

special relationships
T-15.V.4-10; T-17.IV.4;
T-24.II.4-5

suffering
T-27.VIII.10-12

Teacher
T-12.V.5,9; T-15.II.2-6;
T-16.III.1; T-25.I.5-7
W-pI.95.8
M-29.2-7

teacher of God
W-pI.125; **W-pI.154.2-11**;
W-pII.296
M-9.2; M-14.4; M-29.8
C-6.5
P-1.5

time
T-15.I.7-15; T-26.V.1-4
W-pI.97.4

Translator
T-6.V-A.2-5; T-7.II.4-6; T-7.IV.4;
T-9.IV.3; T-14.VII.5; T-14.X.11;
T-15.II.2; T-16.II.5
W-pI.157.8; W-pI.192.3

Trinity
T-5.I.4; T-5.III.1; T-25.I.5

Voice for God
T-5.II.5-8
W-pI.49.1-5; W-pI.106.1-6;
W-pI.151.3-15;
W-pI.186.4-7,11-13
C-6

world
T-17.II.5; T-25.III.5-8
W-pI.64.2,5

humility–arrogance

humility is of the right mind, which recognizes its dependence on God, while arrogance is of the wrong mind, which feels it is in competition with Him; spirit rests in the grandeur of God, from Whom it derives its power, while the ego's grandiosity comes from believing that *it* is God, with the power to determine our function in God's plan; in this way the ego confuses humility with arrogance, telling us we are unworthy to be God's instruments of salvation.

---

ego
T-4.I.12; T-9.III.7

forgiveness-to-destroy
S-2.II.2-3

function
W-pI.61.1-3; W-pI.154.1;
W-pI.186.1-12

grandeur–grandiosity
T-9.VIII

healing
S-3.III.4

holy instant
T-18.IV.2-4

Holy Spirit
T-16.I.4

Jesus
T-15.III.7-10

littleness–magnitude
T-15.III; T-15.IV.1-4

love
T-10.V.14

prayer
S-1.V.1-3

sin
T-19.II.2-4; T-19.III.7;
T-19.IV-C.4; T-25.IX.1

teacher of God
M-14.5

truth
W-pII.319.1

wish–will
T-22.VI.10; T-26.VII.18

world
W-pI.132.5-6; **W-pI.152.6-10**

"I am as God created me"

an expression of the principle of the Atonement; the statement that acknowledges that the separation from God never truly occurred; denial of this principle reinforces belief in our separated ego self and body; accepting it heals the separation, restoring to awareness our true Identity as God's Son, our Self.

---

arrogance
T-26.VII.18

Atonement
W-pI.139.11-12
M-23.2

body
W-pI.rVI.In.3

Cause–Effect
W-pII.326.1

changelessness
T-30.III.5
W-pI.152.5; W-pII.230.2;
W-pII.277.1

Christ
T-13.VI.3
W-pII.6.1,5; W-pII.303.2;
W-pII.354
C-6.1
S-2.III.7

decision
W-pI.139.1

ego
C-2.2

forgiveness
W-pI.192.10; W-pII.249.2;
W-pII.304.2; W-pII.350.1

freedom
T-26.V.11
W-pI.57.2

Great Rays
W-pII.360

guiltlessness
T-13.I.5; T-13.VI.3

holiness
W-pII.285.2; W-pII.299
M-28.5

Holy Spirit
M-29.4,7

illusions
T-24.II.14
W-pII.272.1

judgment
W-pII.243.1; W-pII.268.1
M-22.7

justice
T-26.II.8

light
W-pI.61.1; W-pII.237.1

love
W-pII.239.1; W-pII.274.1;
W-pII.282

mind
T-6.V-C.5

resurrection
T-11.VI.4

sacrifice
W-pII.322.2; W-pII.343.1

salvation
W-pI.93.7; **W-pI.94**; **W-pI.110**;
W-pI.162

Self
W-pI.197.8; W-pII.261.2;
W-pII.287

sin
T-19.II.4

suffering
T-10.V.9; **T-31.VIII.5-6**
W-pII.248; W-pII.281
M-5.III.3

truth
T-23.I.7
W-pI.136.13; W-pI.191.4

unity
W-pI.95.1; W-pI.185.14;
W-pII.307; W-pII.11.4
M-12.1

will
W-pII.309.1

world
T-24.VI.3
W-pI.132.9-15

the expression of the law of cause and effect, for cause and effect cannot be separate: an idea cannot leave the mind that thought it.

knowledge: the extension of God's Thought, His Son, has never left its Source, for what is of God can never be separate from Him.

perception: the world of separation has never left its source in the separated mind, though it appears to be external to it; thus, there is no material world, only a projected illusion of one.

w-m: projecting guilt from our minds by attack reinforces its presence in the mind that thought it.

r-m: extending the Love of the Holy Spirit through forgiveness—seeing Him in others—increases the awareness of His loving Presence in ourselves.

---

attack
T-24.IV.3
W-pI.26.1; W-pI.170.4

body
T-22.III.6
W-pI.72.4; W-pII.228.2
S-3.I.2

Christ
W-pI.159.9; W-pII.6.1

creation
T-6.II.8; T-26.VII.13
W-pI.158.1

creations
T-16.III.5

extension
T-6.III.1

giving
T-5.I.1
W-pI.187.2

Holy Spirit
T-19.IV-C.5

idol
T-29.VIII.3

life–death
T-19.IV-C.2
W-pI.167.3-12

love–fear
T-7.VI.1

mind
T-19.I.16; T-21.VII.13
W-pI.45.2-3

projection
T-26.VII.4,12-13

salvation
W-pI.85.3; W-pI.96.7

separation
T-19.I.7; T-22.II.9

sharing
T-5.IV.3; T-6.III.4

sin
W-pI.156.1

Thought of God
T-30.III.6; **T-31.IV.9-10**
W-pI.165.2; W-pII.260.1;
W-pII.280.1; W-pII.326.1

world
W-pI.130.6; W-pI.132.5-10;
W-pII.3.1

idol

symbol of the substitution of the ego for our true Self or God; a false belief that there can be something other than, or more than God, and thus separate from Him, a belief which is then projected onto the special relationship: people, things, or ideas; the anti-Christ.

---

anti-Christ
T-29.VIII

body
T-20.VI.2-7,9,11
W-pII.277.2

death
T-29.VII.3-10
W-pI.163.4

decision
T-30.I.14; **T-30.III**

dream
T-29.IX.1-4

fear
T-7.V.9; T-29.IX.9-10
W-pI.170.5-13

holy relationship
T-30.V.7,10

illusions
T-30.IV.1-6
W-pI.70.9

Jesus
C-5.5

real world
T-30.V.1-6

self-concept
T-31.V.2-4
W-pI.61.1; W-pI.84.1-2

sickness
T-10.III; T-30.VI.6-10

special relationships
T-30.III.3

illusion

something that is believed to be real but is not; the ultimate illusion is the separation from God, upon which rest all the manifestations of the separated world which may be understood as distortions in perception; i.e., seeing attack instead of a call for love, sin instead of error; the illusions of the world reinforce the belief that the body has a value in and of itself, a source of either pleasure or pain; forgiveness is the final illusion as it forgives what never was, and leads beyond all illusion to the truth of God.

---

attack
T-8.VII.15-16; T-13.III.6;
T-30.IV.1-5

death
M-27

decision
T-26.III.4-7; T-31.IV.8

defense
T-22.V
W-pI.135.1-10; W-pI.rIV.In.3;
W-pI.153.7
M-16.6

ego
W-pI.13.3
C-2.1-8

fear
T-11.V.1-4; T-16.V.8

forgiveness
T-16.VII.9-12; T-24.III.1-6;
T-29.III.3
W-pI.46.1-2; W-pI.134.7-10;
W-pI.198.2-10

form–content
T-4.VII.1; T-13.V.1

holy instant
T-16.VII.7-11

Holy Spirit
T-7.VI.6; T-8.V.6

mind
T-7.VI.5; T-7.VII.4; T-28.IV.2-4
W-pI.45; W-pI.66.7-9
C-1.2-6

miracle
W-pI.89.1

resurrection
M-28

sacrifice
W-pII.322

sin
T-17.I.1; T-26.VII.3; T-27.VII.7

special relationships
T-16.IV.3-12; T-16.V.8-17;
T-17.VII.9

truth
T-6.V-C.9; T-17.I.4-5;
T-22.II.1-4; **T-23.I.6-12**;
T-28.V.3-4
W-pI.107.1-7; W-pI.155.2-11

innocence

knowledge: used rarely to denote God or His attributes.

perception: w-m: the face of innocence the ego employs to conceal its true intent of attack, making others guilty for seemingly having inflicted suffering upon an innocent victim.

r-m: the Holy Spirit's correction for our belief in sinfulness; awareness of our innocence and purity as God's Son is restored to us through the forgiveness of our guilt and attainment of true perception.

Atonement
T-3.I.6-7; **T-14.V.3-11**

attack
T-25.IV.1; T-25.V.2; T-27.I.1-3

child
W-pI.182.4

dream
T-27.VII.13

face of Christ
W-pI.198.10

face of innocence
T-26.VII.12; T-26.X.4-5; T-28.II.7; **T-31.V.2-6**

forgiveness
T-27.I.3-5
W-pI.60.1

God
T-3.I.8; T-14.V.3; T-15.XI.2-3; T-28.I.10
W-pI.187.9-11; W-pI.199.1-2; W-pII.309

guilt–guiltlessness
T-13.IX.6-8; T-14.IV.1-2; T-23.In.4; T-26.X.4; **T-27.VIII.13**; T-31.I.9-10

healing
T-27.II.5-8

holy relationship
T-20.II.9-11; T-26.II.5; T-27.VII.15

Holy Spirit
T-15.IV.9; T-19.IV-D.8-9; T-25.VIII.8-12

invulnerability
T-3.I.5-7; T-19.IV-C.10; T-20.III.11; T-23.In.1-5

Jesus
T-3.I.5

justice
T-25.IX.4-6

mind
T-28.II.2

real world
T-20.III.6; T-21.III.9; T-31.I.7-8
W-pI.189.1-4,9

salvation
M-1.3

Self
T-25.VIII.12
W-pI.187.10

sin
T-21.IV.8; T-26.I.6; T-28.V.7

true perception
T-3.II.2-5

truth
W-pI.134.7-10

vision
T-31.VII.13
W-pII.263

invulnerability

our natural state as a Son of God; our true nature being spirit and not the body, nothing of the ego's world can harm us; recognizing our invulnerability becomes the basis for our defenselessness, the condition for forgiveness.

Atonement
T-14.III.7-10

attack
T-6.I.1-6; T-6.III.3; **T-12.V.1-3**; T-23.IV.1; T-25.IV.1
W-pI.26.1-4; W-pI.68.6; W-pI.87.3

defenselessness
W-pI.153.1-10
M-4.VI

forgiveness
W-pI.62.3; W-pI.121.1; W-pI.122.1-2

gentleness
M-4.IV

God
T-10.IV.6; T-12.VIII.1-2; T-23.IV.1; T-24.VII.5
W-pI.47.3-8; W-pI.50.3; W-pI.87.3; W-pI.194.7; W-pII.244; W-pII.261; W-pII.330.2

guiltlessness
T-13.I.8-11; **T-14.III.7**
W-pI.98.3

holy instant
T-31.II.8

Holy Spirit
T-6.I.19; T-6.III.3
W-pII.275
M-16.6-8

innocence
T-19.IV-C.10; T-23.In.1-3

Jesus
T-6.I.1-15; T-8.V.5

love
T-10.III.3
W-pII.5.5

real world
W-pII.8.1-3

sickness
T-8.VIII.3

sinlessness
W-pII.337; W-pII.341

spirit
T-1.IV.2; T-4.I.13; T-31.VI.6

unity/wholeness
T-4.III.1; T-5.IV.4
W-pII.11.3

Jesus

the source of the Course, its first person or "I"; the one who first completed his part in the Atonement, enabling him to be in charge of the whole plan; transcending his ego, Jesus has become identified with Christ and can now serve as our model for learning and an ever-present help when we call upon him in our desire to forgive.

(Note—not to be exclusively identified with Christ, the Second Person of the Trinity.)

A Course in Miracles
M-23.7

Atonement
T-1.III.1-4; T-4.VI.6; **T-5.IV.6-8**
C-6.2

awe
T-1.II.3; T-1.VII.5

body
T-7.V.10; T-19.IV-A.17

Christ
T-1.V.6
C-5

Christmas
T-15.III.7; T-15.X.1-3;
T-15.XI.7-10

comforter
W-Ep.6

communion
T-19.IV-A.16-17

crucifixion
T-6.I.1-16; T-11.VI.7-10;
T-19.IV-A.17

decision
T-3.IV.7; T-5.II.9-11; **T-8.IV.3-6**;
T-12.VII.11-12

Easter
T-20.I.2-4

ego
T-4.I.13; T-4.IV.10-11; T-8.V.4-6

elder brother
T-1.II.3-4; T-4.IV.2

fear
T-2.VI.1-4; **T-4.III.7-8**;
T-12.VII.10

forgiveness
T-19.IV-A.17; T-19.IV-B.6-8;
T-20.I.2-4; T-20.II.4-6
W-pII.241.2
C-5.5

God
T-8.VI.8-10; T-13.X.13;
T-15.IV.3; **T-31.VIII.7-11**
M-23.2-4

gratitude
T-4.VI.7; T-6.I.17; T-18.II.7
M-23.4-5

holy instant
T-15.IV.5; T-15.X.2

holy relationship
T-9.II.4-8; T-17.III.10;
T-18.III.4-7; T-19.IV-B.5-8;
T-19.IV-D.17-19; T-20.III.9-11

Holy Spirit
T-5.II.10-12; T-5.IV.4;
T-12.VII.6; T-13.VII.17;
T-19.IV-D.17
C-6

illusions
W-pI.70.9

light
T-7.V.10-11; T-8.IV.2

miracle
T-1.III.1,3-4,8; T-2.II.1; T-2.V.11

model
T-3.IV.7; T-5.II.9-12; T-6.In.2;
T-6.I
M-23.5
C-5.3-6

resurrection
T-3.V.1; T-4.In.3; T-11.VI.4-7;
T-12.II.7; T-12.VII.15; T-14.V.10
W-pI.rV.In.7
C-5.3-6

sacrifice
T-15.X.2; T-15.XI.7-8

Second Coming
T-4.IV.10

sickness
T-8.IX.7; T-10.III.6-7

teacher
T-4.I.6-7; T-5.IV.5; T-14.V.8-9;
T-15.III.9
W-pI.rV.In.6-8

time
T-2.V.17; T-2.VII.7

world
T-8.IV.3

joining

despite the dream of separation, the Sons of God remain joined with each other as Christ, and joined with God in perfect oneness; however, since we share the illusion of being separate, we must first share the illusion of joining with each other, which reflects the process of forgiveness occurring in our minds; only then can we awaken and remember that we are already joined; joining with Jesus or the Holy Spirit is the prerequisite for joining with our brothers.

(Note—not to be confused with external joining)

Jesus
T-4.IV.8,10-11; T-5.I.3; T-5.II.11; T-8.IV.5-7; **T-8.V.2-6**; T-11.In.4; T-13.V.7; T-13.VIII.8; **T-15.III.7-11**; T-15.VI.6-7; T-16.IV.12; **T-18.III.2-8**; T-19.IV-A.16; T-20.I.2; T-31.VIII.4-11
W-pII.221.2; W-pII.264.2; W-pII.313.2
C-5.5-6; C-6.5

mind
T-6.II.13; **T-18.VI.3,7-14**; **T-21.VI.2-10**; T-25.IV.1; **T-28.IV.2-10**
W-pI.18.1; W-pI.19.2; **W-pI.185.3-6**
P-3.II.8

miracle
T-20.V.1-2; **T-28.III.2-9**

prayer
P-2.VII.2
S-1.IV.1-3; S-1.V.2-4

psychotherapy
P-2.III.2-3; P-2.VI.7; P-2.VII.2-3

real world
T-18.II.9; T-30.V.6-11

Sonship
T-13.VI.7-12; T-13.VIII.8-9

teacher of God
M-4.IV.2; M-12.1-2; M-16.4; M-26.1-3

world
T-27.VII.4

joy (happiness, gladness)

joy is one of the characteristics of a teacher of God, shared with all of Heaven; happiness is God's Will for us, attained through fulfilling our function of forgiveness and awakening from the dream of death.

---

decision
T-5.VII.5-6; T-10.II.2; T-21.II.1; **T-21.VII.12-13**; **T-21.VIII**

depression/misery
T-4.IV.2-3; T-8.VII.8,13; T-22.II.2-12

extension
T-5.III.11; T-7.I.5-6; T-7.V.9; T-7.VI.12-13; T-7.IX.3-6; T-22.VI.14

forgiveness/function
T-17.IV.1-2
W-pI.64.4; **W-pI.66**; W-pI.83.3; W-pI.121.13

God/Heaven
T-4.VII.5-8; T-6.V.1; T-7.XI.1-3; **T-8.VI.3-6**; T-13.II.9; T-25.II.9; T-26.IV.2-6
W-pI.41.4; W-pI.104; **W-pI.105**; W-pI.190.6-11; W-pII.355

guilt
T-5.VI.2; T-13.IX.6

healing
T-5.In; T-5.I.1; T-7.V.6; T-29.II.2-5

holy relationship
T-17.V.10-15; T-20.II.9-11; T-20.III.8; T-20.V.2-4; **T-20.VIII.2-3**; T-22.IV.4

Holy Spirit
T-5.I.5; T-5.II.2-3,10; T-6.IV.1; T-7.X.3-8; T-8.III.1-2; **T-9.VI.1-2**; T-13.VII.6; T-14.II; T-14.III.6-8
W-pI.106.3-4

love
T-16.II.8
W-pI.103

real world
T-13.VII.9-10; T-16.VI.11; T-17.II.1; T-29.VI.6; T-30.V.3-9
W-pII.301
M-14.5

resurrection/Easter
T-11.VI.6; T-20.I.4

spirit
T-4.I.9-10; T-4.VI.5

teacher of God
T-14.V.8-9
M-In.4; **M-4.V**

vision
T-24.V.1-7; T-25.IV.1-3

Will of God
T-1.VII.1; T-8.II.6; T-8.III.2; T-8.IV.1; T-8.V.3; T-9.VII.1; T-11.III.3
W-pI.100.2-8; W-pI.101; W-pI.102; W-pI.193.1; W-pI.210; W-pII.235.1

world
T-6.II.5-6; T-21.I.4; T-29.VI.6
W-pI.135.20; W-pI.153.8-14

judgment

knowledge: strictly speaking God does not judge, since what He creates is perfect and at one with Him; the Course's references to God's Judgment reflect His recognition of His Son *as* His Son, forever loved and one with Him.

perception: w-m: condemnation, whereby people are separated into those to be hated and those to be "loved," a judgment always based upon the past.

r-m: vision, whereby people are seen either as expressing love or calling for it, a judgment inspired by the Holy Spirit and always based upon the present.

see: *Last (Final) Judgment*

---

attack
T-13.In.1; T-30.I.3-5
W-pII.347.1

body
T-20.VII.5-8
W-pI.151.3-8

dream
T-29.IX

ego
T-4.IV.8; T-5.VI.4; T-8.VIII.4;
T-14.X.7-9

fear
T-30.VII.3

forgiveness
W-pI.198.2-12; W-pII.1.2-4;
W-pII.352

God
T-2.VIII.2-5
W-pII.10.3-5
M-11.2-4; **M-15**; M-19.4-5

Holy Spirit
T-6.V-C.2; T-9.III.3-8;
T-12.I.3-10; **T-14.X.5-11**
W-pI.125.2-3; W-pI.151.7-13;
W-pII.311; W-pII.347
M-9.2; M-28.6

love
T-25.VIII.8-12
W-pI.127.2-3

past
T-15.V.1

perception
T-3.VI; T-12.VII.12-13
W-pI.51.2; W-pII.312.1
M-8.3-4

psychotherapy
P-2.VII.5; **P-3.II.2,6-7**

sickness
P-2.IV.1

special relationships
T-24.II.1

teacher of God
M-4.III; **M-10**

vision
T-20.V.3-4; T-20.VIII.7; T-21.I.2
W-pII.349.1

justice

the Holy Spirit's correction for the world's injustice; the belief that God's Sons are equally loved and equally holy, undoing the judgments based on separation; the end of sacrifice and the belief that one's gain is another's loss; called "the rock on which salvation rests."

---

attack
T-26.X

forgiveness
T-26.IV.1

God
T-26.I.8; T-26.II.5-8; T-26.V.9
M-19.4-5

Holy Spirit
T-25.VIII.3-14; T-25.IX.3-7

judgment
T-29.IX.3

mercy
T-3.VI.6

miracle
T-25.IX.5-10; T-26.II.4-6

sin
T-25.VIII.3-14

Kingdom of God, Heaven

(see: *Heaven*)

knowledge

Heaven, or the pre-separation world of God and His unified creation in which there are no differences or forms, and thus it is exclusive of the world of perception; not to be confused with the common use of "knowledge," which implies the dualism of a subject who *knows* and an object which is *known*; in the Course it reflects the pure experience of non-duality, with no subject-object dichotomy.

(Note—since perception and knowledge are usually discussed together, *perception* is not cross-referenced below.)

see: *Heaven*

A Course in Miracles
T-18.IX.11
W-pI.138.5

Christ
T-12.VI.7
W-pI.158.5,11

creation
T-3.III.7; T-3.VII.3-4
W-pI.158.1-2

ego
T-3.IV.2-3; T-4.II.3;

faith
T-19.I.12

forgiveness
W-pI.198.2-3,12; W-pII.336.1
M-4.X.2
C-3.2-5; C-4.7

grace
W-pI.168.4; W-pI.169.1-3,12-15

Holy Spirit
T-5.I.4-7; **T-6.II.7**; T-10.II.2;
T-12.VI.7
W-pI.43.1; W-pII.7.1,4
C-6.3

Jesus
T-3.IV.7

mind
T-3.IV.4-5

miracle
T-3.V.6,8-10; T-16.II.5

peace
T-8.I.1

real world
T-11.VII.3-4; T-11.VIII.1;
T-13.VII.8-9
W-pI.129.4

reason
T-21.V.7-9

resurrection
T-3.V.1

revelation
T-3.III.4-5

spirit
T-3.IV.6-7; T-4.In.2; T-4.I.2

true perception
T-3.III; T-4.II.11; T-4.VI.2;
T-5.I.4-7; T-12.VIII.8;
T-13.VIII.2-8
W-pI.15.3
C-4

truth
T-26.VII.3-4
W-pII.4.1

wholeness
T-3.V.8; T-8.VIII.1; T-13.VIII.2

world
W-pII.3.2

Last (Final) Judgment

knowledge: contrasted with the traditional Christian view of judgment and punishment to reflect God's loving relationship with *all* His Sons: His Final Judgment.

true perception: contrasted with the traditional Christian view of judgment and punishment and equated with the end of the Atonement when, following the Second Coming, the final distinction is made between truth and illusion, all guilt is undone, and awareness is restored to us as Christ—the Son of the living God.

---

fear
T-2.VIII.2-5; T-9.IV.9

God
W-pII.10.3-5
M-15

Holy Spirit
T-13.XI.4
M-28.6

miracle
T-2.VIII.2

perception–knowledge
T-3.VI.1
W-pII.10.1-2

Second Coming
W-pII.9.3

truth–illusion
T-26.III.4

last step

this step, belonging to God, occurs when the Atonement is complete and all ego interferences have been removed; when nothing remains to separate us from God, He takes the last step, raising us unto Himself; strictly speaking God does not take steps, and the term actually refers to *our* experience of returning to our Source Which we never truly left.

Atonement
T-15.IX.1

face of Christ
C-3.4-6

forgiveness
T-14.IV.3; T-27.III.6; **T-30.V.3-4**
W-pI.60.1; **W-pI.193.13**

grace
W-pI.168.3; W-pI.169.3

Holy Spirit
T-5.I.6; T-6.V-C.5; **T-7.I.6-7**;
T-19.IV.3
W-pII.In.4

Jesus
T-4.VI.7

memory of God
T-28.I.15

miracle
T-13.VIII.10; T-28.III.6

real world
T-11.VIII.15
W-pI.129.5; W-pII.289.2;
W-pII.8.5
C-1.5
S-1.V.4

resurrection
M-28.1

true perception
T-13.VIII.3
C-4.8

laughter

the Course asks us not to take the ego and its world seriously, for this makes them real in our minds; rather, we are urged to laugh gently at the ego thought system and all its seeming consequences, remembering at last to laugh at the "tiny, mad idea."

---

cause–effect
T-27.VIII.8-9

fear
T-11.VIII.13-14
W-pI.41.10

forgiveness
T-19.IV-D.16
W-pI.134.6

guilt/sin
T-27.VII.14
W-pI.151.8; W-pI.153.13-14;
W-pI.156.6

idols
T-29.VIII.9

judgment
T-3.VI.5

sacrifice
W-pI.187.6

self
W-pI.166.8

suffering
T-27.II.8
W-pI.195.2

teacher of God
W-pI.100.2-3; W-pI.155.1

tears
T-27.I.5
W-pI.54.5; W-pI.183.3;
W-pI.193.9
M-10.5; M-14.5

time
T-27.VIII.5-6; T-28.I.9

laws of God

the principles that express God's existence and the extension of His Kingdom.

knowledge: include creation, love, truth, and eternal life.

true perception: reflected in this world as forgiveness, the miracle, healing, and freedom, in contrast with the ego's laws of projection, specialness, suffering, and death—the laws of chaos.

---

body
W-pI.158.7; W-pII.277;
W-pII.278.1

Christ
W-pII.354

creation
T-7.V.11; T-10.I.1; T-25.IV.2

death
T-24.VI.4-5
W-pI.137.9

decision
W-pI.133.3-12

ego
T-5.V.6; T-13.IX.1

extension–projection
T-7.II.2-5; T-7.VIII.1-4

forgiveness
T-25.VI.5
W-pI.198.2-3

freedom
T-10.IV.4-5
W-pI.57.4; W-pI.88.3

giving
T-7.VII.2
W-pI.159.1-2; W-pII.13.2;
W-pII.349.1
P-3.III.5

healing
T-7.IV.1-6; T-24.VI.4-5;
T-27.II.7; T-27.V.9-10

holy instant
T-15.VI.5

holy relationship
T-20.IV.2-7; T-20.V.6-7;
T-24.VI.10

Holy Spirit
T-7.II.4-5; T-7.VIII.1
W-pI.154.4

inviolate
T-8.IV.1; T-9.I.11; T-10.In.1;
T-11.I.5; T-27.V.9-10

laws of chaos
T-10.IV.4-5; T-23.II.14-15

love
T-13.VI.12-13; T-25.III.1
W-pI.127.3-9; **W-pII.344.1**

miracle
T-27.VI.6-8
W-pI.77.2-4; **W-pII.345.1**

perception
T-25.III.1-4; T-25.IV.2

protection
T-10.In.1; T-11.IV.2-3; T-30.IV.4

truth
T-26.VII.4-6

world
T-7.XI.1
W-pI.76
M-4.I.1; M-18.3

light

knowledge: metaphor to describe the essence of spirit—God and Christ.

true perception: metaphor to describe the vision of Christ, or forgiveness, which joins us in holy relationships and removes the darkened veils of guilt that keep us rooted in the ego's dream.

see: *bringing darkness (illusions) to the light (truth)*
Great Rays

Atonement
T-2.III.1; T-3.I.6-7

body
T-24.VII.4-9; T-25.I.4;
T-25.II.7-11; T-25.III.5-7

darkness
T-1.IV.3; T-4.III.5; T-13.VI.2-12;
T-14.X.5; T-15.XI.2;
T-25.IV.3-5; T-25.VI.2-7
W-pI.88.1; W-pI.97.6
M-1.1-2

dream
T-2.I.4; T-29.IX.4

enlightenment
T-4.In.1; T-7.V.10; T-8.III.1;
T-12.II.4; T-12.VI.7
W-pI.188.1

forgiveness
T-23.In.6; T-26.IV.2-5;
T-29.III.3-5
W-pI.57.5; W-pI.62.1;
W-pI.63.1-3; W-pI.81.3;
W-pI.82.1; W-pI.121.10-13;
W-pII.332.1

God/Heaven
T-3.VII.5-6; T-4.IV.9;
T-8.VII.12; T-11.III.4-8;
T-11.IV.3; T-26.IX.4-7; T-30.II.3;
T-30.III.8-11; T-31.VIII.11-12
W-pI.44; W-pI.59.4; W-pI.94.2;
W-pII.225.1; W-pII.239.2;
W-pII.249.1; W-pII.283.1

guilt
T-13.IX.7-8; T-13.X.8-14;
T-14.V.4; T-18.IX.5-9

healing
T-5.In; T-12.II.1-2; T-14.III.6
W-pI.108.1-3

holy instant
T-20.V.5; T-26.V.11

holy relationship
T-18.I.13; **T-18.III**; T-20.II.9-11;
T-20.III.7-11; T-22.II.12;
T-22.IV.3-4; **T-22.VI.4-15**;
T-23.IV.4-6; T-31.II.11
W-pI.153.11

Holy Spirit
T-5.II.4; T-5.III.7; T-6.V-C.1;
T-13.VII.12-14; T-14.II.4
C-6.3

Jesus
T-8.IV.2; T-19.IV-B.6-8

mind
T-7.III.4-5; T-7.XI.5; T-9.II.5;
T-9.V.7

miracle
T-1.I.33; T-3.V.10; T-13.VIII.8
W-pI.78; W-pI.91; W-pI.92;
W-pII.345
C-2.5-6

real world
T-13.VI.11; T-18.IX.8-13
W-pI.73.4-5; W-pI.75;
W-pI.131.13-14;
W-pI.135.20-25; W-pI.182.4;
W-pI.189.1-5

veil/cloud
T-15.VI.6; T-19.IV-D.2;
T-29.VIII.3-5; T-31.VII.6-15
W-pI.41.5; W-pI.56.4; **W-pI.69**;
W-pI.70.8-9; W-pI.95.12

vision
T-13.V.8-11; T-13.VIII.2-5;
T-20.VIII.3-4; **T-21.I.8-10**
W-pI.15.2-3; W-pI.158.7-11;
W-pII.265.1

world
T-5.II.10; T-6.II.13
W-pI.61; W-pI.81.1-2;
W-pI.100.3; W-pI.124.2-7;
W-pI.156.4-8; W-pI.157.4-7;
W-pI.188

lilies

the Course's symbol of forgiveness and the innocence of God's Son; the gift of forgiveness that we offer each other, contrasted with the ego's gift of thorns (attack, crucifixion).

---

altar
T-20.VIII.4
W-pI.187.9-11

face of Christ
T-20.I.4

innocence
T-20.II.9-10

Jesus
T-20.II.4-6

light
W-pII.12.5

miracle
W-pII.13.3

truth
W-pII.336.1

vision
W-pI.159.8

looking at the ego

the essence of forgiveness: looking with the Holy Spirit's or Jesus' non-judgmental gentleness and patience at our ego thought system; since it is guilt that prevents us from looking at our specialness, thus sustaining the ego and keeping its true nature hidden, it is looking without judgment at our attack thoughts that undoes the ego: thus, looking at the ego without guilt and fear is the essence of the Atonement.

see: *bringing darkness (illusions) to the light (truth)*

---

attack
T-13.III.1-7
W-pI.68.5; W-pI.92.3-11;
W-pI.136.19-20
M-17.9
S-1.IV.1

body
T-20.II.1,4-5

decision
T-10.II.6; T-30.I.11-12;
T-31.II.2; T-31.VII.7,11-15

dreams
T-27.VIII.3-9
W-pI.185.5-8
M-12.6

ego
T-7.X.1; **T-8.III.6**; T-10.III.5;
T-11.In.2-4; **T-11.V.1-5**;
T-12.V.8; T-14.II.5; **T-15.IX.2**;
T-17.VII.5; T-18.VIII.8;
T-19.IV-D.6-7; T-22.II.9-10;
T-22.VI.10; **T-23.II.1,15,18**
W-pI.133.8-10; W-pI.152.10;
W-pII.254.2

fear
T-11.VIII.13-14; T-12.I.10;
T-14.VII.1-2; T-19.IV-A.10-11;
T-19.IV-D.8-11
W-pI.170.3-12; **W-pI.187.7-10**;
W-pI.196.3-12

forgiveness
T-25.VI.1
W-pI.46.3-5; **W-pI.134.6-12**;
W-pI.192.4; **W-pII.1.1-4**;
W-pII.333; W-pII.352
P-2.VI.6-7

forgiveness-to-destroy
S-2.I.9

guilt
T-13.I.3; T-13.II.4-5;
T-15.VII.2-5; T-18.IX.4-9
W-pI.47.4-8

healing
P-2.VI.1-2

Holy Spirit
T-2.V.7; T-5.III.11; T-5.IV.1; T-12.II.9-10; T-14.I.5; **T-14.VII.6-7**; T-16.III.1; T-19.IV-C.11; T-25.VII.8
W-pI.49; W-pI.138.8-10; W-pI.151.13-15

idols
T-29.VII.4-6; **T-30.IV.4-8**; T-30.V.10

illusions
T-16.V.14,16; T-20.II.7
W-pII.344.1

Jesus
T-4.III.7-8; T-11.In.4; T-11.V.1; T-31.VIII.11

judgment
T-6.V-C.2

mind searching
W-pI.5.3-7; W-pI.6.2; W-pI.8.2-6; W-pI.10.4-5; W-pI.16.3-6; W-pI.19.3; W-pI.21.2-4; **W-pI.23.4-7**; W-pI.24.2-4; W-pI.35.4-9; W-pI.38.4; W-pI.94.3-4

miracle
T-28.II.7; T-29.II.2
W-pII.13.1-4
C-2.4-8

nightmares
T-12.II.4-5

pain
W-pII.235.1; W-pII.347.1

real world
T-12.VIII.5-8

reason
T-21.VII.5-13; T-22.II.4-5; **T-22.III.1-7**; T-22.VI.5

sacrifice
T-15.X.5-9

sanity–battleground
T-9.VII.6; T-13.III.12; T-13.VII.7; T-23.III.6; **T-23.IV.4-8**

separation
T-28.V.7

sin
T-22.V.5-6; T-31.V.5-6

special relationships
T-16.IV.1,6-7; T-16.V.1,10; T-16.VI.3; **T-17.IV.6-9,12-15**; T-24.I.7

thoughts
T-2.VI.2; T-4.IV.2-8
W-pI.31.3; W-pI.32.2-3; W-pI.34.1-3; W-pI.39.6-8; W-pI.41.5-10; W-pI.42.4-8; W-pI.43.5-6; W-pI.44.4-11; **W-pI.45**; W-pI.65.3-8; W-pI.100.7-9; W-pI.131.11

time
W-pI.158.4; W-pI.164

vision
T-20.VIII.5-11; T-21.In;
T-24.V.1-7

within
T-12.VII.8-10; T-13.V.11;
T-13.IX.7-8; **T-13.X.1-12**;
T-21.IV; T-22.In.3
W-pII.309

world
T-13.In.2; T-13.V.6; T-17.II.5;
T-18.I.5; **T-27.VII.2-11**
W-pI.198.7
C-4.4-6

love

knowledge: the essence of God's being and relationship to His creation, which is unchanging and eternal; beyond definition and teaching, and can only be experienced or known once the barriers of guilt have been removed through forgiveness.

true perception: impossible in the illusory world of perception, yet expressed here through forgiveness; the emotion given by God, in contrast to the ego's emotion of fear, and reflected in any expression of true joining with another.

A Course in Miracles
T-In.1; T-13.IV.1

Atonement
T-2.II.4; T-2.VI.7-8; T-16.VII.10

attack
T-7.VI.2; T-12.V.1-7;
T-23.II.14-20; T-23.IV; T-26.IX.6
W-pI.68
M-7.4

body
T-1.VII.2; **T-18.VI.4-5**;
T-18.VIII; **T-20.VI.2-12**;
T-29.I.5-9

charity
T-2.V.9

Christ
T-11.IV.6-7; T-12.II.3-6;
T-12.VI.5-6; T-30.V.7-8

creating
T-7.I.3-6; T-7.V.9-11; T-8.VI.5;
T-10.I.1
S-1.In.1

death
T-19.IV-C.7-9
M-27

ego
T-7.VI.4; T-12.IV.1-3; T-15.V.1

extension
T-7.I.3; T-7.VIII.1; T-11.I.6-7;
T-13.I.6; T-15.V.11; T-24.I.1;
T-28.II.2

faith
T-19.I.10; T-21.III.2

fear
T-1.VI.5; T-5.In.2; T-11.V.10-12;
T-12.I.8-10; **T-13.III.2-9**;
T-13.V; T-15.X.4-7; T-18.I.3;
T-19.IV-A.10-15; T-19.IV-D.2-7;
T-29.I.1-8
W-pI.103; W-pI.170.3-10
P-2.IV.6

forgiveness
T-18.IX.10-13; T-25.V.6;
T-29.III.4
W-pI.46.1-2; W-pI.186.14
W-pI.193.8-13

God
T-7.VII.6-7; T-9.I.9-11;
T-10.V.6-10; **T-12.VIII.2-8**;
T-13.III.2-8; T-14.IV.8;
T-15.VII.1; T-16.VI.1-2
W-pI.99.5-12; **W-pI.127**

grace
W-pI.168; W-pI.169.1-2

gratitude
T-12.I.6
W-pI.195; W-pII.298

guilt
T-13.In; T-13.I.1; **T-13.X.8-12**;
T-15.VII.10; T-19.IV-A.10-11

happy dream
T-13.VII.9; T-29.IV.6

healing
T-8.IX.5; T-27.V.11

holy instant
T-15.V; T-15.VI.5-6; T-15.XI.7;
T-18.VIII.11

Holy Spirit
T-9.VII.3; T-14.III.15-17;
T-14.V.10; T-14.X.7-11;
T-15.IX.5
W-pII.7.2-5; W-pII.295.2

identity
T-6.I.13; T-6.III.2-4; T-7.IV.7;
T-7.VI.4
W-pI.67; W-pI.rV.In.4;
W-pII.229; W-pII.282;
W-pII.14.1

invulnerability
T-10.III.3; T-12.VIII.2
W-pI.50.3-4; W-pII.5;
W-pII.264.1; W-pII.348.1

Jesus
T-7.I.5; T-13.X.13-14;
T-15.XI.7-8
M-23.4-5

judgment
T-20.VII.9
W-pII.352

justice
T-25.VIII.8-14; T-26.II.8

law
T-13.VI.12-13
W-pII.345.1; W-pII.349.1

messengers
T-12.VII.8; **T-19.IV-A.10-15**

miracle
T-1.I.1,3,9,11,35; T-27.VI.6-8
W-pII.356

prayer
S-1.I.5

real world
T-11.VII.2; T-12.III.8;
T-13.VII.4-6
W-pI.189

sacrifice
T-15.X.5-7; T-15.XI.3-8;
T-26.II.7

sharing
T-5.IV.3; T-10.V.14; T-12.VIII.1

sickness
T-12.II.1-3

sin
T-1.IV.3; T-5.VII.5; T-19.III.4;
T-25.VII.1-6

sinlessness
T-23.In.2-3
W-pI.60.5; W-pII.235

special relationships
T-16.IV; **T-16.V.2-15**; T-24.I;
T-24.II.1-12

magic

the attempt to solve a problem where it is not, i.e., trying to solve a problem in the mind through physical or "mindless" measures: the ego's strategy to keep the real problem—the belief in separation—from God's Answer; guilt is projected outside our minds onto others (attack) or our bodies (sickness) and sought to be corrected there, rather than being undone in our minds by bringing it to the Holy Spirit; referred to as "false healing" in "The Song of Prayer."

---

attack
M-17; M-18.1-2

body
W-pI.92.1

defenses
W-pI.98.3; W-pI.136.3;
W-pI.138.8

ego
T-2.VIII.1; T-4.II.9

guilt
M-17.5-8

healing
T-7.V.3-4; T-9.V.6
S-3.I.5; **S-3.II.1**,6; **S-3.III.1-3**

Holy Spirit
T-6.V.2
M-25.1-4

mindlessness
T-1.I.14; T-2.V.2
M-27.6

psychotherapy
P-2.In.2-4

sickness
T-2.IV.2-4; T-2.V.2; T-5.V.5;
T-10.IV.1
W-pI.140.1-10
P-2.IV.4-7

special relationships
T-23.II.12

temptation
M-16.8-11

time
W-pI.158.4

world
T-25.VII.1
W-pI.50.1; W-pI.76.6-9

spirit creates, while the ego makes.

knowledge: creation occurs only within the world of knowledge, creating truth.

perception: making, also referred to as miscreating, leads only to illusions; used rarely for the Holy Spirit, Who is described as the Maker of the real world.

see: *creation*

---

ego–Holy Spirit
T-5.V.6

ego–spirit
T-4.I.7-12

fear–love
T-2.VII.3; T-7.VI.1

forgiveness
T-18.IX.10

healing
T-2.V.12

Holy Spirit
T-25.III.1-5,8

mind
T-2.VIII.1; **T-3.IV.5**; T-5.V.4

projection–extension
T-11.In.3

Self
W-pI.93.9

separation
T-3.IV.3; **T-3.V.2-3**

teacher of God
M-4.VI; M-5.III.3

thought
T-1.I.12; T-3.VII.1
W-pI.16.1

wish–will
W-pI.73.1

world
T-11.VII.4

despite the multitude of means in the world, there remain but two ends or goals: truth or illusion; the body can serve either end, as the mind elects.

w-m: the body is used as a means to bring about the goal of sin and guilt, reinforcing illusion through the special relationship.

r-m: the body is used as a means to achieve the goal of forgiveness, leading us to truth through the holy relationship.

---

body
T-8.VIII; T-18.VII.1;
T-19.IV-B.10; T-20.V.5
W-pII.4.2; **W-pII.5.3-4**;
W-pII.294

forgiveness
W-pI.82.1; **W-pII.256**

God
T-24.VII.6
W-pII.257; W-pII.258

grace
W-pI.168.2-4

holy relationship
T-17.V.14; T-18.V.3-4

Holy Spirit
T-20.VII; **T-21.III.6**
W-pII.7.2-3; W-pII.302.2

perception
T-24.VII.5-11; T-25.I.3

reason
T-21.VI.7-8; T-22.II.5

salvation
W-pII.318

truth
T-17.VI; T-17.VIII.5-6

vision
W-pII.269.1

world
T-31.IV.2
W-pI.25.1-5

memory of God

the Atonement's final stage, which follows seeing the face of Christ in all our brothers and precedes the last step, taken by God Himself; we remember God through forgiveness, undoing all beliefs in separation that obscured His Presence to us.

---

body
T-23.I.5

Christ's vision
W-pII.271

decision
T-12.VIII.5
W-pI.185.1

face of Christ
T-26.IV.3; T-26.IX.2; T-30.V.7
W-pI.122.3
C-3.4

fear
T-13.III.2; T-19.IV-D.1; T-28.I.13
W-pI.48.3

forgiveness
T-18.IX.14
W-pI.60.2; W-pII.2.3; W-pII.7.4;
W-pII.335.2; W-pII.350
P-2.II.3

function
W-pII.11.4; W-pII.FL.In.3-4

grace
W-pI.168.2

gratitude
W-pII.315.2

guilt
T-13.II.1,9; T-13.X.8-9

healing
T-12.II.2

holy instant
T-15.VI.8; T-28.I.11-12

holy relationship
P-2.II.5

innocence
T-31.I.9-10

Jesus
T-8.IV.7
C-5.2

last step
T-28.I.15
W-pII.8.5

psychotherapy
P-2.VII.9

resurrection
M-28.2

sacrifice
T-26.I.4; T-26.II.7

special function
T-26.II.8

true perception
C-4.6

mind

knowledge: the activating agent of spirit, to which it is roughly equivalent, supplying its creative energy.

perception: the agent of choice; we are free to believe that our minds can be separated or split off from the Mind of God (wrong-mindedness), or that they can be returned to it (right-mindedness); thus, the split mind can be understood as having three parts: the wrong mind, the right mind, and the part of the mind (decision maker) that chooses between them; not to be confused with the brain, which is a physical organ and thus an aspect of our bodily self.

see: *Mind of God, split*

---

abstraction
T-4.VII.1
W-pI.161.2

attack
T-7.VI.2; T-18.VI.3-7

body
T-2.IV.2-4; T-2.V.1-6;
T-18.VI.2-8; T-19.I.2-3;
T-19.IV-B.10
W-pI.96.1-5; **W-pI.135.4-13**;
W-pI.192.5
M-8.3-4,6
P-2.VI.3

creation
T-2.IV.2-3; T-2.V.1-2; T-2.VI.9

death
W-pI.167.3-11

decision
T-7.VI.2; **T-8.IV.3-6**;
T-10.In.2-3; T-12.III.9
M-5.II.1-2

denial
T-7.VII.1

ego
T-4.V.4; **T-7.VI.4-9**; T-12.IV.2

extension
T-6.III; T-7.VI.12; T-8.VII.10-16

guilt
T-5.V.3-5
W-pI.70.1-3

healing
T-9.V.4,7; T-28.II.11
P-In

Holy Spirit
W-pI.199.1-2

Jesus
T-3.IV.7; T-8.IV.4-6

joining
T-11.III.8; **T-18.VI.3-7**;
T-28.III.2-5
W-pI.18.1

law of mind
T-6.II.9-12; T-7.II.2-3; T-12.VII.7

make–create
T-3.IV.5; T-3.VII.1-4

mind training
T-1.VII.4
W-In.1,4; W-pI.95.4-6

miracle
T-28.I.11; T-28.II.11-12

sickness
T-8.VII.10-12
W-pI.135.13
M-5.II.1-3
P-2.IV.4-5

sin
T-21.III.10; **T-31.III.3-5**

spirit
T-1.V.5; T-3.IV.5-6
W-pI.96.4-5; W-pI.97.1-4;
W-pII.330.1
C-1.1-4

world
T-12.III.6-10
W-pI.132; W-pI.190.5-7

equated with the creative function of God which represents the activating agent of spirit, supplying its creative energy; as an extension of God, the Mind of Christ—God's Thought—shares in the attributes of the Mind of God—One-mindedness; after the separation, the Mind of Christ *appeared* to be split in two: Mind and mind.

---

changelessness
T-10.In.3; T-12.I.6; T-16.V.12;
T-18.V.3

Christ
T-5.I.5
C-1.1,6

creation
T-4.IV.9; T-7.VIII.1; **T-11.I.3-6**;
T-25.VII.4

guiltlessness
T-13.I.5

healing
T-19.I.2

Holy Spirit
T-5.I.5; T-5.III.1; T-6.II.11;
T-13.VIII.4; T-14.IV.10
W-pI.99.4-5; W-pI.169.8

identity
T-9.VI.7; T-9.VIII.5-10;
T-13.VIII.2
W-pI.139.8

innocence
T-14.V.3

Jesus
T-5.II.10-12; T-5.IV.4-5; T-7.V.10

light
T-18.III.8; T-25.II.7-8
W-pII.265.1

love
T-10.V.10
W-pI.123.8

miracle
T-28.I.11

sinlessness
W-pI.36.1

thoughts
W-pI.43.3; **W-pI.45**; W-pI.59.5;
W-pI.96.7; W-pI.rIV.In.2-5

Thoughts
T-6.II.8; T-11.III.7; T-24.VI.3
W-pI.56.5; W-pII.280.1;
W-pII.326.1

Trinity
T-3.II.5

unity
T-7.V.10; T-8.V.1; T-10.IV.6;
T-30.III.6-11
W-pI.38.1

will
T-5.II.1; T-24.III.5

miracle

the change of mind that shifts our perception from the ego's world of sin, guilt, and fear, to the Holy Spirit's world of forgiveness; reverses projection by restoring to the mind its causative function, allowing us to choose again; transcends the laws of this world to reflect the laws of God; accomplished by our joining with the Holy Spirit or Jesus, being the means of healing our own and others' minds.

(Note—not to be confused with the traditional understanding of miracles as changes in external phenomena.)

Atonement
T-2.II.6-7; T-2.IV

body
T-1.VII.1
W-pII.13

cause–effect
T-28.II.4-12

correction
T-1.IV.2
W-pII.13.1-2

decision
T-14.III.5
W-pI.78

dream–happy dream
T-29.IV.1-2
C-2.7

ego
T-21.V.3
C-2.5-10

extension
T-7.IX.4-7; T-16.II.1

forgiveness
T-27.VI.6
W-pII.13.1-3
C-2.10

God
T-14.X.11-12; T-28.I.9-11
W-pI.77; W-pI.89.1

healing
T-2.IV.1; T-24.IV.3; T-27.II.5-7;
T-27.V.1; T-28.III.1-3,7-8;
T-30.VI.5-8; **T-30.VIII.3-5**

holy instant
T-27.V.1-4
W-pI.169.12-13

Holy Spirit
T-5.II.1; T-9.IV.6; T-10.IV.7;
T-12.VII.1-4; T-14.X.2-3,6;
T-14.XI.7,10-11; T-16.II.5-7
W-pI.151.14

Jesus
T-1.III.1,3-4,8; T-1.V.6

justice
T-25.IX.5-10

mind
T-21.V.3

principles
T-1.I; **T-2.V.11-18**

revelation
T-1.II.1-3

salvation
W-pI.90.1

sin
T-27.VI.4-7

time
T-1.II.6; T-1.V.2; T-2.VIII.2;
T-9.VI.6; T-28.I.1
W-pI.97.3-4

vision
T-3.III.4
W-pI.91; **W-pI.159.3-10**

Name of God

used as a symbol for the Identity of God, Which Self we share as His Son; the symbol of God's holiness, which is our own as well.

Christ
T-12.I.7; T-15.III.6
M-22.5

creations
T-10.V.11-13; T-11.III.3

forgiveness
W-pII.240.2

Holy Spirit
T-5.VI.11; T-12.VI.4;
T-15.VII.5; T-19.IV.3
W-pI.78.7; W-pI.169.9

illusions
T-16.IV.9

Jesus
T-8.IX.7; T-17.III.10
M-23.1-4

love
W-pII.282.2

psychotherapy
P-3.I.3

salvation
W-pI.106.6; W-pII.2.3

Son of God
T-8.IX.7
W-pI.183; W-pI.204;
W-pII.223.2; W-pII.224.2;
W-pII.262.1; W-pII.288.1;
W-pII.356
M-5.III.2
C-Ep.3

Teacher of teachers
M-26.2

unity
T-26.VII.20
W-pI.139.12; **W-pI.184.10-15**

no order of difficulty in miracles

the first principle of miracles; something is either true or false, with no real levels existing within each category; there is no order of difficulty in correcting illusions as they are all equally unreal, requiring only the miracle's shift from illusion to truth; similarly, there is no order of difficulty in healing as any form of sickness (illusion), even unto death, is undone in the mind—where it truly is—when brought to the truth there; the correction for the ego's first law of chaos: there is a hierarchy of illusions.

A Course in Miracles
T-26.V.1

Atonement
M-22.1

death
T-19.IV-C.6

forgiveness
M-14.3

generalization
T-12.VII.1

healing
T-5.VII.2; T-7.IV.5; T-3O.VI.5-8
M-8.5
P-3.II.2,7-9

holy instant
T-18.IV.8

Holy Spirit
T-6.V-A.4; T-7.IV.2;
T-14.X.2-12; T-26.II.1-2
M-16.7

Jesus
T-4.IV.11

justice
T-25.IX.6

laws
T-1.III.9

Lessons of the Holy Spirit
T-6.V-B.8; T-6.V-C.4

love
T-1.I.1; T-19.IV-A.5

perception–vision
T-1.I.49; **T-2.I.5**; T-20.VII.5;
T-21.In.1
M-8.1

relationships
T-20.VI.8

sickness
P-2.IV.8

Sonship
T-11.VI.10

true perception
T-16.II.3

truth
T-17.I.3-4; T-23.II.2-3

workbook exercises
W-pI.19.4

world
T-7.XI.1; T-14.X.2-3; T-20.VIII.8

not to make error real

one of the key elements in the Holy Spirit's plan of forgiveness, correcting the ego's plan to make sin real which inevitably leads us either to erect defenses against it out of fear, or to forgive it falsely; true forgiveness, on the other hand, recognizes the error as a call for love and correction; making the error real, as when we falsely empathize with another, or magically hope to solve an external problem, roots us still further in the ego's thought system, while seeing all problems or forms of suffering as external reflections of internal guilt allows the true healing of the mind to occur.

---

attack
T-9.III.7

cause–effect
T-28.II
W-pI.41.2

ego
T-9.III.1-7; **T-9.IV.4**;
T-11.V.14-15

forgiveness
T-9.III.8; **T-9.IV.1-5**

Holy Spirit
T-13.X.6

Holy Spirit's judgment
T-12.I; T-12.II

illusions
T-17.I.5; T-30.VIII

investment
T-12.III.2-4

magic
M-16.10; M-17

miracle
T-28.II.7-12; **T-30.VIII**

sickness–healing
T-10.IV.1-7; T-28.II.2-3
W-pI.136.1-11
P-2.IV.6-7

sin
T-14.III.15; T-21.II.9
W-pI.101; W-pI.156.1
S-2.I.3

unhealed healer
T-9.V

One-mindedness

the Mind of God or Christ; the extension of God which is the unified Mind of the Sonship; transcending both right- and wrong-mindedness, it exists only at the level of knowledge and Heaven.

Christ
T-3.IV.3
C-1.6

Holy Spirit
T-4.II.10; T-5.I.6

oneness

knowledge: the reality of God and Christ, Whose perfect unity constitutes Heaven.

perception: reflected in the world through forgiveness, the undoing of our belief in separate interests; our joining together with others, through the undoing of our thoughts of specialness, is simply the acceptance of our inherent oneness as God's Son; sharing this purpose of forgiveness is our one and only function, reflecting our function of creating in Heaven.

see: *One-mindedness*

Father-Son
T-1.III.7; T-3.II.4; T-7.VI.10; T-8.III.3; **T-8.VI.9**; T-11.I.5-7,11; T-11.II.1; T-13.X.7,14; T-19.IV-B.7; **T-20.VI.1**; **T-21.II.12-13**; T-22.VI.12-15; T-24.II.3; T-24.VI.2; T-28.VII.1
W-pI.124; **W-pI.132.11-13**; W-pI.184.15; W-pI.185.13; W-pI.201; W-pII.239.2; W-pII.6.1-2; W-pII.326.1; W-pII.329
C-3.8
S-1.In.1-2; S-2.III.4

forgiveness
T-13.I.6
C-3.5; C-4.3

God
T-6.II.1; T-11.I.2-3; T-14.IV.1-2; T-15.XI.2,9; T-26.III.1-3; T-26.VII.10; T-29.I.1
W-pI.56.4-5; W-pI.83.3; W-pI.169.1,4-6
P-2.VII.1

holy instant
T-15.IV.8; T-15.V.10; T-15.VI.5

holy relationship
T-11.VIII.11; T-20.V.2; T-25.II.11

Holy Spirit
T-14.VIII.2-5; T-14.XI.11; T-16.III.5; T-27.II.16; T-28.IV.7-9
C-6.4

Jesus
T-3.IV.7; T-8.IV.3; **T-8.V.1-4**
W-pII.225.2

Kingdom
T-3.V.8; T-3.VII.6; T-4.III.1; T-6.II.12-13; T-7.I.6; T-7.II.7; T-7.VIII.7; **T-7.IX**; **T-18.VI.1**; T-20.III.10; T-26.VII.15
W-pI.187.10

love
T-5.In.2; T-12.VIII.7; T-16.V.3-8; T-19.IV-A.10; T-21.VI.9-10
W-pI.127.1-3

mind
T-5.VII.2; T-14.III.8-9

miracle
T-5.II.1

Self
T-18.VIII.6-7
W-pI.93.9; **W-pI.95.1-2,10-15**; W-pI.96; W-pI.97.1-2; W-pI.137.3; W-pI.rV.In.4; W-pII.253.2

Sonship
T-2.VII.6; **T-5.IV.1-7**; T-6.V-C.8; T-8.IX.7-9; T-9.VI.4-5; T-10.IV.3; T-11.III.7-8; T-13.VI.8; **T-16.IV.8-13**; **T-17.III.7**; **T-18.I.2,9-13**; T-24.V.9

Sonship (continued)
W-pI.57.5; W-pI.139.10-12; W-pI.160.8-10; W-pI.195.5-6; W-pII.262; **W-pII.11.1-4**; W-pII.14.1,4; W-pII.354
M-12.1-2
S-1.II.5-6; S-3.III.4-5

Thoughts
T-6.II.8; **T-30.III.2-11**; T-31.IV.9-11

Trinity
T-3.II.5; T-3.IV.1; **T-8.IV.8**; T-13.VIII.3-6; **T-25.I.4-7**

truth
T-14.VII.1

pain

(see: *suffering*)

peace

the goal of the Course; the condition for attaining knowledge and returning home; obscured by four obstacles—our attraction to attack (guilt), pain, death, and the fear of God—which are overcome by teaching and learning forgiveness.

A Course in Miracles
T-8.I.1; T-24.In.1

Atonement
T-5.VII.6; T-9.VII.2; T-13.IX.7; T-14.III.12; T-20.IV.8

attack
T-11.VI.7; T-19.IV-A.1-9; T-25.IX.6-7
W-pII.261.1

body
T-1.VII.1; T-2.I.5; T-19.IV-B.1-4

Christ
T-12.VI.5; T-24.VI.13
W-pI.182.5-12; W-pII.305

death
T-19.IV-C.1; T-27.VII.10

Easter
T-20.I.1

eternity
T-5.III.8-10; T-5.VI.2; T-7.I.5

extension
T-7.VI.12; T-7.IX.4-7; T-12.III.10; T-12.VII.10-11; T-19.IV.1-3; T-25.IV.4
W-pI.34.1; **W-pII.245.1**; W-pII.360

forgiveness
T-1.VI.1; T-24.V.3; T-29.VI.1
W-pI.63; W-pI.68.3; W-pI.121.1; **W-pI.122.1-11**; W-pII.352; W-pII.359
M-20.3
C-3.2-3

God/Heaven
T-7.VII.6; T-8.IV.1; T-10.III.10-11; T-10.IV.4-6; T-11.III.1,7; T-11.IV.3-8; T-13.VI.9; **T-13.XI**; T-15.IV.2-4; T-19.IV-D.1-5
W-pI.50.3; W-pI.104; W-pI.105; W-pI.109; W-pI.170.9-13; W-pII.221; W-pII.255

holy instant
T-18.VI.14

holy relationship
T-18.I.13; T-19.IV-D.19; T-22.VI.6-9; T-24.VI.1,7; T-26.VII.19; T-29.V.3-8

idols
T-29.VII.1-2,6; T-29.VIII.5-6

Jesus
T-8.V.4-5; T-10.III.6; T-12.II.7;
T-15.VI.7; T-15.XI.7-8;
T-31.VIII.7
W-pII.225.2
C-5.6

judgment
T-3.VI.2-3; T-21.VIII.2

obstacles
T-19.IV
W-pI.170.9; W-pI.193.10-12;
W-pI.195.8; W-pI.196.12

peace of God
T-In.2; T-2.II.1; T-7.VII.10;
T-13.VII.8-9,13-15
W-pI.185; **W-pI.188**; W-pI.200;
W-pI.205; W-pI.220; W-pII.230;
W-pII.267; W-pII.273; W-pII.346
M-20

salvation
T-12.III.5; T-20.VIII.3
W-pI.70.1-2

special relationships
T-13.III.10-12; T-13.X.3-5,9-11;
T-16.IV.6; T-24.II.2-3; T-24.IV.5;
T-24.V.2

teaching
T-6.III.4; T-6.V-B.1-7;
T-6.V-C.5-6; **T-14.V.6-9**
M-4.II.2

truth
T-14.XI.5-6,12-15; T-17.VI.5-7;
T-17.VIII.2-6; T-19.I.1

war
T-5.II.7; T-7.III.3; T-8.I.3;
T-23.I; T-23.III.4-6; T-24.I.1-2;
T-25.III.6; T-27.V.3; T-29.II.3
W-pII.2.2
M-11.4; M-14.5; M-20.3-4

perception

level I: the post-separation, dualistic world of form and differences, mutually exclusive of the non-dualistic world of knowledge; this world arises from our belief in separation and has no reality outside of this thought.

level II: comes from projection: what we see inwardly determines what we see outside ourselves; crucial to perception, therefore, is our *interpretation* of "reality," rather than what seems to be objectively real.

w-m: perception of sin and guilt reinforces the belief in the reality of the separation.

r-m: perception of opportunities to forgive serves to undo the belief in the reality of the separation.

(Note—since perception and knowledge are often discussed together, "knowledge" is not cross-referenced below.)

see: *true perception*

---

body
T-3.IV.6

change
T-3.III.1-6; T-20.III.1-3;
T-26.VII.3

consciousness
T-3.IV.2
C-1.7

decision
T-11.V.18; T-12.VII.5-8;
T-21.V.1; **T-25.I.3**; **T-25.III**
W-pI.130

dream
T-13.VII.9; T-18.II.5

forgiveness
W-pI.198.2; W-pII.7.1;
W-pII.336.1
C-3.2-4

God
W-pI.43.1-2; W-pI.193.2

Holy Spirit
T-5.I.5-7; T-6.II.7-11; T-12.VI.7;
T-13.VIII.2; T-21.III.6
W-pI.43.1-2; W-pII.3.4
C-6.3-4

interpretation
T-3.III.2; T-3.IV.6; T-3.V.5;
T-11.VI.2-3

judgment
T-3.V.7-8; T-3.VI.1-3
W-pII.312.1
M-8.1-4

law
T-6.II.9; T-25.III.1-2; T-31.V.12
W-pI.189.5

learning
M-4.I.1

mind
T-3.IV.4-5; T-21.V.1,8

miracle
T-3.III.2-5
W-pII.13.1-3; W-pII.345.1

part–whole
T-8.VIII.1; T-13.VIII.2-5

prayer
T-3.V.10

projection
T-12.III.7-9; T-13.V.3; **T-21.In.1**;
T-24.VII.8-9
W-pI.51.3; W-pII.304.1

real world
T-11.VII; T-12.VIII.8;
T-18.IX.9-14
W-pII.8

specific
T-4.II.1

thoughts
W-pI.15.1; W-pI.17.1

world
T-14.I.2;
W-pI.184.1-3; W-pII.3
C-4.3-4

our guilt and fear cannot be undone without dealing with them through the opportunities for forgiveness used by the Holy Spirit; this honest looking within our minds with the Holy Spirit or Jesus—a process the ego counsels *against*—is what leads to the periods of discomfort and anxiety we almost inevitably feel in the process of shifting from wrong- to right-mindedness.

---

darkness–light
T-11.In.3; T-11.IV.4;
T-18.III.2-3; T-20.III.9

development of trust
M-4.I.3-8

ego
T-4.I.3; T-4.II.5; **T-9.VII.3-4**;
T-9.VIII.2-4

fear/terror
T-2.VII.4; T-13.III.1-6;
T-18.IX.3; T-19.IV-D.6-7;
T-20.VI.7
W-pI.196.10-11
S-1.III.4

Holy Spirit
T-6.V-A.5-6; T-17.VIII.4;
T-31.V.8-9

illusions
T-1.V.6
C-Ep.1

learning
W-pI.14.3; W-pI.rI.In.4

perception–vision
T-2.III.3; T-2.V.7; T-6.V-A.5-6
W-pI.9.2

special relationships
T-16.VI.7-8; **T-17.V.2-6**;
T-20.VI.12; T-20.VII.1-3;
T-21.III.2; T-22.IV.1-2;
T-24.II.14; T-31.V.16

belongs to the world of perception, as popularly understood, for it asks God for something we believe we need; our only real prayer, on the other hand, is for forgiveness, as this restores to our awareness that we already have what we need; as used in the Course itself, does not include the experiences of communion with God that come during periods of quietness or meditation; compared to a ladder in "The Song of Prayer," emphasizing both the process of forgiveness as well as the communion between God and Christ, the Song that is the very end of the ladder.

Bible
T-9.II.3

forgiveness
T-3.V.6
S-1.III; **S-1.IV**; S-2.In; S-2.III.6; S-3.IV.4

Holy Spirit
T-9.II
M-29.2,6

humility
S-1.V

joining
W-pII.264.2
P-2.VII.2

justice
M-19.5

love
S-1.In.1

miracle
T-1.I.11; T-3.V.6

Name of God
W-pI.183.10; W-pII.In.10

perception
T-3.V.10

process
S-1.I; S-1.II

song
S-1.In.1,3; S-2.I.8

words
M-21

process

A Course in Miracles emphasizes that within the dream of separation forgiveness occurs over time, and is therefore a process of growth; our fear of God's Love is so great that we cling to our specialness as protection, and thus we must learn gently and patiently that the ego's guilt and attack reinforce pain, while the Holy Spirit's forgiveness leads to joy.

(Note—since the workbook as a whole is concerned with the *process* of learning the Course's curriculum, only the more important references have been included below.)

see: *periods of unsettling*

---

journey
T-12.IV.4-5; T-13.VII.12-17;
T-18.VIII.13;
T-19.IV-D.8-11,16-19;
T-20.I.2-3; T-29.II.1
M-19.2
C-Ep

ladder
T-18.V.1-2; T-28.II.12; T-28.III.1

Last Judgment
T-2.VIII.3-4

miracle
T-1.II.6
W-pI.97.3

prayer
S-1.In.2-3; S-1.II.1,**7-8**;
S-1.V.3-4; S-3.In

psychotherapy
P-3.II.8

reawakening
T-5.I.2; T-11.IV.4

teacher of God
M-In.4-5; M-4; **M-9**; M-17.8;
M-24.4-6

teaching/learning
T-4.I.1; T-4.II.4-5; T-4.VI.2-6;
T-11.VIII.3; **T-31.I.1-6**;
T-31.III.1
W-pI.28.1; W-pI.157.1-3;
W-pI.162.1; W-pI.In.181-200
M-3; M-16.1-3

time/holy instant
T-2.VII.5-7; T-15.I.9-15;
T-15.II.5-6; T-15.IV.1-2;
T-16.VII.6-7; T-18.IV.1-2;
T-20.IV.8; T-20.V.5-6; T-26.V.11;
T-26.VIII; T-27.V.1-6
W-pI.158.3-6
M-1

truth
T-16.IV.12; T-19.I.15;
T-31.V.16-17
W-pI.155; **W-pII.284**

undoing
T-5.VII.6; **T-6.V-A.5-6**; **T-6.V-B**;
T-6.V-C

vision
W-pI.124.9-11

world
W-pI.132.6-7

projection

the fundamental law of mind: projection makes perception—what we see inwardly determines what we see outside our minds.

w-m: reinforces guilt by displacing it onto someone else, attacking it there and denying its presence in ourselves; an attempt to shift responsibility for separation from ourselves to others.

r-m: the principle of extension, undoing guilt by allowing the forgiveness of the Holy Spirit to be extended (projected) through us.

---

attack
T-6.In.1; T-6.I.3; T-6.II.2-3;
T-13.V.3-4
W-pI.22.1-2; W-pI.26.1-2;
W-pI.170.4-10; W-pI.196.1-10

authority problem
T-3.VI.8

body
T-18.VI.2-6; T-19.IV-B.15

cause–effect
T-28.II.7
W-pI.17.1; W-pI.32.1

crucifixion
T-6.I.12-16

dream
T-27.VII; **T-27.VIII**

ego
T-6.II.3-4,12; T-7.VII.8-9;
T-7.VIII.1-5
W-pI.71.2

extension/law of mind
T-2.I.1; T-6.II.9; T-7.II.2-3;
T-7.VIII.1; T-11.In.3; T-12.VII.7

fear
T-5.V.3; T-18.II.4
W-pI.13.3; W-pI.130.3;
W-pI.161.8
P-2.VII.7

forgiveness
T-25.V.4-6
W-pII.1.2
P-2.VI.6
S-2.I.4-5

God
W-pI.68.1-2; W-pI.72.1-5

guilt
T-13.In.1; **T-13.II.1-5**;
T-13.IX.6-8; **T-13.X.1-3**
W-pI.70.1
M-17.5-7
S-1.III.1,3-4

perception
T-13.V.3; **T-21.In.1**
W-pI.2.1; W-pI.8.1; W-pI.130.1;
W-pII.325

sacrifice
T-3.I.1-6; T-25.VIII.4; T-26.X.3

separation
T-6.II.1-3

sin
T-31.III.1-2; T-31.V.5-6

special relationships
T-16.IV.3-6; T-16.V.1-14;
T-17.III.1-3; T-22.III.8-9

world
T-12.III.6-10; T-13.IX.3;
T-18.I.4-6; T-20.VIII.9; T-21.In;
T-27.VII.3-6; **T-27.VIII.7-8**
W-pI.11.1; W-pI.12.1; W-pI.35.2;
W-pI.132.4-11
P-1.3-4

questions

the Course presents our basic decision to choose between God and the ego in the form of different questions.

---

communication
T-15.IV.8

dream
W-pI.185.8

forgiveness
T-20.VII.9; T-25.III.7; T-29.VI.1
W-pI.134.9,15
S-2.III.5

God–ego
T-5.V.6; T-11.In.1-2; **T-11.II.7**; T-15.III.5
W-pI.156.8; W-pI.160.7-8

Holy Spirit
C-2.9

identity
W-pI.139.1

problem–answer
T-11.VIII.4

purpose
T-4.V.6; **T-17.VI.2**; T-20.VIII.8; T-24.VII.4,6

real world
T-21.VII.5-6

sin–truth
T-21.VII.8-11

Will of God
T-8.VI.8

world
T-20.III.4

real world

the state of mind in which, through total forgiveness, the world of perception is released from the projections of guilt we had placed upon it: thus, it is the mind that has changed, not the world, and we see through the vision of Christ which blesses rather than condemns; the Holy Spirit's happy dream; the end of the Atonement, undoing our thoughts of separation and allowing God to take the last step.

---

bridge
T-16.VI.6-7; T-26.V.11

consciousness
C-1.7

death
M-27.5
S-3.II.3-4

decision
T-26.III.2-6
W-pI.129.5-9

face of Christ
C-3.4-8

forgiveness
T-17.II; **T-18.IX.9-14**; T-23.In.6;
T-30.V.1-6; T-30.VI.1-3
W-pII.249.1; W-pII.289; **W-pII.8**
S-3.IV.2

God
T-2.VII.5; T-12.III.8-10;
T-12.VIII.8

happy dream
T-13.VII.9; T-29.IX.7
W-pII.2.4

holy relationship
T-17.V.2; T-30.V.7

Holy Spirit
T-11.VII.4; T-12.VI.3-5;
T-17.II.8; T-21.III.4;
T-25.III.5-8; T-25.VII.5

Jesus
T-12.VII.11

judgment
T-20.III.5-6
W-pII.312.2

last step
T-11.VIII.15
W-pII.8.5

light
T-18.IX.9
W-pI.75; **W-pI.189.1-3**

perception–knowledge
T-11.VII; T-11.VIII.1;
T-18.IX.9-11

prayer
S-1.II.7; S-1.V.4; S-2.II.8

sickness
T-11.VIII.10

sin
T-21.VII.11
W-pI.181.9

vision
T-12.VI.4-5; T-13.VII.1-9
W-pI.159.3-10; W-pII.290

reason

right-mindedness; thinking in accordance with the Holy Spirit, choosing to follow His guidance and learn His lessons of forgiveness, seeing sinlessness rather than sin, and choosing vision instead of judgment.

(Note—not to be confused with rationalism.)

---

defenselessness
T-22.V.1

ego
T-21.IV.4-6; T-22.III.1-5

forgiveness
T-27.II.3

guilt
T-13.X.6-10

holy instant
T-21.VI.7-9; T-21.VIII.5

holy relationship
T-22.III.9

Holy Spirit
T-21.IV.4-6; T-21.V.5-9;
T-21.VI.8
M-7.2

madness
T-21.VI.3-8

perception–knowledge
T-21.V.7-10

real world
T-17.II.5

separation
T-21.V.4

sin–error
T-21.VI.1-2; T-22.III.2-9

truth–falsity
T-22.II.4-7

world
T-22.I.2-3

resurrection

the awakening from the dream of death; the total change in mind that transcends the ego and its perceptions of the world, the body, and death, allowing us to identify completely with our true Self; also refers to the resurrection of Jesus.

(Note—since crucifixion and resurrection are often discussed together, "crucifixion" is not cross-referenced below.)

Atonement
T-3.I.1; T-14.V.10

Christ–ego
T-11.VI.1

death
T-26.V.10
M-28.1-2

decision
T-14.III.4

Easter
T-19.IV-D.17; T-20.II.8-10
W-pI.135.25

face of Christ/happy dream
M-28

forgiveness
T-19.IV-C.10; **T-20.I.1-2**

healing
T-26.IX.8; T-27.VI.8

Holy Spirit
T-21.II.1
W-pI.151.11-12

Jesus
T-3.V.1; T-4.In.3; **T-11.VI.4-7**;
T-14.V.10; T-19.IV-D.17-18
W-pI.rV.In.7
C-5.3-6

joy
T-11.VI.6

reawakening
T-6.I.7,10,12

sharing
T-6.I.12; **T-19.IV-D.17**

truth
T-3.I.7

revelation

the direct communication from God to His Son which reflects the original form of communication present in our creation; it proceeds from God to His Son, but is not reciprocal; brief return to this state is possible in this world.

---

communication
T-1.II.1; **T-4.VII.7**

ego
T-4.III.3

fear
T-1.I.28; T-1.II.1; T-1.VII.5

grace
W-pI.169.14

healing
T-5.I.1

Jesus/Holy Spirit
T-1.II.5

knowledge
T-3.III.4-5

miracle
T-1.I.28,46,48; **T-1.II.1-3**

time
T-1.I.48; T-2.V.10
W-pI.158.2-5,11; W-pI.169.4

unity
W-pI.158.2; **W-pI.169.4-10**

right-mindedness

the part of our separated minds that contains the Holy Spirit—the Voice of forgiveness and reason; we are repeatedly asked to choose it instead of wrong-mindedness, to follow the Holy Spirit's guidance rather than the ego's, and thus return to the One-mindedness of Christ.

---

charity
T-2.V.9

denial
T-2.II.2

ego
T-4.I.8; T-6.IV.4

forgiveness
T-2.V.14-15
C-1.5-6

healing
T-2.V.4

holy instant
W-pII.227

Holy Spirit
T-5.I.3-6; T-9.I.10
W-pI.66.7
C-1.5

Jesus
T-3.IV.7; T-4.IV.11; T-5.I.3

Last Judgment
T-2.VIII.3,5

miracle
T-2.V.3,13-14; T-3.II.3; T-21.V.3

perception–knowledge
T-3.IV.4

reason
T-21.V.9

salvation
T-4.II.10

spirit
T-5.I.1
W-pI.96.4

vigilance
T-4.III.10

sacrifice

a central belief in the ego's thought system: someone must lose if another is to gain; the principle of giving up in order to receive (giving to get); e.g., in order to receive God's Love we must pay a price, usually in the form of suffering to expiate our guilt (sin); in order to receive another's love, we must pay for it through the special love bargain; the reversal of the principle of salvation or justice: no one loses and everyone gains.

Atonement
T-3.I

attack
T-15.X.5; T-26.I.1

body
T-19.IV-B.2-3; T-21.III.8-12;
T-26.I; T-29.II.9-10;
T-29.VII.4-5; T-31.III.5

Christ
T-15.XI.2

ego
T-7.X.3-5
W-pII.319.1

fear
T-3.I.4; T-29.I.7
W-pII.323

giving
T-4.II.6
W-pI.105.1-5; **W-pI.187.1-8**
M-6.3

God
T-3.I.1-4; T-15.X.2-9;
T-25.VII.11-13; T-31.III.7
W-pI.100.7; W-pI.185.13;
W-pII.322; W-pII.343

guilt
T-15.X.5; T-15.XI.4

Holy Spirit
T-21.III.9-12; T-25.IX.3-7;
T-26.II.2
W-pI.76.9

Jesus
T-15.XI.3-8

judgment
T-30.VII.5-6

justice–injustice
T-25.VIII.3-6,13-14;
T-25.IX.4-10; T-26.X.3

laws of chaos
T-23.II.9-11

sacrifice (continued)

love
T-15.X.5-9; **T-15.XI.3-8**

miracle
W-pI.77.4

psychotherapy
P-3.I.1

real world
T-25.VII.5

salvation
T-23.III.3; **T-25.VII.12-13**;
T-26.VII.14

special relationships
T-15.VII.6-9; **T-16.V.7-12**

suffering
T-27.I.1-3
W-pI.101.1-4; W-pI.187.6-8

teacher of God
T-21.I.3-5
W-pI.155.4-8
M-4.I-A.3-7; **M-13**

truth
W-pI.92.5

vision
W-pI.27.2; W-pI.37.1-2;
W-pI.192.6

salvation

the Atonement, or undoing of the separation; we are "saved" from our *belief* in the reality of sin and guilt through the change of mind that forgiveness and the miracle bring about.

---

cause–effect
T-27.VIII.10-12; T-28.II.8-9

compromise
T-23.III.3-4

face of Christ
C-3.4

forgiveness
T-30.IV.7-8
W-pI.46.2; W-pI.62.1; **W-pI.99**; W-pI.122.5-9; W-pI.186.14; W-pII.297.1
M-14.3

function
W-pI.99; W-pI.100; W-pI.169.9-11; W-pI.186; W-pII.317

God
T-13.In.3; T-15.IV.2-4
W-pI.71

guilt
T-14.III.10-15
W-pI.70

happy dream
T-17.II.7; T-30.IV.7-8
W-pII.2

healing
W-pI.137.1
P-2.IV.11

holiness
T-22.III.8
W-pI.37.3; W-pI.39.1-4

holy relationship
T-4.VI.8; T-8.III.4; T-19.IV-B.7
P-3.III.7

Holy Spirit
T-14.III.13-14
W-pI.96.7-8; W-pI.169.9; W-pI.198.5

illusions
T-16.V.14
W-pI.70.7-10

justice
T-25.IX.10
M-19.4-5

mind
T-12.III.5,10
W-pI.132.1-10; W-pI.152.1-3

miracle
T-30.VIII.2
W-pI.97.3

perception
T-26.III.5
W-pI.43.2

real world
T-11.VII.4; T-17.II.8; T-26.III.3-5

reason
T-22.III.3

right-mindedness
T-4.II.10

rock of salvation
T-25.VII.12

sacrifice
T-26.VIII.2-3
W-pII.343

simplicity
T-15.X.9; T-31.I.1-2
W-pI.77.1; W-pI.90.1

sin
W-pI.101.1-4

teacher of God
M-1.1-3; M-3.1-3

thoughts
W-pI.14.3; W-pI.16.3; W-pI.23.4

vision
T-20.VII.9; T-31.VI.2-3

world
T-25.VI.4-7; T-30.II.5; T-31.V.17

scarcity principle

an aspect of guilt; the belief that we are empty and incomplete, lacking what we need; this leads to our seeking idols or special relationships to fill the scarcity we experience within ourselves; inevitably projected into feelings of deprivation, wherein we believe others are depriving us of the peace which in reality *we* have taken from ourselves; in contrast to God's principle of abundance.

---

attack
T-7.VII.7-8

body
T-15.XI.5; **T-29.VII.2-4**

decision
T-4.IV.3

ego
T-4.II.6; T-12.III.6

God
T-28.VII.1
W-pI.165.6;

Holy Spirit
T-5.IV.7

love
T-15.VI.5

miracle
T-1.I.34

need
M-14.1

perception
T-1.I.41; T-3.V.6-10

prayer
S-1.II.1-3

projection
T-2.I.1; T-2.V.14

psychotherapy
P-3.II.4

separation
T-1.VI.1-2; T-3.V.2

sin
T-5.V.4

special relationships/idols
T-16.V.9; T-22.In.2;
T-29.VII.4-10; T-30.III.3
P-3.III.5

truth–error
T-1.IV.2-3

Second Coming

the healing of the mind of the Sonship; the collective return to awareness of our reality as the one Son of God, which we had at our creation, the First Coming; precedes the Last Judgment, after which this world of illusion ends.

---

awareness of reality
T-9.IV.9-10

ego
T-4.IV.10

forgiveness
W-pII.9

Jesus
T-4.IV.10

Last Judgment
T-9.IV.9
W-pII.9.3; W-pII.10.1

Self

our true Identity as Son of God; synonymous with Christ, the Second Person of the Trinity, and contrasted with the ego self we made as a substitute for God's creation; used rarely to refer to the Self of God.

---

attack
T-24.I.3
W-pI.68.1-2; W-pI.181.1

body
W-pII.5.1

Christ/Son
T-5.III.8; **T-15.V.10**; T-31.VIII.3
W-pI.92.9-10; W-pI.94.3;
W-pI.95.12-13; W-pI.97.2;
W-pI.110.9-11; W-pII.252;
W-pII.253.2; **W-pII.6**;
W-pII.303.2

ego/self
T-4.II.4; T-18.VIII.6-11;
T-31.V.15
W-pI.93.9; **W-pI.96.1-7**

fear
W-pI.160

forgiveness
T-24.V.7

God
T-15.V.11
W-pI.183.5; **W-pII.253**

healing
W-pI.137.3,12-14

Holy Spirit
W-pI.96.7-11; W-pI.121.6;
W-Ep.3-5

humility
S-1.V.2

illusions
T-1.VII.1; T-28.V.3-4

Jesus
W-pI.rV.In.9

love
W-pI.67; W-pI.rV.In.4;
W-pII.252.1; W-pII.5.5

salvation
T-11.IV.1
W-pI.77.1; W-pI.132.1,10

sinlessness
W-pI.181.9

unity
W-pI.95; W-pI.187.10

world
W-pI.127.6; W-pI.128.1-3;
W-pII.252; W-pII.253

most often used to denote attempts by the ego to understand ideas from the world of knowledge that are beyond our comprehension; occasionally used for attempts to understand the ego thought system.

---

ego
T-4.II.1; T-7.VI.11
W-pI.51.3
C-In.3

forgiveness
S-2.III.2

God/Heaven
T-11.III.3; T-14.IV.8;
T-24.VII.6-7; T-30.V.4
M-23.6
S-1.II.8

identity
W-pI.139.8; W-pII.14.2

knowledge
T-18.IX.11

oneness
T-26.III.1
W-pI.169.10-11

salvation
T-30.IV.6; T-31.VI.3
M-14.3; M-26.4

Teacher of teachers
M-26.2

separation

the belief in sin that affirms an identity separate from our Creator; seemed to happen once, and the thought system which arose from that idea is represented by the ego; results in a world of perception and form, of pain, suffering, and death, real in time, but unknown in eternity.

Atonement
T-2.II.4; T-2.III.2; T-6.II.10;
T-17.III.5

attack
T-13.III.2; T-22.VI.11-13

body
T-18.VI.3; **T-19.I.3-7**;
T-28.VII.3-4; T-29.I.4-5;
T-31.VI.2

decision
T-16.V.15

dissociation
T-6.II.1

ego
T-4.III.3-4; T-5.V.2; T-11.V.10-13
W-pII.12.1-2

fear
T-4.I.10
W-pI.130.4

guilt
T-13.In.2; **T-15.V.2**

Holy Spirit
T-5.I.5; T-17.III.5-6; T-17.IV.4

magic
M-17.5-6
S-3.III.1-3

mind/thought
T-3.VII.3-5; T-13.VIII.3;
T-22.II.9
W-pI.54.3

origin
T-2.I.1-3; T-3.VII.3-4;
T-28.II.8-9

perception
T-3.IV.1-3; T-3.V.9-10
W-pI.184.2-3

projection
T-6.II.1-3; T-28.II.8

salvation
W-pI.100.1; W-pII.2.1

sickness
T-26.VII.2; **T-28.III.2-5**
W-pI.137.1-4
M-22.6

sin
T-21.VI.2-6

world
T-12.III.9
W-pI.132.12-13

sickness

a conflict in the mind (guilt) displaced onto the body; the ego's attempt to defend itself against truth (spirit) by focusing attention on the body; a sick body is the *effect* of the sick or split mind that is its *cause*, representing the ego's desire to make others guilty by sacrificing oneself, projecting responsibility for the attack onto them.

see: *suffering*

Atonement
W-pI.140.4
M-22.3

attack
T-8.VIII.3-5; T-28.VI.4-5

body
T-8.VIII.3-9; T-29.II.7-10
W-pI.136.8-9,16-20

cause–effect
T-28.II.2-3,11-12; T-28.III.2-8
S-3.I

decision
W-pI.136
M-5; M-22.4

God
T-10.III; T-10.IV; T-11.I.10;
T-28.V.5

guilt
T-27.I.4-8
W-pI.140.4
M-5.II.3-4
P-2.VI.4-5

healing
T-19.I.4-6; T-28.IV.10
W-pI.70.3-5; W-pI.137;
W-pI.140.1-10

love
T-12.II.1-2

magic
T-2.IV.4; T-5.V.5

mind
T-2.IV.2-4; **T-8.IX.1-8**;
T-28.II.11-12; T-28.III.2
M-5.II-III;
P-2.IV

miracle
T-1.I.23-24; T-28.II.10-12;
T-30.VI.7-8

separation
T-8.VII.11; T-11.II.1;
T-28.III.2-5; T-28.IV; T-28.V.1-4
W-pI.137.1-4
M-22.6
S-3.III.4

sin
T-26.VII.2
W-pII.356

sin

the belief in the reality of our separation from God, seen by the ego as an act incapable of correction because it represents our attack on our Creator, Who would therefore never forgive us; leads to guilt, which demands punishment; equivalent to separation, and the central concept in the ego's thought system, from which all others logically follow; to the Holy Spirit, an error in our thinking to be corrected and therefore forgiven and healed.

Atonement
T-18.VII.1,4

attack
T-25.V.1

body
T-20.VI.11; T-20.VII.4-9;
T-27.VI.2-6; **T-31.III.3-5**

death
T-19.II.3; T-19.IV-A.17;
T-19.IV-C.2-4; T-25.VII.1-2;
T-25.VIII.3
W-pI.101.2-4

defenses
T-5.VII.5; T-20.III.1; T-22.V.2

error
T-19.II; **T-19.III.1-9**;
T-21.VI.1-2,6; **T-22.III.2-8**;
T-25.IX.1
M-18.3

fear
T-2.I.4; **T-21.IV.1-4**; T-23.In.1-3;
T-26.VIII.5
W-pII.259

forgiveness
T-25.III.5-9
W-pI.121.3-6; **W-pI.134.2-16**;
W-pII.1.1
C-5.3-4

forgiveness-to-destroy
S-2.I.2; **S-2.II.2-3**

guilt
T-5.V.4; T-19.III.1-7
M-17.5-7
C-4.5

illusion
T-17.I.1; T-26.VII.3
W-pI.101; W-pI.134.3-6;
W-pII.4
C-4.1-3

projection
T-26.VII.12; T-31.III.1-2;
T-31.V.5-6

punishment
T-19.II.1; T-19.III.2-4; T-23.II.4

sacrifice
T-21.III.9-12; T-25.VIII.3-4,11

separation
T-21.VI.2-6; T-30.III.3

sickness
T-26.VII.2; T-27.I.4-10
W-pII.356

special relationships
T-21.III.1-8; T-22.In.1-2;
T-22.III.8-9; **T-24.II.3-5**;
T-24.III.2; T-24.IV.4-5; T-24.V.4

suffering
T-27.VI.6-8

world
T-20.VIII.7-10; T-25.VII.1-11
W-pI.181.8-9
M-14.1-3

sleep

usually denotes the state of separation from God, in Whom we are awake as Christ; our experiences within the ego thought system constitute our dreams of specialness, in which we believe we have accomplished the impossible of separating from our Creator; less frequently used in the popular sense of physical sleep, where it is emphasized that there is no difference between our sleeping dreams at night and our "waking" ones during the day.

see: *dreams*

Adam
T-2.I.3-4

death
T-11.I.9; T-27.VII.9-10
W-pI.191.10; W-pII.282.1

dreams
T-10.I.2-4; T-29.VII.9

ego
T-13.XI.1
W-pI.68.2

forgiveness
W-pII.256.1

God
T-16.VII.12
W-pI.168.1-3

guilt
T-14.IV.6

happy dreams
T-27.VII.11-16
W-pI.140.2-3

Holy Spirit
T-5.II.10; T-12.VI.4-5;
T-13.XI.9-10

mind
T-2.VI.9
W-pI.167.6-12

miracle
T-28.II.4-6; T-29.IV.1-2

nightmares
T-6.IV.6; T-11.VI.8;
T-13.VI.12-13

physical
T-8.IX.3-4; T-10.I.2; T-15.XI.1

real world
W-pII.8.4

sickness
T-8.IX.3

sleeping dreams
T-13.V.8; T-18.II.1-5,9

special relationships
T-18.II.6-9; T-24.III.7

Son of God

knowledge: the Second Person of the Trinity; the Christ Who is our true Self.

perception: our identity as separated Sons, or the Son of God as ego with a wrong and right mind; the biblical phrase "son of man" is used rarely to denote the Son as separated.

Cause–Effect
T-21.II.10; T-28.I.14

Christ/Self
T-11.IV.6-7; **T-31.VIII.3-5**
W-pI.93.9; W-pI.94.3;
W-pI.110.6-11; **W-pII.6**;
W-pII.354
M-12.1-2
C-1.1

creation
T-2.I.1-2; T-6.I.18; T-28.VI.6
W-pI.rIV.In.2; **W-pII.11.2-4**

crucifixion
T-11.VI.5-8

forgiveness
T-30.VI.7-10
W-pI.78.7

God
T-1.V.3-4; T-11.I.9-11;
T-14.VIII.1-3; T-15.VIII.2-4;
T-20.V.8; T-20.VI.1
W-pII.10.4-5
S-3.IV.6

grace
T-7.XI.2

guiltlessness
T-13.I; T-13.II.9; T-14.IV.7-10;
T-31.I.8-10
M-1.3

Heaven
T-26.I.7

holy relationship
T-18.I.11; T-20.V.1; T-20.VI.10

Identity
W-pI.191; W-pII.252; **W-pII.14**
S-1.II.2

immortality
T-11.I.9; T-29.VI.2

Jesus
T-1.II.4; T-5.IV.5

light
W-pI.61.1

Name
T-8.IX.7
W-pI.78.7; W-pI.169.9

son of man
T-6.I.15; T-13.II.9; T-24.VII.11;
T-25.In.2
M-12.1-2

Sonship
T-2.VII.6; T-11.I.1; T-11.IV.1

Trinity
T-3.II.5

unity
T-5.IV.2; T-8.V.3; T-11.VIII.11
W-pI.95.2-3; W-pI.139.10

symbol of the love and gratitude that unites God and His Sons, who once believed they were separate from their Creator; in "The Song of Prayer," used as a symbol of the soundless communion between God and Christ.

---

ancient
T-21.I.6-9
W-pI.161.10

Christ
T-24.V.7
W-pI.164.1-2

Easter
T-20.II.8

form–content
S-1.I.2-3

freedom
T-13.XI.2; T-17.V.10; T-21.IV.7; T-26.I.6

gratitude
T-13.VI.8-9; **T-26.IV.3-5**; T-31.VIII.11
M-4.V

healing
S-3.IV.1

holy relationship
T-17.V.1; T-26.V.2

Holy Spirit
W-pI.198.6

love
T-24.II.4; T-26.I.4; T-26.IV.6; T-31.I.10
S-3.IV.8

praise
T-13.X.14; T-22.V.4

prayer
S-1.In.1,3; S-2.I.8

resurrection
M-28.4

salvation
T-31.VIII.10

special relationships
T-24.II.4

time
T-26.V.5; T-29.IX.8
C-Ep.4

relationships onto which we project guilt, substituting them for love and our true relationship with God; the defenses that reinforce belief in the scarcity principle while appearing to be undoing it—doing what they would defend against—for special relationships attempt to fill up the perceived lack in ourselves by taking from others who are inevitably seen as separate, thereby reinforcing a guilt that ultimately comes from our believed separation from God: the thought of attack that is the original source of our sense of lack; all relationships in this world begin as special since they begin with the perception of separation and differences, which must then be corrected by the Holy Spirit through forgiveness, making the relationship holy; specialness has two forms: special hate justifies the projection of guilt by attack; special love conceals the attack within the illusion of love, where we believe our special needs are met by special people with special attributes, for which we love them: in this sense, special love is roughly equivalent to dependency, which breeds contempt or hatred.

---

attack
T-15.VII.1-10; **T-16.IV.1-11**;
T-24.IV; T-24.V.2-8

body
T-16.VI.4-5; T-17.III.2-5;
T-20.VI.2-11; T-24.IV.2;
T-24.VI.6-13

death
T-17.IV.9-13; T-24.V.4

dreams
T-18.II.5

ego
T-16.I.1; **T-17.IV.2-13**; T-20.III.2

fear
T-16.IV.7; T-24.I.8

forgiveness
T-24.II.7-9; **T-24.III**; T-25.III.5;
T-25.VI

forgiveness-to-destroy
S-2.II.6

God
T-1.V.3; T-15.VII.1; **T-16.V**;
T-24.III.6-8
S-1.III.6

guilt
T-13.X.2-4,11; T-15.V.2-5;
T-15.VI.1; T-15.VII.2-12;
T-16.IV.3-4; T-16.V.1-10;
T-16.VI.3-10

healing
T-27.II.7
S-3.IV.1

holy instant
T-15.V

holy relationship
T-17.V

Holy Spirit
T-15.V.4-10; T-15.VIII.2;
T-16.VI.12; T-17.IV.4; T-25.I.5-6;
T-25.VI.4-7

past
T-16.VII.1-4; **T-17.III**
S-1.IV.3

psychotherapy
P-3.II.9-10

sacrifice
T-15.VII.6-9; T-16.V.7-11

scarcity
T-22.In.2; T-29.VII.2-9;
T-30.III.3
P-3.III.5

separation
T-15.V.2-3; T-29.I.3-4

sin
T-22.In.1-2; T-22.III.8-9;
T-24.II; T-24.III.2; T-24.IV.4-5

substitution
T-15.V.6-7; T-18.I.1-7; **T-24.I**

spirit

the nature of our true reality which, being of God, is changeless and eternal; contrasted with the body, the embodiment of the ego, which changes and dies; the Thought in God's Mind which is the unified Christ.

---

body
T-2.V.6; T-19.IV-D.5; **T-31.VI**
W-pI.96.3-4

communication
T-1.V.1; T-4.VII.3

creating
T-1.V.5; T-3.IV.5; T-4.III.1;
T-5.I.1; **T-7.IX.1-4**

ego
T-4.In; **T-4.I.2-13**; T-4.II.8-9;
T-4.VI.4-5

God
T-3.V.7,9
C-1.1-4

grace
T-1.III.5

Holy Spirit
T-5.III.7; T-7.IX.1

immortality
T-4.II.11

mind
T-1.IV.2; T-1.V.5; **T-3.IV.5-6**
W-pI.96.4-10; W-pII.9.3;
W-pII.330.1
C-1.1-4

miracle
T-1.I.12,20,29,30,34

Self
W-pI.96.4-10; **W-pI.97**

soul
C-1.3

without enumerating them as such, the Course describes four levels of splits, which are mirrored in the world by our special relationships: 1) the original thought of separation when we believed we had *split* ourselves off from God, leading to the belief in two minds: the Mind of Christ and the split mind; 2) the further *split* of the split mind into the wrong and right minds: the homes of the ego and the Holy Spirit; 3) the *splitting* off of the wrong from the right mind through the belief in the ego's thought system of sin, guilt, and fear; the Holy Spirit's Love now being buried beneath the ego's specialness, with God feared rather than accepted; 4) the final ontological *split* wherein the guilt in our minds is denied and projected out, making a separated world of attack and death, a world which appears to be split off from the mind that thought it.

see: *dissociation*

---

abstract–concrete
T-4.VII.1
W-pI.161.2

attack–guilt
T-7.VIII.4; **T-13.In.1**; **T-13.II.1-3**
W-pI.170.3-4;
W-pI.196.5-6,9-11
M-13.7

behavior
T-2.VI.5; T-12.I.2

body
T-8.VII.9-10; T-8.VIII.9;
T-18.VI.2-4; **T-18.VIII.2-3,5**;
T-19.I.6-7; T-29.VII.2-8

creations
T-10.I.1

ego
T-5.V.2-4

ego–Holy Spirit
T-3.VI.7; **T-5.II.5-8**; T-7.IV.5;
T-7.VI.8; **T-8.I.5-6**
W-pI.66.7; W-pI.71.5

fear
T-2.VI.5; T-9.I.1

God/Heaven
T-6.V.1; T-7.VI.12; T-9.I.4-6;
T-12.VIII.2; T-18.IX.1;
T-23.I.11-12
W-pI.68.1-2; W-pI.110.4;
W-pI.131.7-8

Holy Spirit
T-3.VII.4; T-12.I.6
W-pII.2.1-2

love
T-12.IV.1-3; **T-12.V.1-4**,7;
T-25.VIII.8

oneness/wholeness
T-4.IV.2; T-8.IV.5; T-10.IV.3; T-14.VIII.2; T-16.II.2-3; T-17.VI.6-7; T-25.I.7
W-pI.95.1-2; W-pI.195.5-6
M-19.3-4

perception
T-3.IV.2-3,5; T-6.II.9; T-11.V.13-15; **T-13.V.2-6**; T-22.III.4-5

projection
T-6.II.1-3,9; **T-12.III.6-10**; T-12.VII.6-7

Self
T-7.IX.4; T-18.VIII.6-7
W-pI.96.1-5; W-pI.97.1; W-pI.139.1-5

separation
T-1.VI.2; T-5.III.9; T-6.II.1
C-1.2

sickness
T-8.IX.8; T-10.III.4; T-28.V.1
W-pI.70.3-4; **W-pI.136.2,6-8**; W-pI.137.1-3

sin
T-19.III.6-8; T-26.VII.7

special–holy relationships
T-11.VIII.9-11; T-15.V.6-7; T-16.IV.1,3; T-17.III.3; T-18.I.1-3,12-13; T-24.III.2; T-25.II.11; **T-27.II.11-16**

world
T-12.III.6-10; **T-18.I.4-6**
W-pI.184.1-4

star

symbol of Christ, of the light and Presence of God that always shines in us, and which forgiveness reveals.

Christmas
T-15.XI.2

grace
W-pI.183.3

psychotherapy
P-2.VII.8

real world
C-Ep.5

teacher of God
W-pI.134.12

Thought of God
T-30.III.8-11

truth
T-31.VI.7

suffering

one of the basic ego witnesses to the reality of the body and the nonexistence of spirit, since the body appears to experience suffering or pain; to be in pain, therefore, is to deny God, while being aware of our true invulnerability as God's Son is to deny the reality of pain.

(Note—suffering and pain are used as virtual synonyms.)

see: *sickness*

---

attack
T-27.VII.12; T-28.VI.4;
T-31.V.15

body
T-13.In.2; T-18.VI.3
W-pI.76.5; W-pI.92.3

decision
W-pI.190
M-5.II.1-2

forgiveness
W-pI.193.5-8; W-pI.198.9

forgiveness-to-destroy
S-2.II.4-5

God
T-10.III.3; T-10.V.9; T-11.III.1;
T-13.III.12; T-13.VII.7
W-pI.190

guilt
T-13.IX.2; T-19.III.1;
T-19.IV-B.15; T-30.V.2

Holy Spirit
T-7.X.3,7; T-16.I.1;
T-27.VIII.10-12

illusions
T-4.VI.3; T-13.IV.6; T-22.II.1-3

judgment
M-10.6

pleasure–pain
T-19.IV-B.3,12-13

projection
T-27.I.2-4; **T-27.VII.1-12**

sacrifice
W-pI.187.6-8

sin
W-pI.101

special relationships
T-15.VII.9; T-16.V.1

at the instant we decide to join with another, a decision to join the Atonement, we become teachers of God; teaching the Holy Spirit's lesson of forgiveness, we learn it for ourselves, recognizing that our Teacher is the Holy Spirit Who teaches through us by our example of forgiveness and peace; also referred to as "miracle worker," "messenger," and "minister of God"; used as a synonym for students of *A Course in Miracles*.

A Course in Miracles
M-16.3-5; M-29.1

Atonement
T-2.V.5
M-22

body
W-pI.157.5-7; W-pI.199.7
M-12

characteristics
M-4

Christ
W-pI.166.13; W-pII.353

death
W-pI.163.8-9
M-27.4-7

defenselessness
W-pI.153.9-20
P-2.IV.9-10

forgiveness
P-2.II.1
S-2.In

giving
W-pI.154.5-13
M-7.1-3

God
S-3.IV.8-9

gratitude
W-pI.123.6-8; W-pI.195.7

healing
W-pI.137.10-15
M-5.III; M-6; M-7; M-22
S-3.IV.1-3

Holy Spirit
W-pII.267.1; **W-pII.296**
M-16.1,7; M-21.3-5; M-29.2-8
P-1.5; P-2.III.1

Jesus
T-4.VI.6; T-4.VII.8
W-pI.rV.In.8-9
C-5.6; C-6.5

judgment
M-9.2; M-10.2-6; M-15

light
T-18.III.7
W-pI.63; W-pI.81.1; W-pI.124.2; W-pI.188.3-10; W-pII.245
M-1.1-2

magic
M-16.8-11; **M-17**

miracle
T-2.V
W-pII.350

psychotherapy
P-2.I.4; **P-2.II.7-9**; P-2.V.2-3; P-2.VII.6; P-3.I; P-3.II

pupils
M-2; M-3

reincarnation
M-24.3-5

salvation
W-pI.98.3-8; W-pI.100; W-pI.187.3; **W-pII.14.3-5**

Teacher of teachers
M-26.2
C-5.6
P-2.III.3-4; P-2.V.3; P-3.II.7

Word of God
W-pI.125.1-4; W-pII.276.2

world
W-pI.155
M-In.4-5; M-14.2-5; M-26.1-3

what we believe we are is what we always teach, and what we teach reinforces our belief; thus teaching and learning occur all the time, are really identical, and therefore cannot be separated from each other; our choice of what we teach and learn comes from our identity as spirit or ego.

Atonement
T-14.V.2-11; T-14.XI.3
M-3.3

attack
T-6.III.3
M-17.1-3

body
T-8.VIII.9; T-29.II.7-9; T-31.III.4

change/contrast
T-13.XI.6; T-14.II.1;
T-17.IV.12-15; T-31.V.16-17;
T-31.VII.1

decision
W-pI.138.3-5

ego
T-4.I.2-6; T-6.III; T-7.III.2;
T-16.III.2

equality
T-4.I.1; T-5.II.3; T-6.I.10;
T-6.V-B.1; T-9.VI.3
W-pII.296.2
M-In

forgiveness
W-pI.121.6-9; W-pI.193.4-13
M-4.X.2

God
T-6.IV.11; T-14.III.18-19;
T-14.XI
W-pI.193

grace
W-pI.169.1-3

guilt–guiltlessness
T-14.III; T-14.V.2-9; T-31.I.4-7
M-1.3

happy learner
T-14.II; T-14.V.3

holy relationship
M-2

Holy Spirit
T-6.V; T-7.II.6; T-7.IV.2-4;
T-8.II.1-6; T-8.VII.7-8; T-9.III.5;
T-12.V.5,9; T-13.I.1;
T-14.XI.10-14; T-15.I.1-2;
T-16.III.1; T-27.V.8-10;
T-31.V.8-9
W-pI.121.6-7

Jesus
T-4.I.3-7,13; T-5.IV.5; **T-6.I**;
T-14.V.9
W-pI.rV.In.6-8

learning handicaps
T-12.V.5-6

levels
M-3

love
T-In.1; T-6.I.13; T-6.III.2-4

mind
T-4.I.4; T-6.V-B.2-6; T-7.V.2

peace
T-6.V-B.7-9; T-14.V.6-9;
T-14.XI.5-6,12-14

projection
T-7.II.3

psychotherapy
P-2.I.4; P-3.I.4

Self
T-16.III.3-7

transfer
T-12.V.6; T-27.V.8-10
W-In.4-7

truth
T-14.In; T-14.I; T-14.II;
T-14.XI.1-5

vision–knowledge
W-pI.157; W-pI.158

world
T-31.I.3-13
W-pI.184.5-10

temptation

seeing ourselves and others as egos or bodies, denying our true Identity as Christ by wishing to make illusions real.

---

attack
T-6.I.11; T-23.IV.6; T-25.III.6; T-31.III.1
W-pI.71.10; W-pI.93.11; W-pI.161.12; W-pI.194.9
M-7.4

body
T-31.VIII.1
W-pI.64.1-2

decision
T-31.I.11; **T-31.VIII.1-6**

ego
T-17.V.3-7

God
T-16.VII.12; T-25.VII.13
W-pII.In.10

guilt
T-26.X.4; T-30.VIII.6

illusions
T-30.VIII.3-6
W-pI.61.4; W-pI.64.3; W-pII.272.2

Jesus
T-6.I.11; T-31.VIII.11

littleness–glory
T-23.In.5

psychic powers
M-25.4-5

salvation
W-pI.70.1

self
T-31.VII.10-14
W-pI.97.8

teacher of God
M-16.8-10; M-23.1-2

world
T-24.VI.4
W-pI.76.12; W-pI.79.4; W-pI.128.4-8

thorns

the Course's symbol of crucifixion, the sin and guilt of God's Son; the gift of the ego which projects guilt onto others and attacks them for it; contrasted with lilies, the gift of forgiveness.

---

body
T-20.II.1-10
W-pI.161.11

crucifixion
T-20.I.2-3; T-27.I.1

Holy Spirit
T-26.II.4

Thoughts of God

knowledge:	the non-spatial extension of God's Mind or spirit; includes all of creation, our true Self as well as our own creations; being part of God, His Thoughts share in His attributes: unified, eternal, formless, creative, and changeless.
true perception:	used infrequently to refer to thoughts of the real world; e.g., peace, salvation, healing, and the miracle.

---

changeless
T-30.III.6-10
W-pI.167.8

Christ/Self
W-pI.197.9; W-pII.6.1

creation
T-6.II.8; T-7.I.2
W-pI.107.8; W-pI.132.11;
W-pI.151.9; **W-pII.11**;
W-pII.326.1

ego
T-4.V.2; T-18.VIII.5,9

eternal life
T-19.IV-C.2; T-30.III.6-10
W-pI.167.1,8-11

giving–receiving
W-pI.108.4-6

healing
T-7.II.1

Holy Spirit
T-13.VIII.4
W-pI.186.13-14

limitless
W-pII.280.1

miracle
T-3.V.9-10

peace
W-pII.2.1-2
M-11.4
C-3.3

real world
T-16.VI.9
W-pII.265.2

salvation
W-pI.99.4-9; W-pII.338.2

spirit
T-3.V.7
C-1.1

truth
W-pI.136.13; W-pI.198.8;
W-pII.281.1

unity
T-6.II.8; **T-31.IV.10**
W-pI.56.5; W-pI.91.10;
W-pI.165; W-pII.260.1

vision
W-pI.157.5

world
T-25.VII.3

time

level I: an integral part of the ego's illusory world of separation, in contrast to eternity, which exists only in Heaven; while time appears to be linear, it is all contained in a tiny instant which has already been corrected and undone by the Holy Spirit, and in truth never happened at all.

level II: w-m: the means of maintaining the ego by preserving the sins of the past through guilt, projected by fear of punishment into the future, and overlooking the present which is the closest approximation to eternity.

r-m: the means of undoing the ego by forgiving the past through the holy instant, the medium of miracles; when forgiveness is complete, the world of time has fulfilled the Holy Spirit's purpose and will simply disappear.

Atonement/plan
T-2.II.6; T-15.II.1
W-pI.99.5; W-pI.135.20;
W-pI.158.4; W-pI.169.9

carpet
T-13.I.3

cause–effect
T-28.I.5-15

decision
T-In.1; T-22.II.8; T-25.III.6
W-pI.138.7

ego
T-5.III.5-6; **T-13.IV.4-9**;
T-15.I.2-7

eternity
T-5.VI.1-2; T-10.In.1; T-10.V.14;
T-11.III.8
W-pII.234.1

forgiveness
T-17.III.1-8; T-25.VI.5;
T-29.VI.2-4

God
T-11.I.4
M-2.2-4; M-29.7

guilt
T-5.VI.2; T-13.I.3-9

holy instant
T-13.VI.5-8; T-15.I.8-15;
T-16.VII.6-9; T-17.V.12;
T-18.VII.4; T-20.V.6
W-pI.194.3-5; W-pII.308

holy relationship
T-18.VII.5-6

Holy Spirit
T-13.IV.7-8; **T-15.I**;
T-26.V.3-4,12
W-pII.8.5

illusions
T-13.I.5
W-pI.131.6-9; W-pI.136.13;
W-pI.167.9
M-2.2-3
P-3.II.10

miracle
T-1.I.13,15,19,25,47,48;
T-1.II.6; T-1.V.2; T-2.VIII.2
W-pI.97.3-4

past
T-13.VI.1-6; T-13.VIII.1;
T-14.IX.1; T-17.III.1-8
W-pI.7

perception
T-3.III.1-3

revelation
T-1.I.48
W-pI.158.2-5,11; **W-pI.169.4-10**

Second Coming
W-pII.9.3-4

separation
T-3.VII.3; **T-26.V**; T-26.VIII.1-4
M-2.2-4

teacher of God
M-1.2-4; M-3.3; M-14.3;
M-16.2-3

toys

symbol of the world of sin, reflecting its inherent meaninglessness and harmlessness, despite its seeming solidity and strength.

---

dream
T-29.IX.4-7

fear
T-29.I.9; T-30.IV.8
W-pI.153.12

gap
T-29.I.9

guilt
W-pI.153.13

idols
T-29.IX.4; **T-30.IV.2-5**

sin
W-pI.151.8; W-pII.4.4-5

time
W-pII.346.1

war
W-pI.182.12

world
T-18.IX.7
W-pII.258.1
M-13.4

the unity of Its Levels is not understandable in this world; consists of 1) God, the Father and Creator, 2) His Son, Christ, our true Self, Which includes our creations, and 3) the Holy Spirit, the Voice for God.

---

creations
T-8.VI.5-8

God
T-7.I.7; T-14.IV.1

Holy Spirit
T-5.I.4; T-5.III.1

Son of God
T-3.II.5

unity
T-3.II.5; T-3.IV.1; T-8.IV.8; **T-25.I.5**

true perception

seeing through the eyes of Christ, the vision of forgiveness which corrects the ego's misperceptions of separation by reflecting the true unity of the Son of God; not to be equated with physical sight, it is the attitude that undoes the projections of guilt, allowing us to look upon the real world in place of the world of sin, fear, suffering, and death.

see: *perception*

---

forgiveness
T-17.II.3
W-pII.313
C-4.3-7

gratitude
W-pI.130.9

holy relationship
T-19.IV-B.8; T-22.I.9-10

Holy Spirit
T-7.IV.5; T-13.XI.4; T-25.VII.5
W-pI.43.2; W-pI.193.2;
W-pII.269.1
C-6.3

innocence
T-3.II.2

knowledge
T-3.III; T-4.II.11; T-5.I.4-7;
T-12.VI.6-7; T-13.VIII.2-3;
C-4.3-8

light
W-pI.15.3

miracle
T-13.VIII.5

real world
T-12.VIII.8
W-pI.181.8

right-mindedness
T-4.II.10

world
W-pI.187.1

something is either true or false, reality or illusion; there can be no compromise: we are either created by God or made by the ego; this principle explains why there is no order of difficulty in miracles, since all that is needed for healing or the miracle to occur is to shift from the illusions of the ego to the truth of the Holy Spirit.

A Course in Miracles
T-3.II.1; T-16.V.16; T-22.II.7

Atonement
T-13.IX.4; T-16.VII.10
M-22.1

attack
T-26.X.2
M-17.4

body
T-27.VI.3

decision
T-14.III.4; T-17.III.9
W-pI.88.1; **W-pI.133.3-12**;
W-pI.138.4; W-pI.152.3-12;
W-pI.190.11

dream
T-18.II.8; T-29.IV.1

ego
T-7.VI.8;
P-2.I.2

fear
T-11.V.11
W-pI.160.4

forgiveness
W-pI.134.8-10

form–content
T-19.IV-C.11; T-23.I.6-12;
T-23.II.2-3,19-20
M-7.5

God
T-25.VII.3
W-pI.190.3
C-3.6
P-1.5

healing
T-19.I.5-6
W-pI.137.4; **W-pI.140**
M-6.1; **M-8.5-6**
S-3.II.5

Holy Spirit
T-1.I.38; T-5.IV.1; **T-6.V-B.6-7**;
T-6.V-C.1; T-8.IX.5; T-12.VIII.3;
T-14.II.2-7; T-17.VI.4
W-pI.66.7; W-pII.10.1

Jesus
T-4.III.2
C-5.2-3

Last Judgment
T-2.VIII.3-5; **T-26.III.4**

life–death
T-3.VII.6
W-pI.163.6; W-pI.167.1
M-27.4-7

perception
T-11.VII.3; T-26.VII.3-4
W-pI.28.2

reason
T-22.II.4-7

sacrifice
M-13.7

salvation
T-16.V.14; T-26.VII.10; T-31.I.1
W-pI.99.1-2; W-pI.152.3

sin–sinlessness
W-pI.36.1

special relationships
T-16.IV.5-8

spirit–ego, body
T-4.I.2; T-4.VII.3; T-31.VI.1
W-pI.96.3

thoughts
W-pI.16.1-3

world
W-pI.130; W-pI.132.11

vision

the perception of Christ or the Holy Spirit that sees beyond the body to the spirit that is our true Identity; the vision of forgiveness and sinlessness through which is seen the real world; purely internal, reflecting a decision to accept reality rather than judge it; a shift in attitude from the ego's purpose for the body (specialness) to the Holy Spirit's (forgiveness), and thus is not to be equated with physical sight.

Atonement
T-2.III.4

body
T-24.VI.6-7
W-pI.158.7

Christ
T-12.VI.4-5; T-13.V.9-11;
T-13.VIII.2
W-pI.158.5-11; W-pII.305.1

decision
T-31.VI.1
W-pI.20.3; W-pI.27.1;
W-pI.28.1-4; W-pII.271

extension
W-pI.29.1-3; **W-pI.30**;
W-pI.36.1

faith
T-21.III.4-12

forgiveness
W-pI.75.7-11; W-pI.78.2-8;
W-pI.158.9-10; W-pI.159.8-10;
W-pI.192.6-7; W-pII.270.1
P-2.VII.3

God
W-pI.42.1-4
S-2.I.6

holy relationship
P-2.II.5

Holy Spirit
T-12.VI.4-6; T-20.II.5-6;
T-20.VIII.3-10
W-pI.151.10; W-pII.3.4
C-6.3

innocence
T-31.VII.11-13
W-pI.187.11; W-pII.263

Jesus
M-23.5
C-5.5

judgment
T-20.V.4; T-21.II.8
W-pI.51.2

justice
M-19.5

light
T-13.V.8-11; T-13.VIII.2-5;
T-21.I.8-10
W-pI.15.2; W-pI.108.1-3;
W-pI.168.4

miracle
T-3.III.4
W-pI.91; **W-pI.159.3-10**

projection
W-pI.8.1-3; W-pI.10.3

real world
T-12.VI.4-5; T-12.VIII.4-8;
T-31.VIII.8
C-1.5

reason
T-22.III.1

sinlessness
T-20.VII.4-9; **T-20.VIII**;
T-22.II.13; T-24.II.5-6
W-pII.313

Voice for God

(see: *Holy Spirit*)

war

symbol of the ego's belief in conflict between itself and its image of a vengeful God Who seeks to destroy it; this conflict is projected onto the experience of ourselves at war with the world and with everyone in it.

---

death
M-27.2

ego
T-7.III.3; T-8.I.3; **T-21.VII.2-4**

God
T-23.I; T-23.IV.1

illusions
T-13.XI.1-2; T-23.I.6-12

miracle
T-23.IV.4-9; **T-27.V.3**

peace
T-5.II.7; T-25.III.6; T-29.II.3
M-20.3-4

Self
T-27.VII.13; T-28.V.3

sin
T-23.In.2

special relationships
T-24.I; T-25.III.3

Thought of God
T-30.III.10

truth
T-31.II.1
W-pI.136.16

Will of God

the expression of God's being, which can only create; though seeming to be split by the separation and the ego's wishes, its wholeness and unity with the will of the Sonship remain unchanged and unbroken.

---

changelessness
T-8.IV.1; T-25.VII.2
M-1.4

Christ
T-13.VII.6; T-13.X.9
W-pI.158.5; W-pI.197.7
C-1.6

creation
T-4.VII.3; T-9.I.6; T-10.IV.5
W-pII.In.7; W-pII.11.3-4
C-1.4

ego/self
T-7.IV.6; T-18.IV.3-4; T-21.II.6;
T-23.I.2
W-pI.93.1-5; W-pII.12.1-2

extension/creations
T-7.IX.6; **T-8.II.7**; **T-8.III.3**;
T-8.VI.2-8; T-11.I.5-9
W-pI.76.11; W-pI.193.1;
W-pII.320; **W-pII.329**

fear
T-9.I.1-8; T-11.I.10

forgiveness
T-26.VII.9-10
W-pI.193.3; W-pII.1.1;
W-pII.331.2
C-3.5

happiness/joy
T-1.VII.1; T-8.III.2; T-11.I.10
W-pI.100.2-10;
W-pI.101.1-2,6-7; W-pI.102;
W-pII.235.1

holy relationship
T-22.I.11; T-30.V.11

Holy Spirit
T-5.II.6,8,12; T-8.II.3-6;
T-9.I.4-5; T-18.III.4-5; T-25.I.5-6;
T-31.I.6

Identity
T-7.VII.10; T-7.X.6-8;
T-8.II.3-7; T-8.V.2

immortality
T-11.I.9; T-11.VI.8; T-12.IV.6
W-pI.163.4-9

Jesus
T-8.IV.3-7; **T-8.V.2-5**; T-8.VI.8;
T-15.III.10; T-31.VIII.10

magic
W-pI.76.6
M-16.9-11; M-17.5

miracle
T-7.X.8; T-8.V.3

Will of God (continued)

peace
T-8.IV.1; T-10.IV.4; T-13.XI.8;
T-24.In.1
M-20.6

real world
T-18.II.9
W-pI.54.5; W-pI.73.4

resurrection
T-11.VI.4

salvation
T-8.VI.2; T-9.VII.1

sickness/suffering
T-10.IV.1-3; T-10.V.4;
T-11.III.1-4; T-13.VII.7;
T-25.VII.13
W-pI.99.4-7; W-pII.328

sin
T-19.III.8; T-19.IV-C.3-4;
T-26.V.9-11; **T-26.VII.7-10**;
T-30.VI.5-9
W-pII.4.3

sinlessness
W-pI.181.9; W-pII.334.2

special relationships
T-24.I.9; T-24.II.2; T-24.III.2-8;
T-24.VI.10

unity
T-3.II.4-5; T-8.V.2-3; T-8.IX.9;
T-9.I.5-9; T-11.I.11; T-11.II.1;
T-14.VIII.5; T-19.IV-A.3;
T-21.V.5-9; **T-25.II.10-11**
W-pI.74.1-3; W-pI.125.9;
W-pI.186.1; W-pII.246;
W-pII.309.1; W-pII.326
M-5.III.3

vision
W-pI.42.1; W-pI.59.3; W-pI.75.7

wish–will
T-7.X.4-8; T-11.V.5; T-30.IV.7
W-pI.56.4; W-pII.307
C-3.7
S-1.IV.3

world
W-pI.166.2

wish–will

the ego wishes, spirit wills.

knowledge: willing expresses creation, which is truth.

perception: wishing can reflect wrong- or right-mindedness, both inherently illusory, since wishing implies that there exists a reality other than the unity of Heaven.

---

death–life
T-26.VII.16

decision
T-7.X.4-7

dream
T-30.IV.7

forgiveness
C-3.5-7

free will
T-3.VI.11; T-8.IV.5-7

learning
T-31.I.5

make–create
T-24.V.1

mind
T-3.IV.5; **T-26.VII.13**

spirit
T-7.IX.2

truth
T-26.VII.6
W-pI.56.4

world
T-12.III.9
W-pI.73

Word of God

God's "answer" to the separation; used variously for different aspects of this answer: e.g., forgiveness, peace, Atonement, and the Holy Spirit.

(Note—does not refer to Jesus or Christ, as it does in the Bible.)

Atonement
M-22.1

attack
M-13.7; M-18.3

body
M-12.5

Christ
S-3.II.3

creation
W-pI.162.2; **W-pII.276**

faithfulness
M-4.IX

forgiveness
W-pI.192.4; W-pII.336.2;
W-pII.13.3

function
W-pI.114.2

healing
P-2.V.4
S-3.III.5

Holy Spirit
W-pI.106.4-10; W-pI.123.5;
W-pI.125; W-pII.357; **W-Ep.3**
C-6.4
P-2.IV.5

Jesus
M-23.4

last step
W-pII.In.4

Name of God
W-pI.184.13

resurrection
M-28.3

Second Coming
W-pII.9.1

sinlessness
W-pII.341.2

teacher of God
W-pI.125.1-4; W-pII.245.2;
W-pII.14.5
M-5.III.2; M-13.8; M-14.2;
M-21.5

thoughts/words
W-pI.12.5; W-pI.14.3;
W-pI.188.7-8; W-pII.2.1

world
M-11.1-2

world

level I: the *effect* of the ego's belief in separation, which is its *cause*; the thought of separation and attack on God given form; being the expression of the belief in time and space, it was not created by God, Who transcends time and space entirely; unless specifically referring to the world of knowledge, refers only to perception, the post-separation domain of the ego.

level II: w-m: a prison of separation which reinforces the ego's belief in sin and guilt, perpetuating the seeming existence of this world.

r-m: a classroom wherein we learn our lessons of forgiveness, the Holy Spirit's teaching device to help us transcend the world; thus the purpose of the world is to teach us that there is no world.

see: *real world*

---

attack
W-pI.23; W-pI.73.2-3;
W-pI.153.1-2; W-pII.3.2

body
T-27.VIII.1-5; T-31.VI.2-6
W-pI.72.6-7
M-5.II.1-3
C-4.5

death
T-13.In.2; T-29.VI.2-5
M-27

dream
T-18.II.1-8; **T-27.VII**;
T-28.II.3-12

fear
T-30.V.7-9
W-pI.13.1-3; W-pI.130.2-4;
W-pI.135.2; W-pII.3.2

forgiveness
T-25.III.5-8; T-26.IV.2;
T-30.II.4-5
W-pI.64.1-3
M-14
P-2.II.3
S-2.I.10

God
T-8.VI.1-3; T-11.VII.1; T-31.IV.9
W-pI.14; W-pI.152.6-7;
W-pI.166.2-5
M-11
C-4.1-2

guilt
T-13.In.2-4; T-18.IX.3-9;
T-27.I.6; T-31.I.7

healing
T-2.III.5; T-24.VI.4
W-pI.132.7

Holy Spirit
T-5.III.11; T-25.VII.5-8
W-pII.3.4
M-25.2

idea
T-5.I.1

illusion
T-18.IX.4
W-pI.53.3; W-pI.155.2;
W-pI.166.2; W-pI.184.2-8;
W-pII.240.1; **W-pII.3**

insanity
T-14.I.2

judgment
T-20.III.5-8
M-9.2; M-10.1-3

love
T-13.III.3-4
W-pI.127.5-11

mind
W-pI.132

projection
T-12.III.7-10; T-13.IX.3,7;
T-18.I.4-6; **T-20.VIII.9-10**;
T-21.In; T-27.VII.1-13;
T-27.VIII.4-13
W-pI.11.1; W-pI.13.2-3

sacrifice
T-26.I
M-13

self-concept
T-31.V

separation
T-4.I.4; T-12.III.9; T-28.III.7;
T-28.VII.5
W-pI.184.1-11

sin
T-25.VII.1-11; T-26.VII.12
W-pI.181.9

suffering
T-27.VII.1-5
W-pI.190.5-8

valueless
W-pI.128; W-pI.133.2-12;
W-pII.226
P-3.III.7

wrong-mindedness

the part of our separated and split minds that contains the ego—the voice of sin, guilt, fear, and attack; we are repeatedly asked to choose right-mindedness instead of wrong-mindedness, which imprisons us still further in the world of separation.

---

ego
T-3.IV.2-4; T-4.III.10; T-4.IV.11
W-pI.66.7
C-1.6

fear
T-2.V.4

right-mindedness
T-2.V.4; T-3.IV.4; T-4.II.10

sickness
T-2.IV.2

Part III

SCRIPTURAL INDEX

(King James Version)

ABBREVIATIONS FOR SCRIPTURAL REFERENCES

Old Testament

Gn	Genesis
Ex	Exodus
Lv	Leviticus
Nb	Numbers
Dt	Deuteronomy
Jos	Joshua
Jg	Judges
1 K	1 Kings
Jb	Job
Ps	Psalms
Pr	Proverbs
Qo	Ecclesiastes
Is	Isaiah
Jr	Jeremiah
Ezk	Ezekiel
Dn	Daniel
Ho	Hosea
Jl	Joel

New Testament

Mt	Matthew
Mk	Mark
Lk	Luke
Jn	John
Ac	Acts
Rm	Romans
1 Co	1 Corinthians
2 Co	2 Corinthians
Ga	Galatians
Ep	Ephesians
Ph	Philippians
Col	Colossians
1 Th	1 Thessalonians
1 Tm	1 Timothy
2 Tm	2 Timothy
Heb	Hebrews
1 P	1 Peter
1 Jn	1 John
Rv	Revelation

A Course in Miracles

text
workbook for students
manual for teachers
clarification of terms

"Psychotherapy: Purpose, Process and Practice"

"The Song of Prayer"

Reference	Quote	Bible Reference
T-1.I.14:1	Miracles bear witness to truth	Jn 1:7-8; 18:37c
T-1.I.16:1	as blessed to give as to receive	Ac 20:35
T-1.I.18:3	loving your neighbor as yourself	Lv 19:18; Mt 22:39
T-1.I.24:1	heal the sick and raise the dead	Is 26:19; 35:5-6; Mt 10:1,8a; 11:5
T-1.I.24:2	likeness of your Creator	Gn 1:26-27
T-1.II.3:7	elder brother [Jesus]	Rm 8:29
T-1.II.4:1	"No man cometh…but by me"	Jn 14:6b
T-1.II.4:5	elder brother [Jesus]	Rm 8:29
T-1.II.4:7	"I and my Father are one"	Jn 10:30; 14:20
T-1.II.4:7	the Father is greater	Jn 14:28c
T-1.III.1:2	you do it to *yourself* and me	Mt 25:40
T-1.III.2:1	"Heaven and earth…pass away"	Mt 24:35
T-1.III.2:2	the resurrection and the life	Jn 11:25a
T-1.III.2:4	This is how a man must think	Pr 23:7
T-1.III.4:7	"Lead us not into temptation"	Mt 6:13a
T-1.III.6:2	The Golden Rule	Mt 7:12
T-1.III.7:6	bring in the stranger	Mt25:35; Heb 13:2
T-1.IV.4:2	"There is no death"	Rv 21:4b; 2Tm 1:10
T-1.IV.4:3	I came to fulfill the law	Mt 5:17
T-1.IV.4:8	Those who witness for me	Ac 1:8; Is 43:10,12
T-1.V.3:4	"Except ye…little children"	Mt 18:3
T-1.V.4:3	"God is not mocked"	Jb 13:9; Ga 6:7b
T-1.V.5:3	cannot serve two masters	Mt 6:24
T-1.V.6:2	choosing to follow Him [Christ]	Mt 4:19
T-1.V.6:3	All shallow roots	Lk 8:13
T-1.V.6:4	the Golden Rule	Mt 7:12
T-1.VI.1:6	"separation"…"fall"	Gn 3:1-7
T-1.VI.5:4	*Perfect love casts out fear*	1 Jn 4:18b

Reference	Quote	Bible Reference
T-1.VI.5:10	this faith *is* His gift	Ep 2:8
T-1.VII.1:4	All real pleasure...God's Will	Ps 40:8
T-1.VII.3:3	who know not what they do	Lk 23:34
T-2.I.1:5	likeness to your Creator	Gn 1:26-27
T-2.I.3:1-4:5	The Garden of Eden	Gn: Chaps. 2-3
T-2.I.3:4	the twinkling of an eye	1 Co 15:52a
T-2.I.3:6	a deep sleep fell upon Adam	Gn 2:21
T-2.I.4:5	the deep sleep fell upon Adam	Gn 2:21
T-2.I.4:9	you *are* free	Jn 8:32
T-2.I.5:9-10	find it...searching	Mt7:7b,8b; Dt4:29
T-2.II.1:2	I have asked...perform miracles	Mt 10:1,8a; 11:5
T-2.II.1:3	cannot be performed in...fear	Mt 17:19-20
T-2.II.1:5	your heart...your treasure	Mt 6:21
T-2.II.1:9	"peace of God...understanding"	Ph 4:7
T-2.II.4:8	a two-edged sword	Ps 149:6; Rv 1:16
T-2.II.7:4	"The meek shall inherit the earth"	Mt 5:5; Ps 37:11
T-2.III.1:5	body as a temple	1 Co 6:19; 3:16
T-2.III.5:10	daily bread	Mt 6:11
T-2.V.16:3	"Father forgive them..."	Lk 23:34
T-2.V.17:1	"Be of one mind"	2 Co 13:11
T-2.V.17:2	"Do this in remembrance of me"	Lk 22:19; 1 Co 11:24-25
T-2.V.18:4	*I do not have to worry*	Mt 10:19
T-2.VI.9:8	belief...move mountains	Mt 17:20a,b; 1 Co 13:2
T-2.VII.5:4	the darkness is abolished	1 Jn 1:5; 2:8
T-2.VII.5:14	"For God so loved the world..."	Jn 3:16
T-2.VIII	Last Judgment	Mt 11:22

Reference	*Quote*	*Bible Reference*
T-2.VIII.4:3	God Himself…it was good	Gn 1:31
T-3.I.3:1	"Vengeance is Mine…"	Dt32:35; Rm12:19
T-3.I.3:9	Adam…Garden of Eden	Gn 3:23-24
T-3.I.4:3	be merciful even as your Father	Lk 6:36
T-3.I.5:1	"lamb of God…sins of the world"	Jn 1:29
T-3.I.5:3	The lion and the lamb	Is 11:6; 65:25
T-3.I.5:4	"Blessed are the pure…"	Mt 5:8; Ps 24:4
T-3.I.6:4	lamb "taketh away…world"	Jn 1:29
T-3.I.7:7	light abolishes forms of darkness	1 Jn 1:5; 2:8
T-3.I.8:3	Atonement, not sacrifice	Ho 6:6; Mt 9:13
T-3.II.4:1	likeness of His Own	Gn 1:26-27
T-3.II.5:1	commends his spirit	Lk 23:46; Ps 31:5
T-3.II.5:8	their hearts are pure	Mt 5:8; Ps 24:4
T-3.II.5:10	"When He shall…as He is"	1 Jn 3:2
T-3.III.5:1	Bible tells you to know yourself	Mt 7:3-5; 23:25-26
T-3.III.6:5	"Alpha and Omega…"	Rv 21:6; 22:13
T-3.III.6:5	"Before Abraham was I am"	Jn 8:58
T-3.III.6:7	"Fear God…commandments"	Qo 12:13; Dt 5:29
T-3.IV.7:12	"Many are called…are chosen"	Mt 20:16b; 22:14
T-3.IV.7:15	find rest unto their souls	Mt 11:29b; Jr 6:16
T-3.V.5:7	truth that shall set you free	Jn 8:32
T-3.V.7:1	"God created man…likeness"	Gn 1:26-27
T-3.VI.1:1-2	Last Judgment	Mt 11:22
T-3.VI.1:4	"Judge not that ye be not judged"	Mt 7:1
T-3.VI.7:3	"root of all evil"	1 Tm 6:10
T-3.VI.11:8	"Seek ye first…"	Mt 6:33
T-3.VII.2:4-6	"devil"…opposition to God	Mt 4:1-11; Rv 12:7-10

Reference	*Quote*	*Bible Reference*
T-3.VII.2:7	"sell" him their souls	Mt 16:26
T-3.VII.3:4	The fruit…garden	Gn 2:16-17
T-3.VII.5:11	There is no death	Rv 21:4b; 2 Tm 1:10
T-3.VII.6:1	The branch that bears no fruit	Jn 15:2
T-3.VII.6:9	Your kingdom is not of this world	Jn 18:36
T-4.In.1:1	twice as far as he asks	Mt 5:41
T-4.In.2:2	"Be still and know that I am God"	Ps 46:10
T-4.I.8:6	be still and know that God is real	Ps 46:10
T-4.I.8:6	you are His beloved Son	Mt 3:17; 17:5
T-4.I.9:1	God is not the author of fear	1 Co 14:33
T-4.I.11:2	Do not try to make…house stand	Mt 7:24-27
T-4.I.11:3	Its weakness is your strength	2Co 12:9b;Ph 4:13
T-4.I.12:1	Of your ego you can do nothing	Jn 5:19,30
T-4.I.12:4	The meek shall inherit the earth	Mt 5:5; Ps 37:11
T-4.I.13:5	if I had not once been tempted	Mt 4:1-11; Heb2:18
T-4.I.13:10-11	*I have overcome the world*	Jn 16:33
T-4.II.5:8	Be patient a while	Ps 46:10
T-4.III.1:1	"Kingdom…is within you"	Lk 17:21
T-4.III.1:12	*the ego will not prevail against it*	Mt 16:18b
T-4.III.5:3	The Bible gives…you must ask	Mt 7:7a,8a; 21:22
T-4.III.6:6	no other gods before Him	Ex 20:3
T-4.III.7:2	Holy One	Ps 16:10; Mk 1:24
T-4.III.8:3	Holy One	Ps 16:10; Mk 1:24
T-4.IV.1:6	The glass…is dark indeed	1 Co 13:12
T-4.IV.2:3	darkened glass	1 Co 13:12
T-4.IV.9:2	To the ego's dark glass	1 Co 13:12
T-4.IV.9:3	the Holy One shine…in peace	Ps 16:10; Mk 1:24; Nb 6:25-26
T-4.IV.10:2-4	Second Coming	Mt 16:27; 25:31

Reference	*Quote*	*Bible Reference*
T-4.IV.11:6	your brother...in my name	Mt 18:20
T-4.IV.11:7	I raised the dead	Jn 11:43-44; Mt 9:24-25
T-4.V.1:1	All things work together for good	Rm 8:28
T-4.V.5:2	"Seek and ye shall find"	Mt 7:7b,8b; Dt 4:29
T-4.VI.6:4	Holy One	Ps 16:10; Mk 1:24
T-4.VII.6:1	The Bible...should praise God	Ps 150:1-6; Rm 15:11
T-5.In.3:6	love his neighbor	Lv 19:18; Mt 22:39
T-5.I.3:4	"May the mind...in Christ Jesus"	Ph 2:5
T-5.I.4:2	the Comforter	Jn 14:16a
T-5.I.4:4	"If I go...He will abide with you"	Jn 14:16b; 15:4,10; 16:7
T-5.II.6:8	God did not leave...comfortless	Jn 14:18
T-5.II.7:11	What profiteth...soul	Mt 16:26
T-5.II.8:4	God's Will...earth...Heaven	Mt 6:10b,c
T-5.II.9:2	all power in Heaven and earth	Mt 28:18
T-5.II.10:3	the light of the world with me	Mt 5:14; Jn 8:12
T-5.II.11:4	"My yoke is easy..."	Mt 11:30
T-5.III.11:5	truth...set you free	Jn 8:32
T-5.III.11:7	in remembrance of me	Lk 22:19; 1Co 11:24-25
T-5.IV.1:10	The ego cannot prevail	Mt 16:18b
T-5.IV.2:7	thoughts can make you...free	Jn 8:32
T-5.IV.3:9	the Kingdom of Heaven	Mt 19:14
T-5.IV.4:3	The Mind that was in me	Ph 2:5
T-5.IV.4:6	"turning the other cheek"	Mt 5:39
T-5.IV.6:5	I will never leave you	Heb 13:5
T-5.IV.6:8	rendering unto God	Mt 22:21

Reference	Quote	Bible Reference
T-5.IV.8:7	depart in peace	Lk 2:29
T-5.IV.8:7	I have loved you as I loved myself	Lv 19:18; Mt 22:39
T-5.IV.8:13	have our being	Ac 17:28
T-5.VI.3:2	The Mind that was in me	Ph 2:5
T-5.VI.6:1	"As ye sow, so shall ye reap"	Ga 6:7c; 2 Co 9:6
T-5.VI.7:1	"Vengeance…sayeth the Lord"	Dt 32:35; Rm 12:19
T-5.VI.8:1	"I will visit the sins…"	Ex 34:7
T-5.VI.9:1	"The wicked shall perish"	Ps 37:20
T-5.VI.10:3	bearing false witness	Ex 20:16; Mt 19:18
T-5.VI.10:8	"thine is the Kingdom"	Mt 6:13b
T-5.VI.11:1	"I am come as a light…"	Jn 12:46
T-5.VII.1:4	cast your cares upon Him	1 P 5:7
T-5.VII.2:2	moved mountains…faith	Mt 17:20a,b;1 Co 13:2
T-5.VII.2:3	healed the sick…the dead	Is 26:19; 35:5-6; Mt 10:1,8a; 11:5
T-5.VII.3:2	God commended His Spirit	Lk 23:46; Ps 31:5
T-6.I	Crucifixion [of Jesus]	Mt 27:26-50
T-6.I.7:6	"agony in the garden"	Lk 22:39-46
T-6.I.8:2	build my church	Mt 16:18a
T-6.I.10:3	the way, the truth and the life	Jn 14:6a
T-6.I.14:3	"wrath of God"	Ezk 7:19; Jn 3:36
T-6.I.15:2	"…peace…sword"	Mt 10:34
T-6.I.15:5	"Betrayest…with a kiss?"	Lk 22:48
T-6.I.15:7	The "punishment"…upon Judas	Mt 26:24
T-6.I.16:1	the Apostles…understand later	Jn 16:12
T-6.I.19:3	learned of me	Mt 11:29a
T-6.II.7:6	everything was created by Him	Jn 1:3
T-6.II.10:2	He uses everything for good	Rm 8:28
T-6.II.10:8	The ego cannot prevail	Mt 16:18b
T-6.II.13:2	The ego is legion	Mk 5:9

Reference	Quote	Bible Reference
T-6.II.13:4-5	light of the world	Mt 5:14; Jn 8:12
T-6.III.4:2	the truth that will set you free	Jn 8:32
T-6.V-A.3:4	To be of one mind	1 P 3:8; Rm 12:16
T-7.I.6:2	your joy may be complete	Jn 15:11; 16:24
T-7.I.7:8	true...forever	Heb 13:8
T-7.III.1:7	"I am with you always"	Mt 28:20
T-7.III.1:9	the way, the truth and the life	Jn 14:6a
T-7.IV.7:1	Seek ye first	Mt 6:33
T-7.IV.7:4	God is All in all	1 Co 15:28; Ep 1:23
T-7.IV.7:5	All being is in Him	Ac 17:28
T-7.V.10:4	remembrance of me	Lk 22:19; 1 Co 11:24-25
T-7.V.10:12	Blessed are you	Mt 5:3-11
T-7.V.11:1	Come therefore unto me	Mt 11:28a
T-7.VII.5:8	Sons of the living God	Jn 6:69
T-7.VII.6:2	His beloved Sons	Mt 3:17; 17:5
T-7.VII.11:6	All power and glory are yours	Mt 6:13b
T-7.IX.2:2	spirit's own fullness	Ep 3:19
T-7.IX.2:3	The ego cannot prevail	Mt 16:18b
T-7.X.7:2	not left you comfortless	Jn 14:18
T-7.XI.1:3	Following Him	Mt 4:19
T-7.XI.6:1	"What is truth?"	Jn 18:38
T-8.II.7:1,7	power and glory	Mt 6:13b
T-8.II.8:1	power and glory	Mt 6:13b
T-8.III.1:1	Glory to God in the highest	Lk 2:14

Reference	Quote	Bible Reference
T-8.III.1:2	Ask and it shall be given you	Mt 7:7a,8a; 21:22
T-8.III.2:6	power and glory	Mt 6:13b
T-8.III.4:8	For I am…with you	Mt 28:20
T-8.III.4:8	in remembrance of *you*	Lk 22:19; 1 Co 11:24-25
T-8.III.5:3,5	power and glory	Mt 6:13b
T-8.III.5:10	imprisoned or released	Mt 16:19b; Jn 20:23
T-8.III.7:2,8	power and glory	Mt 6:13b
T-8.III.8:1	Power and glory	Mt 6:13b
T-8.IV.1:3	Yet He is All in all	1Co 15:28; Ep 1:23
T-8.IV.2:1	I am come as a light	Jn 12:46
T-8.IV.2:4	I am with you always	Mt 28:20
T-8.IV.2:5	I am the light of the world	Mt 5:14; Jn 8:12
T-8.IV.2:8	to overcome the world	Jn 16:33
T-8.IV.2:13	The remembrance of me	Lk 22:19; 1 Co 11:24-25
T-8.IV.2:13	of Him Who sent me	Jn 8:16; 20:21b
T-8.IV.3:7	The world…reject me	Jn 15:18
T-8.IV.7:3	Of yourself you can do nothing	Jn 5:19,30
T-8.IV.7:5	I will always remember you	Lk 22:19; 1 Co 11:24-25
T-8.V.2:1	likeness of God	Gn 1:26-27
T-8.VI.3:1	over His Kingdom…no power	Jn 18:36
T-8.VI.4	the prodigal son	Lk 15:11-32
T-8.VI.9:4	Whom God has joined	Mt 19:6
T-8.VI.10:3	Your heart…your treasure	Mt 6:21
T-8.VII.5:3	power and glory	Mt 6:13b
T-8.VII.6:1	Rejoice…you can do nothing	Jn 5:19,30
T-8.VII.6:3	power and glory	Mt 6:13b

Reference	*Quote*	*Bible Reference*
T-8.VII.7:1	"The Word...made flesh"	Jn 1:14
T-8.VII.9:6	temple of the Holy Spirit	1 Co 6:19; 3:16
T-8.VII.11:2	through the body, but not *in* it	Jn 15:19;17:14,16,18
T-8.VII.14:1	thought cannot be made flesh	Jn 1:14
T-8.IX.3:2	sickness...unto death	Jn 11:4
T-8.IX.7:1	be perfect	Mt 5:48
T-8.IX.7:1	to heal all errors	Is 26:19; 35:5-6; Mt 10:1,8a; 11:5
T-8.IX.7:1	take no thought of the body	1 Co 6:15-20
T-8.IX.7:1	accomplish all...in my name	Jn 14:13-14; 16:23
T-9.I.6:1	alien tongues	Gn 11:1-9; 1 Co 12:10,28
T-9.I.9:7	God is Love	1 Jn 4:8,16
T-9.II.3:1	all prayer is answered	Mt 7:7a,8a; 21:22
T-9.II.5:9	This light can shine into yours	Mt 5:16
T-9.II.11:8	What you give...exact measure	Mt 7:2
T-9.IV.2:7	is not *of* you but *for* you	Jn 15:19;17:14,16,18
T-9.IV.9:2	Last Judgment	Mt 11:22
T-9.IV.9:3-4	Second Coming	Mt 16:27; 25:31
T-9.IV.11:10	Second Coming	Mt 16:27; 25:31
T-9.V.6:2	"Let there be light"	Gn 1:3
T-9.V.9:6	*By their fruits...know them*	Mt 7:16
T-9.VI.2:4	What you offer...to Him	Mt 25:40
T-9.VI.3:8	what you do to my brother	Mt 25:40
T-10.I.1:3	love your creations as yourself	Lv 19:18; Mt 22:39
T-10.I.1:7	your banishment is not of God	Gn 3:23-24
T-10.III.2:1	What Comforter can there be	Jn 14:16a
T-10.III.6:6	"My peace I give unto you"	Jn 14:27a

Reference	Quote	Bible Reference
T-10.III.7:8	faith...make you whole	Mt 9:22
T-10.III.8:3	no other gods before Him	Ex 20:3
T-10.III.8:4	God is not jealous	Ex 20:5; 34:14
T-10.III.10:3	other gods before Him	Ex 20:3
T-10.III.11:3	no other gods before Him	Ex 20:3
T-10.IV.1:5	other gods before Him	Ex 20:3
T-10.IV.3:4	If you perceive other gods	Ex 20:3
T-10.IV.4:4	no other laws beside His	Ex 20:3
T-10.V.1:5	the wages of sin *is* death	Rm 6:23
T-10.V.4:4	Who alone is his Help	Ps 115:9; 121:2
T-10.V.5:1	of yourself you can do nothing	Jn 5:19,30
T-10.V.5:3	be troubled over nothing	Jn 14:1
T-11.I.2:3	no beginnings...in God	Heb 7:3
T-11.I.2:5	I and my Father...one with you	Jn 10:30; 14:20
T-11.I.11:6	Blessed are you	Mt 5:3-11
T-11.II.3:6	know not what you do	Lk 23:34
T-11.II.4:5	your guest will abide with you	Jn 14:16b; 15:4,10
T-11.II.7:8	the Comforter of God	Jn 14:16a
T-11.III.1:2	Your Comforter will rest you	Mt 11:28b,29b
T-11.III.1:7	root of all evil	1 Tm 6:10
T-11.III.2:1	he knows not what he does	Lk 23:34
T-11.III.3:1	your joy would be complete	Jn 15:11; 16:24
T-11.III.6:1	The children of light	Lk 16:8; 1 Th 5:5
T-11.III.6:3	no other gods	Ex 20:3
T-11.III.7:1	God's Comforter can comfort	Jn 14:16a
T-11.IV.6:4	But love yourself	Jn 13:34
T-11.IV.6:6	Come unto me	Mt 11:28a
T-11.IV.8:1	Blessed is the Son of God	Ps 118:26; Mt 21:9
T-11.IV.8:4	Peace be unto you	Jn 20:19,21a,26

Reference	*Quote*	*Bible Reference*
T-11.V.2:3	Be not afraid	Jn 6:20
T-11.V.18:5	false witness	Ex 20:16; Mt 19:18
T-11.VI.1:5	"Blessed are ye...still believe"	Jn 20:29
T-11.VI.1:7	ascends to the Father	Jn 20:17
T-11.VI.4:1	I am *your* resurrection...*your* life	Jn 11:25a
T-11.VI.4:9	ascend unto the Father together	Jn 20:17
T-11.VI.4:9	as it was...ever shall be	Heb 13:8
T-11.VI.6:6	Father has given you all	Lk 15:31
T-11.VI.7:1	nails...thorn	Mt 27:29,35
T-11.VI.8:1	nailed...crown of thorns	Mt 27:29,35
T-11.VI.9:5	your redeemer liveth	Jb 19:25
T-11.VI.10:8	To God all things are possible	Mt 19:26
T-11.VII.1:4	a new Heaven and a new earth	Is 65:17; Rv 21:1
T-11.VIII.2:1	become as little children	Mt 18:3
T-11.VIII.4:7	you will see it as it is	1 Jn 3:2
T-11.VIII.5:4	if you ask you will receive	Mt 7:7a,8a; 21:22
T-11.VIII.7:7	Blessed are you	Mt 5:3-11
T-11.VIII.8:3	Kingdom...*is* within you	Lk 17:21
T-11.VIII.12:1	If you perceive offense	Mt 5:29
T-12.II.3:4	know your brother as yourself	Lv 19:18; Mt 22:39
T-12.II.7:1	A little while...will see me	Jn 16:16
T-12.II.8:1	There is no fear in perfect love	1 Jn 4:18a,b
T-12.II.9:2	The Lord is with you	Lk 1:28; Jg 6:12
T-12.II.9:3	Yet your Redeemer liveth	Jb 19:25
T-12.II.9:3	abideth in you	Jn 14:16b; 15:4,10
T-12.III.1:1	sell all you have...follow me	Mt 19:21
T-12.IV.Title	Seeking and Finding	Mt 7:7b,8b; Dt 4:29
T-12.IV.1:3	search...do not find	Mt 7:7b,8b; Dt 4:29

Reference	*Quote*	*Bible Reference*
T-12.IV.1:4	"Seek and do *not* find"	Mt 7:7b,8b; Dt 4:29
T-12.IV.2:3	seeking what it is afraid to find	Mt 7:7b,8b; Dt 4:29
T-12.IV.4:2	To seek and not to find	Mt 7:7b,8b; Dt 4:29
T-12.IV.4:5	"Seek and you *will* find"	Mt 7:7b,8b; Dt 4:29
T-12.IV.6:4	death is your treasure...purchase	Mt 13:44-46
T-12.IV.6:7	Your inheritance...nor sold	Gn 25:31-33
T-12.V.5:3	of yourself you cannot learn	Jn 5:19,30
T-12.V.7:1	"Seek and do not find"	Mt 7:7b,8b; Dt 4:29
T-12.VI.1:1	lose your own soul	Mk 8:36
T-12.VI.1:2	world...profits nothing	Pr 10:2; Jn 6:63
T-12.VII.6:3	seek...find	Mt 7:7b,8b; Dt 4:29
T-13.In.3:6	Adam's "sin"	Gn 3:23-24
T-13.I.5:3-5	seeking...finds	Mt 7:7b,8b; Dt 4:29
T-13.I.6:7	Goodness and mercy	Ps 23:6
T-13.II.9:6	joy in Heaven...homecoming	Lk 15:7
T-13.II.9:7	son of man	Ezk 2:1; Mt 8:20
T-13.III.11:3	departing in peace	Lk 2:29
T-13.III.11:3	returning to the Father	Jn 14:12,28b
T-13.IV.1:5	dust...you were made	Gn 2:7; 3:19
T-13.V.7:6	You who know not what you do	Lk 23:34
T-13.V.9:7	And He...return unto the Father	Jn 14:12,28b
T-13.V.11:4	risen in Him to the Father	Col 2:12; 3:1
T-13.VI.3:5	born again	Jn 3:3,7
T-13.VI.4:8	born again	Jn 3:3,7
T-13.VI.5:1	born again	Jn 3:3,7
T-13.VI.5:4	find it if you seek it	Mt 7:7b,8b; Dt 4:29

Reference	*Quote*	*Bible Reference*
T-13.VI.8:1	Now is the time of salvation	2 Co 6:2
T-13.VI.8:4-5	only light…no darkness	1 Jn 1:5; 2:8
T-13.VI.10:1	the light is in you	Mt 5:14; Jn 8:12
T-13.VII.3:5	to return to dust	Gn 2:7; 3:19
T-13.VII.8:1	peace of God…understanding	Ph 4:7
T-13.VII.10:2	you have need of nothing	Mt 6:8,32
T-13.VII.16:8	My peace I give you	Jn 14:27a
T-13.VIII.7:3	seeking…find	Mt 7:7b,8b; Dt 4:29
T-13.VIII.10:6	the gates of Heaven	Gn 28:17
T-13.IX.2:6	For faith is…treasured	Mt 6:21
T-13.IX.6:9	great is the joy in Heaven	Lk 15:7
T-13.X.5:2	born again	Jn 3:3,7
T-13.X.10:4	There is no fear in love	1 Jn 4:18a
T-13.X.11:7	No one who condemns a brother	1 Jn 2:9; 4:20
T-13.X.11:10	*be still*	Ps 46:10
T-13.X.12:6	I thank You, Father	Mt 11:25; Jn 11:41
T-13.X.13:1	my faith…on what I treasure	Mt 6:21
T-13.X.14:6	the gates of Heaven	Gn 28:17
T-13.XI.7:3	They will not prevail against	Mt 16:18b
T-13.XI.7:5	If that suffices Him…for you	2 Co 12:9a
T-13.XI.9:4	His certainty suffices	2 Co 12:9a
T-14.In.1:1	Yes, you are blessed indeed	Mt 5:3-11
T-14.II.1:7	the “treasure” that you seek	Mt 6:21
T-14.II.4:3	the light…into the darkness	Jn 1:5; Lk 1:79
T-14.II.4:3	lets it shine on you	Nb 6:25
T-14.II.6:3	and built on truth	Mt 7:24-27
T-14.II.6:5	you will not look back	Gn 19:26; Lk 9:62

Reference	*Quote*	*Bible Reference*
T-14.III.6:2	replace darkness...and fear	1 Jn 1:5; 2:8;4:18a,b
T-14.III.6:3	If he...binds himself	Mt 16:19b;Jn 20:23
T-14.III.13:6	the innocence that sets you free	Jn 8:32
T-14.III.19:2	*He leadeth me and knows the way*	Ps 23:2-3
T-14.V.2:6	You know not what you do	Lk 23:34
T-14.V.8:1	Peace, then, be unto everyone	Jn 20:19,21a,26
T-14.V.8:7	Abide with me	Jn 14:16b; 15:4,10
T-14.V.9:1	Blessed are you	Mt 5:3-11
T-14.V.9:5	holy ground	Ex 3:5
T-14.V.11:4	Judge not	Mt 7:1
T-14.VI.7:1	You know not what you say	Lk 23:34
T-14.VII.7:9	All honor to you through Him	Rv 5:12,13; 1 Tm 6:16
T-14.X.9:6	two or more join together	Mt 18:20
T-14.X.10:5-7	seeks...find	Mt 7:7b,8b; Dt 4:29
T-14.XI.2:4	His Son, given all power by Him	Mt 28:18
T-14.XI.7:3	no needs his Father will not meet	Mt 6:8,32
T-15.I.14:5	ascend unto your Father	Jn 20:17
T-15.II.2:4	Blessed is God's Teacher	Mt 5:3-11
T-15.II.3:2	For you are...and will forever be	Heb 13:8
T-15.II.3:5	weakness...strength	2 Co 12:9b; Ph 4:13
T-15.II.6:5-6	strength...weakness	2 Co 12:9b; Ph 4:13
T-15.III.6:5	The power and the glory	Mt 6:13b
T-15.III.6:7	All honor...of God	Rv 5:12,13; 1Tm 6:16
T-15.III.8:4	the Prince of Peace	Is 9:6
T-15.III.9:6	Welcome me not into a manger	Lk 2:7
T-15.III.9:7	My Kingdom is not of this world	Jn 18:36
T-15.III.9:7	My Kingdom...is in you	Lk 17:21

Reference	*Quote*	*Bible Reference*
T-15.III.10:1	abide with you	Jn 14:16b; 15:4,10
T-15.III.10:9	needs not seek to find	Mt 7:7b,8b; Dt 4:29
T-15.III.11:3	release...be bound	Mt 16:19b; Jn 20:23
T-15.V.4:4	love, where fear...is not perfect	1 Jn 4:18a,b
T-15.VI.2:1	perfect love is in you	Lk 17:21; 1 Jn 4:18b
T-15.VI.2:2	seek...cannot find	Mt 7:7b,8b; Dt 4:29
T-15.VI.5:12	For the instant...he is not bound	Mt 16:19b; Jn 20:23
T-15.VIII.3:9	everyone seek, and find	Mt 7:7b,8b; Dt 4:29
T-15.XI.6:1-2	seeking...you find not love	Mt 7:7b,8b; Dt 4:29
T-15.XI.7:2	The Prince of Peace	Is 9:6
T-16.II.6:5	glad tidings	Lk 1:19; 8:1
T-16.II.8:5	joyful tidings	Lk 1:19; 8:1
T-16.III.2:2	"By their fruits..."	Mt 7:16
T-16.III.7:7	His Kingdom has no limits	Dn 7:27
T-16.III.9:1	Your bridge is builded stronger	Mt 7:24-27
T-16.IV.6:1	seek and find	Mt 7:7b,8b; Dt 4:29
T-16.V.6:5	"Seek but do not find"	Mt 7:7b,8b; Dt 4:29
T-16.V.7:2-3	seeks...finds	Mt 7:7b,8b; Dt 4:29
T-16.V.13:1	raise other gods before Him	Ex 20:3
T-16.VI.9:3	it will abide with you	Jn 14:16b; 15:4,10
T-16.VII.9:5	Release your brothers	Mt 16:19b; Jn 20:23
T-16.VII.10:4	His help suffices	2 Co 12:9a
T-16.VII.11:1	Seek and *find* His message	Mt 7:7b,8b; Dt 4:29
T-16.VII.12	*Forgive us...Amen.*	Mt 6:9-13
T-17.I.1:1	The betrayal of the Son of God	Lk 22:48

Reference	Quote	Bible Reference
T-17.I.2:4	cannot be faithful to two masters	Mt 6:24
T-17.III.6:3	seeks and finds	Mt 7:7b,8b; Dt 4:29
T-17.III.7:3	Whom God has joined	Mt 19:6
T-17.IV.16:2	Let us ascend…to the Father	Jn 20:17
T-17.IV.16:3	the power and the glory	Mt 6:13b
T-17.V.7:12	justification for your faith	Rm 3:28; 5:1
T-17.V.10:3	will leave you comfortless	Jn 14:18
T-17.VI.5:6	deception cannot prevail	Mt 16:18b
T-18.I.7:1	"God is not fear, but Love"	1 Jn 4:8,16,18a
T-18.I.8:2	the living God	Jn 6:69
T-18.I.9:4	holy ground	Ex 3:5
T-18.III.1:7-8	The light…cannot put it out	Jn 1:5; Lk 1:79
T-18.III.3:2	Who walks beside you	Lk 24:13-16
T-18.V.4:3	"Thy Will be done"	Mt 6:10b; 26:39,42
T-18.V.5:1	love your brother as yourself	Lv 19:18; Mt 22:39
T-18.VIII.9:3	The desert becomes a garden	Is 51:3
T-18.VIII.9:8	living water	Jn 4:10; 7:38
T-18.IX.3:2	bear witness	Jn 1:7-8; 18:37c
T-19.I.9:7	faith is always justified	Rm 3:28; 5:1
T-19.I.11:1	Faith is the gift of God	Ep 2:8
T-19.I.14:6	glad tidings	Lk 1:19; 8:1
T-19.II.3:6	For the wages of sin *is* death	Rm 6:23
T-19.III.11:2	your brother as yourself	Lv 19:18; Mt 22:39
T-19.III.11:3	weary ones can come and rest	Mt 11:28b,29b

Reference	*Quote*	*Bible Reference*
T-19.IV-A. 11:3	Perception...two masters	Mt 6:24
T-19.IV-A. 16:3-4	communion...I will join you there	Mt 26:29; Lk 22:30
T-19.IV-B. 6:5	I...overcame the world	Jn 16:33
T-19.IV-B. 12:1	seek...and not find	Mt 7:7b,8b; Dt 4:29
T-19.IV-B. 17:5-6	seeking...finding	Mt 7:7b,8b; Dt 4:29
T-19.IV-C. 10:8	babe of Bethlehem	Lk 2:12
T-19.IV-C. 10:9	the resurrection and the life	Jn 11:25a
T-19.IV-D. 13:5	the power to forgive your sin	Mt 16:19b; Jn 20:23
T-19.IV-D. 17:1	faith and hope and mercy	1 Co 13:13
T-19.IV-D. 17:9	He leadeth you and me	Ps 23:2-3
T-19.IV-D. 18:4	garden of...agony and death	Lk 22:39-46
T-19.IV-D. 18:5	rise again	Mt 20:19
T-19.IV-D. 19:1	not to be lost but found	Lk 15:24,32
T-20.I.3:3	wander into the temptation	Mt 6:13a
T-20.I.4:3	I was a stranger...took me in	Mt 25:35; Heb 13:2
T-20.II.4:3	is against me still	Mt 12:30; Lk 9:50
T-20.II.8:9	There *is* no fear in love	1 Jn 4:18a
T-20.II.8:11	Let us lift up our eyes	Ps 121:1
T-20.III.9:6	enter with him to Paradise	Lk 23:43
T-20.III.11:2	faith...is justified	Rm 3:28; 5:1

Reference	*Quote*	*Bible Reference*
T-20.III.11:3	no fear in perfect love	1 Jn 4:18a,b
T-20.III.11:5	the pure in heart see God	Mt 5:8; Ps 24:4
T-20.III.11:5	Son to lead them to the Father	Jn 14:6b
T-20.IV.6:5	The ark of peace	Gn 7:9
T-20.IV.8:5	making straight your path	Is 40:3; Jn 1:23
T-20.V.8:4	What is he	Ps 8:4; Heb 2:6
T-20.VI	The Temple of the Holy Spirit	1 Co 6:19; 3:16
T-20.VI.2:5-7	Love…known…misunderstood	1 Co 13:4-7
T-20.VI.7:7	You are an idolater no longer	Ep 2:19
T-20.VI.9:6	look you not back	Gn 19:26; Lk 9:62
T-20.VI.10:5	Everlasting Arms	Dt 33:27
T-21.In.1:6	As a man thinketh	Pr 23:7
T-21.III.3:1	faith can move mountains	Mt 17:20a,b; 1 Co 13:2
T-21.III.6:1	sought to find it	Mt 7:7b,8b; Dt 4:29
T-21.III.9:6	its recognition is at hand	Mt 3:2; 4:17
T-21.V.1:6	The still, small Voice	1 K 19:12
T-21.V.8:1	the great deceiver's needs	Rv 12:9; 20:7-10
T-21.VI.6:1	condemn the Son of God	Mt 16:19b; Jn 20:23
T-21.VI.9:8	To give is…to receive	Ac 20:35
T-21.VI.11:5	God is not mocked	Jb 13:9; Ga 6:7b
T-21.VII.1:8	you are for him or against him	Mt 12:30; Lk 9:50
T-21.VII.2:7	do not know…whom they hate	Lk 23:34
T-21.VII.4:3	*seek*…find	Mt 7:7b,8b; Dt 4:29
T-21.VII.5:5	seek…find	Mt 7:7b,8b; Dt 4:29
T-22.In.1:2	whom God hath joined	Mt 19:6

Reference	*Quote*	*Bible Reference*
T-22.I.7:6	For no two brothers can unite	Mt 18:20
T-22.III.4:7	rock on which its church is built	Mt 16:18a
T-22.V.3:5	separate whom He has joined	Mt 19:6
T-22.VI.1:9	seek…found	Mt 7:7b,8b; Dt 4:29
T-23.In.3:1	fear no evil	Ps 23:4
T-23.In.5:1	lead God's Son into temptation	Mt 6:13a
T-23.I.11:2	house of God…itself divided	Mt 12:25
T-23.I.11:3	Holy One	Ps 16:10; Mk 1:24
T-23.I.11:3	temple…becomes a house of sin	Jr 7:11; Mt 21:13
T-23.II.4:5	Sin cannot be remitted	Mt 26:28; Ac 2:38
T-23.II.11:2	this priceless pearl	Mt 13:46
T-23.IV.7:4	have a mind as one	Ph 2:2
T-24.In.1:4	He will not fail	Dt 31:6,8
T-24.II.7:1	the power to forgive	Mt 9:6
T-24.II.7:6	the key to Heaven	Mt 16:19a
T-24.II.11:1	You *are* your brother's	Gn 4:9
T-24.II.13:4	the gates of hell	Mt 16:18b
T-24.II.14:1	The key you threw away	Mt 16:19a
T-24.III.2:7	given your brother's birthright	Gn 25:31-33
T-24.III.3:6	What rests on nothing	Mt 7:24-27
T-24.III.4:7	a flaming sword	Gn 3:24
T-24.III.5:8	"Thy will be done"	Mt 6:10b; 26:39,42
T-24.III.6:7	Holy One	Ps 16:10; Mk 1:24
T-24.III.7:2	come forth…dream of death	Jn 11:11,43
T-24.III.7:6	Curse God and die	Jb 2:9
T-24.III.8:6,12	the print of nails	Jn 20:25

Reference	*Quote*	*Bible Reference*
T-24.IV.2:10	Of itself…can do nothing	Jn 5:19,30
T-24.IV.3:15	treasure house barren and empty	Mt 6:19
T-24.IV.5:5	So are you bound	Mt 16:19b; Jn 20:23
T-24.V.4:6	hated him before it hated you	Jn 15:18
T-24.VI.5:1-5	your brother…release you both	Mt 16:19b; Jn 20:23
T-24.VI.5:6	lives and shares His Being	Ac 17:28
T-24.VII.1:7	This is your son, beloved of you	Mt 3:17; 17:5
T-24.VII.10:6	"…my own beloved son…"	Mt 3:17; 17:5
T-24.VII.11:8	The son of man	Ezk 2:1; Mt 8:20
T-25.In.2:6	The son of man	Ezk 2:1; Mt 8:20
T-25.I.1:7	everlasting Love	Jr 31:3
T-25.I.2:7	see your brother as yourself	Lv 19:18; Mt 22:39
T-25.II.2:6	seek…found	Mt 7:7b,8b; Dt 4:29
T-25.IV.2:7	that his joy might be increased	Jn 15:11; 16:24
T-25.IV.5:1	In you is all of Heaven	Lk 17:21
T-25.V.3:5	returning unto God…His Own	Mt 22:21
T-25.VII.1:6	the cost of sin is death	Rm 6:23
T-25.VII.4:2	For God and His beloved Son	Mt 3:17; 17:5
T-25.VII.12:7	the rock on which salvation rests	Mt 16:18a
T-25.VIII.2:5	one divided still against himself	Mt 12:25
T-25.VIII.2:7	only little faith is asked of you	Mt 17:20a
T-25.VIII.5:5	Vengeance is alien to God's Mind	Dt 32:35; Rm 12:19
T-25.VIII.6:4	lightning bolts…angry Hand	Ps 144:6-7; 18:13-14
T-25.VIII.7:4	Heaven's gate	Gn 28:17
T-25.VIII.9:11	stand at God's right Hand	Ps 110:1; Mk 16:19
T-25.VIII.9:11	power to forgive…sin	Mt 9:6

Reference	*Quote*	*Bible Reference*
T-25.VIII.13:3	Judge not	Mt 7:1
T-25.IX.1:9	you know not what it is	Lk 23:34
T-25.IX.2:4	Heaven…treasures	Mt 6:20
T-26.I.3:8	see him as you see yourself	Lv 19:18; Mt 22:39
T-26.I.7:6	He is the same forever	Heb 13:8
T-26.I.7:7	Born again	Jn 3:3,7
T-26.III.2:4	the gate of Heaven	Gn 28:17
T-26.III.3:5	gate where Oneness is	Gn 28:17
T-26.III.4:2	final judgment	Mt 11:22
T-26.IV.1:2,4	gate…Heaven	Gn 28:17
T-26.IV.3:1	holy place on which you stand	Ex 3:5
T-26.IV.4:1	gate of Heaven	Gn 28:17
T-26.IV.6:1	Heaven's gate	Gn 28:17
T-26.IV.6:3	how great…the joy in Heaven	Lk 15:7
T-26.V.1:5	gate of Heaven	Gn 28:17
T-26.V.2:4	Heaven's gate	Gn 28:17
T-26.V.10:4	the dead…be peacefully forgotten	Mt 8:22
T-26.V.14:3	Heaven's gate	Gn 28:17
T-26.VI.2:3	in Whom all power…rests	Mt 28:18
T-26.VI.3:5	gifts that are not of this world	Jn 14:27b; 18:36
T-26.VII.4:5	in this world, but not a part of it	Jn 15:19; 17:14,16,18
T-26.VII.15:7	What God calls…forever one	Mt 19:6
T-26.VIII.6:6	everything brings good	Rm 8:28
T-26.VIII.9:4	What profits freedom	Mt 16:26
T-26.IX.2:4	holy ground	Ex 3:5
T-26.IX.3:7	ground so holy	Ex 3:5
T-26.IX.8:1	temple of the living God	1 Co 6:19; 3:16

Reference	Quote	Bible Reference
T-26.X.3:6	you do not know him *as* yourself	Lv 19:18; Mt 22:39
T-27.I.1:3	fear no evil	Ps 23:4
T-27.I.1:4	a crown of thorns	Mt 27:29
T-27.I.1:9	His beloved Son	Mt 3:17; 17:5
T-27.I.5:5	every tear is wiped away	Is 25:8; Rv 7:17;21:4a
T-27.II.1:10	forgive him his transgressions	Mt 6:12,14
T-27.II.2:7	Good cannot *be* returned for evil	Mt 5:44
T-27.II.3:8	removed it from his own [eyes]	Mt 7:3-5
T-27.II.6:7	the last trumpet	1 Co 15:52b; Jl 2:1
T-27.II.6:8	there is no death	Rv 21:4b; 2 Tm 1:10
T-27.III.7:1	eyes...seen or ears have heard	Is 64:4; 1 Co 2:9
T-27.V.4:5	Be not afraid	Jn 6:20
T-27.V.11:1	Peace be to you	Jn 20:19,21a,26
T-27.VI.2:11	Sin's witnesses...call of death	Rm 6:23
T-27.VI.3:8	truth he represents	Jn 1:7-8; 18:37c
T-27.VI.5:9	The dying live, the dead arise	Is 26:19; 35:5-6; Mt 10:1,8a; 11:5
T-27.VII.1:5	he knows not what he does	Lk 23:34
T-27.VII.6:6,8	Seek not...to *find*	Mt 7:7b,8b; Dt 4:29
T-27.VII.14:5	there is no death	Rv 21:4b; 2Tm 1:10
T-27.VIII.8:1	others do...you did to them	Mt 7:12
T-28.III.7:1-2	treasures...thieves	Mt 6:19
T-28.III.8:1	Be not afraid	Jn 6:20
T-28.III.8:7-9:8	door is open...the feast of plenty	Lk 14:16-23
T-28.III.9:7	lean years	Gn 41:27

Reference	*Quote*	*Bible Reference*
T-28.IV.7:2	what is joined in Him is...one	Mt 19:6
T-28.IV.9:1	I thank You, Father	Mt 11:25; Jn 11:41
T-28.V.2:4	fear...love	1 Jn 4:18a
T-28.VI.6:4	"You are beloved of Me..."	Mt 3:17; 17:5
T-28.VI.6:5	"...Be you perfect as Myself..."	Mt 5:48
T-28.VII.2:10	what is joined cannot be separate	Mt 19:6
T-28.VII.3:4	who can build his home	Mt 7:24-27
T-28.VII.5:7-7:4	It is like the house...itself alone	Mt 7:24-27
T-28.VII.7:5	ark of safety	Gn 7:9
T-29.I.8:7	"God is Love"	1 Jn 4:8,16
T-29.I.9:6	self be lost by being found	Lk 15:24,32
T-29.II.4:7	the holy ground	Ex 3:5
T-29.II.10:6	from sickness and from death	Jn 11:4
T-29.III.3:12	Whom you forgive	Mt 16:19b; Jn 20:23
T-29.V.4:2	Be...still and hear God's Voice	Ps 46:10
T-29.V.5:2	Behold His Son	Jn 19:5
T-29.V.6:2	his Father's house	Jn 14:2
T-29.V.6:8	how blessed are you	Mt 5:3-11
T-29.VI.2:12	He will be as he was and as he is	Heb 13:8
T-29.VI.4:1	Heaven would not pass away	Mt 24:35
T-29.VI.4:9	There is no death	Rv 21:4b; 2 Tm 1:10
T-29.VI.5:1	world will bind your feet...hands	Jn 11:44
T-29.VII	Seek Not Outside Yourself	Mt 7:7b,8b; Dt 4:29
T-29.VII.10:2	there is no death	Rv 21:4b; 2 Tm 1:10
T-29.VIII.Title	The Anti-Christ	1 Jn 2:18,22

Reference	*Quote*	*Bible Reference*
T-29.VIII.3:1,5	anti-Christ	1 Jn 2:18,22
T-29.VIII.6:2	anti-Christ	1 Jn 2:18,22
T-29.VIII.9:6	If Heaven is within	Lk 17:21
T-29.IX.1:2	bow down in worship…no life	Ex 32:1-8
T-29.IX.2:7,9	Judge not	Mt 7:1
T-29.IX.6:2-7:5	toys…put away	1 Co 13:11
T-30.I.14:8	anti-Christ	1 Jn 2:18,22
T-30.I.16:8	Whose kingdom is the world	Mt 6:24
T-30.I.17:8	as you have received…you give	Mt 10:8b
T-30.II.4:3	whom God so loves	Jn 3:16
T-30.V.7:2	they still look back	Gn 19:26; Lk 9:62
T-30.V.8:2	the gate of Heaven	Gn 28:17
T-30.V.8:6	His Father's house	Jn 14:2
T-30.V.9:3	Look back no longer	Gn 19:26; Lk 9:62
T-30.V.9:8	coins of suffering	Mt 26:15
T-30.V.10:1	Do not look back	Gn 19:26; Lk 9:62
T-30.V.10:5	Be merciful	Lk 6:36
T-30.VI.4:2	God is just	Is 45:21
T-30.VI.9:4	*I thank You, Father*	Mt 11:25; Jn 11:41
T-30.VI.10:4	graven image	Ex 20:4
T-30.VII.7:6-8	Interpreter…common language	Gn 11:1-9; 1 Co 12:10,28
T-30.VIII.3:7	What you ask *is* given you	Mt 7:7a,8a; 21:22
T-30.VIII.5:9	And when He has appeared	1 Jn 3:2
T-31.I.4:4	Voice…small and still	1 K 19:12
T-31.I.6:1	Voice, so small and still	1 K 19:12
T-31.I.10:6	God is Love	1 Jn 4:8,16

Reference	*Quote*	*Bible Reference*
T-31.I.12:1	be still	Ps 46:10
T-31.I.13:4	born again	Jn 3:3,7
T-31.II.6:4	be still	Ps 46:10
T-31.II.7:2	Be still and listen	Ps 46:10
T-31.II.8:1	Be very still an instant	Ps 46:10
T-31.II.10:5	He asks and you receive	Mt 7:7a,8a; 21:22
T-31.III.7:4	God has said...no sacrifice	Ho 6:6; Mt 9:13
T-31.V.8:2-3	seek...find	Mt 7:7b,8b; Dt 4:29
T-31.VI.1:1	flesh...spirit	Jn 3:6
T-31.VI.4:3-4	Your will be done	Mt 6:10b,c
T-31.VI.4:7	"Your will be done"	Mt 6:10b; 26:39,42
T-31.VI.6:4	forgiven it its trespasses	Mt 6:12,14
T-31.VI.7:1-2,5	Your will be done	Mt 6:10b,c
T-31.VII.7:2	you see...nothing with clarity	1 Co 13:12
T-31.VII.12:4	likeness...whose image	Gn 1:26-27
T-31.VIII.2:3	your weakness...Christ in you	2Co 12:9b; Ph4:13
T-31.VIII.3:5	He...not leave you comfortless	Jn 14:18
T-31.VIII.4:1	cannot prevail against	Mt 16:18b
T-31.VIII.10:1	I thank You, Father	Mt 11:25; Jn 11:41
T-31.VIII.12:7	in Your likeness	Gn 1:26-27
T-31.VIII.12:7	lives and moves in You	Ac 17:28

Reference	*Quote*	*Bible Reference*
W-pI.16.1:6	own likeness	Gn 1:26-27
W-pI.20.2:8	great indeed...your reward	Mt 5:12
W-pI.20.3:6	the resurrection and the life	Jn 11:25a
W-pI.20.3:7	all power is given	Mt 28:18
W-pI.38.5:5	dominion over all	Gn 1:28
W-pI.46.1:4	forgive...binding themselves	Mt 16:19b; Jn 20:23
W-pI.47.2:1	Of yourself...these things	Jn 5:19,30
W-pI.48.3:2	His strength...your weakness	2 Co 12:9b; Ph 4:13
W-pI.49.4:2	Be very still	Ps 46:10
W-pI.50.5:4	Such is the Kingdom	Mt 19:14
W-pI.53.5:6	cannot prevail	Mt 16:18b
W-pI.53.5:7	no other gods	Ex 20:3
W-pI.61.Title	the light of the world	Mt 5:14; Jn 8:12
W-pI.61.1:1	the light of the world	Mt 5:14; Jn 8:12
W-pI.61.2:4	the light of the world	Mt 5:14; Jn 8:12
W-pI.61.4:3	depart in peace	Lk 2:29
W-pI.61.5:3	*I am the light of the world*	Mt 5:14; Jn 8:12
W-pI.61.7:4	to build a firm foundation	Lk 6:48
W-pI.61.7:5	You are the light of the world	Mt 5:14; Jn 8:12
W-pI.62.Title	the light of the world	Mt 5:14; Jn 8:12
W-pI.62.1:3	the light of the world	Mt 5:14; Jn 8:12
W-pI.62.3.1	strength of Christ in you	2 Co 12:9b; Ph 4:13
W-pI.62.5:2	*the light of the world*	Mt 5:14; Jn 8:12
W-pI.63.Title	The light of the world	Mt 5:14; Jn 8:12
W-pI.63.1:2	How blessed are you	Mt 5:3-11

Reference	*Quote*	*Bible Reference*
W-pI.63.2:1	the light of the world	Mt 5:14; Jn 8:12
W-pI.63.3:4	*the light of the world*	Mt 5:14; Jn 8:12
W-pI.64.1:1	"...wander into temptation"	Mt 6:13a
W-pI.64.3:1	the light of the world	Mt 5:14; Jn 8:12
W-pI.67.1:2	you are the light of the world	Mt 5:14; Jn 8:12
W-pI.68.3:1	God in their own image	Gn 1:26-27
W-pI.69.Title	the light of the world	Mt 5:14; Jn 8:12
W-pI.69.1:2,5	the light of the world	Mt 5:14; Jn 8:12
W-pI.69.8:6	the power of God	Mt 22:29
W-pI.69.8:6	His Will and yours be done	Mt 6:10b; 26:39,42
W-pI.69.9:1,4,8	the light of the world	Mt 5:14; Jn 8:12
W-pI.71.4:2	"Seek but do not find"	Mt 7:7b,8b; Dt 4:29
W-pI.71.7:3	All things are possible to God	Mt 19:26
W-pI.72.11:3	Ask and you will be answered	Mt 7:7a,8a; 21:22
W-pI.72.11:4	Seek and you will find	Mt 7:7b,8b; Dt 4:29
W-pI.73.Title	I will there be light	Gn 1:3
W-pI.73.7:7	nothing can prevail against it	Mt 16:18b
W-pI.73.10:2	*I will there be light*	Gn 1:3
W-pI.73.11:3	*I will there be light*	Gn 1:3
W-pI.75.5:3	glad tidings	Lk 1:19; 8:1
W-pI.76.2:2	seek salvation...find it	Mt 7:7b,8b; Dt 4:29
W-pI.76.7:4	truth that keeps us free	Jn 8:32
W-pI.77.3:3	the Kingdom...is within you	Lk 17:21
W-pI.77.5:5	the Will of God be done	Mt 6:10b; 26:39,42
W-pI.rII.In.5:1	the way, the truth and the life	Jn 14:6a

Reference	*Quote*	*Bible Reference*
W-pI.81.1:1	the light of the world	Mt 5:14; Jn 8:12
W-pI.81.1:3	Let me be still	Ps 46:10
W-pI.81.2:2-3	*the light of the world*	Mt 5:14; Jn 8:12
W-pI.81.3:1	the light of the world	Mt 5:14; Jn 8:12
W-pI.82.1:1-3	the light of the world	Mt 5:14; Jn 8:12
W-pI.82.2:3	*the light of the world*	Mt 5:14; Jn 8:12
W-pI.84.1:2,7	likeness of my Creator	Gn 1:26-27
W-pI.85.1:1	the light of the world	Mt 5:14; Jn 8:12
W-pI.85.2:3	*The light of the world*	Mt 5:14; Jn 8:12
W-pI.87.1:1	I will there be light	Gn 1:3
W-pI.91.3:7	impossible...you are not alone	Mt 19:26
W-pI.92.3-10	God's strength...Weakness	2 Co 12:9b; Ph4:13
W-pI.92.3:4	eyes that cannot see	Mk 8:18; Jr 5:21
W-pI.92.4:7	God...should be light	Gn 1:3
W-pI.94.4:2	God has...promised...ask	Mt 7:7a,8a; 21:22
W-pI.97.2:4	He is with you always	Mt 28:20
W-pI.98.9:5	on earth as...Heaven	Mt 6:10b,c
W-pI.99.5:5	God is...Love	1 Jn 4:8,16
W-pI.99.6:8	*God still is Love*	1 Jn 4:8,16
W-pI.99.11:4	*God still is Love*	1 Jn 4:8,16
W-pI.100.2:5	Your joy must be complete	Jn 15:11; 16:24
W-pI.102.4:3-4	seek this...find it	Mt 7:7b,8b; Dt 4:29
W-pI.103.Title	God, being Love	1 Jn 4:8,16

Reference	*Quote*	*Bible Reference*
W-pI.103.2:2,4	being Love	1 Jn 4:8.16
W-pI.103.3:3,5	God, being Love	1 Jn 4:8,16
W-pI.106.Title	Let me be still	Ps 46:10
W-pI.106.2:2	Be still	Ps 46:10
W-pI.106.3:4	Be still	Ps 46:10
W-pI.106.4:2	Hear and be silent	Ps 46:10
W-pI.106.7:5	I will be still	Ps 46:10
W-pI.106.9:1	Be still	Ps 46:10
W-pI.106.10:3	Let me be still	Ps 46:10
W-pI.107.1:7	From dust to dust	Gn 2:7; 3:19
W-pI.109.2:6	born again	Jn 3:3,7
W-pI.109.5:6	Let it be still	Ps 46:10
W-pI.109.6:2	born again	Jn 3:3,7
W-pI.110.5:4	truth…set you free	Jn 8:32
W-pI.110.9:3	graven images…worshipped	Ex 20:4
W-pI.110.10:1	Seek Him…find Him	Mt 7:7b,8b; Dt 4:29
W-pI.110.11:6	Word of God…sets you free	Jn 8:32
W-pI.110.11:7	key…gate of Heaven	Mt 16:19a
W-pI.115.1:2	*My function here is to forgive*	Mt 16:19b; Jn 20:23
W-pI.117.1:1	God, being Love	1 Jn 4:8,16
W-pI.117.3:2	God, being Love	1 Jn 4:8,16
W-pI.118.2:1,2	be still	Ps 46:10
W-pI.118.3:4	be still	Ps 46:10
W-pI.121.5:3	bears witness	Jn 1:7-8; 18:37c
W-pI.122.4:4-5	Seek…You will not find	Mt 7:7b,8b; Dt 4:29
W-pI.124.10:1	transfiguration	Mt 17:2

Reference	*Quote*	*Bible Reference*
W-pI.124.10:1	the glass	1 Co 13:12
W-pI.125.4:2	the tidings of salvation	Lk 1:19; 8:1
W-pI.125.9:3,5	be still	Ps 46:10
W-pI.127.6:1	Seek not…to find your Self	Mt 7:7b,8b; Dt 4:29
W-pI.127.9:5	He will abide with you	Jn 14:16b; 15:4,10
W-pI.128.6:1	be still	Ps 46:10
W-pI.128.7:8	Be still	Ps 46:10
W-pI.130.4:7-8	be sought…not be found	Mt 7:7b,8b; Dt 4:29
W-pI.131.4:1-5	search…find	Mt 7:7b,8b; Dt 4:29
W-pI.131.5:2-3	find…seek	Mt 7:7b,8b; Dt 4:29
W-pI.131.12:1	seek…find	Mt 7:7b,8b; Dt 4:29
W-pI.131.14:5	find…seeking	Mt 7:7b,8b; Dt 4:29
W-pI.131.15:5	seek and find	Mt 7:7b,8b; Dt 4:29
W-pI.132.2:4	seeking…want to find	Mt 7:7b,8b; Dt 4:29
W-pI.132.8:4	sick are healed…dead arise	Is 26:19; 35:5-6; Mt 10:1,8a; 11:5
W-pI.133.14:1	the gate of Heaven	Gn 28:17
W-pI.134.4:4	as white as snow	Is 1:18
W-pI.134.10:4	Heaven's gate	Gn 28:17
W-pI.135.6:4	its [body] value…dust	Gn 2:6-7
W-pI.136.15:2	truth…set us free	Jn 8:32
W-pI.137.6:2	anti-Christ	1 Jn 2:18,22
W-pI.139.10:1	he knows not what he is	Lk 23:34
W-pI.140.5:1	Peace be to you	Jn 20:19,21a,26

Reference	*Quote*	*Bible Reference*
W-pI.140.8:5	but seek it...must be found	Mt 7:7b,8b; Dt 4:29
W-pI.140.10:2	We will be still	Ps 46:10
W-pI.rIV.In.6:3	the Lord of Hosts	Ps 46:7,11
W-pI.151.7:3	bear false witness	Ex20:16; Mt 19:18
W-pI.151.12:2	within the Holy, holy as Itself	Ex 26:33
W-pI.151.16:3	your transfiguration	Mt 17:2
W-pI.153.5:2	You know not what you do	Lk 23:34
W-pI.153.6:3	Christ's strength...weakness	2 Co 12:9b; Ph 4:13
W-pI.153.10:1	Be still a moment	Ps 46:10
W-pI.153.11:2	God has elected all, but few	Mt 20:16b; 22:14
W-pI.153.19:3	We rise up strong in Christ	2 Co 12:9b; Ph 4:13
W-pI.153.20:2	Be not afraid nor timid	Jn 6:20
W-pI.155.1:1	living in the world...not here	Jn 15:19; 17:14,16,18
W-pI.155.5:4	serve them...serve yourself	Lv 19:18; Mt 22:39
W-pI.155.8:2	truth...lighting up the path	Is 42:16
W-pI.155.8:2	ransom from illusion	Ps 49:7; Mt20:28
W-pI.156.2:6	Where you are He is	Jn 14:3
W-pI.156.2:9	apart from Him and live	Ac 17:28
W-pI.156.5:5	unto Its likeness	Gn 1:26-27
W-pI.157.8:2	Holy One	Ps 16:10; Mk 1:24
W-pI.158.11:2	its image...its likeness	Gn 1:26-27
W-pI.159.3:4	The darkened glass	1 Co 13:12
W-pI.159.4:3	on earth, as...in Heaven	Mt 6:10b,c
W-pI.159.5:4	and the blind can see	Is 26:19; 35:5-6; Mt 10:1,8a; 11:5
W-pI.159.6:3	received but for the asking	Mt 7:7a,8a; 21:22
W-pI.159.8:1	holy ground	Ex 3:5

Reference	*Quote*	*Bible Reference*
W-pI.160.4:3	fear…created in His likeness	Gn 1:26-27
W-pI.160.6:1-3	search…find	Mt 7:7b,8b; Dt 4:29
W-pI.160.8:5	Whom God has joined	Mt 19:6
W-pI.160.10:5	denies…brother is denying Him	Mt 25:45
W-pI.160.10:5	the gift of sight	Mk 10:51-52
W-pI.161.11:5	nails which pierce	Jn 20:25
W-pI.161.11:5	lift the crown of thorns	Mt 27:29
W-pI.162.2:4-5	trumpet of awakening…its call	1 Co 15:52b; Jl 2:1
W-pI.162.2:6	will never look on death	Jn 8:51; 11:25b,26
W-pI.163.Title	There is no death	Rv 21:4b; 2 Tm 1:10
W-pI.163.8:5	There is no death	Rv 21:4b; 2 Tm 1:10
W-pI.163.9:3	*We live and move in You alone*	Ac 17:28
W-pI.163.9:5	*There is no death*	Rv 21:4b; 2 Tm 1:10
W-pI.165.4:4	Ask…and it is given you	Mt 7:7a,8a; 21:22
W-pI.167.1:5-7	There is no death	Rv 21:4b; 2 Tm 1:10
W-pI.167.12:2	As we were…forever be	Heb 13:8
W-pI.168.1:11	never-changing Love	Jr 31:3
W-pI.169.4:3	bear witness	Jn 1:7-8; 18:37c
W-pI.169.7:2	bear witness	Jn 1:7-8; 18:37c
W-pI.169.7:2	the time…is now at hand	Mt 3:2; 4:17
W-pI.170.10:1	gods of vengeance	Dt 32:35; Rm 12:19
W-pI.rV.In.2:2	*be quiet and…be still*	Ps 46:10
W-pI.rV.In.4:3	*God is but Love*	1 Jn 4:8,16
W-pI.rV.In.10:2	Hallowed your name	Mt 6:9
W-pI.rV.In.10:8	*God is but Love*	1 Jn 4:8,16
W-pI.171-180	God is but Love	1 Jn 4:8,16

Reference	*Quote*	*Bible Reference*
W-pI.182.Title	I will be still an instant	Ps 46:10
W-pI.182.3:2	seeking...find	Mt 7:7b,8b; Dt 4:29
W-pI.182.4:3	His Father's house	Jn 14:2
W-pI.182.4:5	holy ground	Ex 3:5
W-pI.182.8:1	still an instant	Ps 46:10
W-pI.182.11:1	profits nothing	Pr 10:2; Jn 6:63
W-pI.182.12:9	Be still an instant	Ps 46:10
W-pI.183.3:3-4	The sick...blind...deaf	Is 26:19; 35:5-6; Mt 10:1,8a; 11:5
W-pI.183.3:5	tears of pain are dried	Is 25:8; Rv7:17;21:4a
W-pI.183.8:4	Let all thoughts be still	Ps 46:10
W-pI.185.2:6-7	Many...few	Mt 20:16b; 22:14
W-pI.185.2:9	should any two agree	Mt 18:19
W-pI.185.11:1	seeks...find	Mt 7:7b,8b; Dt 4:29
W-pI.186.1:5	the Will of God is done	Mt 6:10b,c
W-pI.189.7:1	Be still	Ps 46:10
W-pI.189.8:1,2	Is it not He...the way to Him	Jn 14:5
W-pI.189.8:5	Ask and receive	Mt 7:7a,8a; 21:22
W-pI.189.10:9	*Your Will...be done in us*	Mt 6:10b,c
W-pI.191.8:3	Son of God has come in glory	Mt 16:27; 25:31
W-pI.191.8:3	redeem the lost...the helpless	Mt 18:11
W-pI.191.9:1	All power is given unto you	Mt 28:18
W-pI.191.9:2	nothing that you cannot do	Mt 17:20c
W-pI.191.11:1,2	They must await...you are free	Mt 16:19b; Jn 20:23
W-pI.192.8:1	born again in Christ	Jn 3:3,7
W-pI.192.9:2	Release instead of bind	Mt 16:19b; Jn 20:23
W-pI.193.9:4	all tears be wiped away	Is 25:8; Rv 7:17; 21:4a

Reference	*Quote*	*Bible Reference*
W-pI.193.11:1	Give…and give a little more	Mt 19:21
W-pI.193.11:2	arise…our Father's house	Lk 15:18
W-pI.193.11:2	our Father's house	Jn 14:2
W-pI.193.13:5	Heaven's gate	Gn 28:17
W-pI.194.1:3	Heaven's gate	Gn 28:17
W-pI.195.4:5	It will never be…bound	Mt 16:19b; Jn 20:23
W-pI.197.2:1	know not what…do	Lk 23:34
W-pI.197.3:1	The world…offer it release	Mt 16:19b; Jn 20:23
W-pI.197.7:3	live and move in Him	Ac 17:28
W-pI.198.10:3	on earth and…holy home	Mt 6:10b,c
W-pI.198.10:4	as you forgive the trespasses	Mt 6:12,14
W-pI.200.1:1,2	Seek…find	Mt 7:7b,8b; Dt 4:29
W-pI.200.3:5-6	Seek…find	Mt 7:7b,8b; Dt 4:29
W-pI.200.4:2-5	found…find	Mt 7:7b,8b; Dt 4:29
W-pI.200.5:3	You will be bound…as he is	Mt 16:19b; Jn 20:23
W-pI.200.7:2-6	find…find	Mt 7:7b,8b; Dt 4:29
W-pI.200.8:2	gate of Heaven	Gn 28:17
W-pI.200.9:2	the path is straight	Is 40:3; Jn 1:23
W-pI.200.11:1,2	seek…found	Mt 7:7b,8b; Dt 4:29
W-pI.202.1:1	I will be still an instant	Ps 46:10
W-pI.208.1:2	*I will be still*	Ps 46:10
W-pI.219.1:4	*Be still, my mind*	Ps 46:10
W-pII.In.8:1,2	search for truth…found	Mt 7:7b,8b; Dt 4:29
W-pII.In.10:5	we need but be still	Ps 46:10
W-pII.221.Title	Let all my thoughts be still	Ps 46:10
W-pII.221.2:6	let our thoughts be still	Ps 46:10

Reference	*Quote*	*Bible Reference*
W-pII.222.Title	I live and move in Him	Ac 17:28
W-pII.229.1:1	I seek...and find It	Mt 7:7b,8b; Dt 4:29
W-pII.230.Title	seek and find	Mt 7:7b,8b; Dt 4:29
W-pII.230.2:1,5	*seek...find*	Mt 7:7b,8b; Dt 4:29
W-pII.231.1:1-4	*seek...to find*	Mt 7:7b,8b; Dt 4:29
W-pII.231.2:4-5	seek...to find	Mt 7:7b,8b; Dt 4:29
W-pII.237.1:2	arise in glory...shine	Is 60:1
W-pII.3.3:2	find...seek	Mt 7:7b,8b; Dt 4:29
W-pII.246.1:1	if I have hatred in my heart	1 Jn 2:9; 4:20
W-pII.4.4:4	loves him...everlasting Love	Jr 31:3
W-pII.4.5:8	How long, O holy Son of God	Ps 89:46; 13:1
W-pII.251.1:1,2, 3,9	I sought...I find myself	Mt 7:7b,8b; Dt 4:29
W-pII.254.Title	every voice but God's be still	Ps 46:10
W-pII.255.1:4	bear witness to the truth	Jn 1:7-8; 18:37c
W-pII.261.1:5	my refuge and my strength	Ps 46:1
W-pII.261.2:1,3	*Let me not seek...and find*	Mt 7:7b,8b; Dt 4:29
W-pII.262.2:3	be sought and found	Mt 7:7b,8b; Dt 4:29
W-pII.263.2:2	our Father's house	Jn 14:2
W-pII.264.1:1	*before me and...beside me*	Ps 139:5
W-pII.266.2:1	This day we enter into paradise	Lk 23:43
W-pII.6.5:2	let us seek to find	Mt 7:7b,8b; Dt 4:29

Reference	*Quote*	*Bible Reference*
W-pII.277	Let me not bind Your Son	Mt 16:19b; Jn 20:23
W-pII.287.1:4	seek and find	Mt 7:7b,8b; Dt 4:29
W-pII.292.1:6	God's Will is done	Mt 6:10b,c
W-pII.292.1:7	We will seek…find	Mt 7:7b,8b; Dt 4:29
W-pII.296.2:3	seek and find	Mt 7:7b,8b; Dt 4:29
W-pII.9	Second Coming	Mt 16:27; 25:31
W-pII.9.3:1	Last Judgment	Mt 11:22
W-pII.301.Title	God…wipe away all tears	Is 25:8; Rv 7:17; 21:4a
W-pII.303.Title	The holy Christ is born in me	Jn 3:3,7
W-pII.303.1:6	He is born again in me	Jn 3:3,7
W-pII.10	Last Judgment	Mt 11:22
W-pII.10.1	Second Coming	Mt 16:27; 25:31
W-pII.10.4:2	Be not afraid of love	Jn 6:20
W-pII.10.4:3	wipe away all tears	Is 25:8; Rv 7:17; 21:4a
W-pII.319.Title	I came…salvation…world	Jn 18:37b
W-pII.320.Title	My Father…power unto me	Mt 28:18
W-pII.320.1:4	in earth and Heaven	Mt 28:18
W-pII.11.4:6	let God's Will…on earth	Mt 6:10b,c
W-pII.322.1:4	the likeness of Himself	Gn 1:26-27
W-pII.322.1:4	Holy One	Ps 16:10; Mk 1:24
W-pII.323.1:1	*Your beloved Son*	Mt 3:17; 17:5
W-pII.325.1:2	therefore seeks to find	Mt 7:7b,8b; Dt 4:29

Reference	*Quote*	*Bible Reference*
W-pII.326.1:7	*as it is in Heaven, so on earth*	Mt 6:10b,c
W-pII.328.Title	second place to gain the first	Mt 19:30;20:16a
W-pII.332.Title	Fear binds....sets it free	Mt 16:19b; Jn 20:23
W-pII.332.2:1-4	*bind...release*	Mt 16:19b; Jn 20:23
W-pII.334.1:6	I go to find	Mt 7:7b,8b; Dt 4:29
W-pII.334.2:1	*I seek*	Mt 7:7b,8b; Dt 4:29
W-pII.338.1:7	His beloved Son	Mt 3:17; 17:5
W-pII.342.1:5	*gate of Heaven*	Gn 28:17
W-pII346.1:3-4,7	*I do not seek...would find*	Mt 7:7b,8b; Dt 4:29
W-pII346.1:6	*I would abide in You*	Jn 14:16b;15:4,10
W-pII.347.2:2	Be very still	Ps 46:10
W-pII.348.Title	Your grace suffices me	2 Co 12:9a
W-pII.349.2:1	Our Father knows our needs	Mt 6:8,32
W-pII.14.3:5	the gate of Heaven	Gn 28:17
W-pII.14.5:1	it is written on our hearts	Rm 2:15
W-pII.14.5:3	glad tidings	Lk 1:19; 8:1
W-pII.14.5:5	the gate of Heaven	Gn 28:17
W-pII.352.1:6	*not left me comfortless*	Jn 14:18
W-pII.358.1:5	*be still, remembering*	Ps 46:10
W-pII.FL.4:4	the way, the truth and life	Jn 14:6a
W-pII.FL.6:3	"...all I have is his"	Lk 15:31
W-Ep.5:7	For we go homeward	Lk 15:20
W-Ep.6:8	never leave you comfortless	Jn 14:18

manual for teachers

Reference	*Quote*	*Bible Reference*
M-1.1:4	light has entered the darkness	Jn 1:5; Lk 1:79
M-1.1:7	bringer of salvation	Lk 1:77
M-1.2:7	Many hear…few will answer	Mt 20:16b; 22:14
M-2.5:3	any two who join together	Mt 18:20
M-4.I.1:5	*in* them but not *of* them	Jn 15:19; 17:14,16,18
M-4.IX.2:10	seeking…it finds	Mt 7:7b,8b; Dt 4:29
M-4.X.3:8	glad tidings	Lk 1:19; 8:1
M-4.X.3:9	Blessed indeed are they	Mt 5:3-11
M-4.X.3:9	bringers of salvation	Lk 1:77
M-10.3:3	judge anything rightly	Jn 7:24
M-12.2:1	son of man	Ezk 2:1; Mt 8:20
M-13.3:3	to seek without finding	Mt 7:7b,8b; Dt 4:29
M-13.5:8	"Seek but do not find"	Mt 7:7b,8b; Dt 4:29
M-14.5:13	His Will be done	Mt 6:10b; 26:39,42
M-15	Final Judgment	Mt 11:22
M-15.2:8	Judge not	Mt 7:1
M-15.2:12	Learn to be quiet…stillness	Ps 46:10
M-15.3:6	There is no deceit in God	Is 37:10; Jr 20:7
M-15.3:7	His promises are sure	Lk 24:49; Ps 105:42
M-16.11:11	the gate of Heaven	Gn 28:17
M-17.9:10	There is no death	Rv 21:4b; 2Tm 1:10
M-19.5:11	What had been lost…found	Lk 15:24,32
M-20.1:1	peace…not of this world	Jn 14:27a,b; 18:36
M-20.3:2	fail to find…but seeks	Mt 7:7b,8b; Dt 4:29

Reference	*Quote*	*Bible Reference*
M-21.1:3	What you ask for you receive	Mt 7:7a,8a; 21:22
M-22.7:10	"This is my beloved Son"	Mt 3:17; 17:5
M-23.1:4	"Ask...Jesus Christ"	Jn 14:13-14; 16:23
M-23.3:7	Remember his promises	Jn 14:13-14; 16:23
M-23.7:8	he is with you...always here	Mt 28:20
M-25.2:6	the walls...fall	Jos 6:20
M-25.4:9	withheld from love...fear	1 Jn 4:18a
M-26.1:2	His Word...everyone's heart	Rm 2:15
M-27.6:1	"...overcome...death"	1 Co 15:26
M-28.6:6	Final Judgment	Mt 11:22
M-29.4:2	"Of myself I can do nothing"	Jn 5:19,30
M-29.6:5	translate...into His language	Rm 8:26
M-29.6:9-11	A loving father...His Son	Mt 7:9-11
M-29.7:2	your weakness is His strength	2 Co 12:9b; Ph 4:13
M-29.8:4	of all things visible	Col 1:16

clarification of terms

Reference	*Quote*	*Bible Reference*
C-3.3:2	God knows what His Son needs	Mt 6:8,32
C-3.4:9	Heaven...outside the gate	Gn 28:17
C-4.8:2	Hallowed your name and His	Mt 6:9
C-5.1:6	Their names are legion	Mk 5:9
C-5.6:9	*There is no death*	Rv 21:4b; 2Tm 1:10
C-6.1:1	Jesus...ascended into Heaven	Ac 1:8-9; 2:1-4
C-6.1:2	in His likeness or spirit	Gn 1:26-27
C-6.2:3	All power in Heaven and earth	Mt 28:18
C-6.4:6	a far country	Lk 15:13
C-Ep.1:11	the Holy of the Holies	Ex 26:33
C-Ep.2:2	loves you as He loves Himself	Lv 19:18; Mt 22:39
C-Ep.2:3	Ask...help to roll the stone away	Mt28:2;Jn11:38-39
C-Ep.3:1	Be not afraid	Jn 6:20
C-Ep.5:4	morning star	Rv 2:28; 22:16

“Psychotherapy: Purpose, Process and Practice”

Reference	*Quote*	*Bible Reference*
P-1.2:3	the Way, the Truth and the Life	Jn 14:6a
P-2.II.1:5	the temple of the Holy Spirit	1 Co 6:19; 3:16
P-2.II.6:5	If any two are joined	Mt 18:20
P-2.II.9:4	Let him be still	Ps 46:10
P-2.IV.2:2	asked for and...received	Mt 7:7a,8a; 21:22
P-2.V.4:6	helpless of ourselves	Jn 5:19,30
P-2.V.7:5	forgive...trespasses	Mt 6:12,14
P-2.VII.1:2	Physician, heal thyself	Lk 4:23
P-2.VII.6:4	all power in earth and Heaven	Mt 28:18
P-3.II.4:1	God is said to have looked	Gn 1:31
P-3.III.5:1	to him who hath...given	Mt 13:12
P-3.III.6:3,4	Relationships...temple	1 Co 6:19; 3:16
P-3.III.8:1	Physician...heal thyself	Lk 4:23
P-3.III.8:9	glad tidings of salvation	Lk 1:19; 8:1
P-3.III.8:13	God sent His Son	Rm 8:3

“The Song of Prayer”

Reference	*Quote*	*Bible Reference*
S-1.I.1:7	Ask…to receive	Mt 7:7a,8a; 21:22
S-1.I.3:6	sought first the Kingdom	Mt 6:33
S-1.I.4:4	have no gods before Him	Ex 20:3
S-1.II.2:5	prays without ceasing	Th 5:17
S-1.II.2:6	Ask and you have received	Mt 7:7a,8a; 21:22
S-2.I.2:2	seek and find	Mt 7:7b,8b; Dt 4:29
S-2.I.2:5	Forgiveness-to-destroy *is* death	Rm 6:23
S-2.I.3:10	as you see the Son	Mt 25:40
S-2.II.7:7	Christ is for all…in all	1 Co 15:28; Ep 1:23
S-2.III.3:2	arise…your Father’s house	Lk 15:18
S-2.III.3:2	your Father’s house	Jn 14:2
S-2.III.7:5	He will not leave you comfortless	Jn 14:18
S-3.I.1:5	back to dust…will return	Gn 2:7; 3:19
S-3.II.4:4	depart in peace	Lk 2:29
S-3.III.6:6	no fear…for love has entered	1 Jn 4:18a
S-3.IV.2:6	His likeness	Gn 1:26,27
S-3.IV.5:1	as you choose…and God to you	Mt 25:40
S-3.IV.5:6	Vengeance is His	Dt 32:35; Rm 12:19
S-3.IV.7:4	Be still an instant	Ps 46:10
S-3.IV.9:3	the thorns fall…bleeding brow	Mt 27:29

Bible

Old Testament

New Testament

OLD TESTAMENT

Genesis

Chapter and Verse	*Quote*	*Course Reference*
1:3	Let there be light	T-9.V.6:2
		W-pI.73.Title; 10:2; 11:3
		W-pI.87.1:1
		W-pI.92.4:7
1:26-27	make man in our image	T-1.I.24:2
		T-2.I.1:5
		T-3.II.4:1
		T-3.V.7:1
		T-8.V.2:1
		T-31.VII.12:4
		T-31.VIII.12:7
		W-pI.16.1:6
		W-pI.68.3:1
		W-pI.84.1:2,7
		W-pI.156.5:5
		W-pI.158.11:2
		W-pI.160.4:3
		W-pII.322.1:4
		C-6.1:2
		S-3.IV.2:6
1:28	dominion over [all]	W-pI.38.5:5
1:31	God…good	T-2.VIII.4:3
		P-3.II.4:1
Chapters 2-3	garden of Eden	T-2.I.3:1-4:5
2:6-7	God formed man…dust	W-pI.135.6:4

Chapter and Verse	*Quote*	*Course Reference*
2:7 (3:19)	God formed man…dust…………	T-13.IV.1:5
	………………………………………	T-13.VII.3:5
	………………………………………	W-pI.107.1:7
	………………………………………	S-3.I.1:5
2:16-17	tree…good and evil………………	T-3.VII.3:4
2:21	deep sleep…Adam………………	T-2.I.3:6; 4:5
3:1-7	the fall…………………………………	T-1.VI.1:6
3:19 (see Gn 2:7)	dust thou art	
3:23-24	God…garden of Eden……………	T-3.I.3:9
	………………………………………	T-10.I.1:7
	………………………………………	T-13.In.3:6
3:24	flaming sword……………………	T-24.III.4:7
4:9	Am I my brother's keeper?……	T-24.II.11:1
7:9	Noah's ark………………………	T-20.IV.6:5
	………………………………………	T-28.VII.7:5
11:1-9 (1 Co 12:10,28)	tower of Babel……………………	T-9.I.6:1
	………………………………………	T-30.VII.7:6-8
19:26 (Lk 9:62)	his wife looked back……………	T-14.II.6:5
	………………………………………	T-20.VI.9:6
	………………………………………	T-30.V.7:2; 9:3; 10:1
25:31-33	Jacob–birthright…………………	T-12.IV.6:7
	………………………………………	T-24.III.2:7

Chapter and Verse	*Quote*	*Course Reference*
28:17	the gate of heaven	T-13.VIII.10:6
	....	T-13.X.14:6
	....	T-25.VIII.7:4
	....	T-26.III.2:4; 3:5
	....	T-26.IV.1:2,4; 4:1; 6:1
	....	T-26.V.1:5; 2:4; 14:3
	....	T-30.V.8:2
	....	W-pI.133.14:1
	....	W-pI.134.10:4
	....	W-pI.193.13:5
	....	W-pI.194.1:3
	....	W-pI.200.8:2
	....	W-pII.342.1:5
	....	W-pII.14.3:5; 5:5
	....	M-16.11:11
	....	C-3.4:9
41:27	years of famine	T-28.III.9:7

Chapter and Verse	*Quote*	*Course Reference*
3:5	holy ground	T-14.V.9:5
		T-18.I.9:4
		T-26.IV.3:1
		T-26.IX.2:4; 3:7
		T-29.II.4:7
		W-pI.159.8:1
		W-pI.182.4:5
20:3	no other gods	T-4.III.6:6
		T-10.III.8:3; 10:3; 11:3
		T-10.IV.1:5; 3:4; 4:4
		T-11.III.6:3
		T-16.V.13:1
		W-pI.53.5:7
		S-1.I.4:4
20:4	Thou shalt…graven image	T-30.VI.10:4
		W-pI.110.9:3
20:5 (34:14)	I…am a jealous God	T-10.III.8:4
20:16 (Mt 19:18)	false witness	T-5.VI.10:3
		T-11.V.18:5
		W-pI.151.7:3
26:33	the holy place	W-pI.151.12:2
		C-Ep.1:11
32:1-8	molten calf…worshipped	T-29.IX.1:2
34:7	iniquity of the fathers	T-5.VI.8:1

Chapter and Verse	*Quote*	*Course Reference*
34:14 (see 20:5)	the Lord…jealous God	

Chapter and Verse	*Quote*	*Course Reference*
19:18 (Mt 22:39)	thy neighbour as thyself............	T-1.I.18:3
	....	T-5.In.3:6
	....	T-5.IV.8:7
	....	T-10.I.1:3
	....	T-12.II.3:4
	....	T-18.V.5:1
	....	T-19.III.11:2
	....	T-25.I.2:7
	....	T-26.I.3:8
	....	T-26.X.3:6
	....	W-pI.155.5:4
	....	C-Ep.2:2

Numbers

Chapter and Verse	*Quote*	*Course Reference*
6:25	Lord...face shine upon thee	T-14.II.4:3
6:25-26	shine upon thee...peace.............	T-4.IV.9:3

Deuteronomy

Chapter and Verse	*Quote*	*Course Reference*
4:29 (see Mt 7:7b,8b)	seek the Lord...find him	
5:29 (see Qo 12:13)	fear me...commandments	
31:6,8	he will not fail thee	T-24.In.1:4
32:35 (Rm 12:19)	To me belongeth vengeance.......	T-3.I.3:1
	....	T-5.VI.7:1
	....	T-25.VIII.5:5
	....	W-pI.170.10:1
	....	S-3.IV.5:6
33:27	everlasting arms	T-20.VI.10:5

Joshua

Chapter and Verse	*Quote*	*Course Reference*
6:20	sound of the trumpet…wall…….	M-25.2:6

Chapter and Verse	*Quote*	*Course Reference*
6:12 (see Lk 1:28)	The Lord is with thee	

1 Kings

Chapter and Verse	*Quote*	*Course Reference*
19:12	a still small voice	T-21.V.1:6
	....	T-31.I.4:4; 6:1

Job

Chapter and Verse	*Quote*	*Course Reference*
2:9	curse God, and die	T-24.III.7:6
13:9 (Ga 6:7b)	as one man mocketh another......	T-1.V.4:3
	....	T-21.VI.11:5
19:25	my redeemer liveth	T-11.VI.9:5
	....	T-12.II.9:3

Psalms

Chapter and Verse	*Quote*	*Course Reference*
8:4 (Heb 2:6)	What is man	T-20.V.8:4
13:1 (see 89:46)	how long...hide thy face	
16:10 (Mk 1:24)	Holy One..................................	T-4.III.7:2; 8:3
	....	T-4.IV.9:3
	....	T-4.VI.6:4
	....	T-23.I.11:3
	....	T-24.III.6:7
	....	W-pI.157.8:2
	....	W-pII.322.1:4
18:13-14 (see 144:6-7)	Lord...lightnings	
23:2-3	he leadeth me	T-14.III.19:2
	....	T-19.IV-D.17:9
23:4	I will fear no evil.......................	T-23.In.3:1
	....	T-27.I.1:3
23:6	goodness and mercy...follow	T-13.I.6:7
24:4 (see Mt 5:8)	a pure heart	
31:5 (see Lk 23:46)	I commit my spirit	
37:11 (see Mt 5:5)	meek shall inherit the earth	
37:20	the wicked shall perish..............	T-5.VI.9:1
40:8	I delight to do thy will	T-1.VII.1:4

Chapter and Verse	*Quote*	*Course Reference*
46:1	God...refuge and strength	W-pII.261.1:5
46:7,11	The Lord of hosts........................	W-pI.rIV.In.6:3
46:10	Be still...I am God	T-4.In.2:2
	....	T-4.I.8:6
	....	T-4.II.5:8
	....	T-13.X.11:10
	....	T-29.V.4:2
	....	T-31.I.12:1
	....	T-31.II.6:4; 7:2; 8:1
	....	W-pI.49.4:2
	....	W-pI.81.1:3
	....	W-pI.106.Title; 2:2; 3:4; 4:2; 7:5; 9:1; 10:3
	....	W-pI.109.5:6
	....	W-pI.118.2:1-2; 3:4
	....	W-pI.125.9:3,5
	....	W-pI.128.6:1; 7:8
	....	W-pI.140.10:2
	....	W-pI.153.10:1
	....	W-pI.rV.In.2:2
	....	W-pI.182.Title; 8:1; 12:9
	....	W-pI.183.8:4
	....	W-pI.189.7:1
	....	W-pI.202.1:1
	....	W-pI.208.1:2

Chapter and Verse	*Quote*	*Course Reference*
46:10 (cont.)	Be still…I am God	W-pI.219.1:4
	....	W-pII.In.10:5
	....	W-pII.221.Title; 2:6
	....	W-pII.254.Title
	....	W-pII.347.2:2
	....	W-pII.358.1:5
	....	M-15.2:12
	....	P-2.II.9:4
	....	S-3.IV.7:4
49:7 (Mt 20:28)	ransom for him...........................	W-pI.155.8:2
89:46 (13:1)	How long, Lord?........................	W-pII.4.5:8
105:42 (see Lk 24:49)	remembered his…promise	
110:1 (Mk 16:19)	Sit thou at my right hand	T-25.VIII.9:11
115:9 (121:2)	trust thou in the Lord	T-10.V.4:4
118:26 (Mt 21:9)	Blessed…name of the Lord.......	T-11.IV.8:1
121:1	I will lift up mine eyes...............	T-20.II.8:11
121:2 (see 115:9)	My help…from the Lord	
139:5	Thou…behind and before..........	W-pII.264.1:1
144:6-7(18:13-14)	Cast forth lightning....................	T-25.VIII.6:4
149:6 (Rv 1:16)	a two-edged sword.....................	T-2.II.4:8

Chapter and Verse	*Quote*	*Course Reference*
150:1-6 (Rm 15:11)	Praise ye the Lord	T-4.VII.6:1

Chapter and Verse	*Quote*	*Course Reference*
10:2 (Jn 6:63)	Treasures...profit nothing..........	T-12.VI.1:2
	....	W-pI.182.11:1
23:7	as he thinketh in his heart	T-1.III.2:4
	....	T-21.In.1:6

Chapter and Verse	*Quote*	*Course Reference*
12:13 (Dt 5:29)	Fear God…commandments…….	T-3.III.6:7

Chapter and Verse	*Quote*	*Course Reference*
1:18	white as snow..............................	W-pI.134.4:4
9:6	The Prince of Peace	T-15.III.8:4
	....	T-15.XI.7:2
11:6 (65:25)	wolf...dwell with the lamb........	T-3.I.5:3
25:8 (Rv 7:17; 21:4a)	God will wipe away tears	T-27.I.5:5
	....	W-pI.183.3:5
	....	W-pI.193.9:4
	....	W-pII.301.Title
	....	W-pII.10.4:3
26:19; 35:5-6 (Mt 10:1,8a;11:5)	dead...live...eyes...opened	T-1.I.24:1
	....	T-5.VII.2:3
	....	T-8.IX.7:1
	....	T-27.VI.5:9
	....	W-pI.132.8:4
	....	W-pI.159.5:4
	....	W-pI.183.3:3-4
37:10 (Jr 20:7)	Let not thy God...deceive	M-15.3:6
40:3 (Jn 1:23)	make straight...highway...........	T-20.IV.8:5
	....	W-pI.200.9:2
42:16	I will lead them in paths............	W-pI.155.8:2
43:10,12 (see Ac 1:8)	Ye are my witnesses	

Chapter and Verse	*Quote*	*Course Reference*
45:21	a just God....................................	T-30.VI.4:2
51:3	desert…garden of the Lord........	T-18.VIII.9:3
60:1	Arise…thy light is come............	W-pII.237.1:2
64:4 (1 Co 2:9)	not heard…neither…seen..........	T-27.III.7:1
65:17 (Rv 21:1)	new heavens…new earth...........	T-11.VII.1:4
65:25 (see 11:6)	wolf…lamb…feed together	

Chapter and Verse	*Quote*	*Course Reference*
5:21 (see Mk 8:18)	have eyes, and see not	
6:16 (see Mt 11:29b)	find rest for your souls	
7:11 (Mt 21:13)	house...den of robbers..............	T-23.I.11:3
20:7 (see Is 37:10)	Lord, thou hast deceived me	
31:3	loved...everlasting love............	T-25.I.1:7
	....	W-pI.168.1:11
	....	W-pII.4.4:4

Chapter and Verse	*Quote*	*Course Reference*
2:1 (Mt 8:20)	Son of man	T-13.II.9:7
	....	T-24.VII.11:8
	....	T-25.In.2:6
	....	M-12.2:1
7:19 (Jn 3:36)	wrath of the Lord	T-6.I.14:3

Daniel

Chapter and Verse	*Quote*	*Course Reference*
7:27	kingdom…everlasting	T-16.III.7:7

Hosea

Chapter and Verse	*Quote*	*Course Reference*
6:6 (Mt 9:13)	mercy…not sacrifice..................	T-3.I.8:3
	....	T-31.III.7:4

Joel

Chapter and Verse	*Quote*	*Course Reference*
2:1 (see 1 Co 15:52b)	Blow ye the trumpet in Zion	

NEW TESTAMENT

Matthew

Chapter and Verse	*Quote*	*Course Reference*
3:2 (4:17)	kingdom…is at hand	T-21.III.9:6
	....	W-pI.169.7:2
3:17 (17:5)	This is my beloved Son.............	T-4.I.8:6
	....	T-7.VII.6:2
	....	T-24.VII.1:7; 10:6
	....	T-25.VII.4:2
	....	T-27.I.1:9
	....	T-28.VI.6:4
	....	W-pII.323.1:1
	....	W-pII.338.1:7
	....	M-22.7:10
4:1-11 (Rv 12:7-10)	the devil	T-3.VII.2:4-6
4:1-11 (Heb 2:18)	tempted of the devil	T-4.I.13:5
4:17 (see 3:2)	kingdom…is at hand	
4:19	Follow me	T-1.V.6:2
	....	T-7.XI.1:3
5:3-11	Blessed are	T-7.V.10:12
	....	T-11.I.11:6
	....	T-11.VIII.7:7
	....	T-14.In.1:1
	....	T-14.V.9:1
	....	T-15.II.2:4
	....	T-29.V.6:8
	....	W-pI.63.1:2

Chapter and Verse	*Quote*	*Course Reference*
5:3-11 (cont.)	Blessed are	M-4.X.3:9
5:5 (Ps 37:11)	Blessed are the meek	T-2.II.7:4
	....	T-4.I.12:4
5:8 (Ps 24:4)	Blessed are the pure in heart......	T-3.I.5:4
	....	T-3.II.5:8
	....	T-20.III.11:5
5:12	great is your reward	W-pI.20.2:8
5:14 (Jn 8:12)	the light of the world.................	T-5.II.10:3
	....	T-6.II.13:4-5
	....	T-8.IV.2:5
	....	T-13.VI.10:1
	....	W-pI.61.Title; 1:1; 2:4; 5:3; 7:5
	....	W-pI.62.Title; 1:3; 5:2
	....	W-pI.63.Title; 2:1; 3:4
	....	W-pI.64.3:1
	....	W-pI.67.1:2
	....	W-pI.69.Title; 1:2,5; 9:1,4,8
	....	W-pI.81.1:1; 2:2-3; 3:1
	....	W-pI.82.1:1-3; 2:3
	....	W-pI.85.1:1; 2:3
5:16	Let your light so shine	T-9.II.5:9
5:17	the law...fulfil...........................	T-1.IV.4:3
5:29	if thy right eye offend thee.........	T-11.VIII.12:1
5:39	thy right cheek...the other.........	T-5.IV.4:6

Chapter and Verse	*Quote*	*Course Reference*
5:41	go a mile…twain	T-4.In.1:1
5:44	do good…that hate you	T-27.II.2:7
5:48	Be ye therefore perfect..............	T-8.IX.7:1
	....	T-28.VI.6:5
6:8,32	Father knoweth…need	T-13.VII.10:2
	....	T-14.XI.7:3
	....	W-pII.349.2:1
	....	C-3.3:2
6:9	Hallowed be thy name	W-pI.rV.In.10:2
	....	C-4.8:2
6:9-13	Our Father…Amen.	T-16.VII.12
6:10b (26:39,42)	Thy will be done	T-18.V.4:3
	....	T-24.III.5:8
	....	T-31.VI.4:7
	....	W-pI.69.8:6
	....	W-pI.77.5:5
	....	M-14.5:13
6:10b,c	Thy will…earth…heaven..........	T-5.II.8:4
	....	T-31.VI.4:3-4; 7:1-2,5
	....	W-pI.98.9:5
	....	W-pI.159.4:3
	....	W-pI.186.1:5
	....	W-pI.189.10:9
	....	W-pI.198.10:3
	....	W-pII.292.1:6
	....	W-pII.11.4:6

Chapter and Verse	*Quote*	*Course Reference*
6:10b,c (cont.)	Thy will...earth...heaven..........	W-pII.326.1:7
6:11	our daily bread..........................	T-2.III.5:10
6:12,14	forgive...trespasses....................	T-27.II.1:10
	....	T-31.VI.6:4
	....	W-pI.198.10:4
	....	P-2.V.7:5
6:13a	lead us not into temptation.........	T-1.III.4:7
	....	T-20.I.3:3
	....	T-23.In.5:1
	....	W-pI.64.1:1
6:13b	thine is the kingdom..................	T-5.VI.10:8
	....	T-7.VII.11:6
	....	T-8.II.7:1,7; 8:1
	....	T-8.III.2:6; 5:3,5; 7:2,8; 8:1
	....	T-8.VII.5:3; 6:3
	....	T-15.III.6:5
	....	T-17.IV.16:3
6:19	treasures...thieves	T-24.IV.3:15
	....	T-28.III.7:1-2
6:20	treasures in heaven...thieves.....	T-25.IX.2:4
6:21	your treasure...your heart..........	T-2.II.1:5
	....	T-8.VI.10:3
	....	T-13.IX.2:6
	....	T-13.X.13:1
	....	T-14.II.1:7
6:24	serve two masters......................	T-1.V.5:3

Chapter and Verse	*Quote*	*Course Reference*
6:24 (cont.)	serve two masters........................	T-17.I.2:4
	....	T-19.IV-A.11:3
	....	T-30.I.16:8
6:33	seek ye first the kingdom..........	T-3.VI.11:8
	....	T-7.IV.7:1
	....	S-1.I.3:6
7:1	Judge not...be not judged..........	T-3.VI.1:4
	....	T-14.V.11:4
	....	T-25.VIII.13:3
	....	T-29.IX.2:7,9
	....	M-15.2:8
7:2	with what measure ye mete........	T-9.II.11:8
7:3-5	mote...brother's eye	T-27.II.3:8
7:3-5 (23:25-26)	mote...cup	T-3.III.5:1
7:7a,8a (21:22)	Ask...be given you	T-4.III.5:3
	....	T-8.III.1:2
	....	T-9.II.3:1
	....	T-11.VIII.5:4
	....	T-30.VIII.3:7
	....	T-31.II.10:5
	....	W-pI.72.11:3
	....	W-pI.94.4:2
	....	W-pI.159.6:3
	....	W-pI.165.4:4
	....	W-pI.189.8:5
	....	M-21.1:3
	....	P-2.IV.2:2

Chapter and Verse	*Quote*	*Course Reference*
7:7a,8a (21:22) (cont.)	Ask...be given you....................	S-1.I.1:7
	....	S-1.II.2:6
7:7b,8b (Dt 4:29)	seek, and ye shall find...............	T-2.I.5:9-10
	....	T-4.V.5:2
	....	T-12.IV.Title; 1:3-4; 2:3; 4:2,5
	....	T-12.V.7:1
	....	T-12.VII.6:3
	....	T-13.I.5:3-5
	....	T-13.VI.5:4
	....	T-13.VIII.7:3
	....	T-14.X.10:5-7
	....	T-15.III.10:9
	....	T-15.VI.2:2
	....	T-15.VIII.3:9
	....	T-15.XI.6:1-2
	....	T-16.IV.6:1
	....	T-16.V.6:5; 7:2-3
	....	T-16.VII.11:1
	....	T-17.III.6:3
	....	T-19.IV-B.12:1; 17:5-6
	....	T-21.III.6:1
	....	T-21.VII.4:3; 5:5
	....	T-22.VI.1:9
	....	T-25.II.2:6
	....	T-27.VII.6:6,8

Chapter and Verse	*Quote*	*Course Reference*
7:7b,8b(Dt 4:29) (cont.)	seek, and ye shall find...............	T-29.VII
	....	T-31.V.8:2-3
	....	W-pI.71.4:2
	....	W-pI.72.11:4
	....	W-pI.76.2:2
	....	W-pI.102.4:3-4
	....	W-pI.110.10:1
	....	W-pI.122.4:4-5
	....	W-pI.127.6:1
	....	W-pI.130.4:7-8
	....	W-pI.131.4:1-5; 5:2-3; 12:1; 14:5; 15:5
	....	W-pI.132.2:4
	....	W-pI.140.8:5
	....	W-pI.160.6:1-3
	....	W-pI.182.3:2
	....	W-pI.185.11:1
	....	W-pI.200.1:1-2; 3:5-6; 4:2-5; 7:2-6; 11:1-2
	....	W-pII.In.8:1-2
	....	W-pII.229.1:1
	....	W-pII.230.Title; 2:1,5
	....	W-pII.231.1:1-4; 2:4-5
	....	W-pII.3.3:2

Chapter and Verse	*Quote*	*Course Reference*
7:7b,8b (Dt 4:29) (cont.)	seek, and ye shall find...............	W-pII.251.1:1-2, 3,9
	....	W-pII.261.2:1,3
	....	W-pII.262.2:3
	....	W-pII.6.5:2
	....	W-pII.287.1:4
	....	W-pII.292.1:7
	....	W-pII.296.2:3
	....	W-pII.325.1:2
	....	W-pII.334.1:6; 2:1
	....	W-pII.346.1:3-4,7
	....	M-4.IX.2:10
	....	M-13.3:3; 5:8
	....	M-20.3:2
	....	S-2.I.2:2
7:9-11	how much…your Father...........	M-29.6:9-11
7:12	do ye even so to them	T-1.III.6:2
	....	T-1.V.6:4
	....	T-27.VIII.8:1
7:16	know them by their fruits..........	T-9.V.9:6
	....	T-16.III.2:2
7:24-27	built his house upon a rock	T-4.I.11:2
	....	T-14.II.6:3
	....	T-16.III.9:1
	....	T-24.III.3:6
	....	T-28.VII.3:4; 5:7-7:4

Chapter and Verse	*Quote*	*Course Reference*
8:20 (see Ezk 2:1)	the Son of man	
8:22	let the dead bury their dead........	T-26.V.10:4
9:6	power...forgive sins..................	T-24.II.7:1
	....	T-25.VIII.9:11
9:13 (see Ho 6:6)	mercy, and not sacrifice	
9:22	faith hath made thee whole	T-10.III.7:8
9:24-25 (see Jn 11:43-44)	not dead, but sleepeth...arose	
10:1,8a; 11:5	he gave...power...to heal..........	T-2.II.1:2
10:1,8a; 11:5 (see Is 26:19; 35:5-6)	Heal the sick...raise the dead	
10:8b	freely...received, freely give	T-30.I.17:8
10:19	take no thought how or what	T-2.V.18:4
10:34	I came not to send peace...........	T-6.I.15:2
11:22	the day of judgment	T-2.VIII
	....	T-3.VI.1:1-2
	....	T-9.IV.9:2
	....	T-26.III.4:2
	....	W-pII.9.3:1
	....	W-pII.10
	....	M-15
	....	M-28.6:6
11:25 (Jn 11:41)	I thank thee, O Father	T-13.X.12:6
	....	T-28.IV.9:1

Chapter and Verse	*Quote*	*Course Reference*
11:25 (Jn 11:41) (cont.)	I thank thee, O Father	T-30.VI.9:4
	....	T-31.VIII.10:1
11:28a	Come unto me..........................	T-7.V.11:1
	....	T-11.IV.6:6
11:28b,29b	ye that labour...find rest...........	T-11.III.1:2
	....	T-19.III.11:3
11:29a	learn of me	T-6.I.19:3
11:29b (Jr 6:16)	find rest unto your souls	T-3.IV.7:15
11:30	my yoke is easy.........................	T-5.II.11:4
12:25	house divided against itself........	T-23.I.11:2
	....	T-25.VIII.2:5
12:30 (Lk 9:50)	He that is not with me...............	T-20.II.4:3
	....	T-21.VII.1:8
13:12	whosoever hath...given............	P-3.III.5:1
13:44-46	treasure...bought	T-12.IV.6:4
13:46	pearl of great price	T-23.II.11:2
16:18a	upon this rock...church	T-6.I.8:2
	....	T-22.III.4:7
	....	T-25.VII.12:7
16:18b	gates of hell shall not prevail	T-4.III.1:12
	....	T-5.IV.1:10
	....	T-6.II.10:8
	....	T-7.IX.2:3
	....	T-13.XI.7:3
	....	T-17.VI.5:6

Chapter and Verse	*Quote*	*Course Reference*
16:18b (cont.)	gates of hell shall not prevail	T-24.II.13:4
	....	T-31.VIII.4:1
	....	W-pI.53.5:6
	....	W-pI.73.7:7
16:19a	keys of the kingdom..................	T-24.II.7:6; 14:1
	....	W-pI.110.11:7
16:19b (Jn 20:23)	bind…loose	T-8.III.5:10
	....	T-14.III.6:3
	....	T-15.III.11:3
	....	T-15.VI.5:12
	....	T-16.VII.9:5
	....	T-19.IV-D.13:5
	....	T-21.VI.6:1
	....	T-24.IV.5:5
	....	T-24.VI.5:1-5
	....	T-29.III.3:12
	....	W-pI.46.1:4
	....	W-pI.115.1:2
	....	W-pI.191.11:1-2
	....	W-pI.192.9:2
	....	W-pI.195.4:5
	....	W-pI.197.3:1
	....	W-pI.200.5:3
	....	W-pII.277
	....	W-pII.332.Title; 2:1-4
16:26	profited…lose his own soul?.....	T-3.VII.2:7

Chapter and Verse	*Quote*	*Course Reference*
16:26 (cont.)	profited...lose his own soul?.....	T-5.II.7:11
	....	T-26.VIII.9:4
16:27 (25:31)	Son of man...glory	T-4.IV.10:2-4
	....	T-9.IV.9:3-4; 11:10
	....	W-pI.191.8:3
	....	W-pII.9
	....	W-pII.10.1
17:2	transfigured	W-pI.124.10:1
	....	W-pI.151.16:3
17:5 (see 3:17)	This is my beloved Son	
17:19-20	Because of your unbelief	T-2.II.1:3
17:20a	faith...mustard seed..................	T-25.VIII.2:7
17:20a,b (1 Co 13:2)	faith...mountain........................	T-2.VI.9:8
	....	T-5.VII.2:2
	....	T-21.III.3:1
17:20c	nothing shall be impossible	W-pI.191.9:2
18:3	become as little children	T-1.V.3:4
	....	T-11.VIII.2:1
18:11	save that which was lost	W-pI.191.8:3
18:19	if two of you shall agree	W-pI.185.2:9
18:20	two or three are gathered	T-4.IV.11:6
	....	T-14.X.9:6
	....	T-22.I.7:6
	....	M-2.5:3
	....	P-2.II.6:5

Chapter and Verse	*Quote*	*Course Reference*
19:6	What...God hath joined............	T-8.VI.9:4
	....	T-17.III.7:3
	....	T-22.In.1:2
	....	T-22.V.3:5
	....	T-26.VII.15:7
	....	T-28.IV.7:2
	....	T-28.VII.2:10
	....	W-pI.160.8:5
19:14	such is the kingdom	T-5.IV.3:9
	....	W-pI.50.5:4
19:18 (see Ex 20:16)	bear false witness	
19:21	sell...follow me	T-12.III.1:1
	....	W-pI.193.11:1
19:26	with God...possible..................	T-11.VI.10:8
	....	W-pI.71.7:3
	....	W-pI.91.3:7
19:30 (20:16a)	the last shall be first	W-pII.328.Title
20:16a (see 19:30)	the last shall be first	
20:16b (22:14)	called...few chosen	T-3.IV.7:12
	....	W-pI.153.11:2
	....	W-pI.185.2:6-7
	....	M-1.2:7
20:19	he shall rise again......................	T-19.IV-D.18:5
20:28 (see Ps 49:7)	his life a ransom for many	

Chapter and Verse	*Quote*	*Course Reference*
21:9 (see Ps 118:26)	Blessed is he that cometh	
21:13 (see Jr 7:11)	house of prayer...thieves	
21:22 (see 7:7a,8a)	ask...ye shall receive	
22:14 (see 20:16b)	called...few are chosen	
22:21	Render...unto God....................	T-5.IV.6:8
	....	T-25.V.3:5
22:29	the power of God	W-pI.69.8:6
22:39 (see Lv 19:18)	love thy neighbour as thyself	
23:25-26 (see 7:3-5)	cleanse first...within	
24:35	Heaven...pass away	T-1.III.2:1
	....	T-29.VI.4:1
25:31 (see 16:27)	Son of man...glory	
25:35 (Heb 13:2)	I was a stranger	T-1.III.7:6
	....	T-20.I.4:3
25:40	as ye have done it unto one........	T-1.III.1:2
	....	T-9.VI.2:4; 3:8
	....	S-2.I.3:10
	....	S-3.IV.5:1
25:45	as ye did it not to one................	W-pI.160.10:5
26:15	thirty pieces of silver	T-30.V.9:8

Chapter and Verse	*Quote*	*Course Reference*
26:24	woe unto...betrayed	T-6.I.15:7
26:28 (Ac 2:38)	the remission of sins	T-23.II.4:5
26:29 (Lk 22:30)	I drink it new with you..............	T-19.IV-A.16:3-4
26:39,42 (see 6:10b)	thy will be done	
27:26-50	crucifixion.................................	T-6.I
27:29	crown of thorns..........................	T-27.I.1:4
	....	W-pI.161.11:5
	....	S-3.IV.9:3
27:29,35	crown of thorns...crucified	T-11.VI.7:1; 8:1
28:2 (Jn 11:38,39)	rolled back the stone	C-Ep.2:3
28:18	All power is given unto me........	T-5.II.9:2
	....	T-14.XI.2:4
	....	T-26.VI.2:3
	....	W-pI.20.3:7
	....	W-pI.191.9:1
	....	W-pII.320.Title; 1:4
	....	C-6.2:3
	....	P-2.VII.6:4
28:20	I am with you always................	T-7.III.1:7
	....	T-8.III.4:8
	....	T-8.IV.2:4
	....	W-pI.97.2:4
	....	M-23.7:8

Chapter and Verse	*Quote*	*Course Reference*
1:24 (see Ps 16:10)	the Holy One	
5:9	My name is Legion	T-6.II.13:2
	....	C-5.1:6
8:18 (Jr 5:21)	Having eyes, see ye not?............	W-pI.92.3:4
8:36	gain...lose his own soul	T-12.VI.1:1
10:51-52	that I might receive my sight	W-pI.160.10:5
16:19 (see Ps 110:1)	sat on the right hand of God	

Chapter and Verse	*Quote*	*Course Reference*
1:19 (8:1)	glad tidings................................	T-16.II.6:5; 8:5
	....	T-19.I.14:6
	....	W-pI.75.5:3
	....	W-pI.125.4:2
	....	W-pII.14.5:3
	....	M-4.X.3:8
	....	P-3.III.8:9
1:28 (Jg 6:12)	the Lord is with thee	T-12.II.9:2
1:77	knowledge of salvation	M-1.1:7
	....	M-4.X.3:9
1:79 (see Jn 1:5)	light to them... in darkness	
2:7	laid him in a manger	T-15.III.9:6
2:12	babe...swaddling clothes...........	T-19.IV-C.10:8
2:14	Glory to God in the highest	T-8.III.1:1
2:29	depart in peace	T-5.IV.8:7
	....	T-13.III.11:3
	....	W-pI.61.4:3
	....	S-3.II.4:4
4:23	Physician, heal thyself	P-2.VII.1:2
	....	P-3.III.8:1
6:36	Be ye therefore merciful	T-3.I.4:3
	....	T-30.V.10:5
6:48	laid the foundation on a rock	W-pI.61.7:4
8:1 (see 1:19)	glad tidings	
8:13	these have no root	T-1.V.6:3

Chapter and Verse	*Quote*	*Course Reference*
9:50 (see Mt 12:30)	not against us is for us	
9:62 (see Gn 19:26)	No man…looking back	
14:16-23	supper…house may be filled.....	T-28.III.8:7-9:8
15:7	joy…sinner that repenteth..........	T-13.II.9:6
	....	T-13.IX.6:9
	....	T-26.IV.6:3
15:11-32	A certain man had two sons.......	T-8.VI.4
15:13	a far country..............................	C-6.4:6
15:18	arise and go to my father	W-pI.193.11:2
	....	S-2.III.3:2
15:20	he…came to his father...............	W-Ep.5:7
15:24,32	he was lost, and is found...........	T-19.IV-D.19:1
	....	T-29.I.9:6
	....	M-19.5:11
15:31	all that I have is thine................	T-11.VI.6:6
	....	W-pII.FL.6:3
16:8 (1 Th 5:5)	children of light..........................	T-11.III.6:1
17:21	kingdom of God is within..........	T-4.III.1:1
	....	T-11.VIII.8:3
	....	T-15.III.9:7
	....	T-15.VI.2:1
	....	T-25.IV.5:1
	....	T-29.VIII.9:6
	....	W-pI.77.3:3

Chapter and Verse	*Quote*	*Course Reference*
22:19 (1 Co 11:24-25)	in remembrance of me	T-2.V.17:2
	....	T-5.III.11:7
	....	T-7.V.10:4
	....	T-8.III.4:8
	....	T-8.IV.2:13; 7:5
22:30 (see Mt 26:29)	eat and drink...table	
22:39-46	mount of Olives...agony	T-6.I.7:6
	....	T-19.IV-D.18:4
22:48	Judas, betrayest thou...kiss	T-6.I.15:5
	....	T-17.I.1:1
23:34	Father, forgive them..................	T-1.VII.3:3
	....	T-2.V.16:3
	....	T-11.II.3:6
	....	T-11.III.2:1
	....	T-13.V.7:6
	....	T-14.V.2:6
	....	T-14.VI.7:1
	....	T-21.VII.2:7
	....	T-25.IX.1:9
	....	T-27.VII.1:5
	....	W-pI.139.10:1
	....	W-pI.153.5:2
	....	W-pI.197.2:1
23:43	Today...with me in paradise......	T-20.III.9:6
	....	W-pII.266.2:1

Chapter and Verse	*Quote*	*Course Reference*
23:46 (Ps 31:5)	into thy hands…spirit	T-3.II.5:1
	....	T-5.VII.3:2
24:13-16	Jesus…not know him	T-18.III.3:2
24:49 (Ps 105:42)	promise of my Father.................	M-15.3:7

Chapter and Verse	*Quote*	*Course Reference*
1:3	All things were made by him.....	T-6.II.7:6
1:5 (Lk 1:79)	light...darkness..........................	T-14.II.4:3
	....	T-18.III.1:7-8
	....	M-1.1:4
1:7-8 (18:37c)	bear witness...Light [truth]	T-1.I.14:1
	....	T-18.IX.3:2
	....	T-27.VI.3:8
	....	W-pI.121.5:3
	....	W-pI.169.4:3; 7:2
	....	W-pII.255.1:4
1:14	the Word was made flesh	T-8.VII.7:1; 14:1
1:23 (see Is 40:3)	Make straight the way	
1:29	Lamb of God.............................	T-3.I.5:1; 6:4
3:3,7	born again	T-13.VI.3:5; 4:8; 5:1
	....	T-13.X.5:2
	....	T-26.I.7:7
	....	T-31.I.13:4
	....	W-pI.109.2:6; 6:2
	....	W-pI.192.8:1
	....	W-pII.303.Title; 1:6
3:6	born of the flesh...Spirit...........	T-31.VI.1:1
3:16	For God so loved the world	T-2.VII.5:14
	....	T-30.II.4:3
3:36 (see Ezk 7:19)	the wrath of God	

Chapter and Verse	*Quote*	*Course Reference*
4:10 (7:38)	living water	T-18.VIII.9:8
5:19,30	Son…nothing of himself	T-4.I.12:1
	....	T-8.IV.7:3
	....	T-8.VII.6:1
	....	T-10.V.5:1
	....	T-12.V.5:3
	....	T-24.IV.2:10
	....	W-pI.47.2:1
	....	M-29.4:2
	....	P-2.V.4:6
6:20	be not afraid	T-11.V.2:3
	....	T-27.V.4:5
	....	T-28.III.8:1
	....	W-pI.153.20:2
	....	W-pII.10.4:2
	....	C-Ep.3:1
6:63 (see Pr 10:2)	the flesh profiteth nothing	
6:69	the Son of the living God...........	T-7.VII.5:8
	....	T-18.I.8:2
7:24	Judge not…appearance..............	M-10.3:3
7:38 (see 4:10)	living water	
8:12 (see Mt 5:14)	the light of the world	
8:16 (20:21b)	the Father that sent me..............	T-8.IV.2:13
8:32	the truth shall make you free	T-2.I.4:9

Chapter and Verse	*Quote*	*Course Reference*
8:32 (cont.)	the truth shall make you free	T-3.V.5:7
	....	T-5.III.11:5
	....	T-5.IV.2:7
	....	T-6.III.4:2
	....	T-14.III.13:6
	....	W-pI.76.7:4
	....	W-pI.110.5:4; 11:6
	....	W-pI.136.15:2
8:51 (11:25b,26)	he shall never see death	W-pI.162.2:6
8:58	Before Abraham was, I am	T-3.III.6:5
10:30 (14:20)	I and my Father are one	T-1.II.4:7
	....	T-11.I.2:5
11:4	sickness is not unto death	T-8.IX.3:2
	....	T-29.II.10:6
11:11 (11:43)	I go…awake him	T-24.III.7:2
11:25a	I am the resurrection…life	T-1.III.2:2
	....	T-11.VI.4:1
	....	T-19.IV-C.10:9
	....	W-pI.20.3:6
11:25b,26 (see 8:51)	shall never die	
11:38,39 (see Mt 28:2)	Take ye away the stone	
11:41 (see Mt 11:25)	Father, I thank thee	
11:43 (see 11:11)	Lazarus, come forth	

Chapter and Verse	*Quote*	*Course Reference*
11:43-44 (Mt 9:24-25)	he that was dead came forth.......	T-4.IV.11:7
11:44	bound hand and foot	T-29.VI.5:1
12:46	a light into the world.................	T-5.VI.11:1
	....	T-8.IV.2:1
13:34	love one another.........................	T-11.IV.6:4
14:1	Let not your heart be troubled ...	T-10.V.5:3
14:2	In my Father's house.................	T-29.V.6:2
	....	T-30.V.8:6
	....	W-pI.182.4:3
	....	W-pI.193.11:2
	....	W-pII.263.2:2
	....	S-2.III.3:2
14:3	where I am…ye may be also	W-p1.156.2:6
14:5	how can we know the way.........	W-pI.189.8:1-2
14:6a	way, the truth, and the life..........	T-6.I.10:3
	....	T-7.III.1:9
	....	W-pI.rII.In.5:1
	....	W-pII.FL.4:4
	....	P-1.2:3
14:6b	no man cometh…but by me	T-1.II.4:1
	....	T-20.III.11:5
14:12,28b	I go unto my Father...................	T-13.III.11:3
	....	T-13.V.9:7
14:13-14 (16:23)	ask in my name	T-8.IX.7:1
	....	M-23.1:4; 3:7

Chapter and Verse	*Quote*	*Course Reference*
14:16a	another Comforter	T-5.I.4:2
		T-10.III.2:1
		T-11.II.7:8
		T-11.III.7:1
14:16b (15:4,10)	abide with you for ever	T-11.II.4:5
		T-12.II.9:3
		T-14.V.8:7
		T-15.III.10:1
		T-16.VI.9:3
		W-pI.127.9:5
		W-pII.346.1:6
14:16b (15:4,10; 16:7)	abide with you…if I depart	T-5.I.4:4
14:18	I will…comfortless	T-5.II.6:8
		T-7.X.7:2
		T-17.V.10:3
		T-31.VIII.3:5
		W-pII.352.1:6
		W-Ep.6:8
		S-2.III.7:5
14:20 (see 10:30)	I am in my Father…in you	
14:27a	Peace I leave with you	T-10.III.6:6
		T-13.VII.16:8
14:27a,b (18:36)	Peace…not as the world giveth	M-20.1:1
14:27b	not as the world giveth	T-26.VI.3:5
14:28c	My Father is greater than I	T-1.II.4:7
15:2	branch…beareth not fruit	T-3.VII.6:1

Chapter and Verse	*Quote*	*Course Reference*
15:4,10 (see 14:16b)	Abide in me...my love	
15:11 (16:24)	that your joy might be full	T-7.I.6:2
	....	T-11.III.3:1
	....	T-25.IV.2:7
	....	W-pI.100.2:5
15:18	world...hated me	T-8.IV.3:7
	....	T-24.V.4:6
15:19 (17:14,16,18)	ye are not of the world	T-8.VII.11:2
	....	T-9.IV.2:7
	....	T-26.VII.4:5
	....	W-pI.155.1:1
	....	M-4.I.1:5
16:7 (see 14:16b)	if I depart, I will send him	
16:12	many things...cannot bear them	T-6.I.16:1
16:16	a little while...shall see me	T-12.II.7:1
16:23 (see 14:13-14)	ask...in my name	
16:24 (see 15:11)	that your joy may be full	
16:33	I have overcome the world	T-4.I.13:10-11
	....	T-8.IV.2:8
	....	T-19.IV-B.6:5
17:14,16,18 (see 15:19)	not of the world	
18:36	My kingdom...world	T-3.VII.6:9
	....	T-8.VI.3:1

Chapter and Verse	*Quote*	*Course Reference*
18:36 (cont.)	My kingdom…world.................	T-15.III.9:7
	....	T-26.VI.3:5
18:36 (14:27a,b)	not of this world…peace	M-20.1:1
18:37b	came I into the world	W-pII.319.Title
18:37c (see 1:7-8)	bear witness unto the truth	
18:38	What is truth	T-7.XI.6:1
19:5	Behold the man	T-29.V.5:2
20:17	I ascend unto my Father............	T-11.VI.1:7; 4:9
	....	T-15.I.14:5
	....	T-17.IV.16:2
20:19,21a,26	Peace be unto you	T-11.IV.8:4
	....	T-14.V.8:1
	....	T-27.V.11:1
	....	W-pI.140.5:1
20:21b (see 8:16)	as my Father hath sent me	
20:23 (see Mt 16:19b)	sins ye remit…sins ye retain	
20:25	the print of the nails	T-24.III.8:6,12
	....	W-pI.161.11:5
20:29	Blessed…yet have believed.......	T-11.VI.1:5

Chapter and Verse	*Quote*	*Course Reference*
1:8 (Is 43:10,12)	be witnesses unto me	T-1.IV.4:8
1:8-9 (2:1-4)	Holy Ghost…taken up	C-6.1:1
2:1-4 (see 1:8-9)	filled with the Holy Ghost	
2:38 (see Mt 26:28)	the remission of sins	
17:28	in him…have our being	T-5.IV.8:13
	....	T-7.IV.7:5
	....	T-24.VI.5:6
	....	T-31.VIII.12:7
	....	W-pI.156.2:9
	....	W-pI.163.9:3
	....	W-pI.197.7:3
	....	W-pII.222.Title
20:35	more blessed to give	T-1.I.16:1
	....	T-21.VI.9:8

Chapter and Verse	*Quote*	*Course Reference*
2:15	written in their hearts	W-pII.14.5:1
	....	M-26.1:2
3:28 (5:1)	justified by faith	T-17.V.7:12
	....	T-19.I.9:7
	....	T-20.III.11:2
5:1 (see 3:28)	justified by faith	
6:23	the wages of sin is death	T-10.V.1:5
	....	T-19.II.3:6
	....	T-25.VII.1:6
	....	T-27.VI.2:11
	....	S-2.I.2:5
8:3	Son…likeness of sinful flesh.....	P-3.III.8:13
8:26	Spirit…groanings	M-29.6:5
8:28	all things…for good..................	T-4.V.1:1
	....	T-6.II.10:2
	....	T-26.VIII.6:6
8:29	firstborn…many brethren	T-1.II.3:7; 4:5
12:16 (see 1 P 3:8)	same mind…toward another	
12:19 (see Dt 32:35)	Vengeance is mine	
15:11 (see Ps 150:1-6)	Praise the Lord	

1 Corinthians

Chapter and Verse	*Quote*	*Course Reference*
2:9 (see Is 64:4)	Eye hath not seen…ear heard	
3:16 (see 6:19)	ye are the temple of God	
6:15-20	bodies…members of Christ…….	T-8.IX.7:1
6:19 (3:16)	temple of the Holy Ghost………..	T-2.III.1:5
	………………………………………	T-8.VII.9:6
	………………………………………	T-20.VI
	………………………………………	T-26.IX.8:1
	………………………………………	P-2.II.1:5
	………………………………………	P-3.III.6:3-4
11:24-25 (see Lk 22:19)	in remembrance of me	
12:10,28 (see Gn 11:1-9)	diversities of tongues	
13:2 (see Mt 17:20a,b)	remove mountains	
13:4-7	Charity…truth…………………….	T-20.VI.2:5-7
13:11	I put away childish things……….	T-29.IX.6:2-7:5
13:12	see through a glass, darkly………	T-4.IV.1:6; 2:3; 9:2
	………………………………………	T-31.VII.7:2
	………………………………………	W-pI.124.10:1
	………………………………………	W-pI.159.3:4
13:13	faith, hope, charity …………………	T-19.IV-D.17:1
14:33	God is not the author………………	T-4.I.9:1

Chapter and Verse	*Quote*	*Course Reference*
15:26	last enemy…is death..................	M-27.6:1
15:28 (Ep 1:23)	God…all in all...........................	T-7.IV.7:4
	....	T-8.IV.1:3
	....	S-2.II.7:7
15:52a	the twinkling of an eye	T-2.I.3:4
15:52b (Jl 2:1)	the trumpet shall sound.............	T-27.II.6:7
	....	W-pI.162.2:4-5

2 Corinthians

Chapter and Verse	*Quote*	*Course Reference*
6:2	now is the day of salvation	T-13.VI.8:1
9:6 (see Ga 6:7c)	soweth...reap	
12:9a	My grace is sufficient	T-13.XI.7:5; 9:4
	....	T-16.VII.10:4
	....	W-pII.348.Title
12:9b (Ph 4:13)	strength...weakness..................	T-4.I.11:3
	....	T-15.II.3:5; 6:5-6
	....	T-31.VIII.2:3
	....	W-pI.48.3:2
	....	W-pI.62.3:1
	....	W-pI.92.3-10
	....	W-pI.153.6:3; 19:3
	....	M-29.7:2
13:11	be of one mind	T-2.V.17:1

Galatians

Chapter and Verse	*Quote*	*Course Reference*
6:7b (see Jb 13:9)	God is not mocked	
6:7c (2 Co 9:6)	soweth...reap..............................	T-5.VI.6:1

Ephesians

Chapter and Verse	*Quote*	*Course Reference*
1:23 (see 1 Co 15:28)	him that filleth all in all	
2:8	faith...gift of God.......................	T-1.VI.5:10
	....	T-19.I.11:1
2:19	strangers and foreigners.............	T-20.VI.7:7
3:19	the fulness of God.....................	T-7.IX.2:2

Philippians

Chapter and Verse	*Quote*	*Course Reference*
2:2	being…of one mind..................	T-23.IV.7:4
2:5	Let this mind…Christ Jesus	T-5.I.3:4
	....	T-5.IV.4:3
	....	T-5.VI.3:2
4:7	peace…understanding...............	T-2.II.1:9
	....	T-13.VII.8:1
4:13 (see 2 Co 12:9b)	I can do…through Christ	

Colossians

Chapter and Verse	*Quote*	*Course Reference*
1:16	visible and invisible	M-29.8:4
2:12 (3:1)	ye are risen with him..................	T-13.V.11:4
3:1 (see 2:12)	be risen with Christ	

1 Thessalonians

Chapter and Verse	*Quote*	*Course Reference*
5:5 (see Lk 16:8)	children of light	
5:17	Pray without ceasing..................	S-1.II.2:5

1 Timothy

Chapter and Verse	*Quote*	*Course Reference*
6:10	the root of all evil........................	T-3.VI.7:3
	....	T-11.III.1:7
6:16 (see Rv 5:12-13)	honour and power everlasting	

2 Timothy

Chapter and Verse	*Quote*	*Course Reference*
1:10 (see Rv 21:4b)	Saviour…abolished death	

Hebrews

Chapter and Verse	*Quote*	*Course Reference*
2:6 (see Ps 8:4)	What is man…?	
2:18 (see Mt 4:1-11)	he…suffered being tempted	
7:3	neither beginning…nor end.......	T-11.I.2:3
13:2 (see Mt 25:35)	entertain strangers	
13:5	I will never leave thee................	T-5.IV.6:5
13:8	the same yesterday…forever	T-7.I.7:8
	....	T-11.VI.4:9
	....	T-15.II.3:2
	....	T-26.I.7:6
	....	T-29.VI.2:12
	....	W-pI.167.12:2

1 Peter

Chapter and Verse	*Quote*	*Course Reference*
3:8 (Rm 12:16)	be ye all of one mind	T-6.V.3:4
5:7	Casting…care upon him	T-5.VII.1:4

1 John

Chapter and Verse	*Quote*	*Course Reference*
1:5 (2:8)	God is light...no darkness	T-2.VII.5:4
	....	T-3.I.7:7
	....	T-13.VI.8:4-5
	....	T-14.III.6:2
2:8 (see 1:5)	darkness...light now shineth	
2:9 (4:20)	he that...hateth his brother	T-13.X.11:7
	....	W-pII.246.1:1
2:18,22	antichrist	T-29.VIII.Title; 3:1,5; 6:2
	....	T-30.I.14:8
	....	W-pI.137.6:2
3:2	when he shall appear	T-3.II.5:10
	....	T-11.VIII.4:7
	....	T-30.VIII.5:9
4:8,16	God is love................................	T-9.I.9:7
	....	T-18.I.7:1
	....	T-29.I.8:7
	....	T-31.I.10:6
	....	W-pI.99.5:5; 6:8; 11:4
	....	W-pI.103.Title; 2:2,4; 3:3,5
	....	W-pI.117.1:1; 3:2
	....	W-pI.rV.In.4:3; 10:8
	....	W-pI.171-180
4:18a	no fear in love	T-13.X.10:4

1 John (continued)

Chapter and Verse	*Quote*	*Course Reference*
4:18a (cont.)	no fear in love	T-18.I.7:1
	....	T-20.II.8:9
	....	T-28.V.2:4
	....	M-25.4:9
	....	S-3.III.6:6
4:18a,b	perfect love casteth out fear.......	T-12.II.8:1
	....	T-14.III.6:2
	....	T-15.V.4:4
	....	T-20.III.11:3
4:18b	perfect love casteth out fear.......	T-1.VI.5:4
	....	T-15.VI.2:1
4:20 (see 2:9)	hateth his brother	

Revelation

Chapter and Verse	Quote	Course Reference
1:16 (see Ps 149:6)	a sharp two-edged sword	
2:28 (22:16)	the morning star	C-Ep.5:4
5:12-13 (1 Tm 6:16)	honour...be unto him................	T-14.VII.7:9
	....	T-15.III.6:7
7:17 (see Is 25:8)	God shall wipe away all tears	
12:7-10 (see Mt 4:1-11)	the Devil...was cast out	
12:9 (20:7-10)	Satan...deceiveth.......................	T-21.V.8:1
20:7-10 (see 12:9)	Satan...deceive the nations	
21:1 (see Is 65:17)	new heaven...new earth	
21:4a (see Is 25:8)	God shall wipe away all tears	
21:4b (2 Tm 1:10)	there shall be no more death	T-1.IV.4:2
	....	T-3.VII.5:11
	....	T-27.II.6:8
	....	T-27.VII.14:5
	....	T-29.VI.4:9
	....	T-29.VII.10:2
	....	W-pI.163.Title; 8:5; 9:5
	....	W-pI.167.1:5-7

Chapter and Verse	*Quote*	*Course Reference*
21:4b (cont.) (2Tm 1:10)	there shall be no more death	M-17.9:10
	....	C-5.6:9
21:6 (22:13)	Alpha and Omega	T-3.III.6:5
22:13 (see 21:6)	Alpha and Omega	
22:16 (see 2:28)	morning star	

Foundation for "A Course in Miracles"
Academy ✦ Retreat Center

***Kenneth Wapnick** received his Ph.D. in Clinical Psychology in 1968 from Adelphi University. He has been involved with* A COURSE IN MIRACLES *since 1973, writing, teaching, and integrating its principles with his practice of psychotherapy. In 1982, with his wife Gloria, he began the Foundation for "A Course in Miracles," and in 1988 they opened an Academy and Retreat Center in upstate New York. The following is their vision of the Foundation and description of the Center.*

In our early years of studying *A Course in Miracles,* as well as teaching and applying its principles in our respective professions of psychotherapy, and teaching and school administration, it seemed evident that this was not the simplest of thought systems to understand. This was so not only in the intellectual grasp of its teachings, but perhaps more importantly in the application of these teachings to one's personal life. Thus, it appeared to us from the beginning that the Course lent itself to teaching, parallel to the ongoing teachings of the Holy Spirit in the daily opportunities within our relationships, which are discussed in the early pages of the manual for teachers.

One day several years ago while Helen Schucman and I (Kenneth) were discussing these ideas, she shared a vision that she had had of a teaching center as a white temple with a gold cross atop it. Although it was clear that this image was symbolic, we understood it to be representative of what the teaching center was to be: a place where the person of Jesus and his message in *A Course in Miracles* would be manifest. We have sometimes seen an image of a lighthouse shining its light into the sea, calling to it those passers-by who sought it. For us, this light is the Course's teaching of forgiveness, which we would hope to share with those who are drawn to the Foundation's form of teaching and its vision of the Course.

This vision entails the belief that Jesus gave *A Course in Miracles* at this particular time in this particular form for several reasons. These include:

1) the necessity of healing the mind of its belief that attack is salvation; this is accomplished through forgiveness, the undoing of our belief in the reality of separation and guilt.

2) emphasizing the importance of Jesus and/or the Holy Spirit as our loving and gentle Teacher, and developing a personal relationship with this Teacher.

3) correcting the errors of Christianity, particularly where it has emphasized suffering, sacrifice, separation, and sacrament as being inherent in God's plan for salvation.

Our thinking has always been inspired by Plato (and his mentor Socrates), both the man and his teachings. Plato's Academy was a place where serious and thoughtful people came to study his philosophy in an atmosphere conducive to their learning, and then returned to their professions to implement what they were taught by the great philosopher. Thus, by integrating abstract philosophical ideals with experience, Plato's school seemed to be the perfect model for our teaching center.

We therefore see the Foundation's principal purpose as being to help students of *A Course in Miracles* deepen their understanding of its thought system, conceptually and experientially, so that they may be more effective instruments of Jesus' teaching in their own particular lives. Since teaching forgiveness without experiencing it is empty, one of the Foundation's specific goals is to help facilitate the process whereby people may be better able to know that their own sins are forgiven and that they are truly loved by God. Thus is the Holy Spirit able to extend His Love through them to others.

A teacher is defined in the Course as anyone who chooses to be one, and so we welcome to our Foundation all those who wish to come. We offer lectures and workshops for large groups as well as classes for smaller groups that would facilitate more intensive study and growth.

The Foundation, about 120 miles from New York City, is situated on ninety-five acres surrounding beautiful Tennanah Lake in the Catskill Mountains. Its country location and comfortable accommodations provide a peaceful and meditative setting in which students may carry out their plans for prayer, study, and reflection.

RELATED MATERIAL ON *A COURSE IN MIRACLES*

By Kenneth Wapnick

Books and Pamphlets

CHRISTIAN PSYCHOLOGY IN *A COURSE IN MIRACLES.* Second edition, enlarged. Discussion of the basic principles of the Course in the context of some of the traditional teachings of Christianity. Includes a new Preface and an Afterword.
ISBN 0-933291-14-0 • #B-1• Paperback • 90 pages $4.
Audio tape of the first edition of the book, read by Kenneth Wapnick • #B-2 $5.

A TALK GIVEN ON *A COURSE IN MIRACLES*: An Introduction. Fourth edition, revised and enlarged. Edited transcript of a workshop summarizing the principles of the Course; includes the story of how the Course was written.
ISBN 0-933291-16-7 • #B-3 • Paperback • 127 pages $4.

UN CURSO EN MILAGROS: UNA INTRODUCCIÓN BASICA. Spanish translation of A TALK GIVEN ON *A COURSE IN MIRACLES*: An Introduction. Includes a glossary of some of the more important terms used in the Course.
ISBN 0-933291-10-8 • #B-3S • Paperback • 152 pages $4.

BETRACHTUNGEN ÜBER *EIN KURS IN WUNDERN.* German translation of A TALK GIVEN ON *A COURSE IN MIRACLES*: An Introduction. Includes a glossary of some of the more important terms used in the Course.
ISBN 0-933291-12-4 • #B-3G • Paperback • 164 pages US $8 DM 14.

FORGIVENESS AND JESUS: The Meeting Place of *A Course in Miracles* and Christianity. Fourth edition. Discussion of the teachings of Christianity in the light of the principles of the Course, highlighting the similarities and differences; the application of these principles to issues such as injustice, anger, sickness, sexuality, and money.
ISBN 0-933291-13-2 • #B-5 • Paperback • 355 pages $16.

THE FIFTY MIRACLE PRINCIPLES OF *A COURSE IN MIRACLES.* Third edition. Combined and edited transcript of two workshops; line-by-line analysis of the fifty miracle principles, with additional material.
ISBN 0-933291-15-9 • #B-6 • Paperback • 115 pages $8.

AWAKEN FROM THE DREAM. Gloria and Kenneth Wapnick. Presentation of the Course's major principles from a new perspective. Includes background material on how the Course was written.
ISBN 0-933291-04-3 • #B-7 • Paperback • 133 pages $10.

THE OBSTACLES TO PEACE. Edited transcript of tape album; line-by-line analysis of "The Obstacles to Peace"—sections central to the Course's theory—and related passages.
ISBN 0-933291-05-1 • #B-8 • Paperback • 295 pages $12.

LOVE DOES NOT CONDEMN: The World, the Flesh, and the Devil According to Platonism, Christianity, Gnosticism, and *A Course in Miracles*. An in-depth exploration of the non-dualistic metaphysics of *A Course in Miracles*, and its integration with living in this illusory world.
ISBN 0-933291-07-8 • #B-9 • Hardcover • 614 pages $25.

A VAST ILLUSION: Time According to *A Course in Miracles*. A weaving together of various passages from the Course to present a coherent statement of time, including its metaphysical nature, the role of the miracle and forgiveness in collapsing time, and finally the end of time. (Edited and expanded transcription of the tape album "Time According to *A Course in Miracles*.")
ISBN 0-933291-09-4 • #B-10 • Paperback • 301 pages $12.

ABSENCE FROM FELICITY: The Story of Helen Schucman and Her Scribing of *A Course in Miracles*. Discussion of Helen's lifetime conflict between her spiritual nature and her ego; includes some of her recollections, dreams, letters, and personal messages from Jesus—all never before in print; an account of her own experiences of Jesus, her relationship with William Thetford, and the scribing of the Course.
ISBN 0-933291-08-6 • #B-11 • Paperback • 521 pages $16.

OVEREATING: A Dialogue. An Application of the Principles of *A Course in Miracles*. Pamphlet presenting the Course's approach to issues such as food addiction and preoccupation with weight. (Edited and slightly expanded version of the tape "Overeating.")
ISBN 0-933291-11-6 • #B-12 • Paperback • 35 pages $3.

Video Tape Albums

SEEK NOT TO CHANGE THE COURSE. Reflections on *A Course in Miracles*. Talk given by Gloria and Kenneth Wapnick, including questions and answers, on some of the more common misunderstandings about the Course.
#V-1 135 mins. VHS $30 PAL (non-U.S.) $40 Audio tape version $15.

FOUNDATION FOR "A COURSE IN MIRACLES" Conference and Retreat Center. Gloria and Kenneth Wapnick speak about the Course's beginnings, the origin and purpose of the Foundation, and their vision of its development in the future. A visual and verbal portrait of the Center. #V-2 24 mins. VHS $10 PAL (non-U.S.) $20.

Audio Tape Albums

Classes and Workshops

THE SIMPLICITY OF SALVATION. Intensive overview of the Course. The two levels of discourse in the Course; in-depth summary of the major principles; comparison of the Course and Christianity; the story of how the Course was written. #T-1 8 tapes $65.

HOLY IS HEALING. Psychotherapeutic applications of the Course. Workshop weaving together the theory of *A Course in Miracles* with psychotherapeutic and personal examples offered by participants. #T-2 8 tapes $65.

ATONEMENT WITHOUT SACRIFICE: Christianity, the Bible, and the Course. Workshop exploring the relationship between *A Course in Miracles* and the Judaeo-Christian tradition, with special emphasis placed on the role of sacrifice and suffering.
#T-3 2 tapes $15.

THE END OF INJUSTICE. Overview of the Course. The thought systems of the ego and the Holy Spirit; application of principles to problems involving sex, money, injustice, and sickness. #T-4 6 tapes $45.

THE EGO AND FORGIVENESS. Introductory overview of the Course. The ego's thought system of sin, guilt, fear, and special relationships, and its undoing through the Holy Spirit's thought system that includes forgiveness and holy relationships. (Album consists of first two tapes of "The End of Injustice.") #T-5 2 tapes $15.

THE FIFTY MIRACLE PRINCIPLES OF *A COURSE IN MIRACLES*. Line-by-line commentary on the fifty miracles principles which begin the text; introduces students to the central concepts of the Course: Atonement, miracles, healing, time, forgiveness, the Holy Spirit. #T-6 3 tapes $24.

THE WORLD ACCORDING TO *A COURSE IN MIRACLES*. The Course's theory of the world and its role in the ego's plan to usurp God's function and substitute a world of its own for the creation of God. #T-7 3 tapes $24.

THE OBSTACLES TO PEACE. Line-by-line commentary on the "Obstacles to Peace" sections of the text, focusing on the ego's attraction to guilt, pain, and death, and the fear of God's Love, and the undoing of these obstacles through forgiveness.
#T-8 6 tapes $48.

SPECIAL RELATIONSHIPS—PART 1. Line-by-line commentary on sections discussing specialness; explains the unloving nature of most relationships, and how to transform them. #T-9 8 tapes $65.

SPECIAL RELATIONSHIPS—PART 2. Continuation of Part 1, developed through commentary on later chapters in the text including "The Healed Relationship," "The Treachery of Specialness," "The Forgiveness of Specialness."
#T-10 6 tapes $48.

TIME ACCORDING TO *A COURSE IN MIRACLES.* The metaphysics of time—its holographic though illusory nature; the relation of time to the role of the miracle in the plan of the Atonement; the end of time. #T-11 6 tapes $48.

JESUS AND *A COURSE IN MIRACLES.* Discussion of passages in the Course in which Jesus refers to himself: as the source of the Course; his historical teaching example as the manifestation of the Holy Spirit, and perfect model of forgiveness; and his role as our teacher, without whom the undoing of the ego's thought system would be impossible. #T-12 5 tapes $40.

CAUSE AND EFFECT. The importance of this principle in understanding how forgiveness undoes the ego's thought system of guilt and punishment; line-by-line analysis of text sections on our dreams of suffering and victimhood. #T-13 8 tapes $65.

PSYCHOTHERAPY: PURPOSE, PROCESS AND PRACTICE. Line-by-line commentary on the companion pamphlet to the Course, scribed by Helen Schucman from Jesus. #T-14 7 tapes $56.

THE GIFTS OF GOD. A discussion of the inspired poetry of Helen Schucman, scribe of the Course; includes personal reminiscences about Helen. #T-15 3 tapes $24.

LOVE DOES NOT OPPOSE. Gloria and Kenneth Wapnick. The importance of non-opposition as the basis of forgiveness in special relationships. #T-17 8 tapes $65.

THE SONG OF PRAYER. Line-by-line commentary on the companion pamphlet to the Course, scribed by Helen Schucman from Jesus; the role of prayer as a reflection of the process of our acceptance of the true meaning of Jesus' presence in our lives; Jesus' relationship with Helen as the model for understanding the nature of prayer.
#T-18 10 tapes $80.

THE ORIGIN OF *A COURSE IN MIRACLES.* The story of the scribing of *A Course in Miracles*; reflections on Helen Schucman and William Thetford. #T-19 1 tape $6.

I WILL BE STILL AN INSTANT AND GO HOME. A collection of two talks and a meditation by Kenneth Wapnick, and one talk by Gloria Wapnick and Kenneth—given at various Sunday services. #T-20 1 tape $6.

JESUS AND THE MESSAGE OF EASTER. The Course's view of Jesus, and the meaning of his crucifixion and resurrection. #T-21 8 tapes $65.

THE AUTHORITY PROBLEM. The authority problem with God and its reflection in our everyday life. #T-22 5 tapes $40.

OUR GRATITUDE TO GOD. Our gratitude to God, Jesus, and to each other; the obstacles and resistances to this gratitude. #T-23 5 tapes $40.

SICKNESS AND HEALING. Discussion of the cause and purpose of sickness in the ego thought system; analysis of healing as occurring in the mind—the healing of the belief in guilt, by turning to the Holy Spirit and forgiving. #T-24 8 tapes $60.

WHAT IT MEANS TO BE A TEACHER OF GOD. Discussion of the ten characteristics of a teacher of God; also includes discussion of magic and healing.
#T-25 6 tapes $48.

OVEREATING: A DIALOGUE BASED UPON *A COURSE IN MIRACLES*. The ego dynamics involved in food addictions and weight problems; forgiveness through the Holy Spirit as the solution. #T-26 1 tape $6.

TO JUDGE OR NOT TO JUDGE. The Course's teachings on judgment; the process of recognizing our need to judge, and letting Jesus or the Holy Spirit judge for us.
#T-27 4 tapes $32.

HEALING THE UNHEALED HEALER. The characteristics of the unhealed healer; healing through joining with Jesus in understanding all forms of sickness and problems as calls for love. #T-28 8 tapes $65.

THE REAL WORLD: OUR HOME AWAY FROM HOME. A discussion of our true home in Heaven, the ego's home in the world, and the Holy Spirit's correction of the ego's world: the real world. #T-29 8 tapes $65.

TRUE EMPATHY: THE GREATER JOINING. The world's version of empathy contrasted with the Holy Spirit's true empathy. #T-30 8 tapes $65.

JESUS: THE MANIFESTATION OF THE HOLY SPIRIT. A discussion of Jesus and the Holy Spirit in the context of the difference between appearance and reality, and the importance of Jesus as our guide in leading us out of the dream; includes a discussion of the relationship of Jesus to Helen Schucman and to *A Course in Miracles*.
#T-31 5 tapes $40.

THE LAWS OF CHAOS: OUR WAR WITH GOD. An in-depth exploration and discussion of the five laws of chaos that form the foundation of the ego's thought system, and powerfully express the ego's defenses against the Love of God.
#T-32 12 tapes $85.

"THERE MUST BE ANOTHER WAY." The words that led to the birth of *A Course in Miracles* provide the theme of this workshop which discusses forgiveness as the "other way"—rather than specialness—of relating to ourselves, each other, and to God. #T-33 1 tape $6.

THE METAPHYSICS OF SEPARATION AND FORGIVENESS. Summary of the teachings of *A Course in Miracles*, specifically showing how the principle that the thought of separation and the physical world are illusions becomes the foundation for the understanding and practice of forgiveness in our daily lives. #T-34 1 tape $6.

THE WORKBOOK OF *A COURSE IN MIRACLES*: ITS PLACE IN THE CURRICULUM—THEORY AND PRACTICE. Discussion of the metaphysical principles underlying the lessons, the mind-training aspects of the workbook, Jesus' gentle teaching method, and students' common misuses of the workbook. Two charts and an annotated outline of the workbook included. #T-35 8 tapes $65.

MAKING THE HOLY SPIRIT SPECIAL: THE ARROGANCE OF THE EGO. Presentation of the major Course teachings on the role of the Holy Spirit—and Jesus as His manifestation—and the importance of Their Presence in our lives. Discussion of the contrasting attitudes of arrogance and humility in asking help of the Holy Spirit, as well as what it means to hear His Voice. The idea that the Holy Spirit acts in the world is shown to rest on misunderstandings of the principles and language of the Course, as well as on our unconscious desire for specialness. #T-36 7 tapes $56.

THE MEANING OF JUDGMENT. Discussion based on "The Forgiving Dream" from the text, centering on four forms of judgment: 1) the dream of judgment against ourselves; 2) looking with Jesus at this ongoing judgment of guilt without further judgment; 3) judging all things in accord with the Holy Spirit's judgment; 4) joining with Jesus in the judgment of God's Love that is the only reality. #T-37 1 tape $6.

Ordering Information

For orders *in the continental U.S. only*, please add $2.00 for the first item, and $1.00 for each additional item, for shipping and handling.

For orders to *all other countries* (SURFACE MAIL), and to *Alaska, Hawaii*, and *Puerto Rico* (FIRST CLASS MAIL), please add $4.00 for the first item and $1.00 for each additional item.

New York State residents please add local sales tax. (New York law now requires sales tax on shipping and handling charges.)

VISA and MasterCard accepted.

Order from:

Foundation for "A Course in Miracles"
1275 Tennanah Lake Road
Roscoe, NY 12776-5905
(607) 498-4116 • FAX (607) 498-5325

A COURSE IN MIRACLES and other scribed material may be ordered from:

Foundation for Inner Peace
Box 1104
Glen Ellen, CA 95442
(707) 939-0200

A COURSE IN MIRACLES, Second edition:

Hardcover: $30 Softcover: $25

PSYCHOTHERAPY: PURPOSE, PROCESS AND PRACTICE: $3.00

THE SONG OF PRAYER: PRAYER, FORGIVENESS, HEALING: $3.00

THE GIFTS OF GOD: $21.00

Ordering Information

For orders ***in the continental U.S. only***, please add $2.00 for the first item, and $1.00 for each additional item, for shipping and handling.

For orders to ***all other countries*** (SURFACE MAIL), and to ***Alaska, Hawaii***, and ***Puerto Rico*** (FIRST CLASS MAIL), please add $4.00 for the first item and $1.00 for each additional item.

New York State residents please add local sales tax. (New York law now requires sales tax on shipping and handling charges.)

VISA and MasterCard accepted.

Order from:

Foundation for "A Course in Miracles"
1275 Tennanah Lake Road
Roscoe, NY 12776-5905
(607) 498-4116 • FAX (607) 498-5325

A COURSE IN MIRACLES and other scribed material may be ordered from:

Foundation for Inner Peace
Box 1104
Glen Ellen, CA 95442
(707) 939-0200

A COURSE IN MIRACLES, Second edition:

Hardcover: $30 Softcover: $25

PSYCHOTHERAPY: PURPOSE, PROCESS AND PRACTICE: $3.00

THE SONG OF PRAYER: PRAYER, FORGIVENESS, HEALING: $3.00

THE GIFTS OF GOD: $21.00

"THERE MUST BE ANOTHER WAY." The words that led to the birth of *A Course in Miracles* provide the theme of this workshop which discusses forgiveness as the "other way"—rather than specialness—of relating to ourselves, each other, and to God. #T-33 1 tape $6.

THE METAPHYSICS OF SEPARATION AND FORGIVENESS. Summary of the teachings of *A Course in Miracles*, specifically showing how the principle that the thought of separation and the physical world are illusions becomes the foundation for the understanding and practice of forgiveness in our daily lives. #T-34 1 tape $6.

THE WORKBOOK OF *A COURSE IN MIRACLES*: ITS PLACE IN THE CURRICULUM—THEORY AND PRACTICE. Discussion of the metaphysical principles underlying the lessons, the mind-training aspects of the workbook, Jesus' gentle teaching method, and students' common misuses of the workbook. Two charts and an annotated outline of the workbook included. #T-35 8 tapes $65.

MAKING THE HOLY SPIRIT SPECIAL: THE ARROGANCE OF THE EGO. Presentation of the major Course teachings on the role of the Holy Spirit—and Jesus as His manifestation—and the importance of Their Presence in our lives. Discussion of the contrasting attitudes of arrogance and humility in asking help of the Holy Spirit, as well as what it means to hear His Voice. The idea that the Holy Spirit acts in the world is shown to rest on misunderstandings of the principles and language of the Course, as well as on our unconscious desire for specialness. #T-36 7 tapes $56.

THE MEANING OF JUDGMENT. Discussion based on "The Forgiving Dream" from the text, centering on four forms of judgment: 1) the dream of judgment against ourselves; 2) looking with Jesus at this ongoing judgment of guilt without further judgment; 3) judging all things in accord with the Holy Spirit's judgment; 4) joining with Jesus in the judgment of God's Love that is the only reality. #T-37 1 tape $6.

THE AUTHORITY PROBLEM. The authority problem with God and its reflection in our everyday life. #T-22 5 tapes $40.

OUR GRATITUDE TO GOD. Our gratitude to God, Jesus, and to each other; the obstacles and resistances to this gratitude. #T-23 5 tapes $40.

SICKNESS AND HEALING. Discussion of the cause and purpose of sickness in the ego thought system; analysis of healing as occurring in the mind—the healing of the belief in guilt, by turning to the Holy Spirit and forgiving. #T-24 8 tapes $60.

WHAT IT MEANS TO BE A TEACHER OF GOD. Discussion of the ten characteristics of a teacher of God; also includes discussion of magic and healing.
#T-25 6 tapes $48.

OVEREATING: A DIALOGUE BASED UPON *A COURSE IN MIRACLES*. The ego dynamics involved in food addictions and weight problems; forgiveness through the Holy Spirit as the solution. #T-26 1 tape $6.

TO JUDGE OR NOT TO JUDGE. The Course's teachings on judgment; the process of recognizing our need to judge, and letting Jesus or the Holy Spirit judge for us.
#T-27 4 tapes $32.

HEALING THE UNHEALED HEALER. The characteristics of the unhealed healer; healing through joining with Jesus in understanding all forms of sickness and problems as calls for love. #T-28 8 tapes $65.

THE REAL WORLD: OUR HOME AWAY FROM HOME. A discussion of our true home in Heaven, the ego's home in the world, and the Holy Spirit's correction of the ego's world: the real world. #T-29 8 tapes $65.

TRUE EMPATHY: THE GREATER JOINING. The world's version of empathy contrasted with the Holy Spirit's true empathy. #T-30 8 tapes $65.

JESUS: THE MANIFESTATION OF THE HOLY SPIRIT. A discussion of Jesus and the Holy Spirit in the context of the difference between appearance and reality, and the importance of Jesus as our guide in leading us out of the dream; includes a discussion of the relationship of Jesus to Helen Schucman and to *A Course in Miracles*.
#T-31 5 tapes $40.

THE LAWS OF CHAOS: OUR WAR WITH GOD. An in-depth exploration and discussion of the five laws of chaos that form the foundation of the ego's thought system, and powerfully express the ego's defenses against the Love of God.
#T-32 12 tapes $85.

SPECIAL RELATIONSHIPS—PART 2. Continuation of Part 1, developed through commentary on later chapters in the text including "The Healed Relationship," "The Treachery of Specialness," "The Forgiveness of Specialness."
#T-10 6 tapes $48.

TIME ACCORDING TO *A COURSE IN MIRACLES*. The metaphysics of time—its holographic though illusory nature; the relation of time to the role of the miracle in the plan of the Atonement; the end of time. #T-11 6 tapes $48.

JESUS AND *A COURSE IN MIRACLES*. Discussion of passages in the Course in which Jesus refers to himself: as the source of the Course; his historical teaching example as the manifestation of the Holy Spirit, and perfect model of forgiveness; and his role as our teacher, without whom the undoing of the ego's thought system would be impossible. #T-12 5 tapes $40.

CAUSE AND EFFECT. The importance of this principle in understanding how forgiveness undoes the ego's thought system of guilt and punishment; line-by-line analysis of text sections on our dreams of suffering and victimhood. #T-13 8 tapes $65.

PSYCHOTHERAPY: PURPOSE, PROCESS AND PRACTICE. Line-by-line commentary on the companion pamphlet to the Course, scribed by Helen Schucman from Jesus. #T-14 7 tapes $56.

THE GIFTS OF GOD. A discussion of the inspired poetry of Helen Schucman, scribe of the Course; includes personal reminiscences about Helen. #T-15 3 tapes $24.

LOVE DOES NOT OPPOSE. Gloria and Kenneth Wapnick. The importance of non-opposition as the basis of forgiveness in special relationships. #T-17 8 tapes $65.

THE SONG OF PRAYER. Line-by-line commentary on the companion pamphlet to the Course, scribed by Helen Schucman from Jesus; the role of prayer as a reflection of the process of our acceptance of the true meaning of Jesus' presence in our lives; Jesus' relationship with Helen as the model for understanding the nature of prayer.
#T-18 10 tapes $80.

THE ORIGIN OF *A COURSE IN MIRACLES*. The story of the scribing of *A Course in Miracles*; reflections on Helen Schucman and William Thetford. #T-19 1 tape $6.

I WILL BE STILL AN INSTANT AND GO HOME. A collection of two talks and a meditation by Kenneth Wapnick, and one talk by Gloria Wapnick and Kenneth—given at various Sunday services. #T-20 1 tape $6.

JESUS AND THE MESSAGE OF EASTER. The Course's view of Jesus, and the meaning of his crucifixion and resurrection. #T-21 8 tapes $65.

Audio Tape Albums

Classes and Workshops

THE SIMPLICITY OF SALVATION. Intensive overview of the Course. The two levels of discourse in the Course; in-depth summary of the major principles; comparison of the Course and Christianity; the story of how the Course was written. #T-1 8 tapes $65.

HOLY IS HEALING. Psychotherapeutic applications of the Course. Workshop weaving together the theory of *A Course in Miracles* with psychotherapeutic and personal examples offered by participants. #T-2 8 tapes $65.

ATONEMENT WITHOUT SACRIFICE: Christianity, the Bible, and the Course. Workshop exploring the relationship between *A Course in Miracles* and the Judaeo-Christian tradition, with special emphasis placed on the role of sacrifice and suffering.
#T-3 2 tapes $15.

THE END OF INJUSTICE. Overview of the Course. The thought systems of the ego and the Holy Spirit; application of principles to problems involving sex, money, injustice, and sickness. #T-4 6 tapes $45.

THE EGO AND FORGIVENESS. Introductory overview of the Course. The ego's thought system of sin, guilt, fear, and special relationships, and its undoing through the Holy Spirit's thought system that includes forgiveness and holy relationships. (Album consists of first two tapes of "The End of Injustice.") #T-5 2 tapes $15.

THE FIFTY MIRACLE PRINCIPLES OF *A COURSE IN MIRACLES*. Line-by-line commentary on the fifty miracles principles which begin the text; introduces students to the central concepts of the Course: Atonement, miracles, healing, time, forgiveness, the Holy Spirit. #T-6 3 tapes $24.

THE WORLD ACCORDING TO *A COURSE IN MIRACLES*. The Course's theory of the world and its role in the ego's plan to usurp God's function and substitute a world of its own for the creation of God. #T-7 3 tapes $24.

THE OBSTACLES TO PEACE. Line-by-line commentary on the "Obstacles to Peace" sections of the text, focusing on the ego's attraction to guilt, pain, and death, and the fear of God's Love, and the undoing of these obstacles through forgiveness.
#T-8 6 tapes $48.

SPECIAL RELATIONSHIPS—PART 1. Line-by-line commentary on sections discussing specialness; explains the unloving nature of most relationships, and how to transform them. #T-9 8 tapes $65.

THE OBSTACLES TO PEACE. Edited transcript of tape album; line-by-line analysis of "The Obstacles to Peace"—sections central to the Course's theory—and related passages.
ISBN 0-933291-05-1 • #B-8 • Paperback • 295 pages $12.

LOVE DOES NOT CONDEMN: The World, the Flesh, and the Devil According to Platonism, Christianity, Gnosticism, and *A Course in Miracles*. An in-depth exploration of the non-dualistic metaphysics of *A Course in Miracles*, and its integration with living in this illusory world.
ISBN 0-933291-07-8 • #B-9 • Hardcover • 614 pages $25.

A VAST ILLUSION: Time According to *A Course in Miracles*. A weaving together of various passages from the Course to present a coherent statement of time, including its metaphysical nature, the role of the miracle and forgiveness in collapsing time, and finally the end of time. (Edited and expanded transcription of the tape album "Time According to *A Course in Miracles*.")
ISBN 0-933291-09-4 • #B-10 • Paperback • 301 pages $12.

ABSENCE FROM FELICITY: The Story of Helen Schucman and Her Scribing of *A Course in Miracles*. Discussion of Helen's lifetime conflict between her spiritual nature and her ego; includes some of her recollections, dreams, letters, and personal messages from Jesus—all never before in print; an account of her own experiences of Jesus, her relationship with William Thetford, and the scribing of the Course.
ISBN 0-933291-08-6 • #B-11 • Paperback • 521 pages $16.

OVEREATING: A Dialogue. An Application of the Principles of *A Course in Miracles*. Pamphlet presenting the Course's approach to issues such as food addiction and preoccupation with weight. (Edited and slightly expanded version of the tape "Overeating.")
ISBN 0-933291-11-6 • #B-12 • Paperback • 35 pages $3.

Video Tape Albums

SEEK NOT TO CHANGE THE COURSE. Reflections on *A Course in Miracles*. Talk given by Gloria and Kenneth Wapnick, including questions and answers, on some of the more common misunderstandings about the Course.
#V-1 135 mins. VHS $30 PAL (non-U.S.) $40 Audio tape version $15.

FOUNDATION FOR "A COURSE IN MIRACLES" Conference and Retreat Center. Gloria and Kenneth Wapnick speak about the Course's beginnings, the origin and purpose of the Foundation, and their vision of its development in the future. A visual and verbal portrait of the Center. #V-2 24 mins. VHS $10 PAL (non-U.S.) $20.

RELATED MATERIAL ON *A COURSE IN MIRACLES*

By Kenneth Wapnick

Books and Pamphlets

CHRISTIAN PSYCHOLOGY IN *A COURSE IN MIRACLES*. Second edition, enlarged. Discussion of the basic principles of the Course in the context of some of the traditional teachings of Christianity. Includes a new Preface and an Afterword.
ISBN 0-933291-14-0 • #B-1• Paperback • 90 pages $4.
Audio tape of the first edition of the book, read by Kenneth Wapnick • #B-2 $5.

A TALK GIVEN ON *A COURSE IN MIRACLES*: An Introduction. Fourth edition, revised and enlarged. Edited transcript of a workshop summarizing the principles of the Course; includes the story of how the Course was written.
ISBN 0-933291-16-7 • #B-3 • Paperback • 127 pages $4.

UN CURSO EN MILAGROS: UNA INTRODUCCIÓN BASICA. Spanish translation of A TALK GIVEN ON *A COURSE IN MIRACLES*: An Introduction. Includes a glossary of some of the more important terms used in the Course.
ISBN 0-933291-10-8 • #B-3S • Paperback • 152 pages $4.

BETRACHTUNGEN ÜBER *EIN KURS IN WUNDERN*. German translation of A TALK GIVEN ON *A COURSE IN MIRACLES*: An Introduction. Includes a glossary of some of the more important terms used in the Course.
ISBN 0-933291-12-4 • #B-3G • Paperback • 164 pages US $8 DM 14.

FORGIVENESS AND JESUS: The Meeting Place of *A Course in Miracles* and Christianity. Fourth edition. Discussion of the teachings of Christianity in the light of the principles of the Course, highlighting the similarities and differences; the application of these principles to issues such as injustice, anger, sickness, sexuality, and money.
ISBN 0-933291-13-2 • #B-5 • Paperback • 355 pages $16.

THE FIFTY MIRACLE PRINCIPLES OF *A COURSE IN MIRACLES*. Third edition. Combined and edited transcript of two workshops; line-by-line analysis of the fifty miracle principles, with additional material.
ISBN 0-933291-15-9 • #B-6 • Paperback • 115 pages $8.

AWAKEN FROM THE DREAM. Gloria and Kenneth Wapnick. Presentation of the Course's major principles from a new perspective. Includes background material on how the Course was written.
ISBN 0-933291-04-3 • #B-7 • Paperback • 133 pages $10.

Our thinking has always been inspired by Plato (and his mentor Socrates), both the man and his teachings. Plato's Academy was a place where serious and thoughtful people came to study his philosophy in an atmosphere conducive to their learning, and then returned to their professions to implement what they were taught by the great philosopher. Thus, by integrating abstract philosophical ideals with experience, Plato's school seemed to be the perfect model for our teaching center.

We therefore see the Foundation's principal purpose as being to help students of *A Course in Miracles* deepen their understanding of its thought system, conceptually and experientially, so that they may be more effective instruments of Jesus' teaching in their own particular lives. Since teaching forgiveness without experiencing it is empty, one of the Foundation's specific goals is to help facilitate the process whereby people may be better able to know that their own sins are forgiven and that they are truly loved by God. Thus is the Holy Spirit able to extend His Love through them to others.

A teacher is defined in the Course as anyone who chooses to be one, and so we welcome to our Foundation all those who wish to come. We offer lectures and workshops for large groups as well as classes for smaller groups that would facilitate more intensive study and growth.

The Foundation, about 120 miles from New York City, is situated on ninety-five acres surrounding beautiful Tennanah Lake in the Catskill Mountains. Its country location and comfortable accommodations provide a peaceful and meditative setting in which students may carry out their plans for prayer, study, and reflection.

Foundation for "A Course in Miracles"
Academy ✦ Retreat Center

***Kenneth Wapnick** received his Ph.D. in Clinical Psychology in 1968 from Adelphi University. He has been involved with* A COURSE IN MIRACLES *since 1973, writing, teaching, and integrating its principles with his practice of psychotherapy. In 1982, with his wife Gloria, he began the Foundation for "A Course in Miracles," and in 1988 they opened an Academy and Retreat Center in upstate New York. The following is their vision of the Foundation and description of the Center.*

In our early years of studying *A Course in Miracles,* as well as teaching and applying its principles in our respective professions of psychotherapy, and teaching and school administration, it seemed evident that this was not the simplest of thought systems to understand. This was so not only in the intellectual grasp of its teachings, but perhaps more importantly in the application of these teachings to one's personal life. Thus, it appeared to us from the beginning that the Course lent itself to teaching, parallel to the ongoing teachings of the Holy Spirit in the daily opportunities within our relationships, which are discussed in the early pages of the manual for teachers.

One day several years ago while Helen Schucman and I (Kenneth) were discussing these ideas, she shared a vision that she had had of a teaching center as a white temple with a gold cross atop it. Although it was clear that this image was symbolic, we understood it to be representative of what the teaching center was to be: a place where the person of Jesus and his message in *A Course in Miracles* would be manifest. We have sometimes seen an image of a lighthouse shining its light into the sea, calling to it those passers-by who sought it. For us, this light is the Course's teaching of forgiveness, which we would hope to share with those who are drawn to the Foundation's form of teaching and its vision of the Course.

This vision entails the belief that Jesus gave *A Course in Miracles* at this particular time in this particular form for several reasons. These include:

1) the necessity of healing the mind of its belief that attack is salvation; this is accomplished through forgiveness, the undoing of our belief in the reality of separation and guilt.

2) emphasizing the importance of Jesus and/or the Holy Spirit as our loving and gentle Teacher, and developing a personal relationship with this Teacher.

3) correcting the errors of Christianity, particularly where it has emphasized suffering, sacrifice, separation, and sacrament as being inherent in God's plan for salvation.